FORENSIC
RADIOLOGY

FORENSIC
RADIOLOGY

B. G. Brogdon, M.D.

*University Distinguished Professor Emeritus and
Former Chairman, Department of Radiology
University of South Alabama*

*Consultant in Forensic Radiology
Office of the State Medical Examiner
Alabama Department of Forensic Sciences*

CRC Press
Boca Raton   Boston   London   New York   Washington, D.C.

Contact Editor:	Harvey Kane
Project Editor:	Maggie Mogck
Marketing Manager:	Becky McEldowney
Cover design:	Dawn Boyd
Manufacturing:	Carol Royal

Library of Congress Cataloging-in-Publication Data

Brogdon, B.G. (Byron Gilliam)
    Forensic radiology / B.G. Brogdon ; with 13 contributors.
        p.   cm.
     Includes bibliographical references and index.
     ISBN 0-8493-8105-3
     1. Forensic radiography. I. Title.
     [DNLM: 1. Forensic Medicine. 2. Radiology. W 700 B866f 1998]
    RA1058.5.B76 1998
    614'.1—dc21
    DNLM/DLC
    for Library of Congress   97-43645
                                                              CIP

Preface

There are about 25,000 physicians in the U.S. engaged in the practice of Diagnostic Radiology. No more than three dozen of them have had enough experience or interest in Forensic Radiology to have published in the field. Just over a handful have had sufficient involvement to have become members of the American Academy of Forensic Sciences (AAFS), and only three of those have satisfied the requirements for Fellowships in that organization.

There is no set definition or standard for a "Forensic Radiologist". There is no specialized training or fellowship available in that field; there is no separate Society for Forensic Radiology, nor is there certification for a subspecialty or added qualification in Forensic Radiology. It is doubtful that any radiologist in North America, regardless of his level of interest, devotes as much as 10% of his active practice to Forensic Radiology.

Those few of us who do maintain some continuing, albeit sporadic, activity in Forensic Radiology mostly became involved by happenstance, circumstance, curiosity, or just plain good luck. My own introduction to the fascination of forensic problems came in the mid 1960s when I was Radiologist-in-Charge of the Division of Diagnostic Radiology at Johns Hopkins. The famous Dr. Russell S. Fisher (Figure 1), longtime Medical Examiner of the State of Maryland and AAFS President in 1960–1961, first asked for my help in sorting out the commingled body parts of two children (only 15 months apart in age) who were victims of a light aircraft accident. Later, he allowed me to help in other cases. I was hooked for life.

When I left Johns Hopkins to accept the Chair of Radiology at the fledgling School of Medicine at the University of New Mexico, good fortune followed me to Albuquerque. I had several years there of exhilarating experience working with two outstanding forensic

Figure 1   Russell S. Fisher, M.D.

scientists, Jim Weston and Homer Campbell (Figure 2). When Jim came to New Mexico he designed and built both a model state-wide Medical Examiners system and a state-of-the-art Forensic Sciences building on the medical center campus. He already was a world figure in Forensic Pathology and served as President of AAFS in 1976–1977. His untimely death during one of his daily morning runs on the UNM golf course was a great loss to the Forensic Sciences. Homer Campbell at that time was in the practice of General Dentistry and pursued an interest in Forensic Odontology as a part-time avocation. Homer was, in fact, *my* dentist and cleaned my teeth twice a year. (Fortunately, I never needed Jim Weston's professional services!) Later, Homer left his practice in favor of full-time forensic work and became President of the AAFS in 1991–1992.

Since coming to the University of South Alabama in 1978, I have enjoyed an entirely pleasant professional and personal relationship with LeRoy Riddick, a trainee of the legendary Milton Helpern, and now Professor of Pathology and Alabama State Medical Examiner (Figure 3). Roy and his associates and fellows (several of whom have gone on to responsible positions of their own) have invariably treated me with a most gratifying and warm collegiality as their Consultant in Forensic Radiology.

As my participation in forensic activities and meetings increased, I was astounded by the volume of radiologic images presented and/or published by (of necessity) non-radiologists — dentists, pathologists, physical anthropologists, and other forensic scientists. I have been astonished at the good quality of some of those images and saddened by how awfully bad others were. I have seen colleagues struggle with the interpretation of conditions that are well known and easily recognized by almost any radiologist. I have watched others agonize over problems that could be approached rather easily by the radiologic method. I have reviewed elaborate and costly research projects based on null hypotheses both proved and disproved years ago in our discipline. On the other hand, I

Figure 2 Left to right: James T. Weston, M.D., Homer R. Campbell, Jr., D.D.S., and B. G. Brogdon, M.D. on the occasion of a Science Writers' Forum on Forensic Radiology in New York City on April 13, 1977.

Figure 3 LeRoy Riddick, M.D.

have become acquainted with applications of my own technology in forensic sciences that are largely unknown to me and my fellow radiologists. None of this is totally surprising when one recognizes that there is essentially no common fund of radiologic knowledge, comprehensive radiological literature, or data bank of radiologic information readily available to the many disparate disciplines who may wish or need to use the x–ray or other radiologic modalities in their individual forensic pursuits.

The sad truth is that a century after the first x–ray was introduced as evidence in a court of law, there is no general appreciation of the extent of the radiologic potential in the forensic sciences. This was brought most forcefully to my attention when at a recent meeting no less an exemplar than the renowned criminalist, Dr. Henry C. Lee,* showed a slide depicting the 19 disciplines or specialties comprising the body of the forensic sciences; radiology was not among them!

The generally favorable response to my own efforts, and those of a few others, to spread the gospel of forensic radiology through talks, refresher courses, and publications directed to both forensic scientists and fellow radiologists finally has prompted me to undertake this book on *Forensic Radiology*. It represents an attempt to illustrate the applicability of diagnostic radiology to the broad range of the forensic sciences in the hope that it will both assist and stimulate others in the utilization of this useful tool in the solution of their problems. It is not an encyclopedia. It is not, for the most part, a how-to-do-it book. However, the three chapters in Section VIII will serve as a practical technical primer devoted to simplification and solution of technical problems which may mystify or bedevil the relatively untrained person who is forced to undertake unfamiliar tasks.

There is the risk that this volume, in trying to reach a large multidisciplinary readership, will be too difficult for some and too simple for others. As I try to leap unscathed between the horns of this dilemma, I hope the reader will view the attempt with tolerance and understanding.

The goal of this book is to cover the entire scope of radiological applications in the forensic sciences; the range of radiological applicability may be surprising to some readers. To make this volume timely and up to date, both current and anticipated uses of the exciting new modalities and techniques that have graced our discipline in recent years have been included. I am exceedingly fortunate and most grateful that an outstanding group of contributors has agreed to impart a unique body of knowledge and expertise in several chapters. This book would not have been possible without the time-consuming efforts of

---

* Lee, H. C., Advances in the analysis of data/evidence in the laboratory, presented at a conference on Forensic Investigation of Abuse and Violence, Pensacola, FL, September 19, 1995.

those extremely busy colleagues who herein share unstintingly the essence of their own forensic investigations and experience.

I have leaned heavily on other resources in this endeavor. Much information and a number of illustrations have been gleaned from the previously published material of others, and I appreciate the generosity of many authors and publishers in releasing their material for my use.

Sources of material have been acknowledged appropriately whenever possible. Some of the figures were produced from radiographs and slides that have resided in my files for many years; the origin of some of these are lost to both record and memory. My apology is extended for any oversight where credit is due, with the hope that it will be accepted in the same spirit of magnanimity characterized by the original offering.

I cannot apologize for the quality of the illustrations, some of which admittedly are suboptimal. I wish it were not so. But many post-mortem roentgenograms are obtained under most difficult conditions, in the morgue or in the field, by minimally trained or self-taught personnel. Often there is no opportunity for a repeat effort. Furthermore, there is no way to influence the quality of ante-mortem roentgenographs obtained from outside sources. Whatever one gets is considered a benison when the resolution of a case is at stake.

Tolley Tollefson and Teri Deese of the University of South Alabama Department of Radiology's photography section, cheerfully bore the added burden of this book even though they were already heavily laden with the routine work of a busy academic department. The illustrations in this book reflect their high degree of professionalism since, unfortunately, some of the original material with which they worked was of inferior quality, for reasons already given.

Vanessa Brown cheerfully and efficiently typed the several versions of my portion of this manuscript (as well as those of several of the contributors). She has coped with my hillbilly accent on dictated material, interpreted my nearly illegible cursive script and, in all cases, corrected my abominable spelling. This book was added to the exceptional demands she daily faces as Departmental Secretary, with direct responsibility as amanuensis to two senior faculty members and overseer of all other secretarial activities in the department. I thank her for a prodigious effort accomplished with patience and good humor.

My wife, Babs, called upon her experience (in a previous life) as an editor of a biomedical journal to compensate for my well-documented failure as a copyeditor and proofreader. Her influence on this book, and my life, are acknowledged with thanks here and elsewhere.

Steven K. Teplick, M.D., now Professor and Chairman of the Department of Radiology, University of South Alabama, has graciously supported this work by making time and departmental facilities and resources available to me, for which I thank him.

The staff of the Biomedical Library of the University of South Alabama has been unfailingly kind, courteous, and professionally competent in meeting all requests for help in finding and acquiring reference materials.

My editors, first George V. Novotny and later Bob Stern of CRC Press, have provided useful assistance and advice, continuous encouragement, and gentle prodding. They have borne my literary shortcomings, missed deadlines, and other problems with patience and aplomb. I hope the result was worth their effort.

Judge Haskell M. Pitluck, Past President of the American Academy of Forensic Sciences and valued friend, was kind enough to critically review my effort on "Coping with the Courts"; however, any residual errors or inaccuracies are solely my responsibility.

Finally, I must thank an unnamed multitude of friends, acquaintances, associates, and colleagues in Radiology, and a similar horde in the Forensic Sciences, who have been open-handed with their friendship, assistance, case material, and the lore of their respective disciplines. I have gained far more from those associations than have they and, especially, have learned far more than I have taught. I hope they will accept this blanket acknowledgment and my thanks for their contributions — in uncounted ways — to this opus.

Gil Brogdon
Mobile, Alabama

Contributors

Mark L. Bernstein, D.D.S.
Professor of Oral Pathology, Department of Surgical and Hospital Dentistry, University of Louisville Dental School
Diplomate American Board of Forensic Odontology
Forensic Consultant to the Medical Examiner's Office, Commonwealth of Kentucky

B. G. Brogdon, M.D.
University Distinguished Professor Emeritus of Radiology, University of South Alabama College of Medicine
Consultant in Forensic Radiology to the Office of the State Medical Examiner, Alabama Department of Forensic Sciences

Ferdinand Frauscher, M.D.
Department of Radiology II, University of Innsbruck

Blaine L. Hart, M.D.
Associate Professor of Radiology, University of New Mexico Health Sciences Center

A. Everette James, Sc.M., J.D., M.D.
Chair Emeritus, Department of Radiology and Radiological Sciences, Vanderbilt University
Senior Policy Advisor, Institute of Medicine, National Academy of Sciences
Consultant, Smithsonian Institutions
Art Committee, Cosmos Club, Washington, D.C., Explorers Club, New York City, Who's Who in American Art

Chucri M. Jalkh, B.S., R.T.(R)
Instructor in Clinical Radiologic Technology, Department of Radiological Sciences, University of South Alabama

Eric W. Lawson, M.D.
Resident in Diagnostic Radiology, Department of Radiology, University of South Alabama Medical Center

Joel E. Lichtenstein, M.D.
Professor of Radiology, University of Cincinnati College of Medicine

John D. McDowell, D.D.S., M.S.
Assistant Professor and Chairman of Oral Diagnosis, Oral Medicine and Oral Radiology, Department of Diagnostic and Biologic Sciences, University of Colorado School of Dentistry

James M. Messmer, M.D., M.Ed.
Associate Professor, Department of Radiology, Medical College of Virginia, Virginia Commonwealth University
Radiology Consultant, Office of the Chief Medical Examiner's Office, Commonwealth of Virginia

Charles W. Newell, Ed.D., R.T.(R)
Chair and Associate Professor, Department of Radiological Sciences, University of South Alabama

Wolfgang Recheis, Ph.D.
Department of Radiology II, University of Innsbruck

LeRoy Riddick, M.D.
Clinical Professor of Pathology, University of South Alabama College of Medicine
State Medical Examiner, Alabama Department of Forensic Sciences

David Sweet, D.M.D., Ph.D.
Director, Bureau of Legal Dentistry, Department of Oral Biology and Medical Sciences, University of British Columbia

Table of Contents

Section I
Introduction to Forensic Radiology

Section II
Identification

Section III
Gunshot Wounds

Section IV
Radiology in Nonviolent Crimes

Section V
Radiology of Abuse

Section VI
Research and the New Modalities

Section VII
Coping with the Courts

Section VIII
A Primer for Forensic Radiological Technology

this book is dedicated
with love to
BABS
my wife, best friend, sweetheart and partner
who, like our marriage and fine wine,
gets better with the passage of years

SECTION I

Introduction to Forensic Radiology

Definitions in Forensics and Radiology

1

B. G. BROGDON, M.D.

Forensic is derived from the Latin *forens(is)*: of or belonging to the forum, public, equivalent to *for(um)* **forum** + *ens* — **of, belonging to** + *ic*. By extension it came to also mean *disputative, argumentative, rhetorical, belonging to debate or discussion*. From there it is but a small step to the modern definition of **forensic** as *pertaining to, connected with, or used in courts of judicature or public discussion and debate*. Thus the forensic sciences encompass the application of specialized scientific and/or technical knowledge to questions of civil and criminal law, especially in court proceedings.

Forensic Medicine has come to be recognized as a special science or discipline that deals with relationships and applications of medical facts and knowledge to legal problems. Some prefer to call it *legal medicine* or *medical jurisprudence*.

Forensic Medicine is often considered to be synonymous with **forensic pathology** because full-time involvement of a physician with forensic activity is almost exclusively the province of that specialty.[1] The forensic pathologist is concerned principally with the post-mortem examination and, hence, deals mostly with the dead. In acknowledgment of this, Milton Helpern, M.D., the third Chief Medical Examiner of the City of New York, caused to be inscribed upon the lobby wall of his new office building in 1961 the Latin admonition, *TACEAT COLLOQUIA. EFFUGIAT RISUS. HIC LOCUS EST UBI MORS GAUDET SUCCURRERE VITAE,* (Let conversation cease. Let laughter flee. This is the place where death delights to help the living).[2] While other medical specialists may consult with the pathologist in the evaluation of death, virtually all of their other professional activities may have medicolegal ramifications and hazards involving both the living and the dead. These can embrace a large body of legal issues (e.g., age determination, assault, civil rights violations, inheritance, larceny, malpractice, parentage, personal injury, product liability, sexual offenses, smuggling, virginity, and wrongful birth or death).

Thus, in *Gradwohl*[3] the definition of legal medicine was expanded to include "the application of medical knowledge to the administration of law and to the furthering of justice and, in addition, the legal relations of the medical man."

Evidence of the origin of legal or forensic medicine can be found in records of ancient people some thousands of years ago, when occasionally a law appears to influence medicine or medicine is found to influence or modify a law.[3,4] The Egyptian, Imhotep, may have been the first to apply both the law and medicine to his surroundings. Hammurabi codified medical law circa 2200 B.C., and medicolegal issues were covered in early Jewish law. Later, other civilizations — the Greeks, ancient India, the Roman Empire — evolved jurisprudential standards involving medical fact or opinion.

Early cultures recognized the desirability of controlling the organization, duties, and liabilities of the medical profession. They also were acquainted with the importance of the knowledge and opinion of the medical person in the legal consideration of issues of great moment such as the use of drugs or poisons, the duration of pregnancy, virginity, super-fetation, the prognosis of wounds in different body locations (a physician determined that only one of Caesar's 23 stab wounds was fatal), sterility and impotence, sexual deviation, and suspicious death.

Early in the sixteenth century a separate discipline of forensic medicine began to emerge. New codes of law required expert medical testimony in trials of certain types of crime or civil action. The first medicolegal books appeared in the late sixteenth and early seventeenth centuries and, after 1650, lectures on legal medicine were given in Germany and France. The first book on medical jurisprudence in the English language appeared in 1788 and 19 years later the first Regius Chair in Forensic Medicine was recognized by the Crown at the University of Edinburgh. The English coroner's system was imported to the Colonies in North America in 1607, and it was not until 1871 that Massachusetts, later followed by New York and other jurisdictions, established a medical examiner system. Upon this base of professionalism in death investigation, supported by the framework of solid scientific and technical advances during the twentieth century, was erected the modern structure of forensic medicine which covers a heterogeneous, sometimes loosely related, family of numerous disciplines or subspecialties sharing a common interest.

Among those, **Forensic Radiology** usually comprises the performance, interpretation, and reportage of those radiological examinations and procedures that have to do with the courts and/or the law. Until but a few decades ago, **Radiology** could be defined as that special branch of medicine employing ionizing radiant energy in the diagnosis and treatment of disease. Now, the specialty of Radiology is divided into two quite distinct disciplines sharing only a common historical origin and a single certifying body, the American Board of Radiology. One of those two branches is Radiation Oncology, which utilizes high-energy ionizing radiant energy wavelengths and particles in the treatment of (almost exclusively malignant neoplastic) disease.

It is the other major branch of the specialty, **Diagnostic Radiology**, with which this book will be concerned. Diagnostic radiology is devoted primarily to the study of images of the internal structures of the human body. Perhaps Harry Z. Mellins, M.D., a superbly talented radiologist and teacher, best captured the eidolon of the diagnostic radiologist more than 30 years ago when he wrote,[5]

> The [diagnostic] radiologist perceives a shadow, sees a lesion, and imagines a man. The bedside physician sees the man, perceives the signs and images the lesion. They practice from the outside in and we from the inside out.

Nowadays images are acquired by an array of modalities and techniques:

- The *x-ray* or *roentgen ray* is an energy form of ionizing radiation from which may be produced fluorescent or photographic images. The latter are sometimes also called "x-rays" but are correctly termed *roentgenograms*, less accurately *radiographs*, and vulgarly as *films* (e.g., "chest film") (Figure 1-1).
- The *fluorescent image* can be electronically enhanced and directly visualized in real-time motion, cine-photographed, videotaped, or digitized and stored on magnetic tape or disks for replay (Figure 1-2).
- In the subspecialty of *nuclear medicine* or *nuclear radiology*, radioactive materials or isotopes can be directed to internal target organs or tissues by injection, inhalation,

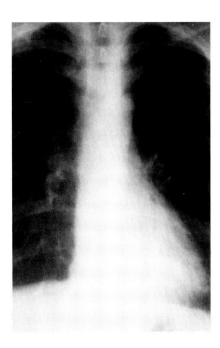

Figure 1-1 Chest roentgenogram, radiograph, or "film". This patient has an intracardiac tumor but it cannot be distinguished from the heart muscles or the blood inside the heart since all have approximately the same ability to absorb x-rays.

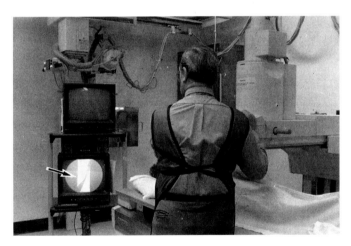

Figure 1-2 A modern fluoroscope with an image intensifier connected to a television camera. The televised image (arrow) can be seen without darkening the room.

or ingestion; the radiant energy escaping from inside the body can be collected on sensitive films or phosphors to create images, *scintiscans*, of the internal targets (Figure 1-3).

- Sound waves generated outside the body by transponders are reflected back from internal structural interfaces to be recaptured and converted into real-time or static images. The modality is called *ultrasound* or *ultrasonography*. The image is a *sonogram* (Figure 1-4).
- With special equipment, a roentgenogram of a thin section or slice of the body or body part can be acquired in the sagittal, coronal, or oblique plains (Figure 1-5). This technique is known as *tomography* and the processed image is a *tomogram* (now qualified as a *conventional tomogram* to distinguish it from a *computed tomogram*).

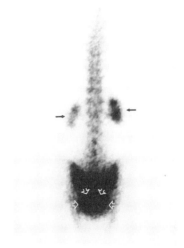

Figure 1-3   This is a nuclear scan using a bone-seeking isotope so the skeleton is imaged. Some of the isotope is taken up by the kidneys (arrows) and excreted into the bladder (open arrows) which should have been emptied before the scan was done. Unfortunately the full bladder obscures a tumor (chordoma) in the sacrum. (See Figure 1-7B-E, same case.)

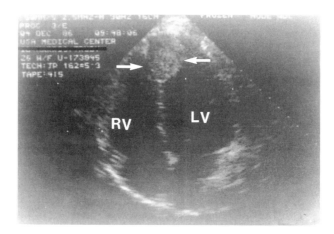

Figure 1-4   The ultrasound image of the same heart shown in Figure 1-1 is displayed as a cross-sectional image of the heart. The tumor is visualized in the interventrical septum (arrows) between the right ventricles (RV) and left ventricle (LV).

- Conventional roentgenograms result when x-ray photons (or light rays from intensifying screen phosphors excited by x-rays) "expose" a sensitive silver halide emulsion which, when processed, leaves a grain of reduced silver where the light-ray or x-ray photon struck. These microscopic black "dots" coalesce where the most x–rays were transmitted to the film and are sparse to absent where the interposed body absorbed the radiation and are intermediately dispersed in a gray scale according to the atomic number of the interposed tissue. This is an analogue image. With proper instrumentation or equipment an *analogue image* can be converted into a *digital image*. Some of the newer radiographic equipment modalities (i.e., digital fluoroscopy, digital subtraction angiography, some ultrasonography, computed tomography, and magnetic resonance imaging) produce a digital image directly. The advantage of a digital image is that it can be manipulated by such techniques as contrast shift, density range adjustment, back/white reversal, and edge enhancement (Figure 1-6). Although the analogue image has better spatial resolution than

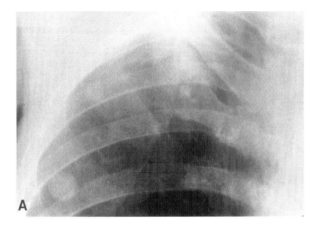

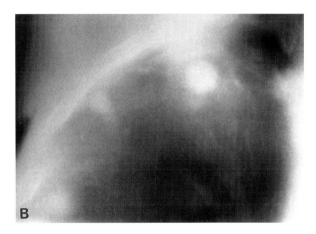

Figure 1-5   Example of conventional tomography. **A**. Chest roentgenogram: close-up of upper lung showing a large plaque of thickened pleura which obscures the underlying lung. **B**. Conventional tomogram: slice through the lung shows a nodular lesion that was hidden by the overlying pleural thickening.

the digital image, maximal contrast resolution is required to exploit the spatial resolution, and shades of gray are not easily separated. Thus the analogue roentgenogram may display muscle, water, blood, or brain in a gray scale in which they are indistinguishable one from another (Figure 1-7). The digital image can be computer processed or manipulated to separate shades of gray, thus permitting, for instance, visual separation of the brain substance from its interventricular fluid or the gallbladder wall from the bile it contains.

- *Computed axial tomography* caught the public fancy as the "CAT Scan" but is now more commonly and properly referred to as *computed tomography* or simply *CT* and the product also called a *CT* or, preferably, a *CT scan*. This device uses an array of photoreceptors to detect slight differences in attenuation of roentgen rays emitted by a rotating x-ray tube as they passed through the body or body part over multiple diametric pathways in the axial or cross-sectional plane. The computer-processed result is a series of images of cross-axial sectional *slices* of the body or part, allowing

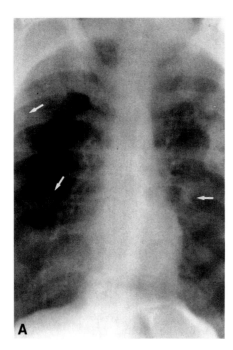 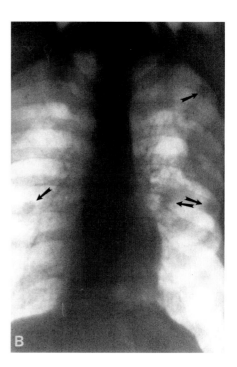

Figure 1-6 **A** and **B** are digital images of a chest containing multiple pulmonary nodules (arrows). The visual effect of black/white reversal image manipulation is demonstrated.

a much higher differentiation between body tissues than can be achieved from a conventional x-ray machine (Figure 1-8). The electronically acquired and computer-processed image can be manipulated in a variety of ways; for instance, to reconstruct images in coronal or sagittal planes or even two-dimensional displays of three-dimensional (3-D) reconstructions.

- *Magnetic resonance imaging (MRI)* utilizes strong magnetic fields to generate electromagnetic signals from elements and compounds found in body fluids and tissues (Figure 1-9). With computer manipulation one can obtain multiplanar, multidirectional, sectional images or *slices (MR scans)*. The signal strengths for individual tissues can be identified or manipulated by varying computer protocols.

- The subspecialty of *interventional radiology* is almost a separate discipline. A complex armamentarium of tools, devices, and instruments (e.g., catheters, balloons, lasers, needles, drains, stints, "wooly worms", macrospheres, enzymes, etc.) are used to invade the body — not only to create images and enhance diagnoses, but also to intervene therapeutically in disease processes or anatomic abnormalities.

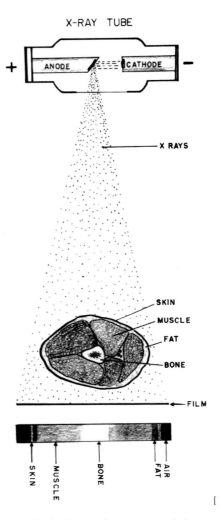

Figure 1-7   Schematic drawing showing differential absorption of x–rays by the tissues of the body in conventional radiography. From most to least radiodense these are (1) bone or calcium; (2) all soft tissues and liquids (muscle, blood, brain, heart, liver, urine, etc.) except (3) fat; (4) air or other gases.

Forensic radiology so far has depended almost exclusively on the x-ray and the static image captured on the roentgenogram. Newer imaging methods have revolutionized the field of diagnostic radiology in a time span so short that it falls within the career experience of radiologists still engaged in active practice. Already, some of these advances are being incorporated into forensic studies. If problems of accessibility and cost can be resolved, other of the newer radiologic techniques and modalities may be appropriated by the forensic sciences.

After all, it took six or seven thousand years of growth and development for forensic medicine to reach its present level of fruition. The flowering of forensic radiology had to wait on Professor Röntgen.

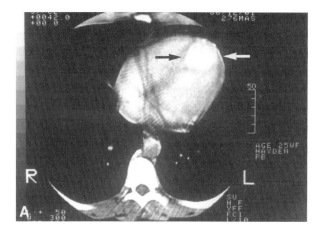

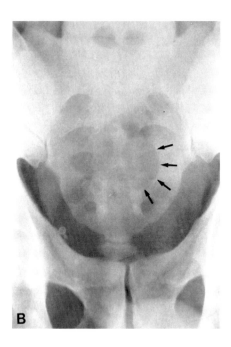

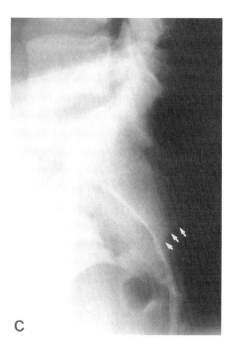

Figure 1-8   Examples of computed tomography. **A**. CT slice of heart showing tumor (arrows) in interventricular septum (same case as in Figures 1-1 and 1-4). **B** and **C**: frontal and lateral roentgenograms of a sacrum being partially destroyed by a tumor (arrows). **D**: CT slice through same sacrum showing bone area of destruction (arrows). **E**: CT reconstruction of sagittal (lateral) view from cross-sectional image. Note similarity to lateral view in **C**.

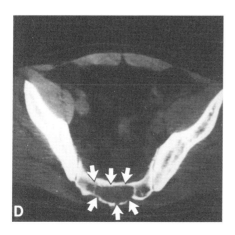
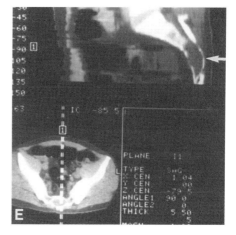

Figure 1-8   (continued)

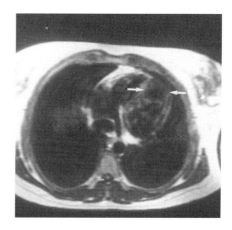

Figure 1-9   Magnetic resonance image (MRI) of cardiac tumor (arrows) shown in Figures 1-1, 1-4, and 1-8A.

References

1. Knight, B., How radiography aids forensic medicine, *Radiography*, 50, 5, 1984.

2. Helpern, M. and Knight, B., *Autopsy*, New American Library, New York, 1979, 184.

3. Camps, F. E., Ed., *Gradwohl's Legal Medicine*, 3rd ed., Yearbook, Chicago, 1976, chap. 1.

4. Wecht, C. H., Forensic use of medical information, in *Legal Medicine: Legal Dynamics of Medical Encounter*, 2nd ed., Am. Coll. Legal Med., Mosby-Yearbook, St. Louis, 1991, chap. 47.

5. Mellins, H. Z., Personal communication, 1963.

Forensic Radiology in Historical Perspective

2

B. G. BROGDON, M.D.
JOEL E. LICHTENSTEIN, M.D.

Contents

Röntgen and His Rays

The discovery of "a new kind of ray" while working alone in the laboratory on an autumn afternoon firmly established the place of Wilhelm Conrad Röntgen among the great investigative scientists of all time. But the mantle of greatness did not descend upon obscurity — Röntgen already enjoyed a solid scientific reputation built on the foundation of academic excellence and painstaking research.

Wilhelm Conrad Röntgen (Figure 2-1) was born on March 27, 1845 in Linnet, a provincial town on the edge of the Ruhr Valley. The family moved to Apeldoorn in Holland when he was three years old. There he enjoyed a pleasant childhood as the only son of a prosperous textile merchant. His schooling was erratic; it was only after considerable difficulty that the 23-year-old Röntgen finally won a diploma in Mechanical Engineering from the Polytechnical School in Zürich. He stayed on in Zürich for some additional courses in mathematics and physics and there found his life-interest in the physics laboratory. He obtained a Ph.D. at the University of Zürich in 1869. There he also met his future wife, Bertha (Figure 2-2), and reached the decision to follow a university career in physics.

Except for some initial delays, the result of his rather informal education, the next quarter of a century brought steady progress in Röntgen's career. At age 43, he received an appointment as Professor of Physics and Director of the Physical Institute at the University of Würzburg; only 6 years later he was elected as Rector of the University, largely as an acknowledgment of his research contributions. Thus, by his 50th birthday in 1895 Röntgen justifiably could look upon his achievements in life with complacent satisfaction. He held the highest office bestowed by the university, and his 48 published communications had brought widespread recognition and admiration from his peers.

The Röntgens enjoyed comfortable living quarters on the top floor of the Physical Institute. His laboratory was readily accessible on the floor below (Figure 2-3). Thus, unlike many present-day researchers whose accomplishments in the laboratory are "rewarded" by appointment to high academic and administrative positions, Röntgen was able to continue to devote a large portion of his time to independent investigation. In an address

Figure 2-1 Wilhelm Conrad Röntgen, 1845–1923. Taken at the time of his discovery of the x-rays. (From Glasser, O., *American Journal of Roentgenology*, 25, 437, 1931. With permission.)

Figure 2-2 Bertha Röntgen, *nee* Ludwig.

upon assuming the rectorship of the university, Röntgen epitomized a strong scientific credo when he said,[1]

> The university is a place of scientific research and mental education ... the experiment is the most powerful and most reliable lever enabling us to extract secrets from nature and ... experiment must constitute the final judgement as to whether a hypothesis should be retained or be discarded. ... if the result does not agree with reality it must necessarily be wrong.

Figure 2-3   The Physical Institute as it stands today on the Röntgenring in Würzburg. The Röntgens' living quarters were on the top floor (arrow) just above the laboratory where Röntgen discovered his rays. The inscription on the front exterior wall of the laboratory reads, "In diesum hause entdeckte W.C. RÖNTGEN im jabre 1895 die nach ihm benannten strahlen."

In the autumn of 1895, Dr. Röntgen became interested in the cathode ray experiments of Hittorf, Crookes, and others. On November 8th of that year he was surprised and immensely excited to observe the fluorescence of a screen coated with barium platinocyanide which was lying on a bench at some distance from an energized Hittorf tube which had been completely light-proofed with a black cardboard. Repetition of the experiment produced the same result even when the barium platinocyanide screen was moved at greater and greater distances from the tube — even up to 2 m. Since no visible light could escape from the heavily shielded tube, and since cathode rays were known to penetrate only a few centimeters of air, the fluorescence must be caused by a completely new kind of emanation from the tube![2] Much later a correspondent from McClure's magazine reported an interview with Röntgen concerning his discovery. He asked the great physicist what his thoughts were upon perceiving that first fluorescent glow in the darkened laboratory. "I did not think," answered Röntgen, "I investigated."[3]

And so he did!

Röntgen embarked upon 50 days of intensive research culminating in the submission of his initial manuscript, "Ueber eine neue Arte von Strahlen" (On a new kind of ray), on December 28, 1895.[4] He worked day and night, taking his meals in the laboratory and often sleeping there.

He had found by accident that the rays penetrated black paper. He then determined that the rays were not stopped by cardboard, cloth, a thick plank, or a book of 2000 pages. Metal such as copper, lead, gold, platinum and silver were less penetrable; the densest of them were almost opaque.[5]

Glasser[6] describes Röntgen's most startling observation,

To test further the ability of lead to stop the rays, he selected a small lead piece, and in bringing it into position observed to his amazement not only that this round shadow of the disk appeared on the screen, but that he suddenly could distinguish the outline of his thumb and finger, within which appeared darker shadows — the bones of his hand.

The professor had just witnessed the first fluoroscopic image of internal structures in a human body!

To better document his findings, Röntgen replaced the fluorescent screen with photographic plates and preserved the images of metal weights in a wooden box, a compass, a piece of welded metal, and a piece of wood wrapped in wire[5,7] (Figure 2-4).

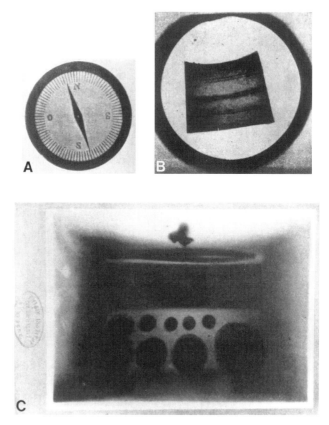

Figure 2-4   Photographic prints of articles Röntgen exposed to the rays during his discovery period. **A**: a compass; **B**: a welded piece of metal; **C**: weights in a wooden box inside a purse.

Bertha Röntgen was somewhat mystified, and more than a little put off by her husband's obsessive and solitary activity: catching naps in the laboratory, being late for meals, and being generally absent-minded and inattentive to ordinary family affairs. Finally, one night she became very angry when he failed to comment upon the excellent dinner she had prepared. Perhaps to mollify her, he led his wife downstairs to the laboratory for a rather disturbing revelation of the reason for his excitement and single-mindedness. Let Glasser tell it:

> At his instruction she placed her hand on a cassette loaded with a photographic plate, upon which he directed rays from his tube for 15 minutes. On the developed plate the bones of her hand appeared light within the darker shadow of the surrounding flesh; two rings on her finger had almost stopped the rays and were clearly visible. When he showed the picture to her, she could hardly believe that this bony hand was her own and shuddered at the thought of seeing her skeleton. To Mrs. Röntgen, as to many others, this experience gave a vague premonition of death.[6]

This one radiograph, when widely circulated, probably did more to change the face of medicine than any other single item in history (Figure 2-5).

Working with his screens and plates, Röntgen made all of the fundamental observations that were the basis for his first two papers on the "x"-rays: so named because "x" was the symbol for the unknown. Röntgen's experimental design was so thorough and his reportage so meticulous and detailed that it was years before other investigators could add anything new to the subject. He showed that the rays were propagated in straight lines and were not influenced by magnetic fields, that the beam could be "hardened" by passing through absorptive material, that secondary radiation could be produced from certain targeted materials, and noted many other basic properties of the strange new ray.[7]

His manuscript was immediately accepted for publication in the December, 1895 issue of the *Annals of the Würzburg Physical-Medicine Society* but, since no meetings or lectures were given in German universities during Christmas vacation, the formal presentation of Röntgen's seminal preliminary communication[4] had to await the January 1896 meeting of the society.

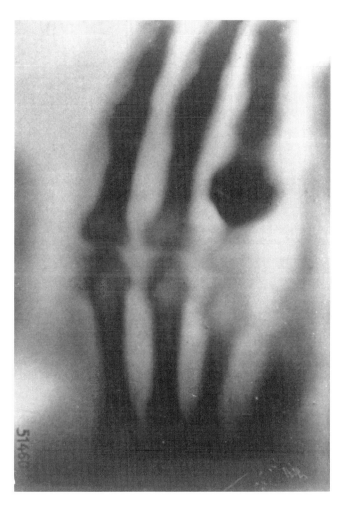

Figure 2-5   The first roentgenogram of a human, Bertha Röntgen's hand, exposed in the laboratory during November 1895.

The alacrity with which Röntgen's offering was accepted is astonishing by today's sluggish standards when months (or years) elapse between the submission and acceptance of a scientific work. Nonetheless, then, as now, it seems there was sufficient impatience with the system to stimulate "leakage" of an important scientific breakthrough to the popular press.

On New Year's Day, 1896 Röntgen sent preprints of "Uber eine neue Arte von Strahlen" and a few of his first x-ray pictures to friends in Bavaria and Austria. Not surprisingly, the news of his discovery ran in *Vienna Presse* on January 5, 1896 and was flashed around the world, hitting the London and New York papers on the following day.

World reaction to this news, often garbled and inaccurate, was as astonishing and sensational as the news itself.[8,9] Lead-lined underclothes for modest young ladies were advertised by a London entrepreneur. A New Jersey assemblyman proposed a bill prohibiting x-ray opera glasses. In New York, a newspaper stated that at the College of Physicians and Surgeons the roentgen rays were used "to reflect anatomic diagrams directly into the brains of the students, making a much more enduring impression than the ordinary methods of learning anatomical details."[10,11] A young man in Jefferson County, IA claimed that with x-rays he was able to transmute 13¢ worth of base metal into pure gold worth $153.[8] The x-ray was proposed as a solution for the issues of vivisection, spiritualism, soul photography, the temperance movement, and telepathy.[7] A private detective, Mr. Henry Slater offered to introduce the "New Photography … in divorce matters free of charge", presumably to discover the skeleton which every closet is said to contain.[8,11]

For the most part, however, physicians and scientists, as well as responsible jurists and journalists, quickly understood that Röntgen's rays were a boon of great potential in the fields of medicine, biological and physical sciences, industry, the arts, and the law:

> The surgeon … could … determine the extent of a complicated fracture without the manual examination … so painful to the patient [or] find the position of a foreign body, such as a bullet or piece of shell … without any painful examinations with a probe.
>
> *Frankfurt Zeitlung*, January 7, 1896

> Knowing the existence of a fracture in a person, who has been burned or mutilated beyond recognition, we can hope to identify him by the x-ray …
>
> *Dr. Fovau d'Courmelles,*
> *Am. X-Ray J.*, October, 1898

It is no wonder then, that on January 23, 1896 a large crowd of representative scientists and members of the Society, university faculty and students, city officials, and representatives from the army filled the auditorium of the Physical Institute for Röntgen's first and only lecture on the x-ray (Figure 2-6). He was modest in demeanor, generous in praise of his scientific forebears, and precise in his description of his "*arbeit*". He showed x-ray pictures of various test objects and actually created an x-ray image of the hand of the famous anatomist, von Kolliker, during the meeting (Figure 2-7). Von Kolliker led three cheers, and amid general applause proposed that the rays be called Röntgen's rays in honor of the great discoverer.[5]

Figure 2-6   Röntgen's lecture to the January 23, 1896 meeting of the Würzburg Physical Medicine Society as portrayed by Robert A. Thom in a painting commissioned by Park, Davis & Co., now a division of Warner-Lambert. Copyright 1962 (with permission). The noted anatomist, von Kolliker (arrow), was a willing subject for the demonstration of "a new kind of ray".

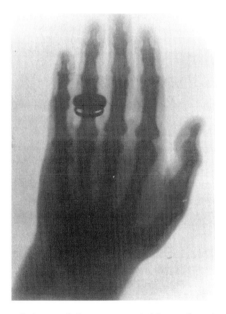

Figure 2-7   Photographic print of the roentgenogram of Professor von Kolliker's hand during the January 23, 1896 presentation by Röntgen.

Never has a new scientific or technological breakthrough been so quickly and universally adopted by the medical/scientific community. The usefulness of the x-ray in non-invasive examinations of persons and objects was self-evident. The relatively simple tools and devices necessary to assemble an x-ray generator were readily available throughout the civilized world. Finally, thanks to a popular press thriving on sensationalism and a scientific press more rapidly responsive than can be even imagined today, the "how-to-do-it" instructions were handy to all interested parties.

The Flowering of Forensic Radiology

By its very nature, the science of radiology solves mysteries as it reveals deep within the body hidden secrets that are otherwise inaccessible to exposure. This potential was obvious from the first few images Röntgen produced in those first fateful 50 days in Würzburg. It seems unsurprising and only natural that the application of x-rays to the solution of problems and mysteries that fall within the purview of law and the courts should have been so quickly realized. Indeed, the first news of Röntgen's discovery in the U.S. in the *New York Sun* on January 6, 1895 reported erroneously — but prophetically — that, "The professor is already using his discovery to photograph broken limbs and bullets in human bodies."[13]

Some credit Professor A. W. Wright of Yale University with being the first American to produce an x-ray image. Wright wrote,

> A rabbit, purchased in one of the markets of the city, after an exposure of one hour to the rays, left upon the plate a complete representation … . Particularly interesting in this photograph were several small round spots which appeared dark on the positive print. These were surmised to be shot … were readily found and extracted. The mode of death of the animal was not previously known.[14]

So this one small animal experiment was a precursor of the familiar forensic activities of localization and extraction of missiles and establishment of cause of death.

Actually, the first court case involving the x-rays in North America commenced on Christmas Eve, 1895 (three days before Röntgen submitted his first communication to the Physical-Medicine Society of Würzburg. In Montreal, a Mr. George Holder shattered the peace of that wintry evening by shooting in the leg a Mr. Tolson Cunning. Attempts to locate the bullet by probing failed; the wound healed but remained symptomatic. A professor of physics at McGill University, John Cox, was requested by Cunning's surgeon, Dr. R. C. Kirkpatrick, to make an x-ray photograph of the wounded extremity. In the Physics Lecture Theater appropriate equipment was assembled and, with a 45-minute exposure, a plate was obtained which showed the flattened bullet lying between the tibia and fibula (Figure 2-8). Dr. Kirkpatrick removed the bullet, and Mr. Cunning was discharged 10 days later. The x-ray plate was submitted to the court during the trial, with the subsequent conviction of Mr. Holder for attempted murder. He was sentenced to 14 years in the penitentiary.[15–17]

The first instance in which a roentgenogram was brought to court in England was a personal injury case tried by Mr. Justice Hawkins and a special jury in Nottingham.[12] Early in September, 1895 a Miss Ffolliott, a burlesque and comedy actress, suffered an injury while carrying out an engagement at a local theater. Hurrying to change costumes between acts, Miss Ffolliott fell on the staircase leading to her dressing room and severely injured her left foot. Even after a month of bed rest, she was unable to resume her professional activities. Finally, early in 1896 a Dr. Frankish sent her to University College Hospital where both her feet were examined by x-rays (the first comparison views?). There, clearly, was demonstrated a displacement of the cuboid bone in Miss Ffolliott's left foot, and when the

Figure 2-8 Tolson Cunning's leg was exposed to x-rays in order to locate the bullet fired by George Holder on Christmas Eve, 1895. The examination took place in the Physics Laboratory at McGill University, Montreal on February 7, 1896. The result was the first x-ray plate to be admitted to a court in North America. (Courtesy of the Center for the American History of Radiology, Reston, VA.)

two negatives were taken into court, both judge and jury could see the difference between the injured and uninjured members. Neither side could further argue the point; the only defense was a charge of contributory negligence against Miss Ffolliott.

Murder was the crime in one of the earliest forensic applications of Röntgen's discovery.[18,19] The murder took place on April 23, 1896 in a Lancashire textile town when Hargreaves Hartley fired four shots from a pistol into the head of his wife, Elizabeth Ann, then killed himself by jumping into the Leeds-Liverpool Canal and drowning. Mrs. Hartley survived the attack and was conscious.

Her physician, Dr. William Little, had learned of the potential of x-rays from a letter calling attention to Röntgen's work in the *Manchester Guardian* from Arthur Schuster, Professor of Physics at Owens College, Manchester. After a local photographer from Burnley tried unsuccessfully to x-ray the head of the victim, Dr. Little called upon Professor Schuster for assistance in locating the bullets. Unfortunately, Professor Schuster was ill and sent two assistants, C. H. Lees and A. Stanton, to the small home at 20 North Street, Nelson on April 29th. The tiny bedroom in this typical working-class terraced house was soon crowded with equipment: three Crookes tubes (two as spares), a high-tension coil, glass photographic plates, and storage batteries (there was no electricity in the house).

The first two radiographs, the results of 60- and 70-minute exposures, were developed by Professor Schuster and showed three of the bullets. On May 2nd, Professor Schuster himself went to Nelson and was able to find the fourth bullet (Figure 2-9). All were beyond the reach of a probe. Because of Mrs. Hartley's weakened condition, no attempt was made

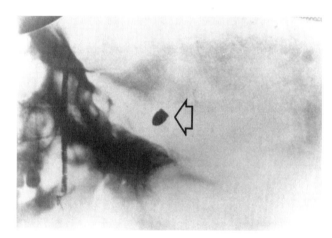

Figure 2-9 Murder in Lancashire.[19] **A**: Professor Arthur Schuster who found **B**: the fourth bullet (arrow). The excitement and stress of the event caused one of Schuster's associates to have a nervous breakdown.

to extract the bullets, no treatment was undertaken, and the patient died on May 9th. (This case can be considered an early manifestation of our tendency to use elaborate procedures and the newest technology, whether or not it will influence the outcome. At best, the radiographs probably replaced an autopsy in this case.)

The entire exercise was quite a spectacle for the town, with the mayor, town clerk, and others crowded into the room where the "experiment" took place, and it was reported extensively in the local press. The excitement and tension associated with the effort was blamed for the nervous breakdown of one of the associates, Mr. Stanton, sometime later.

The first civil case in which x-ray evidence was accepted into a U.S. court took place in Denver, CO.[16,20–22] It all began on June 15, 1895 when James Smith, a poor clerk who was "reading law" and doing odd jobs to make expenses, fell from a ladder while pruning a tree. He procrastinated (perhaps because of financial considerations) for almost a month before calling upon Dr. W. W. Grant for professional services. Dr. Grant was well known as a distinguished surgeon, one of the founders of the American College of Surgeons, who had performed the first appendectomy in this country on a 22-year-old female, Mary Gartside.[23]

Dr. Grant did a thorough examination and found no evidence of fracture; he did not restrict Mr. Smith's activity but asked him to return for an office visit in one week. The second examination disclosed no fracture. Dr. Grant neither saw nor heard from the patient again until April, 1896 when Mr. Smith brought a $10,000 suit for malpractice against Dr. Grant, claiming limb shortening and disability due to a misdiagnosis of an impacted fracture of the left femoral neck (Figure 2-10).

Figure 2-10   Illustration in the *Daily News*, December 3, 1896 of some of the principals and witnesses in *Smith v. Grant*. (From Bruwer, A. J., Ed., *Classic Descriptions in Diagnostic Radiology*, Vol. 2, 1964.[21] Courtesy of Charles C Thomas, Springfield, IL.)

Since James Smith had been employed by several lawyers to take dictation and type up legal instruments and was, himself, studying the law, it should come as no surprise that he appreciated the potential for legal redress for his incapacity and could engage two of the brightest young minds in the legal community to prosecute his case. One, Ben B. Lindsey, later became the founder of the Denver Court of Domestic Relations or Juvenile Court. The other, Fred W. Parks, became the youngest senator from Colorado.

In the interval between the fall from the ladder and the filing of the lawsuit, radiology had come to Denver. Dr. Chauncey Tennant, Jr. of the Denver Homeopathic College, Mr. Harry H. Buckwalter, a local photojournalist, and a Mr. Hall, who was president of the Diamond Lamp Company (and thus could manufacture tubes) had been experimenting with the new rays for some time and had given an exhibition before the Denver and Arapahoe Medical Society. There was speculation at that meeting whether this new science might play a role in the malpractice suit filed against Dr. Grant earlier that same month.

Smith's young attorneys were quick to grasp at new opportunities and, as the trial date drew near, approached Mr. Buckwalter, who agreed to x-ray their client. On November 7, 11, 21, and 29 in 1896 Mr. Buckwalter and Dr. Tennant made several plates of Mr. Smith's hip with exposures ranging up to 80 minutes, the last of which showed the outline of an impacted fracture of the proximal femur. The attempt to admit these roentgenograms in evidence prompted lengthy argument.

There were two issues here: one more medical than legal, the other more legal than medical. The first had to do with whether the shadows on the roentgen plate could accurately represent the condition of the proximal femur, with its complex bends and angles, lying at some distance from both the x-ray tube and the photographic plate. This, basically, was simply a question of proper positioning and alignment of patient, tube, and plate and was resolved by a courtroom demonstration.

The other issue was more fundamental. Photographs had long been accepted as "secondary" evidence; a witness could testify that the photograph was a true representation of what had actually been seen. The roentgenogram, on the other hand, purported to show the true nature of a condition totally hidden from direct observation. For that reason, judges in the eastern U.S. had refused to admit roentgenograms as evidence saying, "It is like offering the photograph of a ghost."

The arguments raged all day before Judge Owen E. LeFevre in the District Court of Arapahoe County. Judge LeFevre was a well-known and colorful character in Colorado. He was a Civil War veteran, University of Michigan graduate, and a respected lawyer and jurist. He had made a fortune in gold mining, bred horses, farmed, had broad social interests, and owned the finest collection of contemporary French paintings in the state. He decided to sleep on the matter, and on the morning of December 2nd or 3rd, 1896 (the record is not clear), handed down his landmark decision in the elegant language of those days:

> We … have been presented with a photograph taken by means of a new scientific discovery … . It knocks for admission at the temple of learning; What shall we do or say? Close fast the door or open wide the portals?

> These photographs are offered in evidence to show the present condition of the head and neck of the femur bone, which is entirely hidden from the eye of the surgeon … . Modern science has made it possible to look beneath the tissues of the human body, and has aided surgery in telling of the hidden mysteries. We believe it is our duty to be the first … in admitting in evidence a process known and acknowledged as a determinate science. The exhibits will be admitted in evidence."

X-rays already had been in court before Judge LeFevre's decision, but not as images. This involved another malpractice case but with x-rays as the cause of the injury. In Chicago, Frank Bolling was thrown from his buggy and suffered a fracture of his right ankle on September 2, 1895. By May, 1896 he was able to return to work but still had symptoms. On September 10, 1896 three x-ray photographs were made under the supervision of Dr. Otto L. Smith and Professor W. C. Fuchs, using exposure times of 35 to 40 minutes with the tube only 6 inches from the ankle. The resultant radiation damage eventuated in amputation of the foot and ankle. The jury awarded $10,000 in damages to Mr. Bolling.[16,21]

The first criminal case in the U.S. involving x-rays was the October, 1897 Haynes murder trial in Watertown, N.Y.[16,21] The victim was shot in the jaw with a .32 caliber bullet. Another foreign object was discovered lodged in the back of the head. Was this a second bullet or a fragment from the first? Dr. Gilbert Cannon gave testimony on the findings of the roentgenogram (not a second bullet) which subsequently was accepted as evidence by Judge Wright.

Acceptance of radiology — and the radiologist — in court was neither immediate, universal, or standardized. As late as 1919, a court in Iowa accepted x-ray photographs as the best evidence, but disallowed expert testimony to explain what they showed. The physician witness might describe the expected roentgenographic manifestations of an injury, then the jury would view the images and draw their own conclusions.[21]

A more sensible approach was that of a Judge Pound in 1915, who denied the doctrine that a photograph is the best evidence of what it contains should be extended to the radiograph. Rather, he said, " … the x-ray picture is not … the best evidence to laymen of what they contain. The opinion of the expert is the best evidence of what they contain — the only evidence."[21]

Dr. Frank W. Ross pointed out that there might be different standards for evidence from a physician who was an x-ray expert and that from his counterpart in general clinical practice. He wrote in 1899, " … evidence which … may be sufficient for us … may count for naught in a court of law … . Best intentions are often looked upon with suspicion by the court and the jury. Especially is this true in regard to new discoveries, which are viewed rather in the light of experiments."[16] (Ross could have been talking about any subsequent technological breakthrough in radiology or in other fields — DNA for instance.)

Other forensic applications of Röntgen's rays were quickly proposed as the news of his experiments spread and others repeated them. The May 30, 1896 issue of *JAMA* mentions an article by Dr. T. Bordas of the Faculty of Medicine of Paris in the May issue of the *Annales d'Hygiene Publique et le Medicine Legale*.[21] Monsieur le Docteur suggested that x-ray be used not only for identification through the visualization of old fractures, bullets, or other known peculiarities, but also recommended its use on suspicious packages suggestive of being infernal machines. Unfortunately, his advice is still timely today (Figure 2-11).

A somewhat logical extension of the concept of examining packages for infernal machines was the use of an x-ray device in customs houses (Figure 2-12). The Bureaux

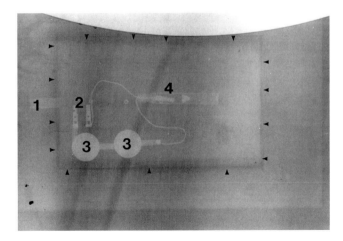

Figure 2-11   Radiograph of a modern letter bomb. Arrowheads indicate plastic explosive inside envelope. The triggering string (1) closes the contact (2) so that current from the batteries (3) energizes the detonator (4). (Courtesy Dr. Rafic E. Melhem. See *Radiology*, 151, 606, 1984.)

Figure 2-12   French customs officer (on right) using a hand-held fluoroscope to examine a piece of luggage. The glass x-ray tube (arrow) is on the table between him and the other official with the chevron on his sleeve. (From Angus, W. M., A commentary on the development of diagnostic imaging technology, *RadioGraphics*, 9, 1225, 1989. With permission.)

de Douanes in 1897 used fluoroscopes to examine passengers' luggage, purses, hats, hair, etc. for contraband at the Pavillion de Rohan and at the Gare du Nord.[21] (A modern version of this initiative is discussed in Chapter 12.)

d'Courmelles' expectations for identification of persons by radiographic comparison seem not to have been realized before the turn of the century. The popular scientific method of human identification at the time of d'Courmelles' prediction had been devised by Alphonse Bertillon, a Parisian anthropologist.[24] In 1879 he had founded an anthropometric department at the prefecture of police. There he introduced an anthropometric system designed to identify an individual throughout his life — this on a classification (small, medium, and large) of 12 precise measurements of the length and breadth of the head; the length of the radius, foot, and left elbow; the height of the trunk and bust; and also color of the iris of the right eye. This description was supplemented by special visible features and front and side photographs. Bertillon's system was accepted widely and used internationally by 1892.[21] Even Bertillon recognized inherent problems in the method — variations in measurements made by different investigators, and changes in individual measurements with variations in body weight or as the result of pathologic processes.

A Berliner, Levinsohn, suggested that direct measurements of the skeleton through x-ray photography would be more accurate.[25] His paper attracted some notice, but apparently his method was not widely employed.

A radiologist and compatriot of Bertillon was the Parisian, Henri Béclère.[26,27] Béclère advocated *dactylography* in which the skin of the fingers is lightly coated with powered lead tetroxide and exposed to soft x-rays. The resultant roentgenogram produced fine fingerprints (Figure 2-13). Béclère also made much of the configuration of the nails; he seemed not to pay much attention to the equally unique patterns of the underlying bones except to note that the skeletal shadows do not compromise the distinctness or clarity of the ungual furrows.

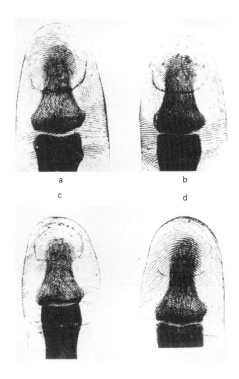

Figure 2-13   Roentgenographic fingerprints obtained by H. Béclère by coating the fingers with lead tetroxide before exposure to soft x-rays. (From Bruwer, A. J., Ed., *Classic Descriptions in Diagnostic Radiology*, Vol. 2, 1964. Courtesy Charles C Thomas, Springfield, IL.)

Béclère may not have known of the work of Dr. David Walsh who, 21 years earlier, also produced images of knuckle folds, palmar lines, and fingerprint furrows on roentgenograms of hands impregnated with bismuth subnitrate.[28] The question of primacy is of no practical importance since both systems quickly were relegated to the status of historical curiosities by the cheap and rapid ink print.

The x-ray has enjoyed a modest resurgence of activity in fingerprint work in the recovery of latent prints from difficult surfaces (i.e., multicolored documents, cloth, polythene, wax, cardboard, hardboard, varnished and untreated wood, rubber, pigskin, and the skin of human corpses or nonvital separated body parts). Thus, by this fingerprint method the corpse may be able to identify his or her assailant. Introduced by Graham[29] and followed up by Winstanley,[30] the method is known as x-ray fluorescence radiography (XFR) or back-scatter radiography. It relies on the emission of low-energy x-rays (secondary or Compton scatter) from heavy metal particles (lead dust) when bombarded with suitable high-energy x-rays (Figure 2-14). Special equipment is required and the lead dust represents a potential health hazard.

As an aid to identification, Angerer in Munich suggested in 1896 the use of wrist bone development as a measure of bone age.[31]

Forensic radiology of celebrities, whether famous or notorious, has a special fascination and has contributed to the public awareness of the field. His Excellency A. von Kolliker, the famous anatomist whose hand Röntgen exposed at the lecture on January 23, 1896

Figure 2-14   Fingerprint raised from the skin of a human corpse by the XFR method of Graham.[29] (By permission of Churchill Livingston Inc., a subsidiary of the Longman Group Ltd., New York.)

certainly was a scientific celebrity and the resultant image was widely circulated. Various early participants in court cases involving x-rays enjoyed fleeting celebrity in the popular press because of the novelty of the method. Perhaps the first American of national or international stature to undergo x-ray examination in a situation with forensic connotations was Theodore Roosevelt. Mr. Roosevelt was the fifth of ten presidents to become the target of an assassination attempt (Jackson, Lincoln, Garfield, McKinley, both Roosevelts, Truman, Kennedy, Ford twice, and Reagan — all but Jackson and T. Roosevelt while in office).

President McKinley was shot by an anarchist while viewing the 1901 Pan-American Exposition in Buffalo, the first such outrage to occur since Röntgen's discovery. Although x-ray equipment was on display at the fair, it was not employed in the unsuccessful search for the bullet and McKinley died eight days later of infection.

Theodore Roosevelt succeeded McKinley as President but was shot after leaving office while running as the Bull Moose Party candidate for a third term. The date was October 14, 1912 in Milwaukee. As Roosevelt was leaving his hotel to speak at a rally, "a half-crazed fanatic" stepped close to his automobile and shot him in the chest. The bullet, which ordinarily would have been fatal, was decelerated and deflected by passing through Mr. Roosevelt's overcoat, suit, shirt, and underclothes. Along the way it penetrated the folded manuscript for his speech and a steel eyeglass case, before entering his heavily muscled chest. Mr. Roosevelt remained upright, calmed the angry crowd, and insisted on proceeding to the hall where he gave his speech and shook hands with some of the crowd. (He did admit that this last activity was somewhat painful.)

Later that evening Mr. Roosevelt went by special train to Chicago, walked to a waiting ambulance, sat up in it en route to the hospital, and walked in for an examination of his wound with x-rays. The bullet had entered his right chest medial and inferior to the nipple and was embedded in a rib, splintering its internal surface so that the pleura was compromised. The bullet was not extracted for fear of massive pneumothorax and/or subsequent empyema. He carried the bullet with him to the grave.[32]

The assassination attempt on Franklin Roosevelt missed him, but killed the mayor of Chicago. The Puerto Rican extremists who assaulted Truman in Blair House never got close to him. But few events in history have had the world impact, or generated so much enduring controversy, as the November 22, 1963 assassination of President John F. Kennedy in plain view of a large crowd and a worldwide television audience. The chronology of that Dallas afternoon, or its aftermath, needs no reiteration here.

The post-mortem radiographs of Mr. Kennedy have added some fuel to the firestorm of debate which burns so fiercely even today, yet seems to cast so little light upon the truth of the matter. The radiographs are central to the controversy about the number of shots, direction and trajectory of the shots, and the number and the location of the shooter(s). The set, a frontal and two lateral views of the skull, are of poor quality, being somewhat overexposed. The location of the bullet wound, trajectory, fracture patterns, and conflicting expert opinion have been used paradoxically in support of opposing theories.[33–39] It is not within the interests or province of this book to enter into those arguments.

In February, 1896 W. Koenig was taking intraoral films of the teeth (Figure 2-15), leading the way for the science of Forensic Odontology which has flourished only since the 1940s.[11,40] The case of Adolph Hitler dates from that decade.

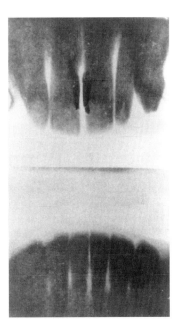

Figure 2-15   Dental x-rays by W. Koenig in 1896. Restorations are seen in the maxillary central incisors.

Following the unsuccessful assassination attempt with the bomb in the Wolf's Lair bunker on July 20, 1944, Hitler had many residual physical symptoms and disabilities. Persistent headaches finally forced him to follow the advice of his otolaryngologist, Dr. Paul Giesler.[41] On September 19th he was driven to an army field hospital at Rastenburg where three roentgenograms of his skull were obtained[42] (Figure 2-16). Those films survived the war; Hitler, of course, did not — although speculation and rumors abounded that he had somehow escaped. The dental work displayed on Hitler's roentgenograms was quite distinctive, however, and the Russians were able to make comparison with the burned remains found in the ruins of the chancellery garden. Although positive identification was made by this dental comparison, the Russians kept secret this information for more than two decades.[43]

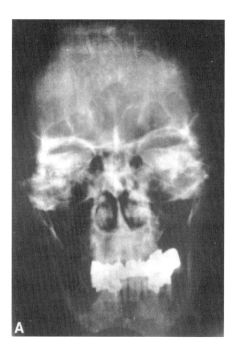
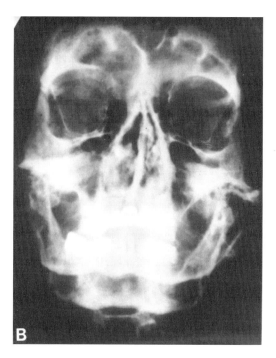
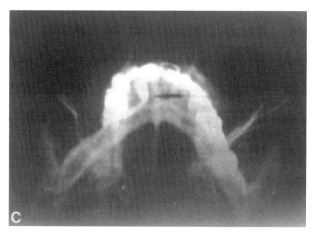

Figure 2-16   **A, B, C**: Ante-mortem roentgenograms of A. Hitler from September 19, 1944. Note the extensive and unusual dental work which confirmed identification of his remains.

One of the worst of Hitler's villains escaped retribution. Dr. Joseph Mengele, the Doctor of Death at Auschwitz, left the camp before its liberation. He lived for some time near Günzberg protected by family influence and local officials. He then went to South America where he practiced medicine in various places under false names; advised General Stroessner, the dictator of Paraguay, on how to annihilate the Indian population; disappeared from Argentina just in time to escape extradition to West Germany; perhaps outsmarted and murdered a female Israeli spy who tried to entrap him; and perhaps was involved in the drug trade. Mengele finally died of a heart attack while swimming in 1979.[44]

In 1985 rumors spread outside South America of a body in Brazil believed to be that of Mengele. A vast team of forensic scientists, representing several disciplines, were employed in the complex identification process.[45] Skeletal abnormalities were found consistent with accidents and illnesses documented in Mengele's history, but there were no ante-mortem radiographs to be found for comparison. Finally, the reluctant family made Mengele's diary available, and in it were references to root canal work. This led to recovery of ante-mortem dental radiographs. These, along with superimposition techniques using the skull and known photographic likenesses of Mengele, and an oral-antral fistula, finalized an inarguable positive identification[46–48] eventually confirmed by DNA typing.

Any reflection on the historical genesis of forensic radiology ultimately must include consideration of early "practical use of roentgen rays for non-medical purposes" as summarized by Glasser in his classic biography.[49] One of Röntgen's first test objects was a piece of welded metal (Figure 2-4). Röntgen was an avid hunter and outdoorsman so it is appropriate that one of his best x-ray pictures, made a bit later, was of his shotgun (Figure 2-17). Röntgen was delighted that not only were the "bullets" there for everyone to see, but also small irregularities in the steel could be discerned. Consequently, early in 1896 the War Ministries of Germany and of Austria proposed using Röntgen's method to detect defects in guns and armor. U.S. ordnance officials were similarly influenced by demonstrations of invisible welds in metal by Professor A. W. Wright of Yale, previously mentioned for his dead rabbit investigation. That same year, the Carnegie Steel Works in Pittsburgh also employed x-rays for nondestructive testing. Industrial radiography is not within the scope of this book, but is still a useful tool for our colleagues in forensic engineering. Apart from mail-bomb searches already mentioned, x-rays were demonstrated to British postal authorities as a means of finding coins in newspapers, embedded in sealing wax, and otherwise posted in violation of existing regulations.

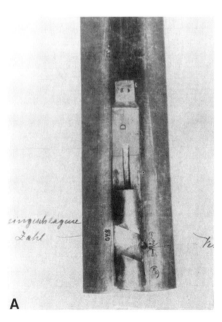
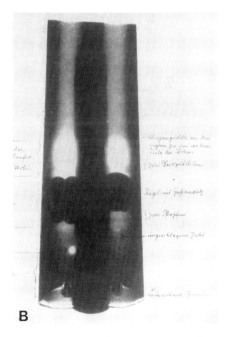

A

B

Figure 2-17   **A**: Photograph, and **B**: roentgenogram of Röntgen's shotgun. Notes alongside pointing out the faithful image reproduction of stampings in the metal as well as the components of the load are in Röntgen's handwriting.

A Mr. B. Hicks made an early excursion into the field of "Questioned Documents" when he used a roentgenogram of a document to show the court how the parchment was extremely thin in one area "as if some names had been erased in order to be replaced by others."

Adulteration of foodstuffs was proven by x-ray in 1896. In the same year roentgenograms of mummies were first obtained. The roentgenogram and its sophisticated progeny, the CT, still are used to nondestrictively evaluate mummies for content, age, sex, embalming methods, hidden valuables, injuries, and disease. Also contemporaneously, roentgen rays were employed to detect fake jewels and alterations in paintings (see Chapters 13 and 14).

Thus, we see that the foundation for most of modern forensic radiology had been laid down before the end of the first decade after Röntgen's discovery. Some seminal work lay ignored for years only to be rediscovered or renovated at a later date. Some building blocks were missing, more from social scotomata than scientific oversight — our blindness to abuse in all of its ugly forms, for instance.

Professor Röntgen furnished the tool. His contemporaries showed us how to use it. Realization of the full scope of forensic radiology was to depend upon the imagination and industry of modern scientists, and the indulgence or approval of the courts.

References

1. Glasser, O., *Wilhelm Conrad Röntgen and the Early History of the Roentgen Rays*, Charles C Thomas, Springfield, IL, 1934, chap. 5.

2. Glasser, O., *Wilhelm Conrad Röntgen and the Early History of the Roentgen Rays*, Charles C Thomas, Springfield, IL, 1934, chap. 2.

3. Glasser, O., *Wilhelm Conrad Röntgen and the Early History of the Roentgen Rays*, Charles C Thomas, Springfield, IL, 1934, chap. 1.

4. Röntgen, W. C., Ueber eine neue art von strahlen, *Sitzgber. Physik-Med. Ges. Würzberg*, December, 132, 1895.

5. Glasser, O., *Wilhelm Conrad Röntgen and the Early History of the Roentgen Rays*, Charles C Thomas, Springfield, IL, 1934, chap. 4.

6. Glasser, O., *Dr. W. C. Röntgen*, 2nd ed., Charles C Thomas, Springfield, IL, 1958, chap. 3.

7. Glasser, O., W. C. Roentgen and the discovery of the roentgen rays, *Am. J. Roentgenol.*, 25, 437, 1931.

8. Glasser, O., *Wilhelm Conrad Röntgen and the Early History of the Roentgen Rays*, Charles C Thomas, Springfield, IL, 1934, chap. 6.

9. Linton, O. W., News of x-ray reaches America days after announcement of Roentgen's discovery, *Am. J. Roentgenol.*, 165, 471, 1995.

10. Glasser, O., *Dr. W. C. Röntgen*, 2nd ed., Charles C Thomas, Springfield, IL, 1958, chap. 7.

11. Dewing, S. B., *Modern Radiology in Historical Perspective*, Charles C Thomas, Springfield, IL, 1962, p. 36.

12. Glasser, O., First roentgen evidence, *Radiology*, 17, 789, 1931.

13. Brecher, R. and Brecher, E., *The Rays: A History of Radiology in the United States and Canada*, Williams & Wilkins, Baltimore, 1969, 9.

14. Brecher, R. and Brecher, E., *The Rays: A History of Radiology in the United States and Canada*, Williams & Wilkins, Baltimore, 1969, 14.

15. Brecher, R. and Brecher, E., *The Rays: A History of Radiology in the United States and Canada*, Williams & Wilkins, Baltimore, 1969, 18.

16. Halperin, E. C., X-rays at the bar, 1896-1910, *Invest. Radiol.*, 23, 639, 1988.

17. Cox, J. and Kirkpatrick, R. C., The new photography with report of a case in which a bullet was photographed in the leg, *Montreal Med. J.*, 24, 661, 1896.

18. Evans, K. T., Knight, B., and Whittaker, D. K., *Forensic Radiology*, Blackwell Scientific, Oxford, 1981, chap. 1.

19. Eckert, W. C., The history of the forensic applications in radiology, *Am. J. Forensic Med. Pathol.*, 5, 53, 1984.

20. Withers, S., The story of the first roentgen evidence, *Radiology*, 17, 99, 1931.

21. Collins, V. P., Origins of medico-legal and forensic roentgenology, in *Classic Descriptions in Diagnostic Radiology*, Vol. 2, Bruwer, A. J., Ed., Charles C Thomas, Springfield, IL, 1964, 1578.

22. Pear, B. L., 1896: The first year of x-rays in Colorado, *Am. J. Roentgenol.*, 165, 1075, 1995.

23. Anon., Associated Press release, *Mobile Register*, January 4, 1989, 1D.

24. Saban, R., Salmar, A., and Potier, M., Biographical notes in: Musees d'Anatomíe Delmar-Orfila-Rouvìere, *Surg. Radiol. Anat.*, 17 (Suppl. 1), 5129, 1995.

25. Levinsohn, Beitraz zur feststellung der identität, *Arch. Krim.-Anthrop. Leipzig*, 2, 211, 1899.

26. Béclère, H., La radiographe anthropométric du pouce (superposition des empreites digitales, du sequelette et de l'ongle), *C. R. Acad. Sci.*, 167, 499, 1918.

27. Béclère, H., La radiographe cutanée, *J. Radiol. Electrol.*, 4, 145, 1920.

28. Walsh, D., Skin pictures with x-rays, *Br. Med. J.*, March 27, 787, 1897.

29. Graham, D., *The Use of X-ray Techniques in Forensic Investigations*, Churchill Livingstone, Edinburgh, 1973, 16-22.

30. Winstanley, R., Recovery of latent fingerprints from difficult surfaces by an x-ray method, *J. Forensic Sci. Soc.*, 17, 121, 1977.

31. Goodman, P. C., The new light: discovery and introduction of the x-ray, *Am. J. Roentgenol.*, 165, 1041, 1995.

32. Bishop, J. B., *Theodore Roosevelt and His Time, Shown in His Own Letters*, Vol. II, Schriber's, New York, 1920, 337.

33. Clark Panel Report, 1968 Panel Review of Photographs, X-ray Films, Documents and Other Evidence Pertaining to the Fatal Wounding of President John F. Kennedy on November 22, 1963 in Dallas, Texas, U.S. Government Printing Office, Washington, D.C., 1969, 12.

34. Warren Commission Report, U.S. Government Printing Office, Washington, D.C., 1964.

35. Breo, D. L., JFK's death — the plain truth from the MDs who did the autopsy, *J. Am. Med. Assoc.*, 267, 2794, 1992.

36. Breo, D. L., JFK's death. II. Dallas MDs recall their memories, *J. Am. Med. Assoc.*, 267, 2804, 1992.

37. Breo, D. L., JFK's death. III. Dr. Finch speaks out: 'two bullets, from the rear', *J. Am. Med. Assoc.*, 268, 1748, 1992.

38. Artwohl, R. R., JFK's assassination: conspiracy, forensic science and common sense, *J. Am. Med. Assoc.*, 269, 1540, 1993.

39. Morgan, R. S., Unpublished data, presentation before The Rocky Mountain Radiological Society, Denver, August 19, 1972.

40. Ford, M. A. and Ashley, K. F., The role of the forensic dentist in aircraft accidents, in *Aerospace Pathology*, Mason, J. K. and Reals, W. J., Eds., College of American Pathologists Foundation, Chicago, 1973, chap. 8.

41. Toland, J., *Adolph Hitler*, Vol. 2, Doubleday, Garden City, NJ, 1976, chap. 28.

42. Toland, J., *Adolph Hitler*, Vol. 2, Doubleday, Garden City, NJ, 1976, chap. 29.

43. Sognnaes, R. F., Dental evidence in the postmortem identification of Adolph Hitler, Eva Braun, and Martin Borman, *Legal Medicine Annual*, 1977, 173.

44. Lifton, R. J., *The Nazi Doctors: Medical Killings and the Psychology of Genocide*, Rare Books, New York, 1986, chap. 17.

45. Joyce, C. and Stover, E., *Witnesses from the Grave*, Little, Brown, Boston, 1991, chap. 9.

46. Joyce, C. and Stover, E., *Witnesses from the Grave*, Little, Brown, Boston, 1991, chap. 10.

47. Curran, W. J., The forensic investigation of the death of Joseph Mengele, *N. Engl. J. Med.*, 315, 1071, 1986.

48. Teixeira, W. R. G., The Mengele report, *Am. J. Forensic Med. Pathol.*, 6, 279, 1985.

49. Glasser, O., *Wilhelm Conrad Röntgen and the Early History of the Roentgen Rays*, Charles C Thomas, Springfield, IL, 1934, chap. 18.

Scope of Forensic Radiology

3

B. G. BROGDON, M.D.

Contents

Introduction

Forensic radiology, as do all other academic and scientific disciplines, rests on the some-times unsteady four-legged stool of service, education, research, and administration. The scope of forensic applications of diagnostic medical radiology as currently understood and practiced is summarized in Table 3-1. As the field of diagnostic radiology has undergone rapid expansion in technology and utilization in the past quarter-century, so may the range of forensic applications burgeon in the near future.

Determination of Identity

Radiological identification depends in the early stages on general biomedical knowledge and utilization of various standards and tables in establishing the basic issues such as animal vs. human remains, commingling, age, sex, and stature. Radiological determination of individual identity may be presumptive upon demonstration of preexisting injuries, illness, or congenital and/or developmental peculiarities (Figure 3-1). Positive radiological identification requires direct comparison of ante-mortem and post-mortem images of the body or its parts (Figure 3-2). The emergence of multiple radiological imaging modalities in recent years has complicated rather than simplified this comparison. This is because, for the most part, the newer modalities display body parts in sectional and planar images quite different from the routine frontal and lateral views typifying most conventional roentgenograms. Identification of human remains by radiological methods is covered extensively in Section II.

Table 3-1   Scope of Forensic Radiology

I.   Service
   A.   Determination of Identity
   B.   Evaluation of Injury and Death
      1.   Accidental
      2.   Nonaccidental
         a.   Osseous injury
         b.   Missiles and foreign bodies
         c.   Other trauma
         d.   Other causes
   C.   Criminal Litigation
      1.   Fatal
      2.   Nonfatal
   D.   Civil Litigation
      1.   Fatal
      2.   Nonfatal
   E.   Administrative Proceedings
II.   Education
III. Research
IV.   Administration

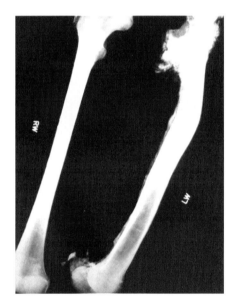

Figure 3-1   Skeletonized remains from the desert show an old healed fracture of the left proximal femoral shaft with residual bowing and shortening. This correlated with the history of a suspected decedent, but a positive identification was not possible because the ante-mortem roentgenograms were no longer available.

Evaluation of Injury or Death

Evaluation of injury or death by radiological methods is greatly enhanced by historical information, physical findings, and appropriate laboratory data when available. Such evaluation frequently requires elements of detection, pattern recognition, interpretation, and comparison, all solidly based on radiologic training and experience with normal and abnormal findings in patients of both sexes and all age groups. The osseous skeleton is the prime target of forensic radiological evaluation, but in many situations the soft tissues of

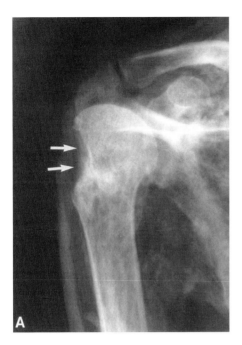 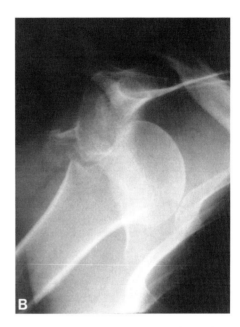

Figure 3-2   **A**: a truck driver who was burned beyond recognition after a wreck had a history of dislocation of the right shoulder. Post-mortem roentgenogram shows a typical Hill-Sachs deformity, an impaction fracture of the humeral head associated with anterior dislocation of the shoulder (arrows). **B**: ante-mortem examination shows the dislocation and Hill-Sachs deformity, a positive identification.

the musculoskeletal framework and the abdominal and thoracic viscera may offer key findings (Figure 3-3).

Osseous injuries are best detected and studied in the post-mortem state if the body parts can be manipulated to replicate the standard positions for those parts normally used for roentgenography in clinical practice (see Chapter 23). Typically, in medical radiology, the patient or his body part is examined in at least two positions or projections (usually at right angles to one another). As a result, objects or parts obscured in one view may be visible in the other (Figure 3-4 is a rather blatant example of this). Also, even though a roentgenogram depicts findings in only two planes or dimensions, the trained observer can use two radiographs taken from different perspectives to conceptualize the third dimension of depth (Figure 3-5).

The location and type of fracture, considered with reference to the age and expected level of activity of the individual, may be highly suggestive of whether the injury is accidental or inflicted. Certain fractures, dislocations, and epiphyseal separations are relatively common in the course of "normal" activities in certain age ranges; others are virtually impossible to sustain accidentally within those parameters (Figure 3-6).

The configuration and direction of fractures in the skull may locate the impact point and direction of impact, indicate the sequence of repetitive blows (Figure 3-7) and, sometimes, the shape of the wounding object or weapon. The appearance and location of some skeletal injuries may be clues to their origin (Figure 3-8). Some skeletal injuries are typically defensive in nature (Figure 3-9). The time span since the original injury often can be estimated with some degree of accuracy and may be important. Of course,

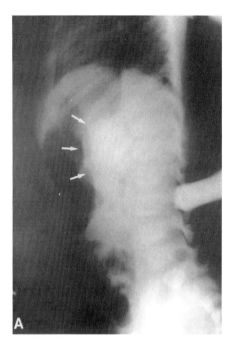
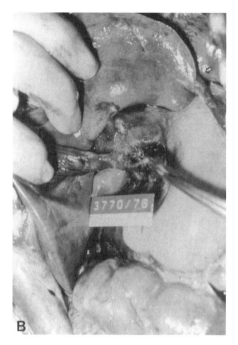

Figure 3-3   **A**: a battered child was moribund on arrival in the Emergency Department. Cross-table lateral view of the abdomen shows a large retroperitoneal mass (arrows) which at autopsy (**B**) was shown to be a collection of blood and other body fluids from laceration of the liver and pancreas and transection of the bile duct. (Dr. Weston made a cast of the stepmother's fist, which exactly matched a bruise of the skin over the epigastrium and led to a conviction.)

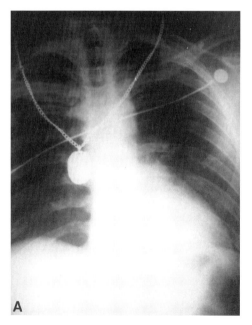

Figure 3-4   **A**: frontal roentgenogram of a body does not reveal a cause of death quite obvious to the autopsy surgeon. **B**: the lateral view, while not necessary for the edification of the medical examiner, makes a powerful display for the jury.

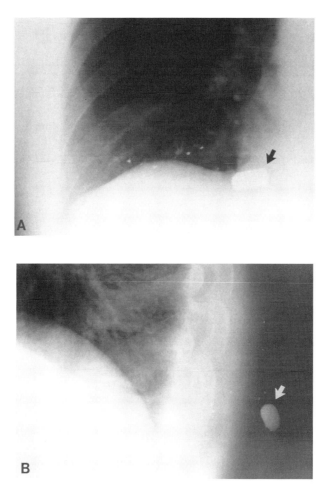

Figure 3-5 A foot patrolman, seeing a man inside a closed and darkened store, called for him to come out. He came out running and fled down the street while the officer fired at him with his service revolver. Sometime later a man was admitted to a local hospital with a bullet wound. **A**: the frontal view of the chest showed a track of lead fragments leading from the midportion of a rib to the major bullet fragment (arrow) overlying the right margin of the heart. It gave no clue as to depth of the missile within the body. **B**: a lateral view showed the slug (arrow) had simply bounced off the rib and came to rest just beneath the skin of the back. With a court order, the slug was popped out through a small incision and matched by ballistics with the officer's weapon.

multiplicity of injuries and injuries in various stages of healing are highly significant findings. Fractures of the hyoid bone or thyroid cornua usually suggest strangulation (Figure 3-10). In vehicular injuries, certain fracture/dislocations may actually suggest the velocity of impact or deceleration. We have seen a pattern-like series of craniocervical distractions and/or dislocations in motorcycle riders, at least some of whom are known to have ridden at speed into a head-high obstacle such as a traffic sign or truck bed (Figure 3-11).

Finally, many diseases leave their "mark" on the skeleton; some of them actually are quite legible "signatures" allowing positive identification of the antecedent process. Those distinctive affectations of the skeleton are too numerous to list here (and are the subject of many volumes of radiological textbooks and at least one excellent anthropological text[1])

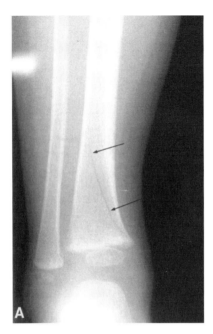 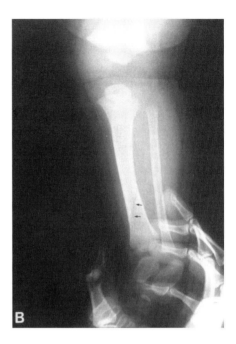

Figure 3-6 **A**: this is a so-called "toddler's fracture" commonly seen in young children in the early years as they begin to walk and run, but are not yet very steady or coordinated. It is a "normal" fracture for this age group. **B**: this nonambulatory infant has a similar-looking fracture, but one impossible to acquire naturally in the course of infantile movement. Rather, this fracture was caused by a twisting force or torsion at the hands of an adult caregiver.

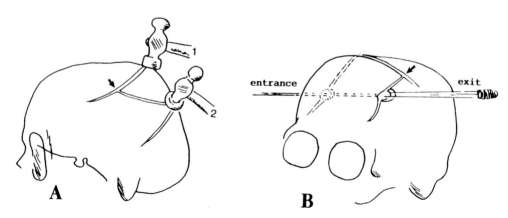

Figure 3-7 Schematic drawings indicate that **A**: a linear fracture from an earlier blow will stop propagation of a fracture from a second blow. **B**: a linear fracture from an entrance wound travels faster than the bullet causing it; a fracture from the exit wound will terminate on meeting the preexisting fracture. (This helps in deciding between entrance and exit wounds when the skull defect is in thin bone, i.e., temporal bone, or when beveling is obscured by fire or decomposition.) Trajectory or direction of fire is suggested by the angle of eccentric beveling. (See Dixon, D. S., Pattern of intersecting fractures and direction of fire, *J. Forensic Sci.*, 29, 651, 1984.)

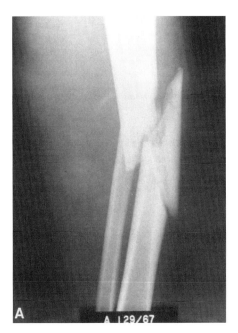 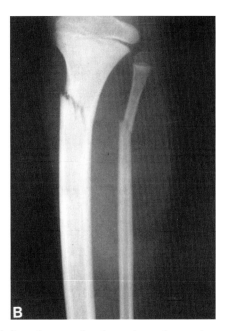

Figure 3-8   **A**: typical "bumper fracture" in an adult pedestrian hit from the right. **B**: "bumper fracture" in a child hit from the left is higher in the leg. Because of the increased elasticity and plasticity of young bones, the impact produced an incomplete or "green-stick" fracture.

but include infections, infestations, metabolic processes, dietary abnormalities, tumors, and even poisons (Figure 3-12).

   Missiles and other foreign bodies are the object of many forensic radiological examinations. Gunshot wounds are the subject of Section III, to follow, and their radiological evaluation may provide important information in a variety of ways.

   Other foreign bodies may be equally important in any given case. All sorts of materials are opaque to x-rays and may be detected by careful radiographic examination and visual search. One may find the snapped-off point of a knife, fragments of broken glass (Figure 3-13), bomb fragments or shrapnel, parts of the automobile or aircraft in which the victim was riding (Figure 3-14), and animal, mineral, or vegetable matter embedded, aspirated, or injected (Figure 3-15). There may be aspirated dirt from a cave-in or sand from drowning in surf (Figure 3-16). Opaque poisons may be seen in soft tissues or the gut. Foreign bodies in the vagina, rectum, bladder or other tissues can indicate sexual abuse, autoeroticism, or psychosis (Figure 3-17).

   Other trauma can include such findings as intracranial hemorrhage from shaking, penetrating wounds which can be demonstrated with injected contrast media, as so can vascular tears or avulsions be revealed. Fractures of the laryngeal soft tissues have been seen with hanging (Figure 3-18) and massive soft tissue contusions may follow beatings.

   Other causes of injury or death may have radiological implications. These would include drowning or near drowning, wherein there usually are radiological findings. (However, one cannot depend upon the radiological appearance of the chest to distinguish between saltwater and freshwater drowning, as once believed.) Poisoning already has been mentioned. Radiography is the best and earliest method of demonstrating air embolism to the heart, brain, or vascular tree. Similarly, the autopsy surgeon can be alerted in advance to the presence of pneumothorax, pneumopericardium, pneumomediastinum,

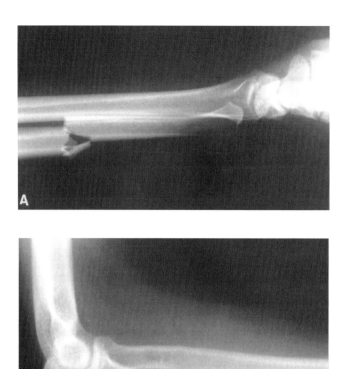

Figure 3-9   **A**: "fending fracture" of the ulna — the result of trying to ward off a blow by blocking it with the upraised forearm. These have also been called "night-stick" or "pool-cue" fractures. **B**: a subtle, undisplaced fending fracture.

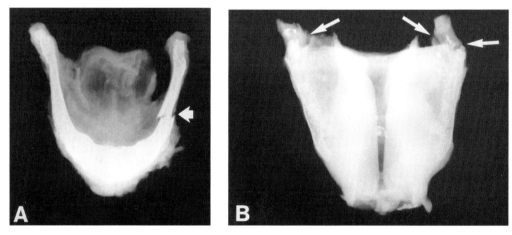

Figure 3-10   **A**: fracture of the hyoid bone (arrow) from strangulation. **B**: fractures of the superior cornua of the thyroid cartilage from strangulation. (Both courtesy of Dr. James C. Downs.)

pneumoperitoneum, or abnormal air collections associated with abscess, obstruction, or paralytic dysfunction (Figure 3-19). Otherwise, the exact location and confines of the air may be difficult or impossible to discern with an ordinary operative approach, even with submersion techniques.

Finally, one must always remember that arson often hides other crimes. It is essential that all bodies burned beyond recognition be investigated radiographically (Figures 3-20 and 3-21).

Criminal Litigation

The usefulness of appropriate radiological images in cases of murder, suicide, attempted murder, manslaughter, mayhem, assault, battery, abuse, terrorism, or any other type of criminal activity directed to the person is self-evident and widely known. Less well-appreciated is the contribution the radiologic method can make in other nonviolent crimes such as smuggling, larceny and fraud, faking, or counterfeiting. Further comments pertinent to nonviolent crimes will be found in Section IV.

Civil Litigation

The radiologist may be called as a defendant, plaintiff, ordinary witness, or expert witness in court cases dealing with liability, be it professional liability or malpractice, personal liability, property liability, or product liability. Expert testimony may be required in civil actions in cases of wrongful death or birth, civil rights violation or, quite commonly, personal injury. These cases may demand a high level of professional knowledge and expertise, but these issues are not within the scope of this treatise. The section on Coping with the Courts (Section VII) contains advice on general courtroom demeanor.

Administrative Proceedings

The radiologist may be called to testify in an administrative legal proceeding that is not, strictly speaking, in a court of law. This would include such actions as a Workman's Compensation Hearing or a Military Board to determine "Line of Duty" status of an injury or illness as well as the extent of any resultant disability and eligibility for a pension or award.

Education

All physicians have an educational obligation dating back to the Hippocratic Oath "… to impart a knowledge by precept, by lecture, and by every other mode of instruction to my sons, to the sons of my teacher, and to pupils who are bound by stipulation and oath, according to the law of medicine …". However, there is no formal curriculum in forensic

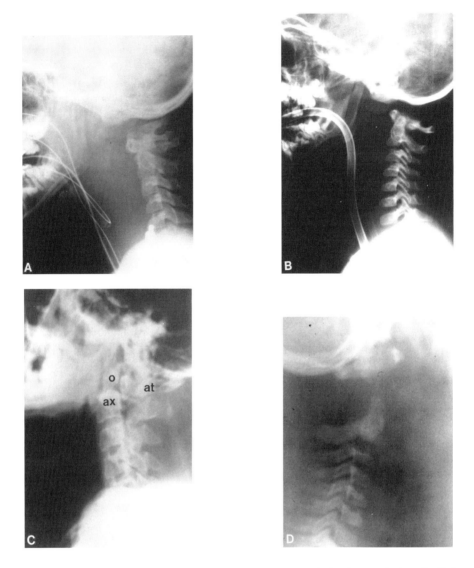

Figure 3-11 Biker injuries. **A**: separation or distraction of the base of the skull from the cervical spinal column. **B**: another craniocervical separation. **C**: the atlas or first cervical vertebra (at), still articulating with the base of the skull, has jumped posteriorly entirely over the odontoid process (o) of the axis (ax) or second cervical vertebra. **D**: wide distraction and separation of the axis and atlas in a child who was riding a motor scooter. **E**: the only "good" motorcycle injury the author has ever seen. This three-year-old was brought to the Emergency Room with a toy motorcycle stuck to his face. Radiography showed that the axle of the front wheel had barely penetrated the outer table of the skull of the forehead. The toy was simply lifted off, leaving only a tiny puncture wound.

radiology nor, to our knowledge, is there any regular course of instruction in forensic radiology in this country. There have been a smattering of "refresher courses" on the subject lasting from one and one-half to six hours presented at random intervals during the annual meetings of the American Academy of Forensic Sciences, the American Roentgen Ray Society, and the Radiological Society of North America. Most instructions, and learning, in forensic radiology is by the individual case study method, hands-on experience, or

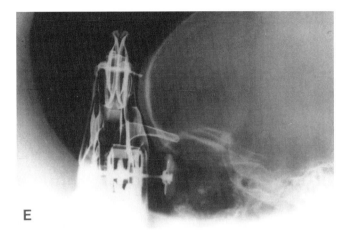

E

Figure 3-11 (continued)

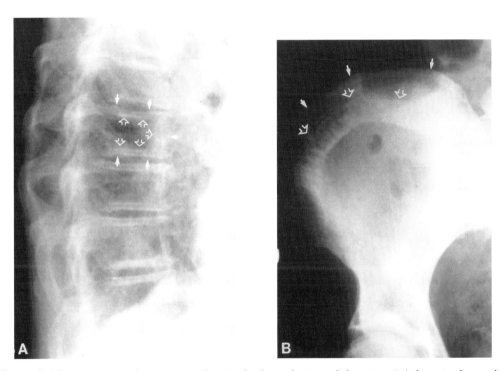

Figure 3-12   Bone-in-a-bone. Note that in the lateral view of the spine (**A**) there is the outline of a smaller vertebra (open arrows) residing inside the adult vertebral margin (closed arrows). Similarly, in the pelvis (**B**) a small pelvic outline (open arrows) is within the adult pelvis (closed arrows). This woman, now 66, had a habit of chewing matches as a teenager. Phosphorus was laid down in the growing margin of the bone at that time. (This finding is not specific to match chewers but can be seen with lead ingestion, severe childhood illness with cessation of growth for several weeks, and with some diseases such as osteopetroses or treated Langerhans-cell lymphoma.)

published reports in a variety of scientific journals. Similarly, there are scattered talks related to the utilization of radiology and forensic matters at meetings of a wide spectrum of scientific disciplines. The quality and quantity of these offerings is as varied as the

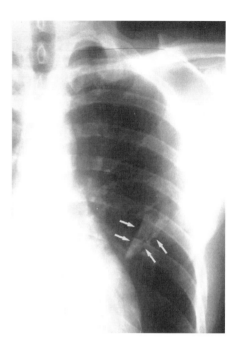

Figure 3-13   Shard of glass (arrows) from a broken beer bottle remain in the lung of this stabbing victim.

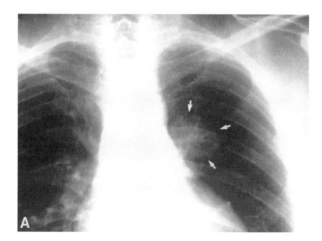

Figure 3-14   This middle-aged man was sent for a chest film (**A**) because of suspected heart disease. A round mass in the left lung prompted a tomogram (**B** and **C**) which defined the mass in frontal and lateral projections. At surgery (**D**) a gearshift knob encapsulated in fibrous scar was removed. The man had been in an automobile accident 22 years earlier but did not recall any penetrating injury at the time!

audience. Many come from non-radiologists. Efforts to develop an organization of individuals interested in the field, or a section in forensic radiology under the aegis of the AAFS, so far have been unsuccessful and discouraging.

Because of the rapid and recent technological developments in the field of diagnostic radiology per se, there is a compelling need for better-planned, better-organized, and systematic educational efforts in forensic radiology. The newer modalities have both great promise and great problems in application to forensic problems. More widespread understanding of, and familiarity with, the discipline will expedite the assimilation of these tools into the forensics armamentarium.

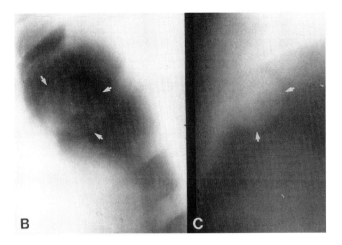

Figure 3-14 (continued)

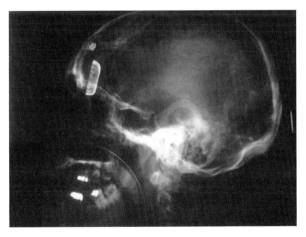

Figure 3-15   A bottle was driven into the victim's face. The cap stayed behind as the bottle was withdrawn.

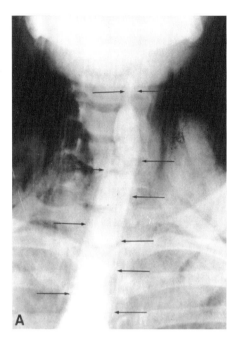 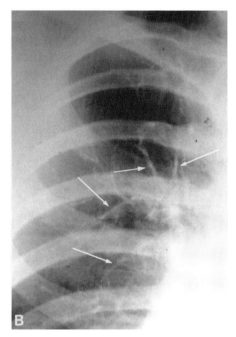

Figure 3-16   **A**: sand completely packs the tracheobronchial tree of a man who drowned in high surf. **B**: a man who recovered from near drowning in surf was found to have sand impactions in upper lobe bronchi. (From Bonilla-Santiago, J. and Fill, W. L., Sand aspiration in drowning and near drowning, *Radiology*, 128, 301, 1978. With permission.)

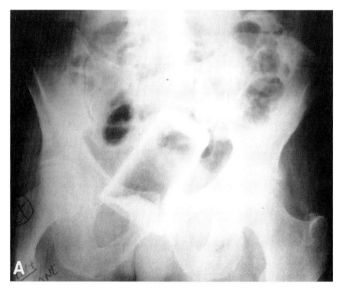

Figure 3-17   **A**: water glass in the rectum. **B**: plastic vibrator lost in the rectum. **C** and **D**: a disturbed youth who obviously is left-handed inserts wires — straightened paper clips — (arrows) beneath his skin. One has traveled through the venous system to the right ventricle (open arrow).

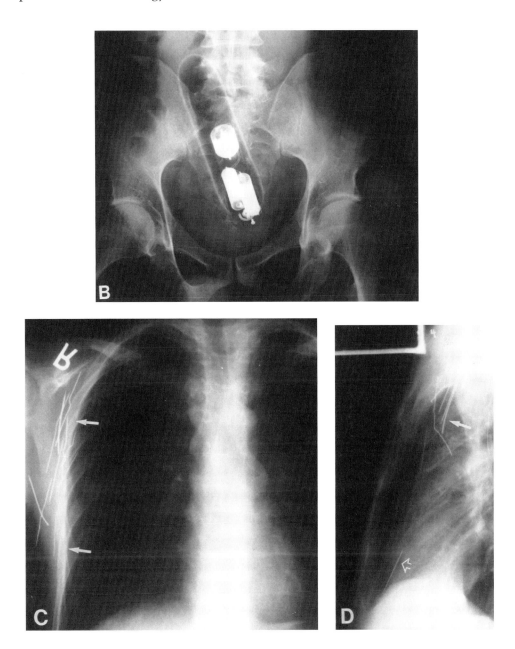

Figure 3-17 (continued)

The forensic sciences have another educational obligation to the public, that is, to alert them to situations discovered to be hazardous to public health or public safety. Examples would be research leading to bicycle helmet laws, warning of the danger of larger water-filled buckets to infants and children (who have a high center of gravity, and cannot extricate themselves after tumbling in), or publicity alerting citizens to the peril of urban hyper- or hypothermia during spells of severe weather. Perhaps the finest example of public education by radiologists has been in the early awareness campaigns concerning child abuse.

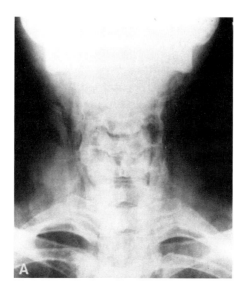

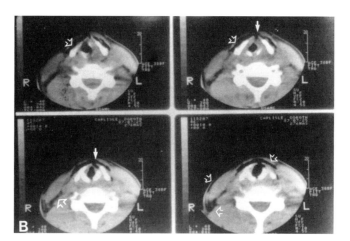

Figure 3-18   Attempted suicide by hanging. **A**: cervical spine examination shows massive dissection of air in the soft tissue planes of the neck. **B**: the CT scan demonstrates the fracture of the anterior commissure of the larynx (arrow) and air dissection in the soft tissues of the neck (open arrows).

Research

Diagnostic imaging methods are, in general, underutilized in forensic biomedical practice and research. Part of this deficiency can be attributed to the cost of, and difficulty of access to, the newer modalities and techniques. These problems may gradually abate as equipment becomes more widely distributed, more commonplace, and, consequently, cheaper and more accessible. Some very promising applications of modern radiological methods to the courts have come about already through individual effort, innovation, and inspiration. Further comments on forensic radiological research and new developments in diagnostic radiology will be found in Section VI.

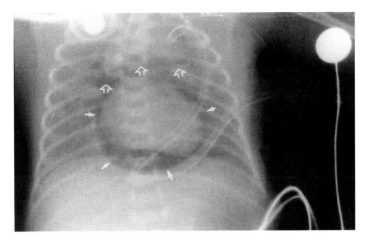

Figure 3-19   Pneumopericardium represented by the dark halo of air surrounding the heart (arrows). There also is pneumomediastinum outlining the inferior border of the thymus (open arrows).

 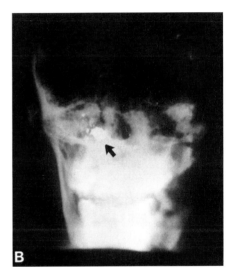

Figure 3-20   **A**: almost totally incinerated body with extremities and half of the head missing. **B**: large caliber bullet (arrow) and smaller fragments found in the remaining part of the skull.

Administration

Administratively, the forensic radiologist usually functions as a consultant to the Office of the Medical Examiner or its local equivalent. He or she may have an official appointment to the Office and serve as a regular member of a team that in large offices may include the pathologist, anthropologist, toxicologist, criminalist, ballistics expert, and others. The radiologist rarely is a sworn officer. In the forensic organization, his or her administrative duties at best are related to selection and maintenance of equipment, development, and ensuring conformity with diagnostic protocols, radiation protection, instruction and

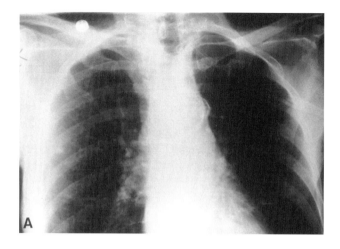

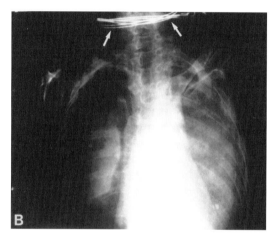

Figure 3-21 A woman, presumably the occupant, was found burned beyond recognition after a house fire. The remains were radiographed in order to try to match them with the occupant's ante-mortem chest film (**A**). The post-mortem study (**B**) revealed several coils of a wire ligature around the victim's neck. (Point-to-point matches of bones, joints, and pulmonary calcifications allowed positive radiological identification.)

supervision of technical personnel responsible for image production, proper identification and storage of images, and proper recording of findings.

In his or her larger activities as a practicing clinical diagnostic radiologist, there may be substantial administrative duties depending on the organization and hierarchy of the parent Department of Radiology. Those administrative responsibilities will not overlap unless local conditions require radiography of forensic specimens and bodies in the clinical facility. In such cases, great administrative and diplomatic skills may be required to ensure optimal handling of competing and conflicting demands for space, equipment, time, and personnel in the provision of both clinical and forensic examinations in shared facilities.

Reference

1. Ortner, D. S. and Putschar, W. G. J., *Identification of Pathological Conditions in Human Skeletal Remains*, reprint ed., Smithsonian Institution Press, Washington, D.C., 1985.

SECTION II

Identification

Identification of the Dead

4

LEROY RIDDICK, M.D.

Contents

The Need to Identify

There is no greater challenge and no heavier responsibility than that facing the professionals charged with identifying the dead. Something deep within the human psyche abhors loss of identity, even for the deceased. The reverence paid to the Tombs of Unknown Soldiers throughout the world attests to the pathos and disquiet we feel about those who have lost their identity in death. Every unidentified body brought to the medical examiner or coroner represents a person missing to friends and family. Without proper identification of these bodies those loved ones bear the heavy burden of a continuing search for that missing person; they are denied the closure which can come with mourning. The religious ceremonies and the social mores concerning the dead bear witness to this need for the living to put the dead to rest. Without proper identification this is impossible. As a corollary of these intense emotional issues, few activities satisfy medicolegal professionals so much as making proper identification of a body originally found as unidentified.

The solution of legal problems associated with death also requires proper identification of the deceased. Without a death certificate, which demands an identifiable decedent (except in cases of fraud), families cannot probate wills, receive death benefits, enter a safety deposit box, etc.; a spouse cannot remarry for a period of seven years, when, in most states, the missing person can legally be declared dead. In homicides and suspicious cases, the detectives have almost no leads upon which to start an investigation when the body remains unidentified. Moreover, if the remains are decomposed or severely mutilated by fire, the investigators may not even have an adequate cause of death, which might be determined from the history if the victim's identify is known. Even in those rare cases in which a suspect is associated with a missing person and all of the circumstantial evidence points to a homicide, without the body and proper identification the case is difficult to adjudicate. And without justice, the loved ones of the decedent are also denied closure.

Methods

In general, the condition of the body, whether the presumed decedent was known in the community in which the death occurred, the number of victims, and the capabilities of the medicolegal professionals will dictate the methods used. Practically, two methods are employed: (1) the least reliable, that is, the least reproducible, method involves the visual review of the remains, photographs of the remains, details such as tattoos on the remains, or personal effects found either on or about the victims by family or friends of the suspected decedent; (2) the most reliable method involves the documentation on or in the body of certain anatomic characteristics such as fingerprints, dental restorations, healed features, surgical sutures, etc. which can be compared with similar documentation, that is, fingerprints, photographs, radiographs, or dental records prepared prior to death. The condition of the body, the age and history of the victim, and the resources of the authorities set stringent parameters on what can be done to make positive, reproducible identification of the dead. The caveat is that some remains cannot be positively identified.

Almost without exception two generalities apply to whatever method is used to make or confirm an identification. Firstly, and almost fatuously, all techniques from visual observation of the remains to sophisticated DNA profiling rely on pattern recognition. The more intact the pattern — whether fingertip pads or teeth — and the more conversant the examiner with analysis of the patterns, the more likely a positive, reliable identification can be made. Secondly, the process of identification requires a team approach. Even in cases where visual inspection of the body is the method, a law enforcement officer will most often notify the family or friends of the death of someone who has to be identified and the medical examiner will witness the observation and confirm the identity. In complex cases requiring a variety of professionals ranging from fingerprint examiners to anthropologists to radiologists, the team can be quite large. All members of the teams should remember that it is the medical examiner certifying the death who bears the ultimate responsibility for assuring the identity of the body and is, thus, *de facto* leader of the team.

Most deaths occur in the community in which the decedent lived and in most instances family members and friends are either in attendance at the death or, in the case of deaths in the hospital or nursing homes, have visited the victim recently. In such cases the health care personnel notify the next of kin about the death and, in many instances, prepare the body to be viewed by the loved ones. Most of those cases, with the exception of medicolegal cases, are released directly to a funeral home and the death certificate completed on the basis of that visual inspection and/or history provided by the caregivers.

In these cases of easily recognizable victims dying at home, in the hospital, or in a location in the community in which they lived, but whose death comes under the coroner's or medical examiner's jurisdiction in which the death occurred, the method of identification will depend upon the resources and the philosophy of the medicolegal authority. In small communities where most people were known in life and readily identified in death, the hospital identification band and/or the police report may suffice. In large urban centers where the living and the dead are often anonymous even to the next-door neighbor, the authorities may require visual identification of the body or an image of the body on video or photograph by someone knowing the victim in life. One caveat about accepting hospital identification must be mentioned: victims who die in transit, or in the emergency department of the hospital, or in the hospital, must be properly identified by relatives or friends and not by documents in or around their bodies at the scene and transported with them to the hospital. These documents can easily have been forged, borrowed, or stolen.

When the body has decomposed or has been mutilated by fire or excessive forces precluding visual identification of the remains, the investigators know from the start that scientific methods must be used and should begin collecting dental and medical records, ante-mortem radiographs, fingerprints, etc. to expedite the process. In cases of badly decomposed but nonskeletonized remains, the skin of the hands sometimes can be carefully peeled off and used as a glove on an investigator's hand to obtain adequate fingerprints. If that skin has sloughed and is not usable, prints of the underlying dermal ridges sometimes can be used. If the fingers are mummified, thus distorting the dermal ridges, the fingerprint analyst may obtain adequate fingerprints after injecting glycerine and saline subcutaneously to rehydrate and expand the tissues. Tattoos and other scars can be delineated by scraping away the discolored dermis. Dental records and radiographs are the most productive tool in identifying such mutilated remains. Radiographs of a variety of anatomic regions and body parts, ranging from those of extremities with healed fractures to scout films of the abdomen with distinctive phleboliths, may prove invaluable.

Example Cases

Two cases illustrate the power of radiographs to establish both the identity and also the cause of death in severely mutilated remains.

Case 4-1 (Figure 4-1) involved the badly decomposed, almost skeletonized, remains of a female. The body was found in the woods near a neighborhood where a 46-year-old mentally retarded female had disappeared 3 months earlier. A search for records revealed a dental x-ray taken some years prior to her death; this was compared with the post-mortem radiograph of the mandible which contained only one tooth (Figure 4-2). Fortuitously, that one tooth had a restoration and next to the tooth in the mandible was the broken bit of a drill; these two findings established the identity beyond any reasonable doubt.

Some days investigators are lucky. Case 4-2 (we gratefully acknowledge Dr. Brian D. Blackbourne, Chief Medical Examiner of San Diego County, CA for this case) involved a dismembered torso of a female which was found in a sewer (Figure 4-3). A radiograph of the torso disclosed a peculiar beak-like configuration of the first ribs at the costochondral

Figure 4-1 Partially skeletonized, badly decomposed remains of a female body.

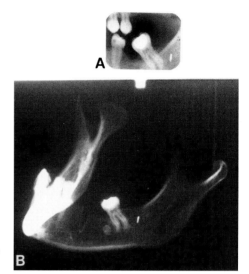

Figure 4-2 Comparison of **A**: ante-mortem dental radiograph, with **B**: post-mortem radiograph of disarticulated mandible. There is a perfect match of both the restoration in the molar and the broken-off drill bit tip.

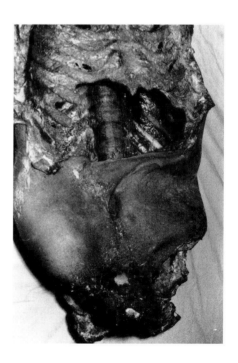

Figure 4-3 Dismembered partial torso of a female found in a sewer.

junctions (Figure 4-4A), which matched those in an ante-mortem chest x-ray of the suspected victim (Figure 4-4B).

In cases of badly decomposed (skeletonized) and severely mutilated bodies for which there are no ante-mortem dental records (assuming the body was not edentulous) or radiographs of the remaining body parts available, the investigators must use more esoteric methods. A physical anthropologist may be able to provide a reasonable evaluation of the age, sex, race, and stature of the decedent and, thus, assist in narrowing the identification process. If the skull is present and reasonably intact, an anthropologist skilled in reconstruction may be able to render a likeness that family or acquaintances can recognize

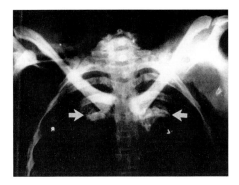 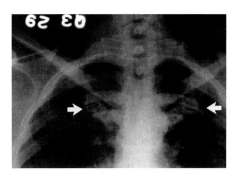

Figure 4-4   **A**: post-mortem radiograph shows peculiar beak-like calcification of the 1st costochondral junction bilaterally (arrows); **B**: ante-mortem chest with identical calcific configuration (arrow).

enough either to identify or to point to other documents which can lead to a positive identification. Similarly, portrait artists (especially those trained in reconstruction) may be able to create a recognizable portrait. With scanners and the hardware and software necessary for digital imaging, a skilled computer guru may be able to superimpose the images from suitable photographs for the missing person onto images of the skull and render a reasonable opinion about the identity.

Biochemical genetic markers may also prove useful in these badly mutilated or decomposed bodies. In those cases in which blood is available (and often enough can be milked out of a limb or other body part to suffice), traditional serological methods used for typing blood for transfusions may be sufficient. In other cases where cells of one type or another (including osteocytes) containing DNA are still present, analysts proficient in the techniques of DNA analysis and the interpretation of the results may be able to determine the identity through comparison with DNA analyses of relatives. This method may be the only reliable means of positively identifying infants and children for whom no ante-mortem dental records or radiographs exist.

When the victim is not known in the community and does not fit the description of anyone missing, that is, the decedent is a John or Jane Doe, the process of identification takes on other dimensions. If the remains have readily identifiable features and if presumptive documents of identification are found on or around the body, the major problem becomes one of searching for the next of kin or someone knowledgeable of the victim. The authorities in the locations listed on the documents and the public media may prove helpful. The next step is having all the pertinent law enforcement agencies search their fingerprint files for a match with the victim (all dead bodies brought to the medical examiner's office should be fingerprinted). Those agencies connected with AFIS (Automated Fingerprint Identification System) can broaden the search to a nationwide data bank. The problem with fingerprint identification is that so few persons, particularly women and children, have their fingerprints on file. If the search to match fingerprints proves fruitless, then those charged with the identification must document and radiograph the teeth and take full body radiographs. Dental and other prostheses may have unique characteristics and, as in the case of dentures, may have the name and/or social security number of the decedent. The data from those examinations coupled with all the observations made during the external examination (clothing, eyeglasses, jewelry, scars, dental or orthopedic prostheses, etc.) and the internal (post-mortem) examinations (congenital anomalies, missing organs, medical devices such as pacemakers, etc.) must be entered into the Federal Bureau of Investigation National Crime Information Center (NCIC) Unidentified Person (UP) and Missing Person (MP) computer data bank for possible matching with features from missing persons entered into the same system. Contacting the local media as well as nationwide TV programs such as "Unsolved Mysteries" may assist in the investigation and identification. The success of such searches depends not only upon the quantity and quality of the information documented and encoded by the professionals examining the dead body, but also upon the quantity and quality of the information available to and encoded by the investigators searching for a missing person. Moreover, someone first must report an individual missing for a search to be initiated. In this land of continual movement, families who have lost contact with members may have no idea that a relative is missing and, thus, data are never entered into the system.

In mass disasters, which for practical purposes means having more bodies than can be handled by the facility available to those charged with making the identifications, all the techniques discussed previously may need to be employed. More pertinent, the organization and management of the personnel involved with the recovery of the remains and their identification are among the most important aspects of processing multiple dead bodies. All professionals with expertise in the various aspects of scene investigation and body identification must work as a team. Plans, practice, and patience are necessary ingredients in assuring that these horrendous tasks are accomplished efficiently. With multiple deaths, extreme care and caution must be exercised at the scene by those charged with the recovery. In airplane crashes and/or bombings, where great forces not only shred the remains into small pieces but also scatter them over broad areas, the investigators must meticulously chart which remains were found where and carefully label them accordingly, both to assist in the identification and also to assist in reconstructing the event. Where body parts are commingled, the assistance of the anthropologists becomes all important.

In transportation-related disasters, manifest lists, seating charts, and other documents will prove indispensable in identifying the bodies. As in individual deaths, the bodies may be, at least at first glance, readily recognizable either directly or through photographs. We recommend, however, that if possible all remains be identified scientifically with conventional means such as dental records or radiographs. In such circumstances relatives and friends may not have seen the victim for years, making visual identification tricky at best. Moreover, comparison of radiographs, dental records, and fingerprints by professionals reduces the involvement of loved ones at an extremely stressful time for everyone. In those trying circumstances where the bodies are mutilated by fire or dismemberment, the patience and stamina of the investigators will prove as valuable as the techniques of identification at their disposal. An articulate spokesperson from the Emergency Management Agency who can deftly deal with the media may prove to be the most valuable member of the identification team.

Whether the remains are those of an individual or a host of persons, the media mavens will hover like vultures around the case, pecking at every tidbit of information whether verifiable or a rumor. One expert who is adroit at dealing with these persons should be appointed to do so, enabling the professionals to get the job done.

Finally, all those having the responsibility of interviewing and communicating with relatives and other loved ones must keep in mind the emotions involved at this most difficult time. The sudden, unexpected loss of a loved one, particularly if the death is a violent one, stresses even the strongest person who then may lash out from frustration at those who are trying their best to help the bereaved. At these moments, Sir William Osler's essay on *Equanimity* should sustain the investigators in their task to positively identify the dead.

Bibliography

Knight, B., *Forensic Pathology*, Oxford University Press, New York, 1991, chap. 3.

Osler, W., *Aequanimitas: With Other Addresses to Medical Students, Nurses and Practitioners of Medicine*, 3rd ed., Blakiston Co., Philadelphia, 1932, chap. 1.

Stahl, J., III and Fierro, F., Identification, in *Handbook of Forensic Pathology*, Froede, R. C., Ed., College of American Pathologists, Northfield, IL, 1990.

Radiological Identification: Anthropological Parameters

5

B.G. BROGDON, M.D.

Contents

Introduction

Common methods of identifying human remains — facial features, scars, birthmarks, tattoos, fingerprints, palm prints, and footprints — depend on preservation of the soft tissue components of the body in question. These methods are thwarted when the remains are so decomposed, burned, mutilated, skeletonized, or fragmented that the surface topography is unrecognizable or featureless. It is then that medical and dental radiological methods may be required.

Sometimes, before any attempt at individual identification of such remains can be undertaken, certain anthropological parameters need be established. Are the remains human or animal? If human, can the sex, age at death, population ancestry, and stature of the individual be determined or estimated within reasonable limits? Are the remains of more than one body commingled?

The radiological evaluation of these anthropological parameters, sometimes called the biological profile, is particularly applicable when the skeletal components are still partially or totally sheathed in soft tissues — however burned, macerated, decomposed, or mutilated. If the remains are completely skeletonized, or there are facilities and time to deflesh the specimen, then the forensic anthropologist can do the job with equal, or in some cases, superior accuracy. Still it is useful to x-ray the bones for possible comparative matching with ante-mortem roentgenograms in the future.

Animal or Human

It is not uncommon for animal parts or bones to be brought to the attention of law enforcement agencies or forensic investigators. Ordinarily, the trained forensic scientist easily can determine the nonhuman nature of the specimen. At times, the true nature of the item may be obscured by its condition. A bear's paw, with claws and terminal phalanges torn away for souvenirs, and with hide and fur removed by the skinning knife or by decomposition, may closely resemble a human hand to the lay hunter or hiker who discovers it. The radiograph quickly reveals the difference (Figure 5-1).

Partially fleshed or skeletonized remains of large mammals may be confusing to the untrained finder. Again, someone trained in human anatomy or osteology — physician, dentist, physical anthropologist — will have no difficulty in detecting nonhuman characteristics of size, architecture, and configuration of intact animal bones (Figure 5-2). However, the most distinctive parts of both animal and human bones, the ends and/or articular surfaces, may be missing because of carnivoral activity, decomposition, or (especially in the case of immature bones with unfused epiphyses) scattering (Figure 5-3).

If only fragments of the shaft or diaphysis of bones remain, roentgenography can be most helpful. Bony ridges, processes, and excrescences related to muscle organs and insertions will be different in four-legged animals. Chilvarquer et al. point out differences in the roentgenographic appearance of the midshafts of human vs. animal bones.[1] The pattern of the human spongiosa and medullary canal is fairly regular, with rounded or ovoid "spaces" between coarse primary trabeculae and finer secondary trabeculae. The zone of transition between the dense cortex and less dense medulla may be 1 to 3 mm wide. (Disease states or aging causing osteoporosis sharpens the transition; conditions producing osteomalacia diffuses the corticomedullary junction.)

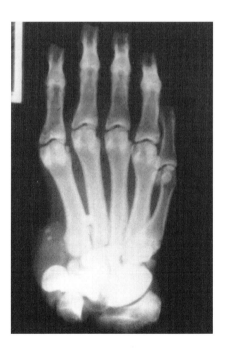

Figure 5-1   Bear paw mistaken for a human hand.

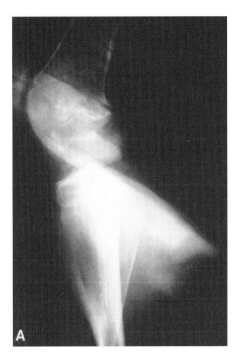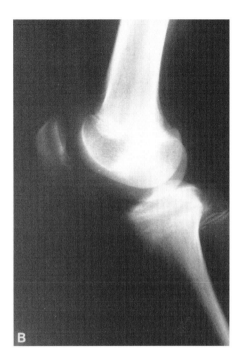

Figure 5-2   **A**: lateral view of knee of immature pig. Compare with **B**: knee of adolescent human.

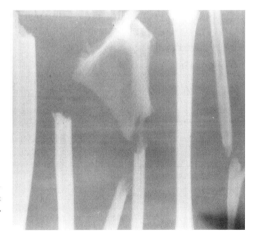

Figure 5-3   Radiograph of human skeletal remains recovered from coastal wetlands. The ends of most of the bones were destroyed or missing.

In animals the corticomedullary junction will be sharp. The spongiosa is less patterned and is more homogeneous or granular in appearance. Cortical spicules or invaginations may extend into the medullary canal from the cortical endosteum.

Age Determination

Determination of age at time of death is an important step toward identification of unknown remains. Age can be established with considerable accuracy by roentgenography of the skeleton from the time of its appearance about the 20th week of gestation until early adulthood. This is possible due to the complex but dependable system by which the osseous framework of the body develops, grows, and matures. Most of the 206 bones of the human adult skeleton develop in cartilage precursors or anlagen from one or more primary centers of ossification (which make up the shaft or diaphysis of a long bone, the centrum of an axial or round bone) and secondary centers which develop the articular ends of the bones (epiphyses) or nonarticular processes (apophyses) for attachment of muscles, ligaments, and tendons (Figure 5-4). The appearance of these centers, and the fusion of secondary centers with the primary, follow a timetable allowing rather precise aging if appropriate skeletal parts are available for evaluation.

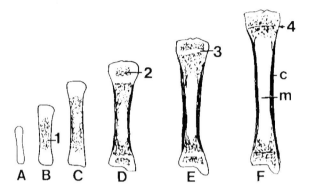

Figure 5-4   Development and ossification of a long bone. **A**: cartilagineous anlage; **B**: (1) appearance of primary ossification center in shaft or diaphysis; **C**: primary center begins reorganization into cortex, medulla, and (with perichondral ossification) the metaphysis or growing end of the shaft; **D**: appearance of (2) secondary ossification center or epiphysis, the diaphysis and metaphyses are continuing to develop and mature; **E**: the differential between cortex and medulla is well established, epiphyseal development continues with growth in length taking place at (3) the epiphyseal cartilagineous plate or physis; **F**: the epiphyseal plates (4) have closed by ossification, growth has ceased; the bone has been modeled into its adult shape and form with well-defined cortex (c) and medullary canal (m).

Fetal age can be measured by crown-rump measurements, fetal length, femoral length, biparietal diameter, or skeletal maturation[2] (Figure 5-5). Fetal parts and soft tissues, if extrauterine, are small enough that radiological magnification will not be a major problem in view of the rather wide range of standard deviations for the various fetal measurements, most of which nowadays are based on real-time intrauterine measurements by ultrasonography. Intrauterine fetuses imaged roentgenographically will be magnified. (Figures 5-6 and 5-7 show systems of correcting for magnification.)

Under ideal conditions, the intrauterine fetal skeleton may be seen as early as the 10th week of gestation,[3] but in practice it is not often visualized before the 18th or 20th week. The ossification centers that appear in the posterior elements of the spine often are the first skeletal components seen radiologically as a chain of densities or "string of beads" sometimes accompanied by tiny rib shadows. The base of the skull and long bones may be visualized between 20 and 25 weeks if not obscured by maternal gas, bones, or other tissues (Figure 5-8).

The ossification center for the calcaneus appears between 24 and 26 weeks of gestation, followed in 2 weeks by the center for the talus (Figure 5-9). In the live fetus, intrauterine

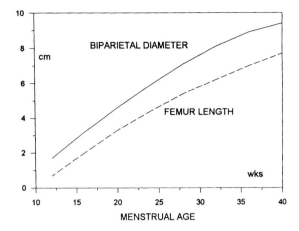

Figure 5-5 Graph presenting average biparietal diameter and femoral lengths in centimeters plotted against menstrual age of fetus. (Plotted from data in Reference 2 by M. D. Harpen, Ph.D.)

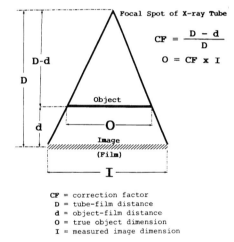

$$CF = \frac{D - d}{D}$$

$$O = CF \times I$$

CF = correction factor
D = tube–film distance
d = object–film distance
O = true object dimension
I = measured image dimension

Figure 5-6 Diagrammatic representation of factors involved in roentgenographic image magnification and formula for magnification correction.

movement often obliterates the image of these small parts. Between 36 and 40 weeks the distal femoral epiphysis, followed by the proximal tibial epiphysis, will appear (Figure 5-10). Before obstetrical ultrasonography, this was the best method of determining fetal maturity. The distal femoral epiphysis will be found in 90% or more of term fetuses, the proximal tibial epiphysis in 85% or more.

At birth the primary ossification centers (diaphyses) of the long bones of the extremities, including the hands and feet, are present. The vertebral bodies and posterior elements have begun their process of ossification, as have the scapulae, pelvic, clavicles, base of the skull, calvaria, and facial bones.[4]

For the next two decades, radiological determination of age is based on the appearance and eventual fusion of the secondary ossification centers (Figure 5-11) (Table 5-1). There are many standards for radiological bone age determination.[4–9] In general, female skeletal maturation precedes that of the male after the first few months of life. The final epiphysis to close is at the medial end of the clavicle during the third decade of life.[4]

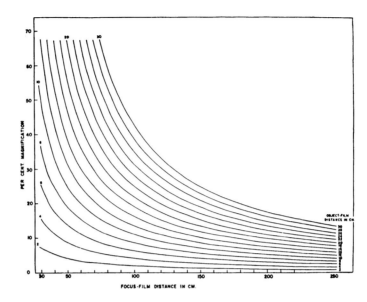

Figure 5-7   Graph constructed by T. H. Oddie, D.Sc., allowing calculation of percent magnification of an object when target-film and object-film distances (in centimeters) are known. (Reproduced from Meschan, I., *An Atlas of Anatomy Basic to Radiology*, W. B. Saunders, Philadelphia, 1975, p1078. With permission.)

The range of standard deviations for skeletal maturation of various ages is quite broad. Most of the radiological standards are based on Caucasian population ancestry, and even greater standard deviations may be found in children of different population ancestries.

For precise age determination in mass casualty studies and sorting out commingled children's remains, we tend to rely heavily on standards of development of the knee, foot ankle, and especially, the hand and wrist[10–12] (Figures 5-12, 5-13, 5-14) (Table 5-2). These standards must be used with reservations, particularly in Black and Hispanic girls and in Asian and Hispanic boys in late childhood and adolescence when their bone age may exceed the chronological age by 9 to 11 1/2 months.[13] It must be pointed out that, for subadults, dental age estimation, when feasible, is a more reliable estimate of chronological age than is bone age evaluation.[14]

From about age 25 to 50, the anthropologists rely heavily on the external appearance of the skull sutures and the pubic symphysis, and these criteria do not lend themselves readily to radiological evaluation.

Beginning about age 40, wear-and-tear degenerative changes start to appear at the margins of the articular surfaces of major joints, especially at the margins of vertebral end-plates (Figure 5-15). These changes of spurring and lipping, sometimes called deforming spondylosis in the spine, are quite variable and modified by occupation, level and kinds of activity, disease, and heredity. These degenerative changes progress with age and are usually more prominent in males. In females vertebral changes of osteoporosis, deformity, and collapse began about the time of menopause and progress. Here again, variability depends on many factors including exercise, diet, and hormonal balance. Ordinarily, an experienced radiologist can estimate adult age from skeletal findings in a range of ±5 to 10 years, that range widening with age.

The costal cartilages tend to become mineralized with age and may be visualized radiographically on prepared "chest plate" specimens as early as age 15 years. (The "chest

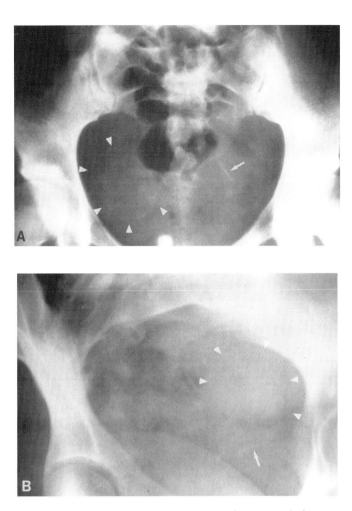

Figure 5-8   **A**: frontal and **B**: oblique roentgenogram of a 20-week fetus *in utero*. The skull (triangles) and long bones (arrows) are seen faintly within the maternal pelvis.

plate" in anthropological terminology consists of the terminal 4 to 6 cm of rib ends, the costal cartilages, the sternum, and [sometimes] the medial ends of the clavicles removed from the body for fine detail radiography.) In a standard chest radiography such ossification is rarely noted before 30 years of age and is not prominent before age 50. Again, there is great variability between individuals. Attempts to establish chronological age or age at death by evaluation of costal cartilage mineralization is imprecise. McCormick[15] found that similar degrees of ossification "over a wide age span during middle years seriously limits the value of this method", and its best recommendations for use were "ease, rapidity and relative inexpensiveness." Barrès and co-workers[16] found that the accuracy of age estimation by radiological evaluation of "chest plates" had a standard error of 8.5 years, which translates to a 95% confidence interval of ±17 years. Stewart and McCormick[17] have described a particular pattern of costal cartilage ossification (which they term Type A) specific to females of advanced age. Type A ossification usually appears no earlier than the mid-50s and becomes well developed and relatively dense only after age 65 years (Figure 5-16).

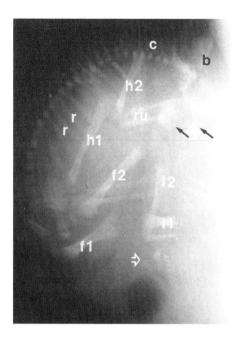

Figure 5-9   A 28-week fetus *in utero* (mother lying on her side). The upside extremities are more magnified than the downside extremities (which are closer to the film). Some bones are parallel to the film; others are angled away from the film and appear distorted and foreshortened. Code: (b) base of skull; (c) cervical vertebrae; (h1) upside humerus; (h2) downside humerus; (ru) downside forearm (radius and ulna) with faint metacarpals at end; overlapping mandible and maxilla (arrows); (r) ribcage; (f1) upside femur, foreshortened; (f2) downside femur; (l1) upside leg (tibia and fibula), foreshortened; (l2) downside leg (tibia and fibula overlapped) with foot at end (open arrow) containing calcaneus, talus, and metatarsal bones.

So far, assessment of age has been discussed in the context of identification of remains. There is another medicolegal indication for radiological age estimation in the living. When the age of a defendant is unknown (usually in primitive cultures) bone age may determine whether he is tried as a juvenile or an adult, or may determine the severity of the punishment. According to newspaper accounts, the young African native who murdered Joy Adamson (of Elsa the lion and "Born Free" fame) was saved from the hangman's rope by a justice who ruled, contrary to a radiologist's expert opinion, the perpetrator was below age 18 when the crime was committed.

Sex Determination

It has been pointed out already that skeletal development maturation in females is accelerated over that of males after the third or fourth year of life. However, differentiation of sexes by skeletal radiology is unreliable until after puberty.[4] It is then that the sexual characteristics discernible by radiography begin to appear.

In general, the male skeleton is more robust and heavier, with more prominent attachment for muscles and tendons. With aging, there is a tendency for more degenerative and hyperostotic changes in the male skeleton. Male long bones are about 110% the length of female long bones. The male femoral head is larger in all dimensions. All of these general findings are helpful but not definitive in establishing the sex of unidentified human remains. There are certain skeletal components, and both skeletal and extraskeletal findings, which are more useful in determining sex.

Pelvis

The bony pelvis often survives the onslaught of factors which diminish or destroy the usefulness of other body parts. This is fortunate since the pelvis offers the most definitive traits of sexual differentiation[18,19] (Figure 5-17).

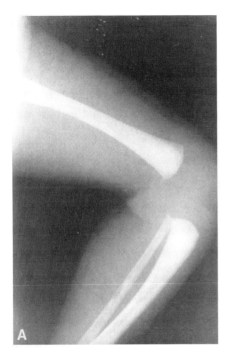
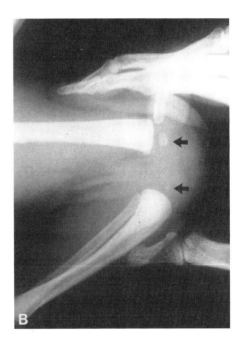

Figure 5-10   **A**: knee of premature newborn. The distal femoral and proximal tibial epiphyses are not ossified. **B**: term newborn with knee epiphyses (arrows) present.

- The *subpubic arch* (subpubic concavity) is narrow and triangular with an inverted V-shape in the male and broad and with an inverted U-shape in the female.
- The *pubic bone* tends to be long and narrow in the male and broad and rectangular in the female.
- The *sciatic notch* is deep and narrow in the male, and is wide and shallow in the female.
- The *preauricular sulcus* (paraglenoid sulcus) when present is one of the most dependable indicators of femaleness. This variable groove in the ilium at the inferior end of the sacroiliac joint is missing or manifest very rarely as a thin groove in the male,[19] and a deep groove is found only in females[20] (Figure 5-18). The groove or sulcus is believed to represent resorption of bone at the insertion of the anterior sacroiliac ligament, much as the costoclavicular ligament produces the rhomboid fossa in the anteroinferior end of the clavicle. Deep grooves are found only in subjects in the mid-fourth decade of life or beyond and only in parous women. The depth of the groove is influenced by multiple pregnancies, genetic differences, level of physical activity, and perhaps, the degree of lumbar lordosis.[20] While a deep groove denotes a female, not all women have a preauricular sulcus. Among the bodies recovered from the Air India disaster, a small notch was found in a 14-year-old female pelvis, and the oldest female without a periglenoid sulcus was 51 at time of death.
- The *obturator foramina* are large and oval or round in the male, but small and triangular in the female.
- The *acetabular fossae* are large and directed laterally in the male, and are smaller and directed anterolaterally in the female.

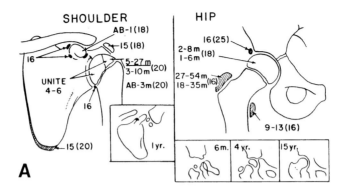

The numbers indicate the range of appearance time for centers of ossification from the 10th to the 90th percentile. Numbers followed by an "m" mean months, all others are in years. When two sets of numbers are given for a single ossification center, the upper one refers to males, the lower one to females. A single get of figures applies to both sexes. AB indicates the center is present at birth. Numbers in parentheses give the approximate time of fusion.

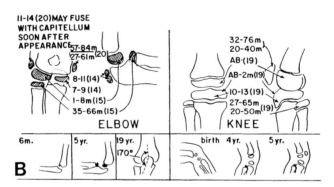

The numbers indicate the range of appearance time for centers of ossification from the 10th to the 90th percentile. Numbers followed by an "m" mean months, all others are in years. When two sets of numbers are given for a single ossification center, the upper one refers to males, the lower one to females. A single get of figures applies to both sexes. AB indicates the center is present at birth. Numbers in parentheses give the approximate time of fusion.

Figure 5-11   Skeletal maturation chart from Girdany and Golden.[6] **A**: shoulder and hip; **B**: elbow and knee; **C**: hand and foot; **D**: vertebra; **E**: sacrum and coccyx; **F**: rib and clavicle. (From Girdiny and Golden, *Am. J. Roentgenol.*, 28, 922, 1952. With permission.)

- The *ilial alae* are high and vertical in the male, and broad and laterally divergent in the female.
- The *sacrum* in the male is narrow, has a relatively flattened curve and has five or more segments. The female sacrum is broad and short with five segments and an anterior concavity.
- The *pelvic inlet* is triangular or heart-shaped in the male, ovoid in the female.

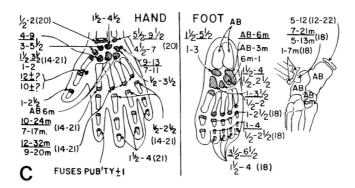

The numbers indicate the range of appearance time for centers of ossification from the 10th to the 90th percentile. Numbers followed by an "m" mean months, all others are in years. When two sets of numbers are given for a single ossification center, the upper one refers to males, the lower one to females. A single get of figures applies to both sexes. AB indicates the center is present at birth. Numbers in parentheses give the approximate time of fusion.

VERTEBRA

OSSIFY FROM 3 PRIMARY CENTERS AND 9 SECONDARY CENTERS – ANY OF THESE SECONDARY CENTERS, EXCEPT FOR ANNULAR EPIPHYSES, MAY FAIL TO FUSE.

ARCH CENTERS FUSE 1-7

BODY & ARCH CENTERS FUSE: CERVICAL AT 3, LUMBAR AT 6

ANNULAR EPIPHYSES APPEAR NEAR PUBERTY – MAY APPEAR BY 7 YRS.

16(25)   16(25)

LUMBAR   AXIS   ATLAS

2(12)   ANT. CENTER APPEARS AB-1(6)

16(25)   AB   FUSE 3

SECONDARY CENTERS FOR MAMMILLARY PROCESSES

D

The numbers indicate the range of appearance time for centers of ossification from the 10th to the 90th percentile. Numbers followed by an "m" mean months, all others are in years. When two sets of numbers are given for a single ossification center, the upper one refers to males, the lower one to females. A single get of figures applies to both sexes. AB indicates the center is present at birth. Numbers in parentheses give the approximate time of fusion.

Figure 5-11 (continued)

- The *muscle markings* are more prominent and rugged in the male. The female bony pelvis tends to be smooth and gracile.
- *Osteitis condensans ilii* is a triangular area of increased bony density on the ilial side of the sacroiliac joint, usually bilateral, found almost exclusively in parous women in the child-bearing years (Figure 5-19). The joint, per se, is unaffected. It may be caused by the stress of pregnancy and childbirth. There is correlation with the presence of deep preauricular sulci. The condition is self-limited and disappears; consequently, it is not to be found in the elderly female.[20–22]

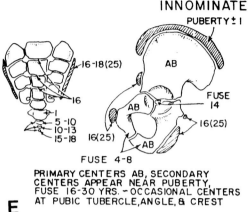

SACRUM & COCCYX
LOWER SACRAL BODIES FUSE
AT 18 ···ALL FUSE BY 30

INNOMINATE
PUBERTY ± 1

FUSE 4-8

PRIMARY CENTERS AB, SECONDARY
CENTERS APPEAR NEAR PUBERTY,
FUSE 16-30 YRS. – OCCASIONAL CENTERS
AT PUBIC TUBERCLE, ANGLE, & CREST

E

The numbers indicate the range of appearance time for
centers of ossification from the 10th to the 90th percentile.
Numbers followed by an "m" mean months, all others are in
years. When two sets of numbers are given for a single
ossification center, the upper one refers to males, the lower
one to females. A single get of figures applies to both sexes.
AB indicates the center is present at birth. Numbers in
parentheses give the approximate time of fusion.

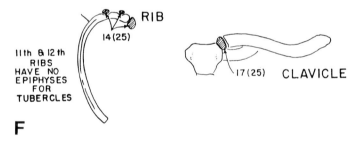

RIB
14 (25)

11th & 12th
RIBS
HAVE NO
EPIPHYSES
FOR
TUBERCLES

17 (25)   CLAVICLE

F

The numbers indicate the range of appearance time for
centers of ossification from the 10th to the 90th percentile.
Numbers followed by an "m" mean months, all others are in
years. When two sets of numbers are given for a single
ossification center, the upper one refers to males, the lower
one to females. A single get of figures applies to both sexes.
AB indicates the center is present at birth. Numbers in
parentheses give the approximate time of fusion.

Figure 5-11 (continued)

Skull and Mandible

Bony characteristics of the skull and mandible may be useful in assigning sexual identification to unknown remains[23–25] (Figure 5-20). The male skull tends to range from mesocephalic to dolichocephalic; the female skull is more likely to be mesocephalic to
brachycephalic. The male has a larger brow or supraorbital ridge and a more sloping
forehead. The male zygomatic arch is wider and heavier. The male inion or nuchal crest
is prominent. The male mastoid process is larger and heavier. The male mandible is larger

and more rugged with a wide ascending ramus. Male orbits tend to be larger and higher. The inferior nasal spine is longer in the male.

Hyperostosis interna frontalis is an overgrowth of the inner table of the frontal bone, often florid, found almost exclusively in middle-aged or older females and is a valuable characteristic for sex determination (Figure 5-21).

Parietal thinning[21,26] is a condition of postmenopausal females in which profound osteoporosis causes symmetrical resorption and virtual disappearance of the outer table and diploë of the parietal bones (Figure 5-22).

Sternum

The gender-predictive value of sternal length is not often used radiographically because it requires cross-table radiographs of the chest with a partially radiopaque ruler in place. With "chest plate" preparations direct measurements can be obtained. A combined length of manubrium and gladiolus of 17.3 cm includes only males; a combined length of manubrium and glandulous of less than 12.1 cm includes only females. Sternal lengths of 14.3 to 15.7 cm were indeterminate.[27]

Other Areas

Bi-partite patella is a common anatomical variant in adolescents, and is nine times more common in boys than girls. It is seen as a separate ossicle (or ossicles) occupying the upper outer quadrant of the patella. It occurs in approximately 2% of the population and is bilateral in 40 to 80% of cases.[28]

Krogman states that the chance of correctly sexing bones is 100% if the entire skeleton is available, 95% with the skull and pelvis or with the long bone and pelvis, and 90% with the skull alone or with the long bones and skull.[25]

Costal cartilage mineralization patterns as a distinctive finding between sexes was first reported by Sanders[29] (Figure 5-23). He noted that the typical male pattern is that of continuous parallel ossification of the upper and lower borders of the cartilage as it extends from the rib end (Figures 5-23A and 5-24). The typical female pattern is a tongue-like or triangular mineralization extending from the rib end into the centrum of the cartilage (Figures 5-23C and 5-25). An uncommon pattern, more common in females, is that of two parallel lines extending from the center of the rib and into the adjacent cartilage (Figure 5-23D). A pitfall is that the male pattern tends to first appear on the inferior images of the costal cartilage (Figures 5-23B and 5-26) and may be mistaken for the female "tongue" which is always central to the cartilage. Finally, the pattern of a central rounded mineral collection in costal cartilage, sometimes with a more lucent center, is believed specific for elderly females[17] (Figures 5-23E and 5-16). Navani et al.[30] believe the predictive value of the parallel marginal male pattern to be 95%, the predictive value of the tongue-like central female-type mineralization to be 93%, and mixtures or combinations of those two pattern to be more likely found in females (predictive value 57%).

Calcification of tracheobronchial cartilage is found in only a small percentage of the people but with an overwhelming female predominance.[21]

Calcification or ossification of the thyroid cartilage anteriorly is more common in males while *arytenoid cartilage* calcification is four times more common in women.[21]

Perhaps the only *absolute roentgenographic indicator of sex* was present in one of the victims of the Air India catastrophe (Figure 5-27). Many of the recovered bodies had

Table 5-1   Age-at-Appearance (Years-Months) Percentiles for Selected Ossification Centers

	Centers	Boys			Girls		
		5th	50th	95th	5th	50th	95th
1.	Humerus, head	—	0-0	0-4	—	0-0	0-4
2.	Tibia, proximal	—	0-0	0-1	—	0-0	0-0
3.	Coracoid process of scapula	—	0-0	0-4	—	0-0	0-5
4.	Cuboid	—	0-1	0-4	—	0-1	0-2
5.	Capitate	—	0-3	0-7	—	0-2	0-7
6.	Hamate	0-0	0-4	0-10	—	0-2	0-7
7.	Capitellum of humerus	0-1	0-4	1-1	0-1	0-3	0-9
8.	Femur, head	0-1	0-4	0-8	0-0	0-4	0-7
9.	Cuneiform 3	0-1	0-6	1-7	—	0-3	1-3
10.	Humerus, greater tuberosity	0-3	0-10	2-4	0-2	0-6	1-2
11.	Toe phalanx 5 M	—	1-0	3-10	—	0-9	2-1
12.	Radius, distal	0-6	1-1	2-4	0-5	0-10	1-8
13.	Toe phalanx 1 D	0-9	1-3	2-1	0-5	0-9	1-8
14.	Toe phalanx 4 M	0-5	1-3	2-11	0-5	0-11	3-0
15.	Finger phalanx 3 P	0-9	1-4	2-2	0-5	0-10	1-7
16.	Toe phalanx 3 M	0-5	1-5	4-3	0-3	1-0	2-6
17.	Finger phalanx 2 P	0-9	1-5	2-2	0-5	0-10	1-8
18.	Finger phalanx 4 P	0-10	1-6	2-5	0-5	0-11	1-8
19.	Finger phalanx 1 D	0-9	1-6	2-8	0-5	1-0	1-9
20.	Toe phalanx 3 P	0-11	1-7	2-6	0-6	1-1	1-11
21.	Metacarpal 2	0-11	1-7	2-10	0-8	1-1	1-8
22.	Toe phalanx 4 P	0-11	1-8	2-8	0-7	1-3	2-1
23.	Toe phalanx 2 P	1-0	1-9	2-8	0-8	1-2	2-1
24.	Metacarpal 3	0-11	1-9	3-0	0-8	1-2	1-11
25.	Finger phalanx 5 P	1-0	1-10	2-10	0-8	1-2	2-1
26.	Finger phalanx 3 M	1-0	2-0	3-4	0-8	1-3	2-4
27.	Metacarpal 4	1-1	2-0	3-7	0-9	1-3	2-2
28.	Toe phalanx 2 M	0-11	2-0	4-1	0-6	1-2	2-3
29.	Finger phalanx 4 M	1-0	2-1	3-3	0-8	1-3	2-5
30.	Metacarpal 5	1-3	2-2	3-10	0-10	1-4	2-4
31.	Cuneiform 1	0-11	2-2	3-9	0-6	1-5	2-10
32.	Metatarsal 1	1-5	2-2	3-1	1-0	1-7	2-3
33.	Finger phalanx 2 M	1-4	2-2	3-4	0-8	1-4	2-6
34.	Toe phalanx 1 P	1-5	2-4	3-4	0-11	1-7	2-6
35.	Finger phalanx 3 D	1-4	2-5	3-9	0-9	1-6	2-8
36.	Triquetrum	0-6	2-5	5-6	0-3	1-8	3-9
37.	Finger phalanx 4 D	1-4	2-5	3-9	0-9	1-6	2-10
38.	Toe phalanx 5 P	1-6	2-5	3-8	1-0	1-9	2-8
39.	Metacarpal 1	1-5	2-7	4-4	0-11	1-7	2-8
40.	Cuneiform 2	1-2	2-8	4-3	0-10	1-10	3-0
41.	Metatarsal 2	1-11	2-10	4-4	1-3	2-2	3-5
42.	Femur, greater trochanter	1-11	3-0	4-4	1-0	1-10	3-0
43.	Finger phalanx 1 P	1-10	3-0	4-7	0-11	1-9	2-10
44.	Navicular of foot	1-1	3-0	5-5	0-9	1-11	3-7
45.	Finger phalanx 2 D	1-10	3-2	5-0	1-1	2-6	3-3
46.	Finger phalanx 5 D	2-1	3-3	5-0	1-0	2-0	3-5
47.	Finger phalanx 5 M	1-11	3-5	5-10	0-11	2-0	3-6
48.	Fibula, proximal	1-10	3-6	5-3	1-4	2-7	3-11
49.	Metatarsal 3	2-4	3-6	5-0	1-5	2-6	3-8
50.	Toe phalanx 5 D	2-4	3-11	6-4	1-2	2-4	4-1
51.	Patella	2-7	4-0	6-0	1-6	2-6	4-0
52.	Metatarsal 4	2-11	4-0	5-9	1-9	2-10	4-1
53.	Lunate	1-6	4-1	6-9	1-1	2-7	5-8
54.	Toe phalanx 3 D	3-0	4-4	6-2	1-4	2-9	4-1

Table 5-1 (continued)   Age-at-Appearance (Years-Months) Percentiles for Selected Ossification Centers

		Boys			Girls		
	Centers	5th	50th	95th	5th	50th	95th
55.	Metatarsal 5	3-1	4-4	6-4	2-1	3-3	4-11
56.	Toe phalanx 4 D	2-11	4-5	6-5	1-4	2-7	4-1
57.	Toe phalanx 2 D	3-3	4-8	6-9	1-6	2-11	4-6
58.	**Radius, head**	**3-0**	**5-3**	**8-0**	**2-3**	**3-10**	**6-3**
59.	Navicular of wrist	3-7	5-8	7-10	2-4	4-1	6-0
60.	Greater multangular	3-6	5-10	9-0	1-11	4-1	6-4
61.	Lesser multangular	3-1	6-3	8-6	2-5	4-2	6-0
62.	Medial epicondyle of humerus	4-3	6-3	8-5	2-1	3-5	5-1
63.	Ulna, distal	5-3	7-1	9-1	3-3	5-4	7-8
64.	**Calcaneal apophysis**	**5-2**	**7-7**	**9-7**	**3-6**	**5-4**	**7-4**
65.	**Olecranon of ulna**	**7-9**	**9-8**	**11-11**	**5-7**	**8-0**	**9-11**
66.	**Lateral epicondyle of humerus**	**9-3**	**11-3**	**13-8**	**7-2**	**9-3**	**11-3**
67.	**Tibial tubercle**	**9-11**	**11-10**	**13-5**	**7-11**	**10-3**	**11-10**
68.	Adductor sesamoid of thumb	11-0	12-9	14-7	8-8	10-9	12-8
69.	Os acetabulum	11-11	13-6	15-4	9-7	11-6	13-5
70.	**Acromion**	**12-2**	**13-9**	**15-6**	**10-4**	**11-11**	**13-9**
71.	**Iliac crest**	**12-0**	**14-0**	**15-11**	**10-10**	**12-9**	**15-4**
72.	**Coracoid apophysis**	**12-9**	**14-4**	**16-4**	**10-4**	**12-3**	**14-4**
73.	**Ischial tuberosity**	**13-7**	**15-3**	**17-1**	**11-9**	**13-11**	**16-0**

Note: P = proximal, M = middle, D = distal. Important "happenings" at various ages are in bold face type.

From Graham, C. B., *Radiol. Clin. N. Am.*, 10, 185, 1972. With permission.

abdominal viscera displaced into the chest. One young female chest contained a fetal skeleton estimated at 18 to 22 weeks.

Determination of Race or Population Ancestry

The physical anthropologists have many elaborate methods of evaluating race or population ancestry if bare bones are available. Some fleshed or partially fleshed remains can be evaluated radiographically.

Skull — The skull reflects certain characteristics of population ancestry that are reasonably dependable[23,24] but may be confused by racial mixing. Figure 5-28 and Table 5-3 summarize differential features in frontal and lateral projections.

Intercondylar shelf angle — A method of determining race from the intercondylar shelf angle can be used with skeletal or fleshed remains[31] (Figure 5-29). It requires only true lateral positioning of the distal femur. The measurement of the angle between the roof of the intercondylar notch (or intercondylar shelf) and the long axis of the femoral shaft is independent of magnification. Figure 5-30 shows the bimodal nature of the racial curves with a fairly narrow overlap range of only 18% between sectioning points.

Long bones — In Blacks, the tibia is long relative to the femur and the radius is long relative to the humerus, but the ratios are variable and overlap in the U.S. population, probably due to racial mixing.[4] Compared to Blacks, the femoral shafts are bowed anteriorly in Whites and Mongoloid populations. Again there is considerable variability, but a markedly bowed femur is unlikely to belong to a Black.[4]

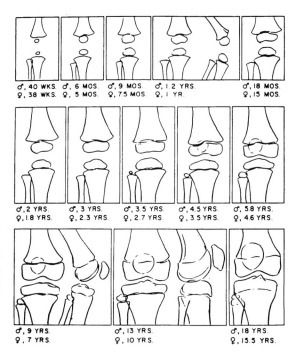

Figure 5-12 Tracings (from Meschan, I., *An Atlas of Anatomy Basic to Radiology*, W. B. Saunders, Philadelphia, 1975, p. 56, with permission) of standard roentgenograms of the maturing knee. (From Pyle, S. I. and Hoerr, N. L., *Atlas of Skeletal Development of the Knee*, Charles C Thomas, Springfield, IL, 1955. With permission.)

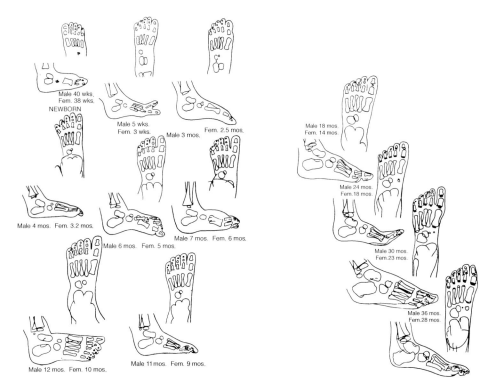

Figure 5-13 Tracings (from Meschan, I., *An Atlas of Anatomy Basic to Radiology*, W. B. Saunders, Philadelphia, 1975, p. 54-55, with permission) of standard roentgenograms of the maturing foot and ankle. (From Hoerr, N. L., Pyle, S. I., and Francis, C. C., *Radiographic Atlas of the Foot and Ankle*, Charles C Thomas, Springfield, IL, 1962. With permission.)

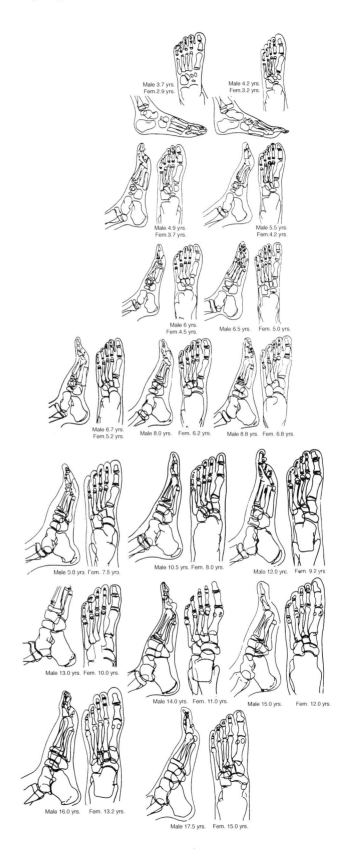

Figure 5-13 (continued)

Stature

Estimations of stature from measurements of long bones have been the province of anatomists and physical anthropologists for many years. Most have been based on extensive research on World War II and Korean War casualties.[32,33] The length of the femur is the most reliable basis for calculation of stature.[25] Controversy has arisen recently concerning the accuracy of tibial measurements in Trotter and Gleser's data.[34]

The equations furnished for stature estimation from long bone measurements are based on direct measurement of the unfleshed bones[35] (Table 5-4). Fleshed remains can be measured radiographically, but correction for magnification is essential. There are four ways in which this correction can be accomplished.

1. Formula to determine correction factor for magnification (see Figure 5-6 and accompanying formula).[36]
2. Use of an excessively long tube-to-specimen distance (72 in. or more) with minimal specimen-to-film distance (table-top grid cassette) will essentially negate magnification and was used in Maresh's seminal studies on long bone growth in children.[37]
3. Direct measurement by computed tomography. This is quick and easy if a CT scanner is readily available.
4. Use of an old technique for measuring long bone to determine correct sizes for intramedullary nails in trauma cases or to measure leg length discrepancies in patients with gait disturbance or scoliosis. This technique depends on carefully collimated x-ray beams at conventional tube-object distances so that only the nondivergent central x-rays are used to expose the end of the bones. A partially radiopaque ruler included in the field of exposure can be used for direct measurement (Figure 5-31).

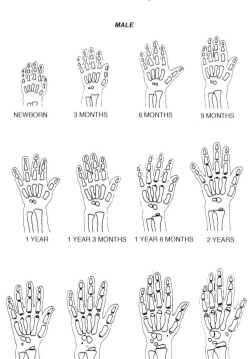

Figure 5-14 Tracings of male and female standards of skeletal development of the hand and wrist. There is no difference between sexes for the first year of life, then development accelerates in females. (Reprinted from Greulich, W. W. and Pyle, S. I., *Radiographic Atlas of Skeletal Development of the Hand and Wrist*, 2nd ed., Stanford University Press, Stanford, CA, 1950. With permission.) (Tracings from Keats[7] with permission of Mosby Yearbook, 1990.)

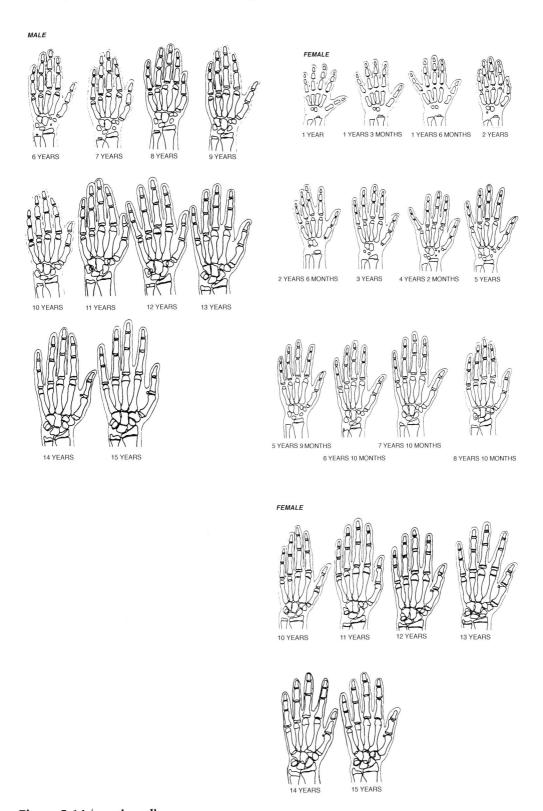

Figure 5-14 (continued)

Table 5-2A   Means and Standard Deviations for Skeletal Age (Hand) — Boys

Chronological Age	Number of Hand-Films	Skeletal Age (in Months)	
		Mean	Standard Deviation
12 mo.	66	12.7	2.1
18 mo.	67	17.5	2.7
2 yr.	67	22.6	4.0
2¹/₂ yr.	67	28.1	5.4
3 yr.	67	33.8	6.0
3¹/₂ yr.	67	39.5	6.6
4 yr.	65	44.8	7.0
4¹/₂ yr.	64	50.3	7.8
5 yr.	64	56.2	8.4
5¹/₂ yr.	64	62.4	9.1
6 yr.	66	68.4	9.3
7 yr.	66	80.6	10.1
8 yr.	63	92.5	10.8
9 yr.	63	104.9	11.0
10 yr.	63	118.0	11.4
11 yr.	65	132.1	10.5
12 yr.	64	144.5	10.4
13 yr.	66	156.4	11.1
14 yr.	65	168.5	12.0
15 yr.	65	180.7	14.2
16 yr.	65	193.0	15.1
17 yr.	60	206.0	15.4

From Greulich, W. W. and Pyle, S. I., *Radiographic Atlas of Skeletal Development of the Hand and Wrist*, 2nd ed., Stanford University Press, Stanford, CA, 1959. With permission.

Table 5-2B   Means and Standard Deviations for Skeletal Age (Hand) — Girls

Chronological Age	Number of Hand-Films	Skeletal Age (in Months)	
		Mean	Standard Deviation
12 mo.	65	12.7	2.7
18 mo.	66	18.4	3.4
2 yr.	66	23.7	4.0
2¹/₂ yr.	65	29.0	4.8
3 yr.	66	34.5	5.6
3¹/₂ yr.	66	40.6	6.5
4 yr.	67	46.4	7.2
4¹/₂ yr.	67	52.3	8.0
5 yr.	67	58.1	8.6
5¹/₂ yr.	67	63.9	8.9
6 yr.	67	70.4	9.0
7 yr.	67	82.0	8.3
8 yr.	67	94.0	8.8
9 yr.	67	105.9	9.3
10 yr.	66	119.0	10.8
11 yr.	66	132.9	12.3
12 yr.	66	147.2	14.0
13 yr.	66	160.3	14.6
14 yr.	63	172.4	12.6
15 yr.	61	184.3	11.2

From Greulich, W. W. and Pyle, S. I., *Radiographic Atlas of Skeletal Development of the Hand and Wrist*, 2nd ed., Stanford University Press, Stanford, CA, 1959. With permission.

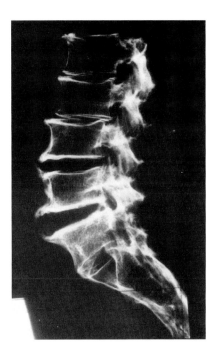

Figure 5-15 Degenerative hypertrophic changes (spurring, lipping, osteophyte production) at the margins of vertebral end-plates.

Figure 5-16 "Chest plate" roentgenogram shows Stewart and McCormick's "Type A" ossification of costal cartilage.[17] Rounded, solitary or coalescent foci confined to the central portions of the cartilage do not extend to the perichondrium. They rarely reach the peristernal junction. The decedent can be identified with great certainty as an elderly female. (From Steward, J. H. and McCormick, W. F., *Am. J. Clin. Pathol.*, 81, 765, 1984. With permission.)

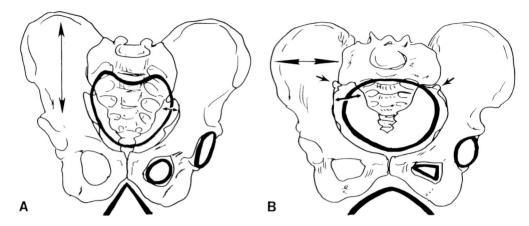

Figure 5-17   **A**: male pelvis. **B**: female pelvis. Differential characteristics are emphasized with bold lines and arrows (see text).

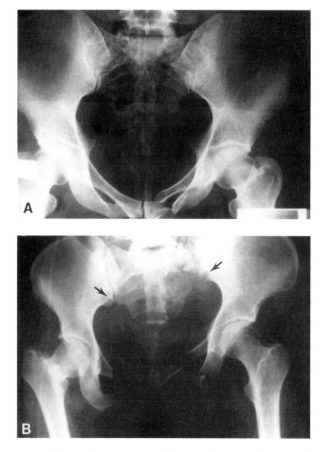

Figure 5-18   **A**: male pelvis and **B**: female pelvis, victims of the Air India disaster. Note the differences in configuration and, especially, the preauricular sulcus (arrows) in the female.

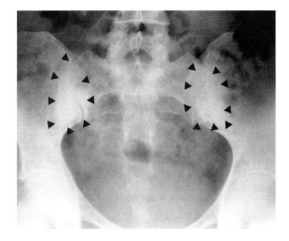

Figure 5-19   Osteitis condensans ilii. A triangular area of increased density (arrowheads) on the ilial side of the sacroiliac joint in women during the child-bearing years.

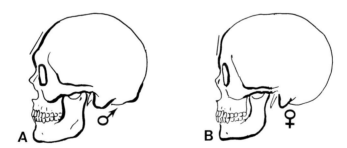

Figure 5-20   **A**: male and **B**: female characteristics in the skull. Differential areas are emphasized by bold lines (see text).

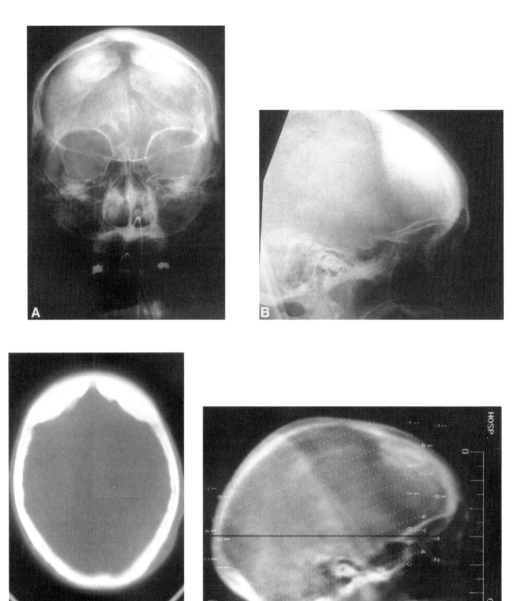

Figure 5-21   Hyperostosis interna frontalis. Dense bony thickening of the inner table of the frontal bone seen in **A**: frontal and **B**: lateral roentgenograms, and **C**: on a CT scan of the skull using a "bone window". The "topogram" preliminary to the CT scan, **D**, is sufficiently detailed that it could be used for purposes of identification comparison.

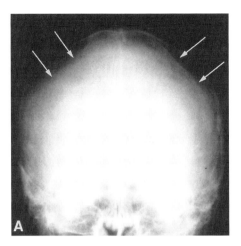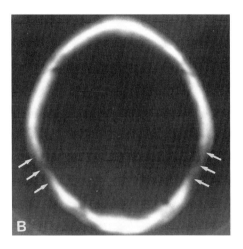

Figure 5-22 Parietal thinning. The resorption of the outer table of the skull and diploë is striking in both the frontal radiograph **A** and the CT scan **B**.

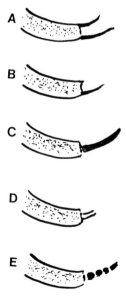

Figure 5-23 Schematic drawing of patterns of costal cartilage ossification useful in determining the sex of human remains. **A**: typical male pattern; **B**: male pattern initially involving only the inferior margin of the costal cartilage; **C**: typical female pattern; **D**: uncommon pattern more often found in females than males; **E**: string of rounded ossifications believed specific for elderly females.

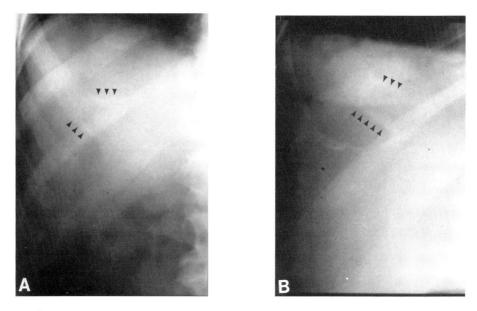

Figure 5-24   **A** and **B**: typical male pattern costal cartilage ossification.

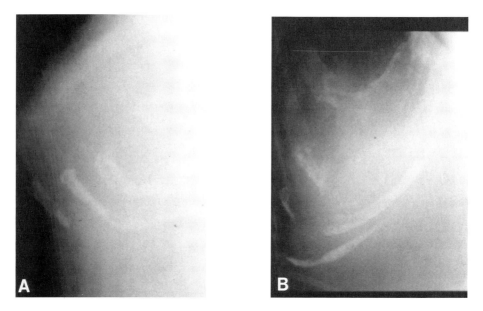

Figure 5-25   **A** and **B**: typical female pattern costal cartilage ossification.

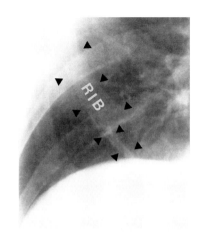

Figure 5-26 Male pattern ossification involving only the inferior border of the costal cartilage, easily confused with female pattern if not traced back to the rib end.

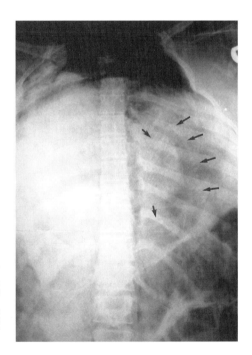

Figure 5-27 Fetal skeleton displaced into the thorax of an Air India crash victim. The chain of ossified vertebral body centers ("string of beads") is marked by long arrows. Short arrows indicate long bones in extremities. The base of the skull is seen at the upper end of the spine.

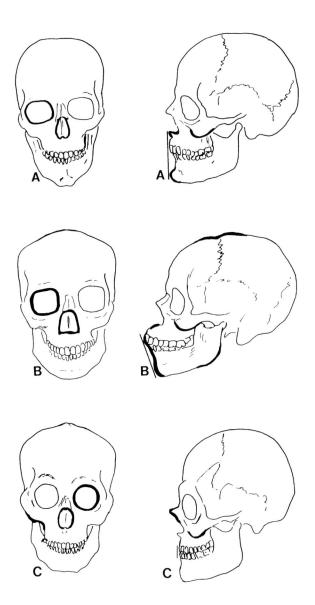

Figure 5-28   Drawings emphasizing characteristic differences in the skull between humans of diverse population ancestry in frontal and lateral views. **AA**: Caucasoid; **BB**: Negroid; **CC**: Mongoloid (see Table 5-3).

Table 5-3   Morphological Features for Racial Assessment of the Skull and Mandible[22,23]

Feature	Caucasoid	Negroid	Mongoloid
General configuration	Mesocephalic	Dolichocephalic	Brachycephalic
Saggital contour	Round	Coronal flat or notching	Arched
Parietal bossing	+ – ++	0	+++
Bite	Slight overbite	Prognathic	Even
Face	Long, narrow	Prognathic	Flat
Orbits	Rectangular	Oval	Rounded
Intraorbital distance	Intermediate	Wide	Wide
Nasal aperture	Narrow, oval	Round	Wide with inferior gully
Inferior nasal spine	Sharp	Short or troughed	Dull
Nasal bones	Intermediate	Short, depressed	Prominent
Zygomatic arches or malar prominence	Slight, retreating	Slight retreating	Prominent, inferior projection
Mandibular angle	Slightly obtuse	Obtuse	Nearly right angle
Chin, mental process	++	–	+

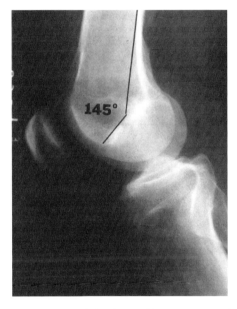

Figure 5-29   Lateral roentgenogram of the knee illustrating method of measuring the intercondylar shelf angle.

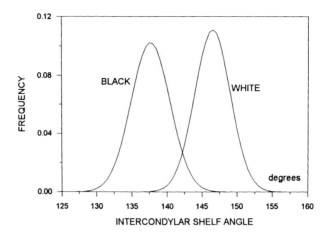

Figure 5-30 Graphic representation of racial distribution of intercondylar shelf angles. (Courtesy Michael D. Harpen, Ph.D., from data presented in Reference 31.)

Table 5-4 Equations to Estimate Living Stature (cm) — with Standard Errors — from the Long Bones of American Whites and Negroes Between 18 and 30 Years of Age[a]

White Males		Negro Males	
3.08 Hum + 70.45	±4.05	3.26 Hum + 62.10	±4.43
3.78 Rad + 79.01	±4.32	3.42 Rad + 81.56	±4.30
3.70 Ulna + 74.05	±4.32	3.26 Ulna + 79.29	±4.42
2.38 Fem + 61.41	±3.27	2.11 Fem + 70.35	±3.94
2.52 Tib + 78.62	±3.37	2.19 Tib + 86.02	±3.78
2.68 Fib + 71.78	±3.29	2.19 Fib + 85.65	±4.08
1.30 (Fem + Tib) + 63.29	±2.99	1.15 (Fem + Tib) + 71.04	±3.53

White Females		Negro Females	
3.36 Hum + 57.97	±4.45	3.08 Hum + 64.67	±4.25
4.74 Rad + 54.93	±4.24	2.75 Rad + 94.51	±5.05
4.27 Ulna + 57.76	±4.30	3.31 Ulna + 75.38	±4.83
2.47 Fem + 54.10	±3.72	2.28 Fem + 59.76	±3.41
2.90 Tib + 61.53	±3.66	2.45 Tib + 72.65	±3.70
2.93 Fib + 59.61	±3.57	2.49 Fib + 70.90	±3.80
1.39 (Fem + Tib) + 53.20	±3.55	1.26 (Fem + Tib) + 59.72	±3.28

Mongoloid Males		Mexican Males	
2.68 Hum + 83.19	±4.25	2.92 Hum + 73.94	±4.24
3.54 Rad + 82.00	±4.60	3.55 Rad + 80.71	±4.04
3.48 Ulna + 77.45	±4.66	3.56 Ulna + 74.56	±4.05
2.15 Fem + 72.57	±3.80	2.44 Fem + 58.67	±2.99
2.39 Tib + 81.45	±3.27	2.36 Tib + 80.62	±3.73
2.40 Fib + 80.56	±3.24	2.50 Fib + 75.44	±3.52
1.22 (Fem + Tib) + 70.37	±3.24		

[a] To estimate stature of older individuals subtract 0.06 (age in years — 30) cm; to estimate cadaver stature, add 2.5 cm.

From Trotter, M., in *Personal Identification in Mass Disasters*, Steward, T. E., Ed., National Museum of Natural History, Smithsonian Institution, Washington, D.C., 1970, 77.

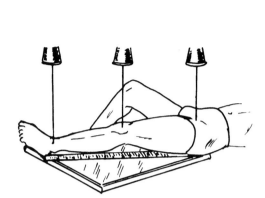

Figure 5-31   A: method of obtaining magnification-free measurements of long bone length using collimated, nondivergent x-rays over the bone ends with a partially radiopaque ruler in the field of exposure. **B**: example of image obtained by above method.

References

1. Chilvarquer, I., Katz, J. O., Glassman, D. M., Prihoda, T. J., and Cattone, J. A., Comparative radiographic study of human and animal long bone patterns, *J. Forensic Sci.*, 32, 1645, 1987.

2. Hadlock, F. P., Deter, R. L., Harrist, D. B., and Park, S. K., Estimating fetal age: computer-assisted analysis of multiple fetal growth parameters, *Radiology*, 152, 497, 1984.

3. Hartley, J. B., Radiological estimation of foetal maturity, *Br. J. Radiol.*, 30, 561, 1957.

4. Krogman, W. M. and Iscan, M.Y., *The Human Skeleton in Forensic Medicine*, 2nd ed., Charles C Thomas, Springfield, IL, 1986, chap. 13.

5. Graham, C. B., Assessment of bone maturation — methods and pitfalls, *Radiol. Clin. N. Am.*, 10, 185, 1972.

6. Girdany, B. R. and Golden, R., Centers of ossification of the skeleton, *Am. J. Roentgenol.*, 68, 922, 1952.

7. Keats, T. E, *Atlas of Roentgenographic Measurement*, 6th Mosby Year Book, St. Louis, 1990, chap. 4B.

8. Meschan, I., *Roentgen Signs in Clinical Practice*, Vol. I, W.B. Saunders, Philadelphia, 1966, chap. 4.

9. Sontag, I. W., Snell, D., and Anderson, M., Rate of appearance of ossification centers from birth to the age of five years, *Am. J. Dis. Child.*, 58, 949, 1939

10. Pyle, S. I. and Hoerr, N. L., *Atlas of Skeletal Development of the Knee*, Charles C Thomas, Springfield, IL, 1955.

11. Hoerr, N. L., Pyle, S. I., and Francis, C. C., *Radiologic Atlas of the Foot and Ankle*, Charles C Thomas, Springfield, IL, 1962.

12. Greulich, W. W. and Pyle, S. I., *Radiographic Atlas of Skeletal Development of the Hand and Wrist*, 2nd ed., Stanford University Press, Palo Alto, CA, 1959.

13. Ontell, F. K., Ivanovic, M., Ablin, D. S., and Barlow, T. W., Bone age in children of diverse ethnicity, *Am. J. Roentgenol.*, 167, 1395, 1996.

14. Sundick, R. I., Age and sex determination of subadult skeletons, *J. Forensic Sci.*, 22,141, 1977.

15. McCormick, W. F., Mineralization of costal cartilages as an indicator of age: preliminary observations, *J. Forensic Sci.*, 25, 736, 1980.

16. Barres, D. R., Durigon, M., and Paraire, F., Age estimation from quantitation of features of "chest plate" x-rays, *J. Forensic Sci.*, 34, 228, 1989.

17. Stewart, J. H. and McCormick, W. F., A Sex and age-limited ossification pattern in human costal cartilages, *Am. J. Clin. Pathol.*, 81, 765, 1984.

18. Sutherland, L. D. and Suchey, J. M., Use of the ventral arc in pubic sex determination, *J. Forensic Sci.*, 36, 501, 1991.

19. Rogers, T. and Saunders, S., Accuracy of sex determination using morphological traits of the human pelvis, *J. Forensic Sci.*, 39, 1047, 1994.

20. Schemmer, D., White, P. G., and Friedman. L., Radiology of the paraglenoid sulcus, *Skeletal Radiol.*, 24, 205, 1995.

21. Kurihara, Y., Kurihara, Y., Ohashi, K., Kitagawa, A., Miyasaki, M., Okamoto, E., and Ishikawa, T., Radiologic evidence of sex differences: is the patient a woman or a man?, *Am. J. Roentgenol.*, 167, 1037, 1996.

22. Wells, J., Osteities condensans ilii, *Am. J. Roentgenol.*, 76, 1141, 1956.

23. Bass, W. M., III, Forensic anthropology, in *CAP Handbook for Postmortem Examination of Unidentified Remains*, Fierro, M. F., Ed., College of American Pathologists, Skokie, IL, 1990, chap. 8.

24. Heglund, W. D., How can the forensic anthropologist help? Handout presented at the American Academy of Forensic Science, Seattle, February 14, 1995.

25. Krogman, W. M., Will Mr. X please come forward?, *Del. Med. J.*, 51, 399, 1979.

26. Steinbach, H. L., The significance of thinning of the parietal bones, *Am. J. Roentgenol.*, 78, 39, 1957.

27. Stewart, J. H. and McCormick, W. F., The gender predictive value of sternal length, *Am. J. Forensic Med. Pathol.*, 4, 217, 1983.

28. Lawson, J. P., Clinically significant radiologic anatomic variants of the skeleton, *Am. J. Roentgenol.*, 163, 249, 1994.

29. Sanders, C. F., Correspondence, *Br. J. Radiol.*, 39, 233, 1966.

30. Navani, S., Shak, J. R., and Levy, P. S., Determination of sex by costal cartilage calcification, *Am. J. Roentgenol.*, 108, 771, 1970.

31. Craig, E. A., Intercondylar shelf angle: a new method to determine race from the distal femur, *J. Forensic Sci.*, 40, 777, 1995.

32. Trotter, M. and Gleser, G. C., Estimation of stature from long bones of American Whites and Negroes, *Am. J. Phys. Anthropol.*, 10, 463, 1952.

33. Trotter, M. and Gleser, G. C., A re-evaluation of estimation of stature based on measurements of stature taken during life and of long bones after death, *Am. J. Phys. Anthropol.*, 15, 79, 1958.

34. Jantz, R. L., Hunt, D. R., and Meadows, L., The measure and mismeasure of the tibia: implications for stature estimation, *J. Forensic Sci.*, 40, 758, 1995.

35. Trotter, M., Estimation of stature from intact long limb bones, in *Personal Identification in Mass Disasters*, Stewart, T. D., Ed., National Museum of Natural History, Smithsonian Institution, Washington, D.C., 1970, 77.

36. Brown, G. H., Jr., Automatic compensation in roentgenographic polycephalometry, *Am. J. Roentgenol.*, 78, 1063, 1957.

37. Maresh, M. M., Growth of major long bones in healthy children, *Am. J. Dis. Child.*, 66, 227, 1943.

Radiologic Applications in Forensic Dentistry

6

MARK L. BERNSTEIN, D.D.S.

Contents

0-8493-8105-3/98/$0.00+$.50
© 1998 by CRC Press LLC

Scope of Forensic Dentistry

Forensic dentistry, simply defined, is the application of dental knowledge to the legal system. The purview of forensic dentistry can be divided into four main areas:

1. Identification of unknown human remains.
2. Analysis of bitemarks.
3. Interpretation of oral and maxillofacial lesions in clinical forensic cases such as child, spouse, and elder abuse.
4. Dental jurisprudence (expert witness testimony, malpractice, and self-policing of the profession).

This chapter concerns only dental identification, particularly as it pertains to the use of radiographs.

History of Dental Radiography[1,2]

The first dental radiograph is attributed to Otto Walkhoff of Braunsweig, Germany on January 14, 1896 — just 14 days after the discovery of x-rays by Röntgen. A glass photographic plate was placed intraorally and exposed for 25 min with x-rays. The resulting silhouetted teeth were not of diagnostic quality. Dr. W. J. Morgan of New York alerted dentists to the diagnostic possibilities of x-rays and illustrated a roentgenogram of an impacted tooth on April 24, 1896. The first practical use of dental radiography was illustrated by C.E. Kells of New Orleans. The long exposure times of 20 min made it impossible for the patient to hold the film and Kells devised a film holder. Ignorant of the dangers of x-ray exposure, early investigators failed to take precautions. Kells had developed squamous cell carcinoma by 1922 and by 1926 had to have an arm amputated. The other arm was also affected and lung metastasis developed. Kells ended his own life with a gunshot on May 7, 1928.

In 1901, W.H. Rollins, a physician and dentist, warned of the dangers of x-rays and was among the first to use a protective screen and an adjustable diaphragm to avoid unnecessary exposure to the patient. By the turn of the century, a single exposure still took 1 to 5 min.

In 1923, the first practical x-ray machine for dental use was introduced. Film for intraoral radiographs was developed 10 years earlier by Kodak. Each film had to be hand wrapped.

The earliest case of an identification on an unknown decedent made through comparison of sinuses in skull radiographs was published in 1926.[3] The first reported use of dental radiography in a forensic identification occurred in 1943.[4] Dental radiology was used to help identify 72 of the 119 victims who perished in the 1949 fire on board the steamship *Noronic* which burned in Toronto.[5] Today, radiographs are routinely used to identify unknown decedents, individually and in mass disasters, and have confirmed identifications in such notable cases as Adolf Hitler, Josef Mengele, and Lee Harvey Oswald.

Identification of the Dead

The Need to Identify

When a person dies at home or in a health care facility with the knowledge of friends or relatives, identity is not in question. However, if death occurs away from home in the absence of acquaintances, or if there is degradation of the body or the possibility of foul play, it might be difficult to confirm or establish the identity of the decedent. This has profound social and legal consequences. The social issues involve the rights of the decedent and his or her family. Our religious and social values entitle all members of society to will the method of their disposal upon death. Even more compelling is the impact on family members. Every unidentified corpse brought to the coroner or medical examiner represents a missing person to a group of loved ones. In cases of homicide, the identity of the individual provides a major clue to the identity of the perpetrator since most murders are committed by people known to the victim. Even if a known homicide suspect is linked to the disappearance of a person, charges are rarely brought if the victim can't be found and the crime proven.

Methods of Identification

Identity can be determined anecdotally by recognition of the decedent, circumstantially through possessions associated with the corpse, or scientifically using verifiable fixed biologic features. Identification by visual means or personal effects, albeit common, is unscientific and subject to accidental or intentional error. Scientific methods are valid and reliable and are not prone to error if proven techniques are correctly applied by trained individuals.

A fingerprint exemplifies a well-established, time-honored scientific means of identification. Regretfully, it is no longer as practical as it once was, since only about 20% of the population has a preexisting fingerprint record on file for comparison to friction ridges of decedents. Also excluded are most burned, decomposed, skeletonized and mutilated remains upon whom soft tissues have been destroyed.

Dental identification is also scientific, relying on the patterns of missing, filled, and decayed teeth as well as anatomic variation of the teeth, jawbones, and sinuses. Teeth and bones are also durable, surviving decompositional and destructive forces. This, combined with the fact that some form of preexisting record of the dentition exists on most people, makes the dentognathic complex well suited for identification.

DNA represents another scientific means of identification which may one day obviate the need for dental techniques. Currently, however, more studies are needed, costs must be contained, and a source of comparative DNA from relatives or the decedent must be available before this method is practical.

Radiographs in Dental Identification

Dental identification is a comparative technique; the dentition of the decedent is compared to dental records of a suspect. Sometimes the decedent's teeth are compared to ante-mortem written records although the most accurate and reliable method is by comparison of ante-mortem and post-mortem radiographs.[6–8] Unlike subjective records which lack detail and can include errors, radiographs supply objective data through the precise recording of the unique morphology of dental restorations and dento-osseous anatomy. A written notation of a filling is of low specificity because other people have similar fillings. A radiographic rendition of that filling, however, shows its specific silhouette which is often unique. The uniqueness of a filling's shape is derived from the fact that it is hand carved by the dentist so that no two are alike. When fillings or teeth are not present, radiographs are particularly important because the written dental record is not likely to have any useable information but the radiographs are apt to show distinctive anatomy.

Limitations of Dental Radiography

A radiograph represents two-dimensional shadows of three-dimensional objects. Fillings on the cheek side of a tooth cannot be distinguished from those on the tongue side. Fillings can be obscured by superimposition of other fillings in the same tooth (see Figure 6-13 C and E). The various metals used in dentistry cannot be distinguished; all are radiopaque. A dentist, however, would recognize outline patterns associated with the various metals. Radiolucent areas in teeth can represent decay, nonmetallic esthetic fillings, congenital defects, physical/chemical injuries, or artifacts. Differentiation of these conditions is important yet radiographically difficult. Artifacts and disparities produced by improper angulation, orientation, exposure, processing, labeling, and storage present potential difficulties which must be controlled. These will be discussed.

Recovery of Ante-Mortem Records

There are two types of identification: confirmatory (directed) and John/Jane Doe. In a confirmatory identification, the authorities believe they know who the decedent might be, either because of a recently reported missing person or personal effects found at the scene. In such cases, a directed search for dental records can be expedited. An example is an immersed body discovered a week following the report of a person who fell out of a boat and was not seen again. Another example is a charred body recovered from a car that crashed and burned. In these cases, the putative victim's family is located and asked for the name of a treating dentist. Complete and original radiographs should be requested of the dentist. If the treating dentist route is not productive, an inquiry of military, prison, employment, or hospital files might turn up a dental record — as long as there is a name to investigate. Military radiographs can be accessed through the Military Panograph Depository (408) 646-1000. Archival military records are stored at National Records Repository, 900 Paige Boulevard, St. Louis, MO (314) 263-7261. One should not overlook the possibility of skull radiographs which fortuitously show teeth. These might be available from hospitals or chiropractors known to have treated the putative victim. In a John/Jane Doe case, there is no *a priori* assumption of identity. There are no local missing persons, no circumstantial clues found with the decedent, and no family members to interrogate. No name is generated. The victim can represent any of the hundreds of thousands of missing people reported nationwide or worldwide. The only hope for an identification is to distill the huge pool of reported missing persons attempting to find records which represent the best possibilities. Such a search is narrowed by determining the age, gender, race, height, weight, hair color, socioeconomic status, etc. from the corpse. This information is distributed to the press and fed into the National Crime Information Center (NCIC) computer which is staffed by the FBI in Washington, D.C. and which stores data including dental information on missing persons. If the decedent is in the computer and the dental information is accurately recorded, the computer can produce a "hit". It is likely that several possible hits will be generated because the pool is so large. Each record can then be individually compared to the decedent by a forensic investigator. Similar computer programs for missing person identification are regulated through state or regional agencies. They might be productive if NCIC fails because states can mandate entry of data whereas federal compliance is not obligatory. For example, NCIC currently contains 75,000 missing persons, but only 1600 have dental information.

Objectives in Radiographic Comparisons

The objective of using radiographs in identification is to compare and evaluate similarities between ante-mortem and post-mortem films. The tasks for the forensic investigator include six steps:

1. Securing ante-mortem radiographs
2. Making post-mortem radiographs
3. Comparing meaningful features (those which are stable and distinctive)
4. Accounting for discrepancies
5. Assessing uniqueness
6. Verbalizing the degree of confidence in the identification

We have already discussed recovery of ante-mortem radiographs. Before we can accomplish the other five steps, we must be familiar with dental terminology, dental and craniofacial anatomy, dental pathology and restorations, and dental radiology.

Review of Terminology and Anatomy

Dental Terminology

The following terms describe anatomic locations on teeth (Figure 6-1):

Mesial — aspect closest to the midline
Distal — aspect farthest from the midline; opposite of mesial
Buccal — aspect facing the outside (lips or cheek)
Lingual — aspect facing the inside (tongue or palate)
Occlusal — the biting surface of posterior teeth (premolars or molars)

Incisal — the biting edge of anterior teeth (incisors and canines)

Cervical — towards the neck of the tooth near the gumline, where the crown meets the root

Proximal — the side of a tooth (either mesial or distal) that contacts a neighboring tooth

Interproximal — in-between two teeth

Fillings are named for the surfaces filled. For instance:

O   = occlusal filling
MOD = multisurface filling extending onto the mesial, occlusal, and distal surfaces
B   = buccal

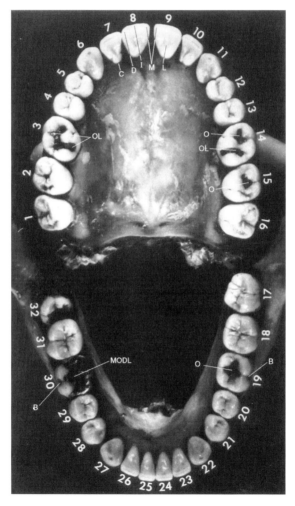

Figure 6-1   Resected jaw specimen with full dentition numbered according to the Universal System. Labels coded as follows: **Surfaces,** M — mesial, D — distal, B — buccal, L — lingual, I — incisal, C — cervical; **Fillings,** O — occlusal amalgams in 14, 15, and 19, OL — occlusolingual amalgams in 3 and 14, MODL — amalgam covering mesial, occlusal, distal and lingual surface in 30, B — buccal amalgams in 19 and 30.

Dental Anatomy

The adult dentition contains 32 teeth, 16 in each jaw. For convenience we divide the jaws into four equal quadrants, upper right, upper left, lower right, and lower left — each of which contains eight teeth. Each quadrant contains two incisors, one cuspid (canine), two premolars (bicuspids), and three molars (Figure 6-1). Each tooth has a crown which protrudes above the gum and is visible when the mouth is examined, and a root which is contained within a socket in the alveolar process of the jaws. Radiographically, the crown is capped by a layer of enamel which is the most radiopaque part of the tooth. Below the enamel is dentin which continues into the root and comprises the bulk of the tooth. Within the center of the tooth is a longitudinal, radiolucent pulp cavity. The coronal extension of the pulp is called the pulp chamber and the root portion is the root canal (Figures 6-2 and 6-3).

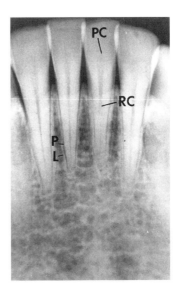

Figure 6-2   Periapical radiograph of the four lower incisors showing the pulp chamber (PC) and root canal (RC), lamina dura (L), and periodontal membrane space (P).

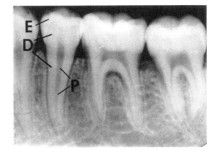

Figure 6-3   Periapical radiograph of lower left premolars and molars showing the basic components of teeth: enamel (E), dentin (D), and pulp (P).

The front teeth (incisors) have flat incisal edges and the canines have a pointed cusp. Premolars typically have two cusps, one buccal and one lingual. The lower second premolar sometimes has two or, rarely, three lingual cusps. Molars have from three to five cusps and occasionally more.

Incisors, canines, and lower premolars have a single, tapered root with a single root canal. The maxillary first premolar typically has a buccal and lingual root which appears overlapped radiographically. Sometimes there is only one root but even so, two root canals are usually present. The maxillary second premolar typically has one root but can have two. Again, two canals are expected. Upper molars generally have three roots, a mesiobuc-cal, distobuccal, and lingual, each with one canal. Roots of the second or third molars may be fused but the three canals are usually present. Lower molars have a mesial and distal root. The distal root canal is wide and the mesial root bears two narrow canals. These mesial canals might be hard to visualize radiographically if superimposed. Fusion of roots is sometimes seen in the second or third molar to form a single tapered conical shape. Pulp chambers and root canals narrow with age and in response to irritations such as decay, drilling, or thermal stimuli. They may be difficult or impossible to visualize radio-graphically in some instances.

Numbering systems are used to conveniently refer to individual teeth. The Universal System is most commonly used in the U.S. It numbers permanent teeth from 1 to 32, beginning at the maxillary right third molar (#1), extending across the maxilla to the left third molar (#16), continuing at the left mandibular third molar (#17), around the man-dibular arch to the right third molar #32 (Figures 6-1 and 6-4). In like manner, the 20 deciduous (baby) teeth are indicated by letters A–T (Figure 6-4).

		A	B	C	D	E	F	G	H	I	J			
1	2	3	4	5	6	7	8	9	10	11	12	13	14	15	16
32	31	30	29	28	27	26	25	24	23	22	21	20	19	18	17
		T	S	R	Q	P	O	N	M	L	K			

Figure 6-4   The Universal System for designating the 32 permanent and 20 deciduous teeth.

Alveolar Bone

In individuals with good oral health, the alveolar bone surrounds almost the entire root of the tooth. A thin layer of cortical bone lines each root socket. Radiographically it forms a thin radiopaque outline called the lamina dura (Figure 6-2). The lamina dura is separated from the root surface by a thin, uniform radiolucency, the periodontal ligament (Figure 6-2). This contains the connective tissue fibers that insert into both the tooth and bone, anchoring the tooth in its socket. The alveolar bone supports the teeth and features bony trabeculae that are oriented for functional support. Blood supply, by way of nutrient canals, penetrates alveolar bone and appears as inconspicuous radiolucent lines coursing vertically (see Figure 6-7). In cross section, they appear as small foramina. Nutrient canals are best seen in the anterior mandible.

Radiographic Anatomic Landmarks of the Jaws

Fixed anatomic features are present in all individuals. These landmarks are relatively similar in most people and, unless showing distinctive variation, should not be considered as individual identifiers. These landmarks are not always visible in radiographs due to tech-nical and anatomic variations.

Mandibular Landmarks (Figure 6-5; see Figure 6-21 A and B)

The mandibular canal is a tubular canal running centrally within the body of each hemi-mandible and appearing as a linear radiolucency outlined both superiorly and inferiorly by a thin opaque border. It begins at the mandibular foramen located in the middle of the ramus, running below the teeth and terminating as the mental foramen, a circular lucency near the apex of the second premolar. The mandibular nerve and vessels are the contents of this canal.

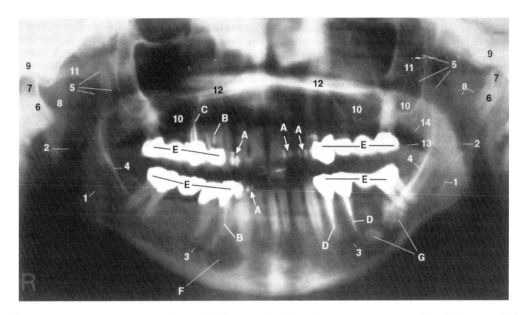

Figure 6-5   Panographic radiograph showing landmarks, restorations, and pathology. Labels are coded as follows: **Landmarks**, (1) mandibular canal (2) mandibular foramen (3) mental foramen (4) external oblique ridge (5) coronoid process (6) condylar neck (7) condylar head (8) sigmoid notch (9) glenoid fossa (10) maxillary sinus (11) zygomatic arch (12) hard palate (13) dorsal rongue (soft tissue density) (14) soft palate (soft tissue density); **Restorations**, (A) "kissing" mesial and distal non-metallic moderately opaque fillings within adjacent teeth (B) gutta percha root canal fillings (C) silver point root canal fillings (more opaque) (D) gutta percha root canal fillings in teeth with metallic posts (E) four metal bridges, one in each quadrant, each consisting of three abutments, and one pontic to replace a missing first molar; **Pathology**, (F) large periapical radiolucency under tooth #28 (G) several radiopaque areas of sclerotic bone in the #19 healed extraction site.

The genial tubercles are the bony attachments for several muscles. They appear as an oval radiopacity sometimes showing a central radiolucency (lingual foramen) below the roots of the central incisors in the mandibular midline (see Figure 6-29).

The internal and external oblique ridges are opaque bony ridges in the superior part of the posterior body extending diagonally toward the anterior ramus. The external ridge is buccal and more superior than the lingual internal ridge, which is at the level of molar root apices.

The coronoid process is a flat triangular protrusion of bone extending superiorly from the anterior ramus. It is the area of attachment of the temporalis muscle. Extending superiorly from the posterior ramus is the condylar neck to which is attached the mushroom-shaped condylar head. The "valley" in-between the two "hills" formed by the coronoid process and condylar neck is the sigmoid notch. The condyle fits into the glenoid fossa of the temporal bone to form the temporomandibular joint.

Maxillary Landmarks (Figures 6-5, 6-12, and 6-21 A and B)

The incisive foramen is a circular opening in the palatal midline between the apices of the central incisors. Superimposition of the radiopaque nasal spine on its superior border renders a heart-shaped rather than circular radiolucency to the foramen. There is variability in the size of this structure.

The floor of the nasal cavity and the maxillary sinuses are visible in dental radiographs. From the maxillary midline above the incisor roots, the floor of the nasal cavity slopes superiorly as it extends distally toward the long canine root. The maxillary sinus presents as a radiolucency extending from the distal aspect of the canine root to the second molar. Its lower border is scalloped and dental roots often project into the sinus floor. The malar bone and inferior border of the zygomatic arch may be projected over the sinus in the molar region, appearing as a U-shaped opacity.

Restorations

Amalgams — Silver amalgam restorations are the most common fillings. They are placed in areas where esthetics isn't important (premolars, molars, and linguals of upper lateral incisors). X-rays do not penetrate amalgams, so they appear white (transparent) on film. Each filling is contained within the crown, often with an irregular shape (see Figures 6-1, 6-11, 6-12, and 6-13).

Esthetic Filling Materials — A variety of tooth-colored, nonmetallic filling materials are used for anterior teeth and, with increasing frequency, in posterior teeth. When radiolucent, they can mimic caries (Figure 6-11). Some have the radiodensity of teeth and are difficult to detect radiographically (Figure 6-13) while others are relatively radiopaque (Figures 6-5 and 6-12).

Crowns — Metal crowns (caps) replace the crowns of natural teeth and appear as large radiopaque restorations (Figures 6-11 and 6-36). Some are surrounded by porcelain which is less radiodense than the opaque metal core. Rarely, the entire crown is made of porcelain and can resemble the density of natural teeth, thereby escaping detection as a restoration. A bridge represents a row of attached crowns, usually fabricated to span a missing tooth or teeth. The crowns that replace the missing teeth are called pontics and have no roots. The abutments are the crowns that cap the remaining teeth and roots (Figures 6-5 and 6-12).

Root canal fillings — Gutta percha is a pink, rubbery substance that is inserted into diseased root canals once they have been cleaned out. The material is moderately radio-paque (Figures 6-5 and 6-13). Less commonly, canals are obliterated with densely radio-paque silver points (Figures 6-5 and 6-11). Sometimes a metal post is inserted part way into the canal to act as a secure attachment for a crown (Figure 6-5). Rarely, broken-off instruments are seen in treated canals (Figure 6-13). If detected in a forensic case this treatment mishap represents a distinctive identifier.

Pathology

Caries (Figures 6-6 and 6-22 A and B) — Dental decay appears as a radiolucency in the crown of the tooth. Interproximal decay begins just below the contact points between two teeth. In early lesions, it penetrates the enamel. In more advanced lesions, caries widens out within the dentin, thus undermining the enamel. Occlusal decay isn't usually apparent until it penetrates into dentin and expands, leaving an intracoronal radiolucent zone beneath the enamel. Buccal or lingual caries developing within mid-coronal pits, similarly, appears as an intracoronal lucency (Figure 6-22 A and B), whereas buccal or lingual cervical caries presents a semilunar lucency lower down on the neck of the tooth. In advanced caries, the entire crown may be destroyed.

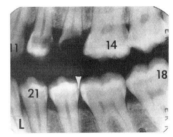

Figure 6-6   Bitewing radiographs of the right (R) and left (L) posterior teeth showing caries. Early interproximal caries seen at white arrows and between teeth 3 and 4 and 30 and 31. Occlusal caries present at black arrow in tooth 31. Massive caries has destroyed teeth 29, 12, and 13.

Periodontal disease (Figures 6-7 and 6-8) — Loss of supporting alveolar bone around roots constitutes periodontal disease. It typically becomes apparent in the fourth to fifth decade, but is variable depending on oral hygiene. Early lesions show blunting and fuzzy, ill-defined lytic destruction of the crestal bone followed by horizontal or, more rarely, vertical bone loss. This may be localized or generalized. Often, calculus is associated with periodontal disease and appears as small radiopaque spurs attached to the interproximal aspects of the cervical portions of the crown.

Periapical radiolucencies (Figures 6-5, 6-11, and 6-12) — Teeth which have become nonvital due to pulpal damage from caries, drilling, large restorations, or trauma often develop an area of inflammatory bone loss at the root apex. It may vary in size from a widening of the apical periodontal ligament space to a large, round, unilocular radiolucency. The associated tooth typically shows gross caries, a large restoration, or fracture.

Radiopacities — Focal radiodensities are occasionally seen within the jaws. The most common represent reactive bony sclerosis and are located in the mandibular first molar region (Figure 6-5). The lesion, measuring 1 to 2 cm, usually has an irregular and varied contour and persists unchanged for years. Tori represent exostoses presenting clinically as

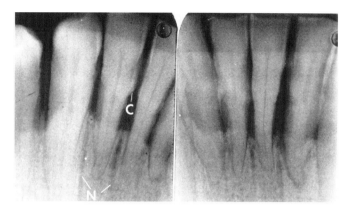

Figure 6-7   Periapical radiograph of lower anterior teeth showing severe periodontal bone loss and associated calculus (C). Compare with normal bone height in Figure 6-2. Nutrient canals (N) are well illustrated.

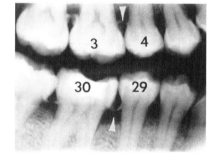

Figure 6-8   Bitewing radiograph of right posterior teeth showing spurs of calculus associated with mild crestal bone loss at white arrows and between teeth 2 and 3 and 30 and 31.

external bony projections. They affect up to 25% of the population. Mandibular tori are found on the lingual aspect in the premolar region bilaterally (Figure 6-9). They are seen in anterior radiographs as smooth, oval, bilateral radiodensities (Figure 6-10). Torus palatinus is a midline bony mass on the mid palate and is seen in anterior films. On panographic views it is projected bilaterally along the hard palate.

Amalgam tattoos — Occasionally, in the process of placing or removing an amalgam filling, metal fragments become implanted in soft tissue where they remain as radiopaque particles. Such tattoos may be found remote from the filling site if they enter a laceration in another location. Some amalgam tattoos are formed when a chunk of amalgam breaks out of a tooth during a mandibular posterior extraction and falls into the socket which subsequently heals. This produces a large opacity in the edentulous crestal bone. Amalgam tattoos are stable and morphologically distinctive findings and are ideal for identification (Figure 6-36).

Impactions (Figure 6-11) — Impactions represent teeth which remain submerged in the jaws after the normal eruption sequence. Third molars are most frequently involved, followed by maxillary canines.

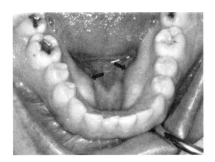

Figure 6-9 Bilateral tori mandibularis (black arrows) projecting into the floor of the mouth.

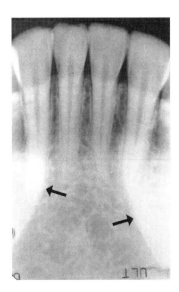

Figure 6-10 Periapical radiograph of lower incisors of patient in Figure 6-9. Note projection of mandibular tori (arrows).

Modern Dental Radiography

Radiography in dentistry differs somewhat from radiography of other sites. The teeth are three-dimensionally arranged around confined, curved arches in proximity to other cranial structures. Detailed study of each tooth and surrounding bone, without overlap, superimposition, magnification, or distortion is required for diagnosis. Such views are not feasible with PA, AP, or lateral skull films. Therefore, modifications in the x-ray machine, films, exposure, and technique are needed.

One advantage of dental radiography is that teeth are not embedded deeply within soft tissue; film can be closely applied to the teeth and jawbones, allowing sharp resolution at anode-to-film distances of 8 to 16 in.

Periapical and Bitewing Films

The standard size 2 dental films measure 1 × 1.5 in. (about the size of 35 mm photographic film) and represent the most common film used for periapical and bitewing views. Entire teeth are visualized with the periapical view. The film is placed within the mouth against the lingual side of the teeth and bone, oriented vertically for anterior teeth and horizontally

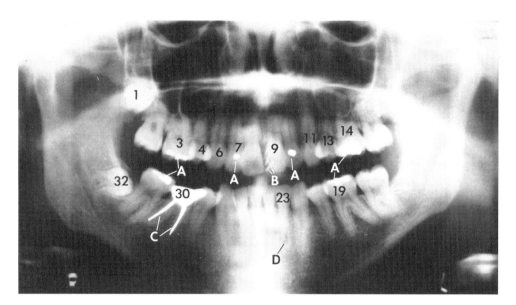

Figure 6-11   Panograph showing restorations, extractions, and pathology. Labels coded as follows: **Teeth 1, 32** — incompletely formed and impacted; **Teeth 3, 14, 19, 31** — occlusal amalgams (A); **Teeth 7, 10** — lingual amalgams (A); **Tooth 9** — two metal retention pins (B) to secure a radiolucent non-metallic filling; **Tooth 30** — metal crown with silver points in root canals (C); **Tooth 23** — small periapical radiolucency (D); **Teeth 5, 12, 21, 28** — missing with spaces closed - indicates orthodontic therapy.

for posterior teeth (Figures 6-2, 6-3, and 6-12). The exposure is between 8 and 15 mA, between 70 to 100 kVp for 0.4 to 1.0 sec (depending on film speed, location, and specific needs). Each periapical view shows about four teeth including the roots and surrounding bone. Ideally, the periapical view should reproduce the actual size of the tooth by using proper angulation. Excessive vertical angulation produces foreshortening while insufficient angulation results in elongation.

Bitewing views center the horizontal axis of the film along the bite line with the jaws closed. This view shows the crowns of both upper and lower opposing teeth (Figures 6-6 and 6-13). Bitewings are best used to illustrate decay and the integrity of crestal alveolar bone and are the most common views made by dentists.[9] For this purpose, increased contrast is helpful and achieved by lowering the kVp to 65 to 70. X-rays should be directed at right angles to the alignment of teeth and parallel to the film so that there is no interproximal overlapping of adjacent crowns.

Left/right orientation — To orient left from right, each film is embossed with a small, circular, dot-like dimple/pimple (Figure 6-14). Looking into the concavity of the dimple renders a lingual view (as if the observer is sitting on the tongue, looking out). Most dentists mount films with the convexity (pimple) facing them. This buccal view is oriented such that the observer is facing the patient. The dot orients the film as it is being read but is not visible when the radiograph is taken because it is obscured by the water-resistant paper which covers intraoral film. During radiography, left/right orientation is ensured by always placing the white (tube) side of the paper facing the lingual surface of teeth. If the colored side is mistakenly placed against the teeth, there is a fail-safe against improper orientation. Each film packet contains textured lead foil on the back surface to block penetration of

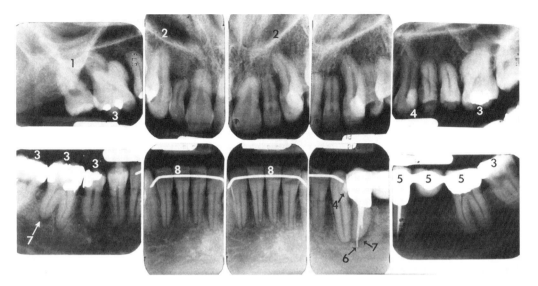

Figure 6-12 Periapical series showing landmarks, restorations and pathology. Labels coded as follows:; 1 — malar eminence; 2 — floor of nasal cavity; 3 — amalgam fillings in teeth 3, 14, 18, 29, 30, 31; 4 — non-metallic, moderately opaque fillings in distal of teeth 11, 22; 5 — three-unit bridge anchored on teeth 19 and 21, replacing missing 20; 6 — overfilled root canal filling in tooth 21; 7 — small periapical radiolucencies at teeth 21 and 30; 8 — orthodontic metal wire retainer splinting the lower anterior teeth. Note the shortening and blunting of roots of 7-10, 12, 13, 22-27, associated with orthodontic movement.

x-rays (Figure 6-14). If the film is reversed, the embossed lead pattern will appear on the processed film signifying the error. In this way, the embossed dot remains a reliable indicator of left/right orientation.

Panographic Radiographs

Panoramic radiographs are tomographs which project the U-shaped jaws onto flat extraoral film with little superimposition. The jaws are rendered flat by having the film and beam simultaneously rotate horizontally around the head during exposure (Figure 6-15). The machine projects a narrow, vertical linear beam as it rotates. Superimposed structures lying outside of the focal trough such as the spinal column and opposite jaw are diffused by the movement and magnification. This view shows the entire maxilla and mandible flattened out (Figures 6-5 and 6-11). It includes the nasal aperture, orbital floor, maxillary sinuses, temporomandibular joint, and styloid process. It demonstrates soft tissue densities such as the nose, ears, lips, tongue, and soft palate as well as air spaces of the pharynx, nasal cavity, and sinuses. Midline structures like the hyoid, spinal column, and torus palatinus are projected bilaterally as double images. The hard palate is seen as a linear opacity running above the roots of the maxillary teeth. Structures are somewhat magnified, geometrically distorted, and soft in focus (see Example Case 6). Left/right identification is accomplished by placing a radiopaque "L" and/or "R" on the cassette or cassette holder. Foreign countries, naturally, have different letter designations; in French-speaking Canada, a G or D represents left (gauche) or right (droit). A long list of artifacts including ghost images, earrings, eyeglasses, and mechanical parts of the x-ray machine can be visualized and require experience when interpreting this projection.

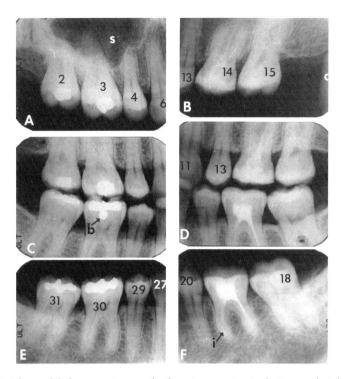

Figure 6-13   Right and left posterior teeth showing: periapical views of right (A) and left (B) maxillary posterior teeth; bitewing of right (C) and left (D) sides; and periapical view of right (E) and left (F) mandibular posterior teeth. Note the following findings: **Teeth 2, 3, 30, 31** — amalgam restorations; **Teeth 14, 19** — gutta percha root canal fillings with non-metallic coronal fillings having the same radiodensity as teeth, causing paradoxical "lack" of coronal restoration in film D.; **Tooth 19** — broken root canal instrument (i) in mesial root in film F; **Teeth 5, 12, 21, 28** — missing with spaces closed following orthodontic therapy; **Teeth 1, 16, 17, 32** — missing due to previous extractions; **Tooth 30** — angulation variation between periapical film E and bitewing C renders different patterns of the restoration, concealing the round buccal amalgam (b) visible only on the bitewing; Coronoid process of left mandible (c) is seen on the left maxillary periapical film B; Maxillary sinus (s) well illustrated in the right maxillary periapical film A.

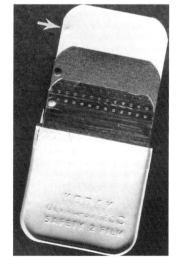

Figure 6-14   Dental film packet size 2 showing, from top to bottom: film with embossed dot (arrow), opaque black paper, lead foil, moisture-resistant plastic-coated outer wrap.

Figure 6-15 Panograph machine with patient positioned.

Other Radiographs

Occlusal (size 4) intraoral film measures 3 × 2 1/4 in. and is meant to show a coronal (overhead) projection of the teeth aligned in their arches. The mandibular view is made with the tube side of the film flat against the biting surfaces of the lower teeth. The tube head is placed under the chin projecting at right angles to the film. The maxillary view places the tube head over the base of the nose and the beam is projected at +65° to the plane of the maxillary arch. The entire maxillary or mandibular arch with the teeth on end is seen, as is the buccal and lingual cortices of bone. These are uncommon views used to show buccolingual positioning of teeth, cortical defects or swellings, extraosseous radiopacities, and in the maxillary projection, the hard palate and nasal cavity.

Orthodontists use lateral cephalometric radiographs to relate the jaws to the skull. This view resembles a lateral skull film.

Making Post-Mortem Dental Radiographs

In general, it is desirable to postpone post-mortem radiography until ante-mortem radiographs on a putative victim are received. In this way, comparative views of existing films can be made. Post-mortem films should reproduce the angulations of ante-mortem films even if the ante-mortem views are not ideal.[7] The point is not to make a perfect diagnostic radiograph but to duplicate the perspective of a previous film. If the jaw specimens cannot be retained and radiographs must be made before ante-mortem films are available, a full set of periapicals (14 for all 32 teeth) and bitewings (4 for all posterior teeth) should be made.[10] If third molars are not visualized clinically, the adjacent bone should be radiographed in case impactions are present. Panoramic views are difficult to produce on specimens and are not routinely made.

Dental radiographs are easiest to make on skeletal remains. *In situ* films are difficult to obtain on intact bodies and jaw resection is often performed to facilitate radiography on decomposing, charred, and mutilated corpses.

Dental radiographic technique on resected specimens or jaw fragments is the same as it is for patients — with the all-white side of the film packet applied to the lingual aspect of the teeth. If film is placed buccally with the tube head on the lingual side erroneous left/right orientation will result. This positioning is impossible in living subjects since the tube head would be inside the mouth. If jaws cannot be resected, rigor mortis, charring decomposition, positioning, and visualization problems complicate radiography, necessitating innovativeness or compromises. A portable dental radiographic unit might be needed (see subsection titled Dental Radiography in Mass Disasters). Mouth props are used to open jaws in rigor, plastic wrap is used to contain odor and contamination, and hemostats, tape, modeling clay, or gauze are used to hold film in place.[10,11]

Film and Exposure

There are two film speeds, D and E. E-speed film requires half the radiation exposure of D-speed film. D-speed film is preferred for post-mortem work as it is less grainy and has better contrast than E-speed film. Exposure time for defleshed bone is about half that for patients[8] (typically 0.4 to 0.5 sec at 15 mA and 70 kVp with size 2, D-speed film). Dried specimens (charred or skeletonized) tend to yield contrasty results which can be compensated for by a higher kVp and lowered mAs.

Double film packets containing two films are recommended. If one set is needed in court or to accompany a report, the investigator can keep the second set of originals.

Processing

For processing film, an automatic dental processing machine develops, fixes, washes, and dries film in less than 5 min and is recommended in a busy laboratory (Figure 6-16). Otherwise, hand processing with a "portable" processor with small tanks and daylight loading capability is an inexpensive alternative (Figure 6-17). Typical medical x-ray film processors tend to lose the smaller dental films in the rollers.

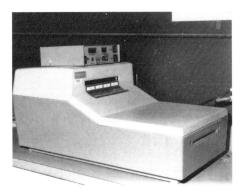

Figure 6-16   Automatic x-ray film processor.

Currently, Kodak recommends the universal GBX-2 (red) safelight which is safe for both panographic and intraoral film as long as unprocessed film is exposed less than 2 1/2 min. The older Kodak ML-2 (light orange) safelight will fog panographic film. Processing chemicals and the water rinse should be fresh, uncontaminated, and at the proper working levels and temperatures. Rollers on automatic processors should be clean and operating

Figure 6-17   Portable manual x-ray film processor for daylight use.

correctly. Otherwise, processed films that appear adequate on initial inspection may fog or discolor months later when they are needed in court.

Periapicals

The film is placed against the lingual aspect of the teeth and root-bearing bone. It is oriented vertically for anterior teeth and horizontally for posteriors. The typical series for a full complement of teeth includes a midline view in each jaw showing the four incisors, a canine view with the canine centered, a premolar view, and a molar view for each quadrant.

The central ray is angled perpendicular to a plane (A) that bisects the angle formed by the film (B) and the trajectory of the tooth within bone (C) (Figure 6-18 A and B). These angles can be modified to duplicate improperly made ante-mortem films.

To hold the mandibular specimen in place, it can be slung over an armrest with the film secured in-between (Figure 6-19). Paper wads or modeling clay can be used to prop the film against the teeth when necessary.

Bitewings

Typically, bitewings are made only for posterior teeth. Two to four films are made depending on the number and size of the teeth. Bitewing films are made by placing a bitewing

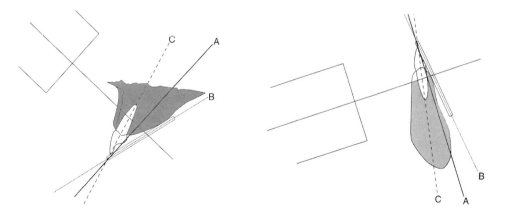

Figure 6-18   (Left) Positioning of film and tube head for the maxillary incisor periapical view (see text). (Right) Positioning of film and tube head for the mandibular incisor periapical view (see text).

Figure 6-19   Use of arm rest to position film against jaw and use of occlusal film to substitute for several periapical views on left posterior mandible.

tab around the film packet. The tab protrudes from the mid-horizontal aspect on the tube side of the film. The jaws are articulated and the film lies flat against the lingual surfaces of upper and lower teeth secured in place by the bite tab held in-between the teeth (Figure 6-20 A and B). If the film slips, "biting pressure" can be exerted by holding the jaws together with rubber bands. The central beam is directed perpendicular to the aligned teeth and at a vertical angle of $+10°$ (Figure 6-21).

Occlusal film

Occlusal film is not often needed to make post-mortem occlusal radiographs but the larger film can be used in place of multiple periapicals (Figure 6-19). The entire posterior dentition of a quadrant can be included in one view (Figure 6-22 A and B). When this larger film is used, the anode-film distance is increased to spread out the beam, and exposure time is increased in accordance with the inverse square law.

Panographic Radiographs

With difficulty, these views can be made on skulls or resected jaw specimens. Since the x-ray tube and film rotate around a standing stationary patient, specimens must be elevated in position, articulated, and oriented with the occlusal line or Frankfort plane parallel to the ground. Odoriferous, wet, or contaminated specimens should be placed in a plastic bag. A setting of 8 mA at 80 kVp is a good starting exposure. If the lowest setting on the machine is too high for proper exposure, a previously exposed black film can be placed in the cassette against the unexposed film to reduce the effect of the intensifying screen. Alternatively, the specimen can be wrapped in aluminum foil. An apple placed in the foramen magnum replaces the density of the missing vertebrae. Some panographic machines accommodate supine patients and can be used on unresected nonskeletonized decedents.

Evidence Management

After radiography is completed, films should be examined for adequacy of results, then stored in envelopes or mounts that are labeled and initialed.

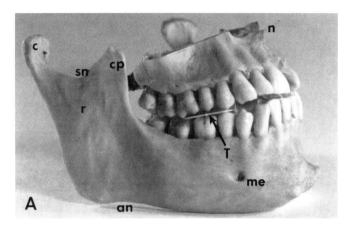

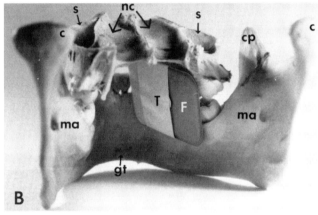

Figure 6-20   Lateral and medial view of resected jaw specimens respectively to show positioning for bitewing radiograph and clinical landmarks. Film (F) is held against lingual surfaces by a tab (T) in-between occluding teeth which then encircles the film. Note clinical landmarks: (**A**) n — nasal spine, c — condyle, sn - sigmoid notch, cp — coronoid process, r — ramus, me — mental foramen, an — antegonial notch; (**B**) nc — nasal cavities, s — maxillary sinuses, c — condyle, cp — coronoid process, ma — mandibular canal, gt — genial tubercle.

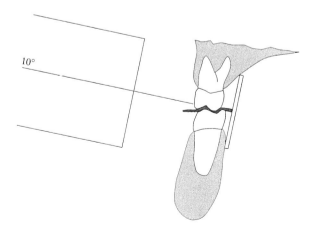

Figure 6-21   Positioning of film and tube head for the posterior bitewing.

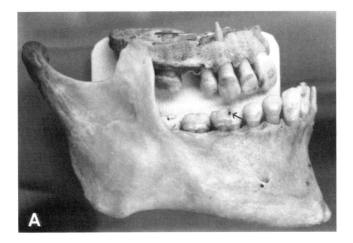

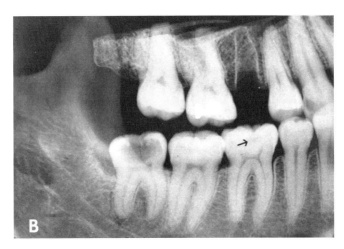

Figure 6-22   Use of occlusal film to include the right posterior maxilla and mandible in one view. Note the following: **Tooth 1** — extracted; **Tooth 3** — two amalgam fillings; **Tooth 4** — lost post-mortem; **Tooth 30** — buccal pit caries seen clinically in **A** as a black spot (arrow) and in **B** as a darkening in the crown (arrow); **Tooth 32** — occlusal carious destruction of crown.

Comparison

Ante-mortem and post-mortem radiographs are compared, noting similarities and differences. Some similarities are commonplace or nonspecific and are of low discriminating value. Others might be so distinctive as to ensure uniqueness. Likewise, apparent differences between ante-mortem and post-mortem radiographs might be explainable and sensible while others are incompatible and rule out the putative victim as the decedent.

A total file of recovered ante-mortem radiographs might contain multiple series of full-mouth, bitewing, and panographic radiographs spanning many years. The most current films are examined first because they will show the greatest similarity to the post-mortem status of the teeth and jaws.

What to Compare

> Number and arrangement of teeth (missing teeth, rotated teeth, spacing, extra teeth, impacted teeth)
> Caries and periodontal bone loss
> Coronal restorations (visible in or on the crown)
> Hidden restorations (bases under fillings, pins, root canal fillings, posts, and implants) seen only radiographically
> Bony pathology
> Dental anatomy
> Trabecular bone pattern and crestal bone topography
> Nutrient canals
> Anatomic bony landmarks
> Maxillary sinus and nasal aperture
> Frontal sinus

Similarities

Although the dentitions of all individuals are unique when fine details are studied, it is equally true that the human dentition is superficially similar. When similarities are noted between ante-mortem and post-mortem radiographs, one must be sure to consider only those which help individualize the person. The term *class characteristics* signifies those features which are expected in all humans (members of a class). When a similarity between an ante-mortem and post-mortem film represents a class characteristic, it is nonspecific and of little value in identification because it is expected in many humans. An *individual characteristic* represents a deviation from normal. Its value in identification depends on its prevalence in the population.

Nonspecific Similarities

The anatomy of virgin teeth can be remarkably alike among individuals and constitutes somewhat of a class characteristic. If typical anatomy is present, its confirmation in an ante-mortem film is of low specificity and might be meaningless. Similarly, anatomic structures such as foramina, canals, ridges, tubercles, and processes are shared human traits and are also typically nonspecific class characteristics. The specificity of missing teeth is determined by which are missing, their patterns, and numbers. Missing third molars are common. First molars are frequently extracted. The preferential absence of all four first premolars with their spaces closed usually signifies that the patient has had orthodontic therapy (Figures 6-11 and 6-13). Canine teeth are stable and usually present in dentulous mouths; their preferential absence would be rather specific.

Specific Similarities

The radiographic outlines of restorations are typically the most distinctive identifiers, particularly if the pattern is complex. Precise positioning of the film and tube head during post-mortem radiography intended to duplicate the angulation of the ante-mortem film is needed in order to reproduce the outline of fillings. Such well-made post-mortem films can be superimposed over ante-mortem films, making a convincing courtroom demonstration.

Unusual dental anatomy has high specificity. Mandibular premolars show the greatest morphologic variation in the patterns and numbers of grooves and cusps, making these teeth typically best for comparison (see Example Case 7).

Supernumerary (extra) teeth or retained deciduous teeth are uncommon, ranging in prevalence from 0.1 to 3.6%.

Dental and bony pathology such as caries, radiolucent lesions, periodontal bone loss, calculus, and dental impactions are of low to moderate specificity because these features are common and unstable, tending to alter their appearance with time. Focal areas of intrabony sclerosis or amalgam tattoos, on the other hand, are often highly distinctive. They are usually unchanging and morphologically unique (see Example Cases 3 and 6). Furthermore, they are asymptomatic and not likely to be removed.

Bone trabeculae and nutrient canals are present in all people but can show individualized patterns that persist over time. Trabecular bone patterns have been studied.[12] They are reproducible between ante-mortem and post-mortem radiographs. Although there is much individualization, some patterns are defined. A horizontal, ladder-like pattern is frequently noted within alveolar bone between widely spaced roots, particularly mandibular incisors and molars (Figures 6-3 and 6-28). When roots are close together, the horizontal trabeculae are cross hatched with vertical trabeculae to form a screen-wire pattern. When a lone tooth is present, trabeculae sometimes radiate perpendicularly from the lamina dura. In edentulous areas, the pattern is random. The body of the mandible features numerous, less defined delicate trabeculae or a smoke pattern.[12]

Both the nasal cavity[6] and maxillary antra[8] show individual variability and are useful in identification. The antra expand during adolescence and reach maximum size during the third decade.[13] Their appearance remains stable in adulthood, but alteration by secondary pathology such as infection, alveolar bone loss, and dental extractions is common.

The uniqueness of frontal sinus patterns has been known for over 60 years. Frontal sinuses can be evaluated according to seven parameters: septum, scalloping of the superior border, partial septum, ethmoid and supraorbital extensions, height, breadth, and midline.[14] Such fastidious metric analyses are seldom necessary in an individual identification. If one is fortunate enough to recover an ante-mortem PA or AP skull radiograph, the same post-mortem projection will reveal a similar pattern if the radiographs are of common origin (Figure 6-23). The stability of frontal sinus morphology has been studied. Sinus growth occurs until after puberty and stabilizes by age 20.[14–16] In the elderly, remodeling causes sinus expansion.[17] Occasionally, minor changes are caused by trauma or pathology. Frontal sinuses are absent in 5% of the population.[14] In a radiographic study attempting identification by comparison of the frontal sinus, 3 observers evaluated 100 cases. Only a single error was recorded in 300 observations and that was attributable to an angulation difference between the ante-mortem and post-mortem films.[16]

Inconsistencies

Discrepancies or inconsistencies between ante-mortem and post-mortem radiographs are either explainable or incompatible. When seen, they must be recognized and accounted for.

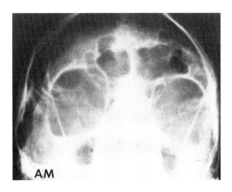 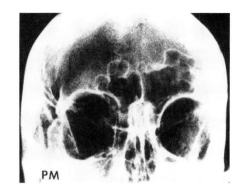

Figure 6-23   Comparison of frontal sinuses between ante-mortem (AM) and post-mortem (PM) skull films showing duplication of distinctive pattern of air cells, margins, and septae.

Explainable Inconsistencies

An explainable inconsistency is a dissimilarity which is plausible or can reasonably be expected to occur. It does not rule out a match. Explainable inconsistencies noted in radiographs are of two types:

Temporal inconsistencies — These are due to a change occurring after ante-mortem radiographs were made. During that period, a filling might have been placed or lost or a tooth erupted or extracted (see Example Cases 1, 2, 3, and 6). The longer the interval between ante-mortem and post-mortem radiographs, the greater the likelihood of temporal discrepancies. Dramatic temporal changes can occur over a short period of time during early adolescence when the first set of teeth are replaced by the permanent dentition. During this period of the mixed dentition, radiographs made several months apart can be unrecognizable as having originated from the same individual. Table 6-1 shows examples of explainable temporal discrepancies.

Table 6-1   Typical Temporal Discrepancies

Ante-Mortem Radiograph	Post-Mortem Radiograph
Tooth present	Tooth extracted
Virgin tooth	Tooth with caries
Unfilled tooth	Tooth with filling
Tooth with filling	Tooth with larger filling
Tooth with filling	Tooth with lost filling
Healthy periodontal bone	Periodontal bone loss
Large pulp chambers	Narrowed pulp chambers with age
Cyst in bone	Larger cyst (growing)
Cyst in bone	No cyst (removal or remission)
Generalized periodontitis	Edentulous jaws
Gross caries	Edentulous jaws
Calculus	No calculus (removed)
No calculus	Calculus (developed)
Incompletely formed tooth	Fully developed tooth

Radiographic technical inconsistencies — These are due to differences in radiographic exposure, dissimilar orientation between ante-mortem and post-mortem films (Figure 6-13 C and E), or comparison of different types of radiographs (see Example Case 6). Filling outlines appear dissimilar and crestal bone height, trabecular pattern, root length, and curvature might seemingly be altered by the positioning of the x-ray machine or film. Spaces between teeth may appear to close or open up, depending on the horizontal positioning of the tube head. Dark or light films may obscure features. All of these can be resolved by retaking the radiograph. Fine details of bony sclerosis or trabecular pattern seen on post-mortem periapical films might be missing from unsharp ante-mortem panographs (see Example Case 6).

Incompatible Inconsistencies

Inconsistencies that cannot be reasonably explained are not compatible with a positive identification and exclude the suspect (see Example Case 7). Examples are set forth in Table 6-2.

Table 6-2 Typical Incompatible Inconsistencies

Ante-Mortem Radiograph	Post-Mortem Radiograph
Missing tooth in adult	Tooth present
Filling	Virgin tooth
Fully formed tooth	Incompletely formed tooth
Severe horizontal alveolar bone loss	Normal bone height
Virgin tooth #20 with 2 cusps	Virgin tooth #20 with 3 cusps

Because a single incompatible inconsistency rules out the putative victim, care must be exercised before declaring a discrepancy to be incompatible. Newer restorative materials and full porcelain crowns can be nearly imperceptible radiographically because they reproduce the density of teeth (Figure 6-13 D). If used to replace an ante-mortem metallic filling, such a restoration could be mistaken as a post-mortem unfilled tooth and can be dismissed as incompatible. Some discrepancies are confusing to interpret but still reasonable. A radiolucent cyst in an ante-mortem film might be larger or smaller in an ante-mortem film, reflecting growth or healing, respectively. Tooth movement occurs dynamically and spaces between teeth may open or close after ante-mortem radiographs are made. Two radiographs of the same location might have literally no features in common, yet originate from the same person if enough elapsed time has allowed sweeping changes. Thus, to rule out a person, the discrepancy must represent an impossibility.

Confirmation of Identity

The ante-mortem and post-mortem concordance of fillings, with their complex shapes, confirms identification (see Example Cases 1, 3, 4, and 5). Yet, restorations are not required to establish person identification. Identifications are possible on unrestored dentitions by comparing dental anatomy and also on edentulous jaws, using individual characteristics within bone (see Example Cases 2 and 6). The ability of observers to establish dental identifications radiographically has been studied. In a study of edentulous remains, one half of the observers could correctly identify all 20 cases. The error rate was small for most other observers. When mistakes were made, they were due to unrecognized temporal changes or dissimilar angulations between ante-mortem and post-mortem films.[18] In another experiment judging accuracy in identification, 20 cases were submitted to 7 observers. A single bitewing film was available for comparison on each case. In cases where a few restorations were present, all examiners identified all cases. When no restorations were present three examiners missed 10% of the cases. When extensive dentistry was present, five examiners missed 20% of cases due to the extent of temporal changes.[19] The above studies had inadequate sample size to determine statistical significance.

Acknowledging that a declining caries rate predicts fewer fillings in future victims, MacLean et al. designed a project to validate the use of bitewing radiographs in identification using dental anatomy.[9] A statistically valid sample of 140 matched pairs of bitewings and 140 unmatched pairs of bitewings was given to three observers, including an experienced forensic dentist and a senior dental student. The matched pairs were taken from patients at intervals of from 1 to 15 years and contained either no restorations or restorations that would not morphologically assist in identification. In a blinded fashion, each case was categorized as a match or mismatch. This simulates actual cases where ante-mortem radiographs are proffered as originating from decedents. Sensitivities of 71% and 99% were recorded. The specificity was 94% for the dental student and 99% for the experienced forensic dentist, indicating a low false positive rate. The overall accuracy was 93%. Factors that produced errors were angulation differences between films, elapsed time over 10 years, and comparisons involving deciduous teeth that were no longer present in later radiographs.

Similarly, validity studies were performed on bitewings of children. This pertinent investigation tested the impact of the rapid temporal changes seen in the deciduous and mixed dentition as well as the value of dental anatomy in a group with few restorations. The average sensitivity was 86% and 77% for children and adolescents, respectively. The average specificity was 88% and 97%. These results were similar to those obtained in the adult sample.[20]

There is no requisite number of points needed to establish person identity. When sufficient characterization exists in the absence of unexplainable discrepancies, identity can be confirmed. A single unique feature may suffice, or a multitude of less specific features may combine to confer uniqueness.

In confirmatory identifications where circumstantial evidence has generated the name of a probable victim, the threshold of features needed for identification is somewhat less than for a John/Jane Doe case. This is because other corroborating evidence exists to support identification and because a blindly selected ante-mortem dental record would not be expected to have much similarity to a random decedent if it were the wrong person. However, in a Doe identification, the ante-mortem dental records have been computer-selected from an enormous record pool; such a record, even from the wrong individual, is similar to the decedent's dentition by design. There also are no additional links between the missing persons and the decedent to circumstantially support the identification. In order to establish identity in the Doe case, there must be sufficient distinctiveness in the match to unconditionally exclude all other people.

Terminology for Reporting Identification

It would be unusual for a non-dentist to bear the responsibility of formalizing a dental identification. Forensic investigations are fastidious and the courts ensure that opinions are rendered by experts who have been qualified through credentials. A dental identification is best made by a forensic odontologist with mastery of dental radiology, record keeping, and clinical dentistry. Nevertheless, dental radiographic comparisons alone can be so compelling that another member of the forensic team might feel confident in rendering an opinion.

If overwhelming evidence of uniqueness is present and there are no exclusionary discrepancies, one can conclude a positive identification. If fewer, less specific similarities are noted between ante-mortem and post-mortem evidence and there are no unexplainable discrepancies, a lower order of confidence can be stated. For example, if the case represents a confirmatory identification in which the medical examiner or coroner has other evidence to support identification, the dental component may combine with the other evidence to allow identification. In this case, the dental evaluator would conclude a probable or confirmatory identification. If there is only scant or nonspecific similarity, identification cannot be proven but neither can it be ruled out. Lastly, if there is even one irreconcilable inconsistency, the putative victim should be excluded. In exclusionary cases, there will usually be other inconsistencies and any similarities will be of low specificity.

Special Problems

Laboratory Procedures

In the course of handling radiographs for dental identifications certain problems arise. Sometimes old, damaged original ante-mortem radiographs are sent to the forensic investigator. Often, duplicated ante-mortem radiographs are received instead of originals. Occasionally, duplicates need to be made by the forensic investigator. Courtroom exhibits might be needed in the form of enlarged black and white prints or projectable transparencies.

Repair of Damaged Film [21]
Light, dark, or opacified films can be improved to show detail. Some of these procedures alter the original film and can further degrade the image.

Dense radiographs can be lightened by chemically removing some of the silver halide. Iodine thiourea reducer is used as follows:

Stock Solution A

Iodine	10 g
Potassium iodide	30 g
Water to make	100 ml

Mix potassium iodide with sufficient water to make a solution. Add iodine and agitate until dissolved. Add water to make 100 ml.

Stock Solution B

Thiourea	10 g
Water to make	100 ml

Prepare working solution by mixing:

Solution A	1 part
Solution B	2 parts
Water	1 part

Immerse the film in reducing solution, agitate, and observe every few seconds until desired density is obtained. Wash in water, clear in fixing solution, wash again, and dry. "Spot" reduction can be performed with Q-tip application of the reducer. Stock solutions are stable, but the working solution is good for only a few hours.

A second lightening method is to physically remove the emulsion from one side of the film. Soak the film in water for a few hours, place it on a soft towel and rub the emulsion from the other side with a wet, lightly abrasive plastic scouring pad (e.g., Scotch-Brite©, 3M, St. Paul, MN 55144).

Light radiographs can be intensified by coupling a dye to available silver halide. Iron-toner intensifier is used as follows:

Solution A

Water	750 ml
Diglycolic acid (Aldrich Chemical Co.)	60 g
Sodium hydroxide	36 g

Solution B

Ferric nitrate $9H_2O$	14 g
Potassium fluoride $2H_2O$	1 g
Water	100 ml

Solution C

Potassium ferricyanide	5 g
Sodium nitrate	1 g
Water	100 ml

Add chemicals in the order given and dissolve each chemical completely before adding the next. Add the sodium hydroxide slowly. Slowly add Solution B to Solution A while stirring. Add Solution C slowly to the AB mixture while stirring. The radiograph is dipped and agitated. About 80% of the intensification occurs within 3 to 4 min and is maximized at 8 min. The film is washed for 5 min. The treated film is blue. The mixed solution keeps well in a dark bottle.

Another technique for intensifying a thin emulsion is to duplicate the film and super-impose the duplicate to enhance detail.

Making Duplicate Radiographs

Duplicating radiographs is easily accomplished with Kodak X-OMAT duplicating film, available in sheets of various sizes including size 2.

Duplicating is accomplished in the darkroom by placing the film to be copied between the duplicating film and a visible or ultraviolet light source. For busy laboratories, a contact printer with built-in light source is available through Lester A Dine, Inc., Rinn Corp., Ada

Products, or Star X-ray Co.[21] (Figure 6-24). The amount of light needed to render a properly exposed duplicate can be optimized by trial and error. Dark originals can even be lightened and improved with more exposure.[10,21] Smudges, fingerprints,[10] and fixer spots are accentuated in duplicates and surface contaminants should be removed from the original before duplicating. Left/right orientation, as imparted by the embossed dot in intraoral film, is lost in duplication. Large plates imprinted with L or R retain these designations.

Figure 6-24   Lester Dine® x-ray film duplicator for use in the darkroom.

Unlike the larger sheets of X-OMAT which are bulk-wrapped in a single envelope, size 2 duplicating film is individually wrapped in packets with lead foil, like x-ray film. The packets are not really necessary since they must be removed for the film to be exposed. The lead foil is completely superfluous since the film is not used on patients or exposed with x-rays. The film contains an embossed dot which serves as a left/right indicator <u>only</u> if the original film and duplicating film are correctly oriented. If either is accidentally reversed, the dot will misidentify right/left. There is no fail-safe way to ensure proper orientation of the developed copy. Because of these problems, plus the additional expense of size 2 X-OMAT film, it is preferable to copy periapicals with larger X-OMAT film. One can cut a sheet of duplicating film larger than the film(s) to be copied. The border can be marked with indelible ink to include demographic data (name, date, orientation, source, etc.). A fine-point Sharpie® marker or, for finer printing, a Rapidograph® draftsman pen with waterproof ink for writing on acetate is useful (Figure 6-25). X-OMAT film is processed with the same chemistry as x-ray film.

Figure 6-25   Rapidograph® pen and waterproof ink for fine line writing on acetate film.

Receiving Duplicate Films

Duplicates rarely show the quality of the original and there might be no indication of left/right orientation. Even the orientation dot on size 2 X-OMAT film is not a trustworthy indicator of right/left. Duplicates are acceptable if they can be used, but if questions arise, originals should be requested.

Identification of a film as a duplicate is relatively easy. Original films have dull emulsion on both sides. Duplicating film has emulsion on one side only. The other side is shiny. Size 2 duplicating film, in addition, is marked "DUP".

Photographing Radiographs

Radiographs should be photographed with a 35-mm single-lens reflex camera equipped with a macro lens with any focal length from 50 to 105 mm. In most applications the lens need only to allow a 1:2 (1/2 life-sized) reproduction. However, if one wishes to fill the frame with a single standard size 2 film, the lens must allow a 1:1 or life-sized reproduction.

The camera should be placed on a copy stand and the radiograph(s) set up on a table-top fluorescent viewing box which transilluminates the film (Figure 6-26). Strips of acetate can be marked with any information to be included in the photograph and then the image is composed and focused (Figure 6-36).

Prints are made using black and white print film such as Kodak Plus X. Direct camera metering for proper exposure works well if the meter can read off an area that is neither too light nor dark. If direct light from the light box enters the camera lens the meter will be fooled into underexposing the image, in which case the aperture should be opened to compensate and the camera used on manual mode. It is always wise to bracket exposures. When made for jury use, one print for every two jurors is recommended.

Transparencies for projection can be made with slide film. Since most slide film is of the daylight color variety, the fluorescent light of the light box renders an undesirable greenish hue which can be partly remedied with an FL-D filter. The best transparencies are made with Kodak Rapid Process Copy Film, which is a black and white slide film having excellent image resolution, grain qualities, and gray scale. Copies retain the contrast characteristics of the original. The slow film speed requires a copy stand because exposures of

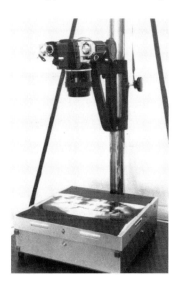

Figure 6-26 Copy stand and fluorescent light box for copywork onto photographic film. Note masking of x-ray film with black paper to block out light leak.

25 to 45 sec at f.4 are needed. Dark films are improved by using exposures as long as 4 min and, since the film is black and white, there are no color distortions from lighting or discolored radiographs. The light penetrates surface smudges, fingerprints, and does not accentuate these imperfections as with X-OMAT duplication. RPCF film can be developed within minutes in a dental x-ray processor and can be handled under an orange or red x-ray safelight.

The most simple and expedient way to project a size 2 radiograph is to insert the original film directly into a plastic 35-mm slide mount.

Dental Radiography in Mass Disasters

Field Equipment for Mass Disasters

In mass disasters involving multiple bodies in remote sites or under compromised conditions, radiographs are often made on location. A tripod-mounted portable dental x-ray unit such as the Min-X-ray® is used. A power source is provided by a generator. Proper shielding is needed.[22]

Considering the workload and urgency in a mass disaster, one does not have the luxury of waiting for ante-mortem radiographs. All bodies and recovered dental fragments should be x-rayed.[23] Full-mouth radiographs are preferred[22] but when individual periapical views are too time-consuming and jaw removal is permitted, occlusal-sized film can include the entire posterior dentition in two to four exposures[24] (Figure 6-22). Double film packets should be used.[25]

The films can be processed with an automatic dental x-ray film processor equipped with a daylight loading hood. If incoming ante-mortem films are being duplicated, a second processor should be used to avoid mixups. If a processor is not practical, there is Polaroid TPX radiographic film, an 8 × 10 in. film with self-contained chemistry for instant processing.

X-ray film mounts, folders, and labels must be on hand to keep radiographs separate and identifiable back to their source. A computer at the mass disaster site can electronically digitize and export radiographic images for rapid comparison.

Commingled, Skeletonized, Carbonized, and Mutilated Remains

When human remains appear to be missing jaws or teeth or when scattering and displacement has occurred, it is worthwhile to make flat plate radiographs with location grids of the entire body or recovered rubble in search of teeth or surviving prostheses[25] (Figure 6-27). Such dispersion and destruction occurs in some house fires, skeletonized remains, and in mass disasters when bodies are mutilated or commingled.

Skeletonized teeth are fragile and brittle. They tend to fracture, usually at right angles and with smooth cleavage through both enamel and dentin. These wedges of fractured tooth structure can be glued in place with Duco® cement or cyanoacrylate cement. Specimens can be preserved so as to prevent fracture by boiling, bleaching in Clorox, then dipping in a solution of polyvinyl acetate resin. The bones and teeth are then coated and permeated with a clear, thin, invisible preservative.

The effect of intense flash fires upon teeth is to cause boiling of the pulp and explosion of the crowns which then break off at the gumline, leaving roots within their sockets. Heat which develops more slowly causes exfoliation of enamel, leaving dome-shaped mounds of charred coronal dentin (Figure 6-28). These teeth are easily lost from their sockets.

Figure 6-27 Flat plate film of collected charred rubble including body parts found after a house fire. Note a molar tooth (arrow).

Figure 6-28 Charred hemimaxilla. Incisors (i) and canine (c) show exploded crowns indicating rapid evolution of intense heat. Premolars (p) show exfoliated enamel and charred dentin indicating slower, less intense heat. Molars (m) are intact.

Recovered conical roots should not be forced back into sockets because of their fragility. Rather, they should be guided in and checked radiographically. Generally, if a charred root has a gray (ashed) surface and a black (carbonized) surface, the gray side is labial (indicating higher heat and more complete combustion) and the black side is lingual.

Carbonized and ashed teeth and bone are friable and can crumble with the slightest touch or movement. Teeth might disintegrate when the jaws are removed. These teeth can be stabilized with spray acrylic, cyanoacrylate, polyvinyl acetate, or Duco® cement. Spray acrylic is easiest to apply *in situ*. Polyvinyl acetate is acceptable, but most time-consuming.[26]

Despite its delicateness, conflagrated mineralized tissue retains its radiographic characteristics although some shrinkage occurs (Figure 6-29). Lowered kVp is recommended as the specimens require less x-ray penetrating ability.

In remains where teeth have been lost post-mortem, the shape of the roots can be reconstructed by filling the empty sockets with radiopaque material (dental alginate impression material mixed with barium sulfate) before making post-mortem radiographs[27] (Figure 6-30).

Anthropologic Reconstructive Analysis

Profiling a missing person based upon physical attributes of a John/Jane Doe is a necessary first step if the individual is to be identified. Over 200,000 missing persons are reported annually in the U.S.[28] and the pool must be narrowed if there is ever a hope of finding the match. Dental features assist in some of these assessments. In fact, dental radiographs

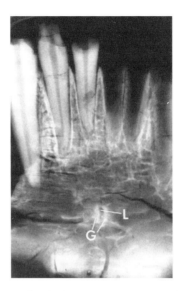

Figure 6-29   Periapical radiograph of charred anterior mandible showing post-mortem loss of the left canine and incisors and heat destruction of the crowns of the right incisors and canine. Note increased contrast which highlights the genial tubercle (G) and lingual foramen (L).

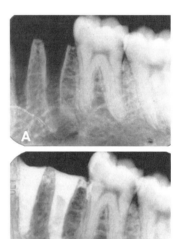

Figure 6-30   The morphology of teeth lost post-mortem (A) can be restored with radiopaque barium sulfate added to alginate dental impression material and pressed into sockets (B).

provide the best method of age determination from the *in utero* period until age 15. This is based on the formation and eruption sequence of deciduous and permanent teeth and is accurate to ±1 year when determined radiographically. Development of the third molars can be used until the age of 20 but is less precise (±2 years for 1 standard deviation).[29] Charts on the sequence and timing of dental development are available.[30–32] In general, the crown of the permanent central incisor begins to mineralize 3 to 4 months after birth and is completed at age 4 to 5. The tooth erupts at age 6 to 7 and its root apex is closed and constricted at age 9 to 10. The first permanent molars follow a slightly earlier schedule, mineralizing at birth, completing crowns at age 3 to 4, erupting at age 6, and completing root closure by age 10. Mineralization of the second molar is first seen radiographically at age 3 to 4 and the crown is fully formed by age 7 to 8. It erupts at age 12 and its root apex is completed by age 15. The third molar crown is fully developed between the ages of 12 and 16 and the apex is completed between 18 and 24 years of age.[29]

Gender is not determinable from dental radiographs, although in PA skull films measurements of total circumfacial height, mastoid height, bicondylar width, and mandibular width yielded the correct sex with 88% accuracy in one study.[6]

Racial determination is not feasible except in the rare instance that shovel-shaped maxillary incisors are visualized radiographically (Figure 6-31 A and B). These are present in about 90% of Asians and Native Americans. Mild shovelling seen in other races is not likely to be seen in radiographs. Absence of radiographic shovelling cannot be used to exclude Mongoloids. Another trait of Mongoloid population is an extra root on mandibular molars (Figure 6-32). The cusp of Carabelli is a tubercle found on the mesiolingual aspect of the maxillary first molar (Figure 6-33 A, B, and C). It is most common in Caucasians.

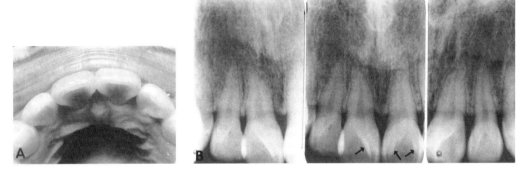

Figure 6-31   Shovel shaped incisors in an Asian woman. Clinically, note the prominent mesial and distal ridges (**A**) that are radiographically opaque (**B**, arrows).

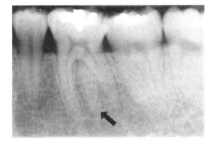

Figure 6-32   Extra roots on mandibular molars (arrow) are most common in mongoloids.

One can speculate socioeconomic status based on dental care. Severe, active caries without much dental intervention tends to suggest lower socioeconomic status while crowns and bridges and root canal fillings in a well-cared-for dentition indicates that much time, effort, and money was spent on dental care. Healthy, unrestored dentitions, edentulous mouths, and mouths with severe periodontal disease cannot be assessed in terms of socioeconomic status. If all four first premolars are missing and their spaces closed, this finding suggests previous orthodontic therapy (Figures 6-11 and 6-13). Blunted root apices, especially of maxillary incisors, also foretells of orthodontic tooth movement as does the presence of orthodontic appliances (Figure 6-12). Such a clue might focus an inquiry of area orthodontists in the search for ante-mortem dental records.

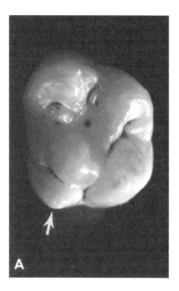

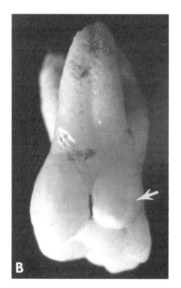

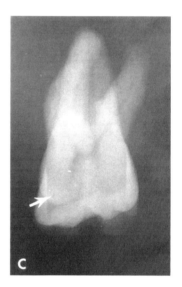

Figure 6-33   The cusp of Carabelli (arrows) of the upper first molar. In large examples, it can be seen radiographically (**C**).

Special Considerations With Children

As mentioned, identification of children by dental radiographs presents many challenges and few opportunities. One is more reliant on dental anatomy because children typically have few fillings yet the anatomy of deciduous teeth is more uniform than the permanent teeth. The child's dentition is also in a state of flux owing to a continuum of tooth development, eruption, movement, resorption, and exfoliation. Lastly, ante-mortem radiographs on children are not frequently made. When recovered, they might show numerous temporal inconsistencies because of the rapid growth changes. Despite these problems, forensic dentists can be expected to establish identity in over 90% of cases based on bitewing radiographs.[20] Mandibular premolars, often visualized in developing crowns between the roots of deciduous molars, offers the most distinctive anatomy. Also, a number of older children and adolescents may have visited an orthodontist and will have comprehensive ante-mortem data (radiographs, close-up intra-oral photographs, and study models of the teeth) for comparison. The alert forensic investigator will look for signs of orthodontic intervention in post-mortem material.

Example Cases

Example Case 6-1 — The nude, partly burned body of a woman was discovered on the banks of the Green River in Kentucky by duck hunters. The dentist of the putative victim was located. His bitewing radiographs, made one year previously, were examined and compared to post-mortem radiographs made on the resected jaw specimens. Figure 6-34 A shows the right ante-mortem film and Figure 6-34 B shows the right post-mortem film. Note that they are nearly identical; both films show a lone maxillary molar, an edentulous area where a molar had been extracted, and two unrestored premolars. The second mandibular premolar shows distal interproximal caries. The first and second mandibular molars show distinctive patterns to the amalgam fillings and the third molar is impacted. Figure 6-34 C and D show the left ante-mortem and post-mortem films, respectively. Note the following similarities. The two maxillary premolars are unrestored. The first molar is missing and another unrestored molar is present. Mandibular teeth show inconsistencies. The two molars seen ante-mortem are not present post-mortem and the two unrestored premolars contain small occlusal amalgams in the post-mortem film. These represent explainable temporal discrepancies. The numerous compatibilities are specific and sufficient to establish a positive identification.

Example Case 6-2 — Following the crash of a small aircraft in Kentucky, the severely charred and mutilated fragmentary remains of a pilot was recovered. The family of the putative victim was located and the name of a treating dentist was proffered. The dentist said that his patient wore an upper denture and had a few natural lower teeth. Although

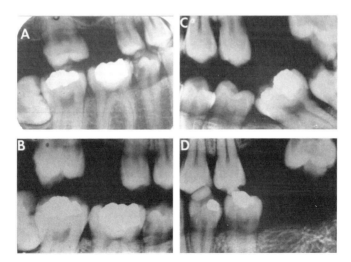

Figure 6-34 Case 6-1 — see text. **A** — right ante-mortem bitewing; **B** — right post-mortem bitewing; **C** — left ante-mortem bitewing; **D** — left post-mortem bitewing.

these characteristics were true of the victim, they were too nonspecific for even a confirmatory identification. When asked about radiographs, the dentist replied that he had a single periapical film, but assumed it would not be helpful because it was eight years old and showed teeth that were no longer present. The film was requested.

The ante-mortem film (Figure 6-35 AM) shows three teeth and supporting bone. The first premolar (28) leans distally and shows a right-angle ledge of abraded tooth structure where the crown and root meet. Attached to the carious root of the canine (27) is a circular periapical radiolucency reflecting inflammation around the dead tooth. The incisor (26) is tipped mesially and shows severe bone loss. Extremely prominent nutrient canals traverse vertically through the bone, below the apex of 27, between 27 and 26, and mesial to 26.

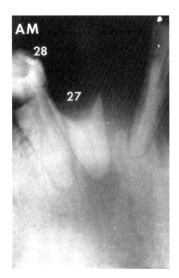 

Figure 6-35   Case 6-2 - see text.

A post-mortem film (Figure 6-35 PM) of the same anatomic area was made with similar angulation. Three compatible temporal discrepancies are seen; 26 and 27 have been extracted and the crown of 28 was broken off in the plane crash. Although the root of 28 and the surrounding alveolar bone are all that remain for comparison, there are sufficient characteristics for comparison. Specific similarities include the distal tilt of 28 and the right-angle ledge which remains just below where the crown snapped off. Distinctive features in bone include the three prominent nutrient canals and the residua of the radiolucency formerly surrounding the apex of 27. There are no incompatible inconsistencies and the similarities are specific enough to confirm a positive identification.

Example Case 6-3 — The putrefied remains of a murdered woman was discovered in a septic tank. The family dentist of the putative victim was located and produced bitewings which were a few months old. Postmortem radiographs were made for comparison. Both ante-mortem (Figure 6-36 AM) and post-mortem (Figure 6-36 PM) radiographs show a wealth of specific comparative features including 15 amalgam restorations and a crown on tooth 18. Three of the larger amalgam fillings in 19, 20, and 31 show retention pins. Bilateral amalgam tattoos are seen interproximally between 18 and 19 and between 30 and 31. These

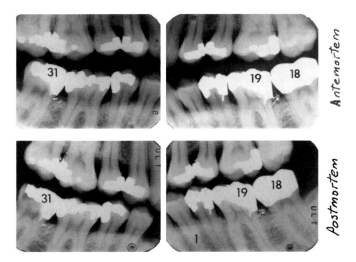

Figure 6-36   Case 6-3 - see text.

appear as small stippled opacities. This constellation of specific comparative features assures an unconditionally positive identification.

Example Case 6-4 — A charred and mutilated body was found in Kentucky in April, 1990. The cause of death was listed as blunt force trauma to the head with jaw fractures, while the manner of death was determined to be homicide. The putative victim was recently released from prison and it was learned that two months earlier, while in prison, he had sustained a blow to the jaw, necessitating a submental vertical radiograph (Figure 6-37 AM). A post-mortem occlusal radiograph was made by positioning the resected jaw specimens in occlusion in order to simulate the ante-mortem view (Figure 6-37 PM). The ante-mortem film shows an unusual arrangement of teeth; there are no maxillary incisors or left maxillary teeth and no mandibular incisors. A single occlusal amalgam restoration is located in 18. The post-mortem films duplicates the number and arrangement of teeth as well as the distinctive outline of the restoration. Even the morphology of the nasal spine and incisive canal of the maxilla are similar. The post-mortem radiograph shows the fracture of the right maxilla and two fractures of the anterior mandible resulting from the agonal trauma. The combination of specific comparative features and absence of any discrepancies confers uniqueness and a positive identification.

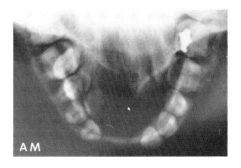
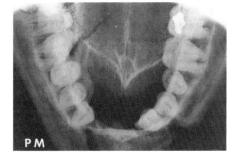

Figure 6-37   Case 6-4 - see text.

Example Case 6-5 — The crash of a small aircraft in Kentucky claimed six victims who were partly burned and mutilated. One victim had no known source of dental records but had a history of chiropractic treatment. A six-year-old radiograph recovered from his chiropractor (Figure 6-38 AM) fortuitously shows teeth, but the fillings were superimposed. Postmortem radiographs (Figure 6-38 PM) were made to duplicate the orientation of the ante-mortem film, resulting in recognizable and unique patterns of the superimposed fillings in all four posterior quadrants. The number and anatomy of lower incisors were also compatible, albeit nonspecific. An unconditionally positive identification could be made on the basis of similarity in the restorative pattern.

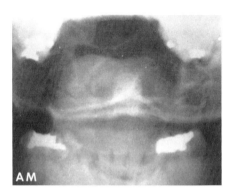 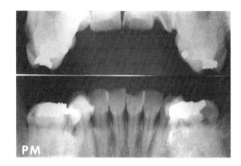

Figure 6-38   Case 6-5 - see text.

Example Case 6-6 — The charred body of a male decedent was recovered from a house fire in Louisville, KY. The resident of the apartment was the presumed victim and it was learned that he had been to the University of Louisville Dental School for emergency treatment. Recovered records included a three-year-old panographic radiograph, a portion of which is shown in Figure 6-39 AM. A lateral view of the left mandible was made with occlusal film to duplicate the panographic view (Figure 6-39 PM). Note the increased magnification and poor resolution of the panographic film. The presence and anatomy of the unrestored 1st and 2nd molars in both ante-mortem and post-mortem films represents a similarity, but it is nonspecific. A more specific similarity includes the prominent antegonial notch (arrows). The most specific similarity which confers identification is the cluster of irregular radiopacities below the 2nd molar. One inconsistency is the absence of the 3rd molar in the post-mortem radiograph. This is a temporal inconsistency. The written record confirms this extraction following the making of the panograph.

Example Case 6-7 — In June, 1983, a 12-year-old girl was reported to have been abducted from a shopping center in Louisville, KY. She was not heard from again. When the skeletonized remains of a young female was found along a Kentucky roadside in July, 1984 an NCIC entry was made on the corpse. The computer offered several possible "hits", but dental records easily ruled them out. The missing 12-year-old from Louisville was also a consideration. Ante-mortem bitewing radiographs of the missing girl were obtained from the family dentist. They had been made three months prior to her disappearance. Post-mortem bitewings on the jaw specimens of the decedent were made for comparison. The

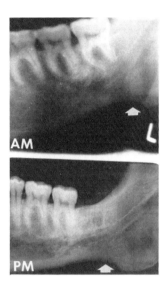

Figure 6-39   Case 6-6 - see text.

two sets are photographed together for comparison (Figure 6-40). The ante-mortem film shows a mixed dentition. The primary molars (A, I, J, T) are on the verge of exfoliation and the underlying premolars are erupting. No fillings are seen. The post-mortem radiograph shows considerable dissimilarity including the presence of four fillings. Such discrepancies, however, are potentially explainable because over a year had elapsed since the girl was reported missing and it was possible that she was not killed immediately, but lived long enough to exfoliate her baby teeth and receive dental fillings. In general, the tooth morphology between the molar teeth is compatible between ante-mortem and post-mortem radiographs. The mandibular second premolars (20 and 29), however, belie the match. The ante-mortem second premolars each show a single lingual cusp in the mid portion of the crown, whereas the post-mortem second premolars each show two lingual cusps. No amount of radiographic angulation on the specimen could recreate the anatomy of the ante-mortem radiograph. The missing 12-year-old was excluded as the missing decedent.

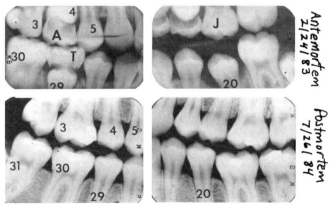

Figure 6-40   Case 6-7 - see text.

References

1. Langland, O. E. and Langlais, R. P., Early pioneers of oral and maxillofacial radiology, *Oral Surg.*, 80, 496, 1995.

2. Langland, O. E., Sippy, F. H., and Langlais, R. P., *Textbook of Dental Radiology*, 2nd ed., Charles C Thomas, Springfield, IL, 1984, chap. 1.

3. Culbert, W. L. and Law, F. M., Identification of a body by comparison of radiographs of the nasal accessory sinuses and mastoid processes, *Trans. Am. Laryngol. Rhinol. Otolaryngol. Soc.*, 32, 248, 1926.

4. Fry, W. K., The Baptist church cellar case, *Br. Dent. J.*, 75, 154, 1943.

5. Brown T. C., Delaney, R. J., and Robinson, W. L., Medical identification in the "Noronic Disaster", *J. Am. Med. Assoc.*, 148, 621, 1952.

6. Nortje, C. J. and Harris, A. M. P., Maxillo-facial radiology in forensic dentistry: a review, *J. Forensic Odonto-Stomatol.*, 4, 29, 1986.

7. DeVore, D. T., Radiology and photography in forensic dentistry, *Dent. Clin. N. Am.*, 21, 69, 1977.

8. Fischman, S. L., The use of medical and dental radiographs in identification, *Int. Dent. J.*, 35, 301, 1985.

9. MacLean, D. F., Kogon, S. L., and Slitt, L. W., Validation of dental radiographs for human identification, *J. Forensic Sci.*, 39, 1195, 1994.

10. Stimpson, P. G., Forensic dental radiology, in *Outline of Forensic Dentistry*, Cottone, J. A. and Standish S. M., Eds., Year Book Medical Publishers, Chicago, 1982, chap. 6.

11. Luntz, L. L. and Luntz, P., *Handbook for Dental Identification: Techniques in Forensic Dentistry*, Lippincott, Philadelphia, 1973, chap. 3.

12. Eastman, J. R., Raibley, S., and Schwartz, L., Trabecular bone patterns in dental radiographs: a further aid to dentists involved in forensic dentistry, *Ill. Dent. J.*, 161, 1982.

13. Sedwick, H. J., Form, size and position of the maxillary sinus at various ages studied by means of roentgenograms of the skull, *Am. J. Roentgenol.*, 32, 154, 1934.

14. Schuller, A., Note on identification of skulls by x-ray pictures of the frontal sinuses, *Med. J. Aust.*, 1, 554, 1943.

15. Messmer, J. M. and Fierro, M. F., Personal identification by radiographic comparison of vascular groove patterns of the calvarium, *Am. J. Forensic Med. Pathol.*, 7, 159, 1986.

16. Kullman, L., Eklund, B., and Grundin, R., The value of the frontal sinus in identification of unknown persons, *J. Forensic Odonto-Stomatol.*, 8, 3, 1990.

17. Ubelaker, D. H., Positive identification from the radiographic comparison of frontal sinus patterns, *Human Identification*, Rathbun, T. A. and Buikstra, J., Eds., Charles C Thomas, Springfield, IL, 1984, 399-411.

18. Borrman, H. and Grondahl, H. G., Accuracy in establishing identity in edentulous individuals by means of intraoral radiographs, *J. Forensic Odonto-Stomatol.*, 10, 1, 1992.

19. Borrman, H. and Grondahl, H. G., Accuracy in establishing identity by means of intraoral radiographs, *J. Forensic Odonto-Stomatol.*, 8, 31, 1990.

20. Kogon, S. L., McKay, A. E., and MacLean, D. F., The validity of bitewing radiographs for the dental identification of children, *J. Forensic Sci.*, 40, 1055, 1995.

21. Mincer, H. H., Kaplan, I., Dickens, R. L., and Harruff, R. C., Salvaging improperly exposed or incorrectly processed radiographs, in *Manual of Forensic Odontology*, Averill, D. C., Ed., American Society Forensic Odontology, Chicago, 1991, 40.

22. Morlang, W. M., Mass disaster management update, *CDA J.*, 14, 49, 1986.

23. Workshop 5: Postmortem Protocol in *Proc. First Natl. Symp. Dentistry's Role and Responsibility in Mass Disaster Identification*, Smith, S. E. and Rawson, R. D., Eds., American Dental Association, Chicago, 1986.

24. Stimpson, P. G., Radiology in forensic odontology, *Dent. Radiogr. Photogr.*, 48, 3, 1975.

25. Morlang, W. M. and Siegel, R., Mass disaster management, in *Outline of Forensic Dentistry*, Cottone, J. A. and Standish, S. M., Eds., Year Book Medical Publishers, Chicago, 1982, chap. 8.

26. Mincer, H. H., Berryman, H. E., Murray, G. A., and Dickens, R. L., Methods for physical stabilization of ashed teeth in incinerated remains, *J. Forens. Sci.*, 35, 971, 1990.

27. Smith, B. C., Reconstruction of root morphology in skeletonized remains with post-mortem dental loss, *J. Forensic Sci.*, 37, 176, 1992.

28. Bernstein, M. L., The identification of a "John Doe", *J. Am. Dent. Assoc.*, 110, 918, 1985.

29. Mincer, H. H., Harris, E. F., and Berryman, H. E., The A.B.F.O. study of third molar development and its use as an estimator of chronologic age, *J. Forensic Sci.*, 38, 379, 1993.

30. Ubelaker, D. H., *Human Skeletal Remains*, 2nd ed., Taraxacum, Washington, D.C., 1989, 63.

31. Gustafson, G. and Koch, G., Age estimation up to sixteen years based on development, cited in Johansen, G., *Odontol. Revy*, 22(Suppl. 21), 1971.

32. Harris, E. F. and McKee, J. H., Tooth mineralization standards for blacks and whites from the middle southern United States, *J. Forensic Sci.*, 35, 859, 1990.

Radiographic Techniques in Bite Mark Analysis — Identification of the Perpetrator

7

DAVID SWEET, D.M.D., PH.D.

Contents

Introduction

Forensic odontologists are often involved in establishing the identification of a deceased person. Comparison of the unique features which are present in natural and artificial teeth and in dental restorations may allow decomposed, burned, mutilated, or commingled human remains to be positively identified as a specific individual. This is the forensic dentist's most common task.

The most challenging area of forensic odontology, however, is the analysis of human or animal bite marks found on skin or objects at a crime scene. Subsequent comparison of any unique characteristics discovered in the injury to similar features present in the suspect's teeth may reveal important links between the suspect and the victim.

The teeth are often used as a weapon when one person attacks another, or in self-defense against an attacker.[1,2] Aggressive offensive bite mark injuries and defensive bite marks have been found in cases of homicide, attempted homicide, heterosexual and homosexual assault, aggravated assault, battery, and in cases involving the physical and sexual abuse of children.[3–8] Biting behavior is the result of the perpetrator's quest to gain dominance through anger and power;[2–9] in cases of self-defense the victim's teeth are often the only available weapon.

A round or elliptical area of contusion or abrasion is the usual presentation of a human bite mark. In other cases, the surface of the skin may be lacerated or a piece of tissue may be completely bitten off.[10] Penetration into deeper layers of the skin with associated bruising is common.

Bite marks are considered to be examples of physical evidence as well as biological evidence.[11–17] The analysis of bite marks most often involves a detailed examination and measurement of the injury patterns and physical comparison of these features to the dental exemplars of the suspect. Imperfections or unique irregularities which are identified in both the injury and the suspect's teeth become valuable indicators of the degree of concordance between them, and appropriate conclusions can be stated in relation to these characteristics.

Methods of analyzing a bite mark typically involve physical comparisons of life-sized photographs or tracings of the injury on the victim's skin to models of the suspect's teeth.[18–20] If there is any distortion, or if imperfections are present in any of the steps leading to the production of the objects used in the comparison, the scientific merit of the final conclusion may be diminished.[10,11]

Bite Marks as Physical Evidence

The premise that the human dentition is unique to each individual is widely accepted.[6,12,21] It is possible to derive the most information from cases in which specific and detailed patterns of the characteristics of individual teeth have been recorded in the injury. If this information is available, it may be possible to identify the teeth which caused the bite mark.

Collection of evidence from the victim's body includes swabbing the site for saliva, photographing the area while employing a reference scale of known dimensions, and producing impressions and molds of the skin's surface.[1,3,22–25] Life-sized photographic prints (color and black-and-white) and models of the bitten surface are produced from these exhibits for later comparison to evidence obtained from suspects.

When suspects are identified, dental evidence should be recovered by a qualified odontologist. A thorough clinical examination of the teeth and oral structures is performed as well as the acquisition of intraoral and extraoral photographs, dental impressions for study models, and a sample of the suspect's bite pattern in materials such as wax, silicone, or styrofoam.[5,7,11,24–26]

Bite Mark Comparisons

Analysis of bite mark evidence involves the detailed examination, measurement, and comparison of evidence recovered from the victim and the suspect. Usually, the odontologist compares life-sized (1:1) photographs of the bite mark (exhibits) to models of the suspect's teeth (exemplars).

Although techniques for evidence collection are well established,[10,27] currently there is no general agreement among odontologists on the best methods of comparing the exhibits and the exemplars. Several comparison techniques are advocated by different odontologists. Methods include production and use of freehand tracings of the bite mark, photocopied acetate overlays of the suspect's teeth, test bites in wax and other materials, or combinations of these procedures.[10,19,20] Other highly sophisticated techniques using CAT scan images, computers, and photographically produced hollow volume overlays have also been evaluated.[28–30] Each method typically involves multiple steps. Care must be taken to avoid the introduction of errors at any stage of the procedures.

The production of overlays to compare teeth to an injury must be completed using a method which faithfully reproduces the contours, shapes, sizes, and arrangement of individual teeth. Photographic and radiographic techniques can be used to achieve consistent and reproducible images of the teeth on clear acetate film which can be used in subsequent physical comparisons.

Radiographic Production of Comparison Aids

Many diverse methods are available for comparing evidence to exemplars. A technique referred to as toneline photography (sometimes called a *line print*)[31] using radiographic images of metal models of the suspect's teeth[32] to produce clear acetate films with life-sized images of the incisal edges is presented here (Figure 7-1).

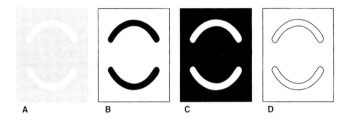

Figure 7-1   Illustration of the steps in producing a toneline photograph from a radiograph. **A**: original radiograph with images of upper and lower dental arches, **B**: high-contrast reversal Kodalith contact print produced from "A", **C**: reversal Kodalith contact print produced from "B" (the result is a high-contrast duplication of "A"), **D**: Kodalith toneline print produced by "stacking" "B" and "C" and exposing film at a 45° angle.

After obtaining upper and lower dental impressions of a suspect, study casts are produced in dental stone. The first pour from the original impressions is retained as a pristine exemplar of the suspect's teeth. Subsequent pours are produced and used as working models. For this reason it is recommended that very accurate and stable dental impression materials, such as vinyl polysiloxane (VPS), be utilized.

To produce a toneline image of teeth, a second set of dental impressions from the suspect's mouth, or a duplicate impression of upper and lower study casts, must be fabricated. Following this, fusible metal (William Dixon Inc., Carlstadt, NJ, catalogue no. Dixon FM), also referred to as "Mellott's" metal, is poured into the VPS impression material to produce a metal cast of the anterior teeth of interest (see Figure 7-2).

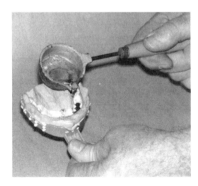

Figure 7-2   A metal cast of the desired teeth is fabricated by pouring fusible metal into a vinyl polysiloxane dental impression.

Radiographic Procedure

1. Melt an ingot of fusible metal in a ladle over a gas flame. Remove oxides from the surface using a 2 × 2 in. gauze square, allow to cool slightly, and then reheat to working temperature (approximately 160°F).
2. Carefully pour the metal from the ladle into the impressions of the crowns of the anterior teeth under consideration. Allow the metal to cool (≤117°F) and harden.
3. Pour ADA Type IV dental stone into the impression to cover the metal teeth and produce a cast of the remaining teeth and a base. Allow the stone to solidify.
4. Remove the study cast from the impression and trim to normal contours (Figure 7-3).
5. Using boxing wax, prepare a mold around the study cast. Seal any voids using a hot wax knife (Figure 7-4).
6. Mix enough clear self-curing denture acrylic (Pour-n-Cure, G. C. America Inc., Chicago, catalogue no. 2670392) to cover the crowns of the teeth and to fill the mold. Vibrate the cast as the acrylic is poured into the mold to avoid inclusion of air bubbles. Subsequently, place the mold in a pressure cooker during polymerization. When acrylic is set, remove the boxing wax.
7. Using a model trimmer equipped with a sandpaper disc, refine the contours of the perimeter of the acrylic and stone cast (Figure 7-5). Then, while holding the acrylic portion of the model and maintaining the occlusal plane parallel to the sandpaper disc, grind the stone base from the model. Slowly remove enough stone and acrylic, while continuing to orient the ground surface parallel to the occlusal plane, to expose the fusible metal near the cervical region of the anterior teeth (Figure 7-6).

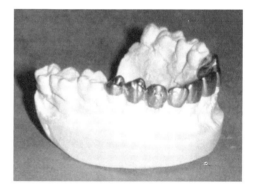

Figure 7-3   A trimmed study cast illustrating the metal crowns and stone base.

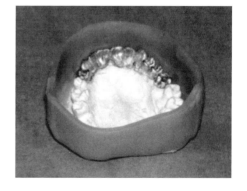

Figure 7-4   A mold surrounding the dental arch is formed from boxing wax. Self-curing acrylic is poured into this mold.

8. Lay the ground surface of the acrylic block on a Kodak Ektaspeed Plus, size 4 dental film (Kodak EO-41P, catalogue no. 876 3500) and position a radiographic scale and appropriate laterality marker in the field. Expose at 90 kVp and 15 mA for 0.35 sec. Process the film and label it as *cross-section no. 1.*

9. Continue removing layers from the surface in 1-mm increments. Expose additional radiographs at each layer and label them as cross-sectional "slices" are made through the metal crowns of the teeth. Select the radiographic film which contains the desired information — usually the incisal edges of the anterior teeth (see Figure 7-7).

The second phase of this technique uses established toneline photographic techniques to produce a high-contrast, thin black outline of the teeth which resembles a pen-and-ink drawing.[33]

Figure 7-5 A trimmed model illustrating acrylic encasing the crowns of the teeth.

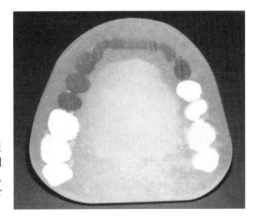

Figure 7-6 A cross section of the dental arch (parallel to occlusal plane) is produced using a model trimmer. The sizes, shapes, contours, and relationship of the teeth near the incisal edges are produced.

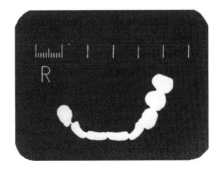

Figure 7-7 A dental radiograph (size 4) illustrating the image produced from the metal teeth in the model.

Photographic Procedure

1. The selected radiograph(s) is placed in contact with the emulsion surface of a Kodak Kodalith Ortho Film 2556 Type 3 reversal film (emulsion-to-emulsion).[34] An exposure is made to produce a negative image of the original radiographic film (Figure 7-8).

2. This procedure is then repeated once more using the product from step 1 above (negative image of original). This produces a high-contrast photographic duplicate of the original radiograph (Figure 7-9).

3. Carefully register the two Kodalith films (positive and negative images) base to base so that no light is able to pass through the images of the teeth when viewed at right angles to the film plane. Viewing this three-layer *film sandwich* from 45° over a view box reveals a fine line which outlines the dimensions of the teeth present in the photographic images.

4. Under darkroom conditions, position the film sandwich in contact with an unexposed Kodalith film as if making a contact print. Place these materials on a turntable which is turning at 45 rpm. Expose the film using a point light source at 45° above the film plane (100 W frosted lamp at 1 m) for 20 sec (15 revolutions). Develop and dry the final Kodalith film. The toneline photograph appears as a black line outlining the perimeter of the teeth (Figure 7-10).

Research projects and use of these methods in actual forensic cases have shown that toneline photography of radiographic images can provide an accurate image of the perimeter of certain human teeth which can be used in comparisons of the shape, pattern, and configuration of a bite mark to the dental exemplars of suspects. The technique is relatively

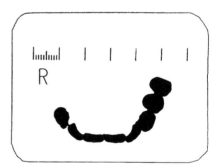

Figure 7-8   A Kodalith contact print of the radiographic image.

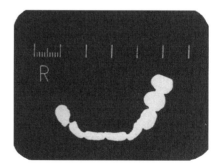

Figure 7-9   A subsequent Kodalith contact print produced using Figure 7-8.

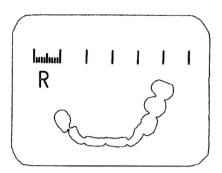

Figure 7-10   A toneline photograph illustrating the perimeter of the desired teeth.

easy and inexpensive and is considered a valuable aid for the production of objective physical comparison tools.

Acknowledgments

The author gratefully acknowledges Dr. Elizabeth Robinson for her collaboration on the subject of toneline photography and the assistance of Dr. John Bull in sharing his experience with these photographic and radiographic techniques. The illustrations were produced with the kind assistance of Bruce MacCaughey of the University of British Columbia Faculty of Dentistry.

References

1. Furness, J., A general review of bite-mark evidence, *Am. J. Forensic Med. Pathol.,* 2, 49, 1981.

2. Walter, R. D., Anger biting: the hidden impulse, *Am. J. Forensic Med. Pathol.,* 6, 219, 1985.

3. Cottone, J. A. and Standish, S. M., *Outline of Forensic Dentistry,* Yearbook Medical Publishers, Chicago, 1982.

4. Vale, G. L. and Noguchi, T. T., Anatomical distribution of human bite marks in a series of 67 cases, *J. Forensic Sci.,* 28, 61, 1983.

5. Johnson, L. T. and Cadle, D., Bite mark evidence: recognition, preservation, analysis, and courtroom presentation, *N. Y. State Dental J.,* 55, 38, 1989.

6. Rawson, R. D., Koot, A., Martin, C., Jackson, J., Novosel, S., Richardson, A., and Bender, T., Statistical evidence for the individuality of the human dentition, *J. Forensic Sci.,* 29, 245, 1984.

7. Sperber, N. D., Bite marks, oral and facial injuries — harbingers of severe child abuse?, *Pediatrician,* 16, 3, 1989.

8. LeRoy, H. A. and Sweet, D. J., Take a bite out of crime — ask a forensic odontologist for assistance, *R. Can. Mounted Gaz.,* 55, 1, 1993.

9. Walter, R. D., An examination of the psychological aspects of bite marks, *Am. J. Forensic Med. Pathol.,* 5, 25, 1984.

10. Rothwell, B. R., Bite marks in forensic odontology; fact or fiction? In *Controversies in Oral and Maxillofacial Surgery,* Worthington, P. and Evans, J. R., Eds., W. B. Saunders, Philadelphia, 1994, 588.

11. Sweet, D. J., Human bite marks — examination, recovery and analysis, in *Manual of Forensic Odontology,* 3rd ed., Bowers, C. M. and Bell, G. L., Eds., American Society of Forensic Odontology, Colorado Springs, 1995..

12. West, M. H., Hayne, S., and Barsley, R. E., Uniqueness of wound patterns, *Am. Soc. Forensic Odontol. Newsl.,* 4, 6, 1992.

13. Mittleman, R. E., Stuver, W. C., and Souviron, R., Obtaining saliva samples from bite mark evidence, *Law Enforcement Bull.,* 1, 1980.

14. Ohashi, A., Aoki, T., Matsugo, S., and Simasaki, C., PCR-based typing of human buccal cell's DNA extracted from whole saliva and saliva stains, *Jpn. J. Legal Med.,* 47, 108, 1993.

15. Clift, A. and Lamont, C. M., Saliva in forensic odontology, *J. Forensic Sci. Soc.,* 14, 241, 1974.

16. Rutter, E. A. and Whitehead, P. H., The fractionation of ABH blood group substances in saliva, *J. Forensic Sci. Soc.,* 16, 241, 1977.

17. Sweet, D. J., Identification of Stains of Human Saliva Using Forensic DNA Analysis, Ph.D. thesis, University of Granada, Spain, 1995.

18. West, M. H. and Barsley, R. E., The use of human skin in the fabrication of a bite mark template: two case reports, *J. Forensic Sci.,* 35, 1477, 1990.

19. Dailey, J. C., A practical technique for the fabrication of transparent bite mark overlays, *J. Forensic Sci.,* 36, 565, 1991.

20. Dailey, J. C., Transparent bite mark overlays, in *Manual of Forensic Odontology,* 2nd ed., Averill, D., Ed., American Society of Forensic Odontology, Colorado Springs, 1991, 164.

21. Beckstead, J. W., Rawson, R. D., and Giles, W. S., Review of bite mark evidence, *J. Am. Dent. Assoc.,* 99, 69, 1979.

22. Benson, B. W., Bite mark impressions: a review of techniques and materials, *J. Forensic Sci.,* 33, 1238, 1988.

23. Dailey, J. C., Shernoff, A., and Gelles, J. H., An improved technique for bite mark impressions, *J. Prosthet. Dent.,* 61, 153, 1989.

24. Dorion, R. B. J., Bite mark evidence, *J. Can. Dent. Assoc.,* 48, 795, 1982.

25. Rothwell, B. R., Bite marks in forensic dentistry: a review of legal, scientific issues, *J. Am. Dent. Assoc.,* 126, 223, 1995.

26. West, M. H. and Barsley, R. E., A second look at wax, *Am. Soc. Forensic Odontol. Newsl.,* 4, 1993.

27. American Board of Forensic Odontology, Guidelines for bite mark analysis, *J. Am. Dent. Assoc.,* 112, 383, 1986.

28. Rawson, R. D., Solarization as an aid to bite analysis, *J. Forensic Dent.,* 3, 10, 31, 1976.

29. Wood, R. E., Miller, P. A., and Blenkinsop, B. R., Image editing and computer assisted bite mark analysis: a case report, *J. Forensic Odonto-Stomatol.,* 12, 30, 1994.

30. Haidle, R., Schlesser, S., and Rawson, R. D., Overlaying hollow volumes on complex 3D surfaces for bite mark case work, in *Proc. Am. Acad. Forensic Sci.,* Cincinnati, 1990, 109.

31. Upton, B. and Upton, J., *Photography,* Little, Brown, Boston, 1976, 114.

32. Bull, J. W., Bite mark analysis of three dimensional pattern production from suspect's teeth, in *Proc. Am. Acad. Forensic Sci.,* Seattle, 1995, 119.

33. Robinson, E. and Wentzel, J., Toneline bite mark photography, *J. Forensic Sci.,* 37, 195, 1992.

34. Young, W. A., Benson, T. A., and Eaton, G. T., *Copying and Duplicating in Black-and-White and Color,* Kodak Publication No. M-1, Eastman Kodak Co., Rochester, 1984, DS-12, DS-14, DS-20, 21.

Radiological Identification of Individual Remains

8

B. G. BROGDON, M.D.

Contents

In the ideal medicolegal facility the use of medical imaging should be as routine as the autopsy and, in point of practical fact, may be used as a substitute for the autopsy under certain situations.

— *J. F. Edland*[1]

Introduction

The radiologic identification of individual human remains depends entirely on matching specific and unique visual findings or features on both ante-mortem and post-mortem radiologic images of that person (Figure 8-1). Post-mortem findings confirming sex, age, stature, or race may be either confirmatory or exclusionary. Post-mortem radiographic evidence of a specific injury, disease, or congenital anomaly known to have been present in a particular missing person can lead to presumptive identification. However, positive radiologic identification requires comparative matches of anatomic features on pre- and post-mortem radiologic examinations. Sometimes a cluster of relatively common or non-specific anatomic changes can establish identification beyond reasonable doubt; on other occasions a single unique finding is sufficient.

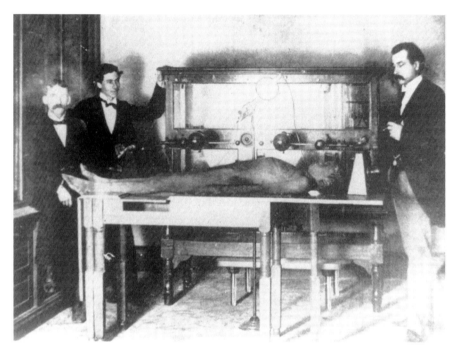

Figure 8-1 Earliest photograph of roentgenography of a cadaver found by the author. It was made in 1898 at the American School of Osteopathy, Kirksville, MO. (Courtesy of the Center for the American History of Radiology, Reston, VA.)

Example Case 8-1 — A 49-year-old male was abducted from his home at gunpoint, in front of a witness, and driven away in his own automobile. On the following morning forest rangers discovered the smoldering hulk of a car in a remote site but left without examining the vehicle after determining that it represented no fire hazard. Later that day, children at play reported a body in the trunk of the burned-out auto, and the sheriff's department undertook a more thorough investigation. The vehicle was identified as that of the abductee. The trunk contained a fragmented, partially carbonized and calcined human skeleton which was removed to the laboratory of the Alabama State Medical Investigator and radiographed. Dissection of some remaining soft tissue in the bony pelvis revealed a prostate, thus confirming that the victim was a male. Fragments of the skull and mandible were edentulous, as had been the owner of the car. A bullet wound in the posterior skull suggested the cause of death (Figure 8-2). The intensity of the fire had exploded the frontal sinuses (Figure 8-3). A roentgenogram of a charred fragment of the right foot and ankle revealed a talotibial fusion (Figure 8-4); the presumed decedent had

Figure 8-2   Case 8-1: gunshot exit wound in posterior skull.

Figure 8-3   Case 8-1: exploded frontal sinuses. The frontal part of the skull (above) is resting on a bed of sand (below) during the process of reconstruction of fragments.

had such an operation 15 years earlier, but the ante-mortem films had been destroyed. Consequently, only presumptive identification was possible. Finally, another search of the nooks and crannies of the automobile trunk turned up a shrunken, calcined, but intact left patella with a punched-out defect on its dorsal surface which was recognized by the radiologist as a classic, albeit uncommon, patellar lesion (Figure 8-5). At about that time films of the car owner's left knee were discovered at a nearby community hospital where he had been treated following a motor vehicle accident two years earlier (Figure 8-6). Radiographs of the isolated patella (Figure 8-7), corrected for size, could be absolutely superimposed on the patella (which also contained a classic dorsal defect) as seen on the frontal view of the knee (Figure 8-8). Thus, positive identification could be based on the precisely matching comparison of a single patella containing a lesion seen in 1% or fewer of the general adult population.[2,3]

Post-Mortem Radiography

In the ideal situation, soon after unidentified remains are brought to the morgue good police work or other information will come up with a presumed identification. Shortly

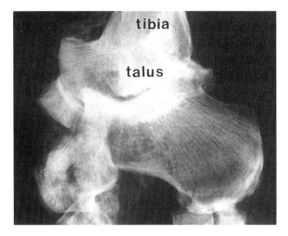

Figure 8-4   Case 8-1: this second-largest (after a portion of the pelvis) of all fragments recovered from the trunk of the car shows fusion of the joint between the talus and the distal tibia as a result of previous surgery. (Copyright ASTM, reprinted with permission.)

Figure 8-5   Photograph of the posterior surface of the left patella found in a second search of the trunk. Arrow marks the "dorsal defect". (Copyright ASTM, reprinted with permission.)

thereafter, ante-mortem roentgenograms of the presumed decedent are discovered at a nearby institution and brought to the morgue for evaluation and are found to reveal several unique anatomic features. These ante-mortem roentgenographs can be duplicated with post-mortem studies of appropriate body parts using a radiographic unit permanently housed within or convenient to the autopsy suite. Ante-mortem views can be replicated by careful positioning of the unknown remains, and positive identification can be quickly substantiated or disproved.

Unfortunately, those ideal conditions are rarely obtained.

Sometimes it is possible to retain the unidentified remains almost indefinitely in the holding vaults or drawers while awaiting ante-mortem materials to surface. In any case, the post-mortem radiographs ideally should precede the autopsy which, at the very least,

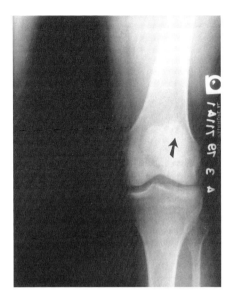

Figure 8-6   Case 8-1: frontal view of left knee of the presumed decedent obtained after an automobile accident 2 years prior to his abduction. A dorsal defect of the patella is present (arrow). (Copyright ASTM, reprinted with permission.)

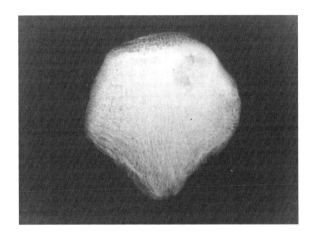

Figure 8-7   Case 8-1: roentgenogram of left patella retrieved from trunk. The dorsal defect is obvious in the upper outer quadrant. (Copyright ASTM, reprinted with permission.)

will disturb the continuity, relationship, and configuration of the skull and anterior thoracic cage.

More often, and especially in mass casualty situations, there will be pressure to process and release the body so that the opportunity for post-mortem radiography is fleeting. Since the availability of ante-mortem studies for eventual comparison is unpredictable, and since those examinations may be quite limited in scope, whole-body radiography of the remains should be undertaken. Furthermore, it is essential that standard radiographic positions or projections be employed in the post-mortem radiography in order that the resultant images can be compared with whatever ante-mortem radiographs may subsequently be discovered (see Section VIII for technical details).

Whole-body radiography takes time and requires a large number of films. In the Air India crash off the coast of Ireland, 12 to 14 large-sized films were required to examine

 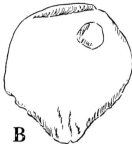

A   B

Figure 8-8   Case 8-1: tracings of patellar roentgenograms (corrected to size) from **A**: the knee x-ray, and **B**: the carbonized and calcined patella from the trunk are exactly superimposable, with identical features and configuration. (Copyright ASTM, reprinted with permission.)

each adult body. The numbers are fairly constant; in the first mass casualty situation in which radiography was used extensively, 13 films per body were required.[4] Thus there may be a temptation to take shortcuts. Furthermore, most morgues do not have the convenience of a fixed radiographic installation and radiologic capabilities are limited to mobile equipment brought into the autopsy suite or to the often erratic availability of adjacent hospital facilities.

Hospital personnel will not be eager to share mobile equipment, which is mostly used for patients in critical care units. There will be even less enthusiasm for bringing bodies or parts, often unsightly and malodorous, into patient care areas and examining rooms, especially during normal duty hours. Such arrangements may demand enormous tact, diplomacy, and negotiating skills on the part of the medical examiner and/or the forensic radiologist. Nevertheless, it is important to obtain the most complete post-mortem radiography possible, as soon as possible. An opportunity missed or postponed is unlikely to return.

Currently, more than 80% of ante-mortem radiologic examinations obtained for clinical purposes are comprised of routine x-ray examinations or roentgenograms. The remainder is made up of other techniques and modalities (Table 8-1). Catheter procedures, nuclear medicine studies, and magnetic resonance examinations collectively add up to about 9% of total examinations and, for the most part, are useless for identification by comparison. Computed tomography (CT) currently accounts for about 9% of all radiologic studies and some of those can be used for comparison with other CTs or even some conventional roentgenograms.

Of the conventional roentgenograms, almost 8% are studies of the breast (mammograms) and are useless for purposes of identification.

The breakdown of conventional roentgenographic statistics shows that more than 40% of all such examinations are chest films. Chest films show remarkable consistency of bony structure appearances over time, but faulty positioning of post-mortem films can seriously jeopardize the chance for comparative identification.

In conventional x-ray studies, the extremities account for about one-fifth of the total and are almost equally divided between upper and lower limbs. Because of their propensity for injury, congenital malformation, or degenerative change, the extremities may contain extremely useful roentgenographic features. Unfortunately, the extremities of unidentified

Table 8-1 Distribution of Radiologic Exams by Body Part and Modality

Type Exam	Body Part	Distribution %	Distribution Number of Cases
Roentgenograms	Chest	43	36
(X-rays)	Lower extremity	11	9
	Upper extremity	10	8
	Spine	8	7
	Breast (Mammogram)	8	7
	Abdomen	7	6
	Head/neck	5	4
	Pelvis/hip	4	3
	Other	4	2
	Total	100	82
Other modalities			
Nuclear medicine			4
MRI			4
Catheter procedures			1
CT	Head/neck	44	
	Abdomen	22	
	Pelvis	10	
	Thorax	9	
	Spine	9	
	Other	6	
	Total	100	9

remains often are made useless for comparative purposes because of separation and scattering, incineration, decay and decomposition, and by the activities of carnivores.

Almost 5% of clinical x-rays are of the head and neck, and the skull contains many features appropriate for comparison identification.

In our experience, the spine and pelvis are most likely to survive as useful post-mortem material and are included (one or the other or both) in about 20% of ante-mortem roentgenographic examinations. Hence, if post-mortem films *must* be limited in number, the odds would favor using them for the carefully positioned chest (including the thoracic spine and lower cervical spine) and the abdomen (to include the lumbosacral spine and pelvis). That strategy will backfire, however, in many individual cases and the foregoing statements should not be construed as an endorsement of limited post-mortem examinations.

Unfortunately, the frequency with which various body areas and parts are examined radiographically for medical purposes is not directly related to the availability of those areas or parts for radiological comparison for purposes of identification.

In Bass and Driscoll's experience with incomplete skeletons in Tennessee,[5] the skull or skull bones, femora, mandibles, and innominate bones were most commonly retrieved (Table 8-2). This may reflect durability, size, or the likelihood of chance discoverers of remains to recognize certain bones and overlook others.

In a series of 30 identifications by ante-mortem and post-mortem radiologic comparisons,[6] Murphy and co-workers found the chest most useful and the pelvis least useful (Table 8-3).

Budgets for coroners and medical examiners rarely will include the luxury of a position for a trained x-ray technologist or radiographer although this is most desirable. In many

Table 8-2 Skeletal Elements Present in 58 Fragmented Skeletons[5]

Bone	Percent
Skull or skull bones	66
Femora	48
Mandibles	41
Innominates	40
Tibias	38
Ulnas	33
Humeri	29
Fibulas	28
Scapulae	28
Clavicles	22
Radius	22
Sacrum	17
Patella	13
Sternum	12

(Copyright ASTM, reprinted with permission.)

Table 8-3 Positive Radiologic Identification by Anatomic Region[6]

Region	Number[a]	Percent
Chest	16 of 30	53
Skull	6 of 30	20
Extremities	6 of 30	20
Lumbar spine	5 of 30	17
Cervical spine	3 of 30	10
Pelvis	1 of 30	3

[a] Some bodies could be identified by comparison of more than one region.

(Copyright ASTM, reprinted with permission.)

facilities an interested assistant or diener can learn on the job to make usable images in frontal and lateral projections (see Section VIII). Sometimes a trained professional hospital or clinic radiographer will become sufficiently interested in forensic work to do it voluntarily in slack or free time, or on a part-time basis, or for periodic rewards such as travel expenses to forensic meetings. However obtained, however trained, and however compensated, the person who actually positions and exposes the roentgenograms is absolutely critical to the success of the entire endeavor. The educated, experienced, and sophisticated eye of the radiologist or other professional observer may be required to detect and interpret the subtle nuances recorded on the film,[7] but without adequate technical support that eye will be blinded.

Film Problems or Problem Films

We previously have alluded to the problem that both the ante-mortem and post-mortem radiographs available for comparison may be of suboptimal quality, and that there often is no opportunity to repeat them or obtain better examples. Dr. Bernstein's suggestions for salvaging radiographs that are overexposed or underexposed in his subsection on "Special Problems" in Chapter 5 are applicable to large films as well as to dental films. Archival films that are simply dirty often can be cleaned with Kodak® film cleaner or by running them through the terminal wash and dry sections of an automatic film processor.

Special attention is called to the paper by Fitzpatrick et al. who were able to overcome the problems of seemingly inadequate comparison films by utilization of selected adjunctive techniques.[8] These include optical (slide projection) and photographic enlargement, photographic contrast enhancement, digitization, and digitization with computer enhancement (Figure 8-9).

Sometimes, injudicious marking of processed radiographs with pens or markers will obscure significant details or, more often, seriously impair the radiographs for reproduction or use as an exhibit or illustration. Sometimes the offending marks can be removed by gentle wiping with a lintless cloth or soft paper after spraying the area with hairspray. (We have found Aqua Net® one of the better and cheaper products for this purpose.)

Identification by Comparison of Soft Tissues

Soft tissues (nonskeletal tissues not ordinarily radiopaque) may play a role in comparative identification with radiological techniques. Murphy[6] found calcifications in the chest helpful or specific in several cases (Table 8-4). Vascular calcifications have been matched on occasion. Calcified scars or posttraumatic calcifications/ossifications (e.g., post-traumatic myositis ossificans) can be distinctive. Certain physiological calcifications may serve for identification; Messmer found a calcified falx cerebri useful in one case (personal communication).

There is increasing use of opaque clips, sutures, stents, filters, and connectors in surgical procedures throughout the body, and these may be useful for future identification.

Inclusions of foreign material in soft tissues (bullets, shrapnel, glass, gravel, etc.) may have unique appearances and locations.

Enteric accretions (gallstones,[9] kidney stones, bladder stones, phleboliths, parasitic encrustations, etc.) can be used for identification.

Identification by Comparison of Skeletal Tissues

Except for teeth, bones are the most durable of body tissues and are the basis for the overwhelming majority of nondental radiological identification. Fortunately for us, bone also is a rather dependable tissue. It is more consistent than most other organs and tissues in its response to all of the insults that befall it — growth and development, disease, trauma, nutritional and metabolic conditions, aging (degeneration), and thermal injury. Consequently, the skeleton also is a good historian.

> "... bones make good witnesses — although they speak softly, they never lie and they never forget. Each bone has its own tale to tell about the past life and death of the person whose living flesh once clothed it. Like people, some bones impart their secrets more readily than others; some are laconic; others are positively garrulous."

> —*Clyde Collins Snow and John Fitzpatrick*[10]

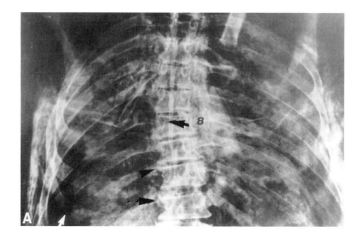

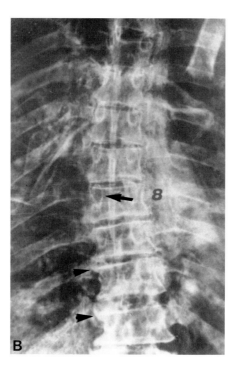

Figure 8-9   **A**: a post-mortem chest roentgenogram shows several features for a potential match including an unusual pedicle on T-8 vertebra (arrow), spurring of vertebral body margins (arrowheads), and costal cartilage ossification (white arrow). **B**: close-up shows some of the above features with better definition. The body was buried. Two years later, **C**, an ante-mortem chest radiograph was found. The bony features could not be seen on this radiograph. **D** and **E** show digitized and computer-enhanced versions of the ante-mortem chest radiograph which bring out the matching features. **F**: diagrammatic analysis of enhanced T-8 pedicle shows the crescentic density of the inferior margin on the left-hand image; on the right the crescent is highlighted by edge enhancement. (Original images courtesy of Dr. John J. Fitzpatrick. Copyright ASTM, reprinted with permission.)

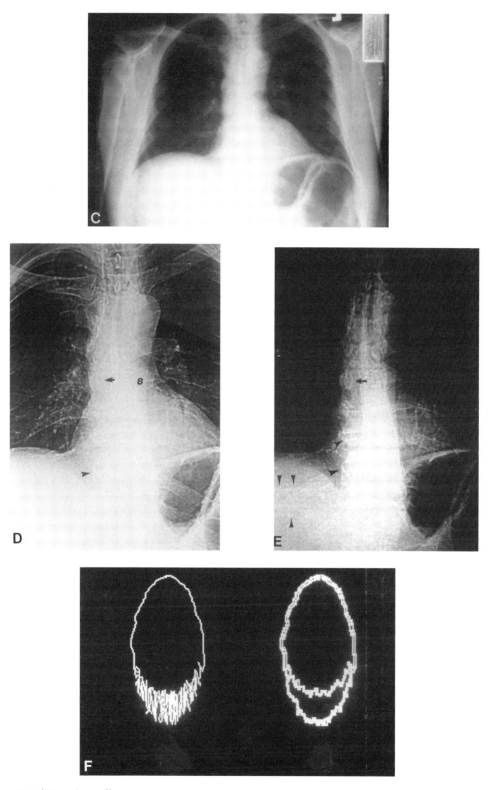

Figure 8-9 (Continued)

11	Chest calcifications
9	Normal anatomic variations
7	Evidence of surgery
5	Fractures
2	Congenital anomaly
2	Abdominal calcifications
2	Arthritis

Upon cessation of skeletal growth, the general configuration of a bone, the shape and direction of its various processes and protuberances, and the pattern of its major trabeculae and vascular structures remain relatively unchanged for a "normal" life. Trauma, destructive disease, and surgery may modify the bone substantially. The slow and insidious changes of aging and wear and tear will gradually alter the configuration of a given bone, but not to the extent that the passage of several years will produce confounding change.[11]

Bones that are burned in the flesh at temperatures of 800°C or less (ordinary house fires) will show shrinkage of about 1% or less and may sustain cracks perpendicular to the long axis of the bone. Burned dry bones may exhibit longitudinal striae. Warping is more common in fat- and muscle-encased incinerated bones. Shrinkage increases between 800°C and 1100°C (cremation temperatures) then levels off. Even at those temperatures, the bone, which will be grayish white in color and extremely fragile, will preserve configuration and internal structures sufficient to be used for comparison identification. The amount of shrinkage is negligible when compared to magnification factors affecting the ante-mortem bone encased in soft tissues.[1,12,13]

Regional Considerations

Skull

Dental Arches

When dealing with a body not clearly recognizable by surface inspection, the contents of the maxillary and mandibular arches, the teeth, are the most productive anatomic areas for individual identification, whether by direct comparison with dental records or by radiologic comparison. This is largely the province of the forensic odontologist and has been extensively covered in Chapter 5. Occasionally, radiography of the unidentified head or skull will reveal dental findings of such characteristic individuality that the expertise of the dentist is not required (Figures 8-10 and 8-11).

Paranasal Sinuses

Culbert and Law[14] are credited with the first identification of human remains by radiological comparison. Culbert had operated for mastoiditis upon a man who, years later, disappeared in the Indus River in India. A skeleton was retrieved from the river two years after the disappearance, and Drs. Culbert and Law were able to confirm the identity by

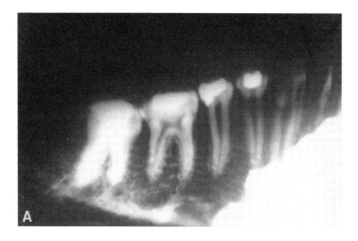

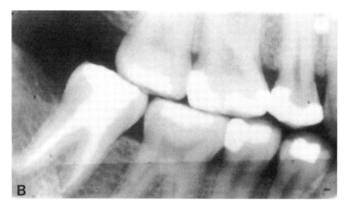

Figure 8-10   **A**: post-mortem radiograph of mandibular fragment compared with **B**: ante-mortem bitewing radiograph. The root canal work and restorations are identical.

comparison of ante-mortem and post-mortem roentgenograms of the man's frontal sinuses and his postoperative mastoid processes. Since their publication in 1927, the value of frontal sinus patterns, especially, has become widely known.

Pneumatization of the maxillary and ethmoid sinuses progresses from birth through the end of the second decade of life. The frontal sinuses develop as extensions of the superior ethmoid group and their appearance may vary from six months to, more commonly, two years of age. Frontal sinus development may be unilateral and is totally absent in about 5% of the population. The sphenoid sinus develops last by extension from the posterior ethmoid cells, and there is considerable variation in time of appearance and ultimate size and configuration in the sphenoid bone.

The frontal sinuses, especially, develop unique scalloped margins with internal septae and pseudoseptae. The frontal sinuses are as unique to the individual as his fingerprints.[15] Even identical twins will have different frontal sinus patterns.[16] The other paranasal sinuses also have individual variations but they are less striking and more difficult to compare.

Comparison of frontal sinus configuration is easy on frontal view radiographs of the skull, even with considerable variations in angulation or projection between two radiographs (Figure 8-12). Elaborate systems of mensuration and classification of the sinuses

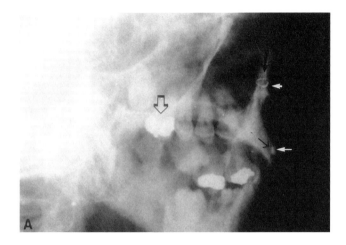

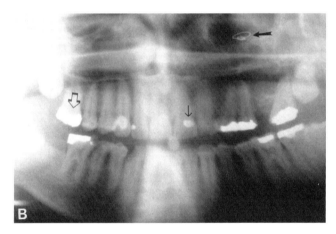

Figure 8-11   **A**: post-mortem facial roentgenogram shows unique restorations and a wire suture in the orbital floor. **B**: ante-mortem panoramic dental examination shows identical findings.

have been proposed,[17,18] particularly by the anthropologists, but such elaboration is not really required. Simple "eyeball" comparison will suffice in virtually every case.

Once paranasal sinus growth has stopped, the appearance will remain relatively stable throughout life. The generalized osteoporosis or absorption of bone that occurs with aging may enlarge the sinuses slightly but will not substantially change the overall pattern. Trauma, tumor, destructive disease, and acromegaly can change the size and configuration of the sinuses substantially. Fortunately, except for trauma, those instances are quite uncommon.

Unfortunately, the frontal sinuses are susceptible to severe fracturing and distortion in automobile and aircraft crashes, and, as previously noted, sinuses may explode in conditions of extreme sudden heat.

Even fragments of frontal sinuses may contain such distinctive patterns that comparative identification is possible[19] (Figure 8-13).

Mastoids

The air cell development in the mastoid processes, the squamous portion of the temporal bone, and the petrous ridges may show characteristic individuality which can lead to

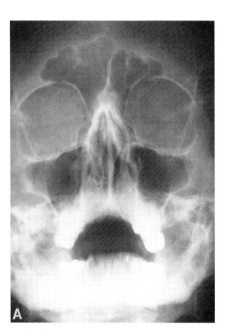 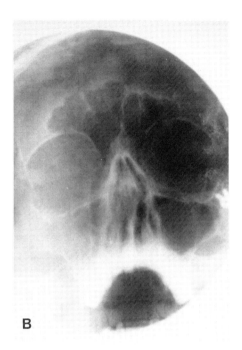

Figure 8-12 **A** and **B**: Water's view of the paranasal sinuses taken 15 years apart and with slight variations in positioning and tube angulation. Still, there is no doubt that the septation and lobulation of the frontal sinuses are identical.

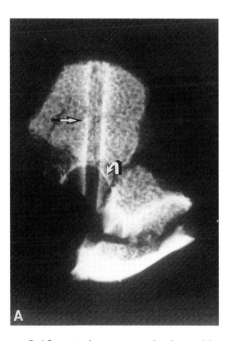 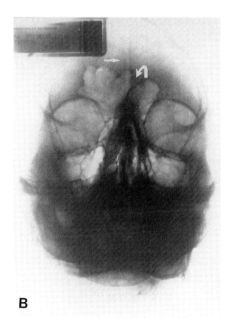

Figure 8-13 **A**: fragments of a frontal bone found at a cremation site in Guatemala. **B**: antemortem Water's view of the skull belonging to a journalist who disappeared in Guatemala four years earlier. A deep sulcus in the frontal crest and the lobulation of the frontal sinuses establish a match. (Original images courtesy of Dr. D. W. Owsley. Copyright ASTM, reprinted with permission.)

successful radiological identification.[20,21] These areas may be seen on lateral views of the skull or cervical spine and on the Townes view of the skull (Figure 8-14). The mastoids usually are not shown in as good detail as the frontal sinuses and evaluation for identification consequently is more difficult and less often successful.

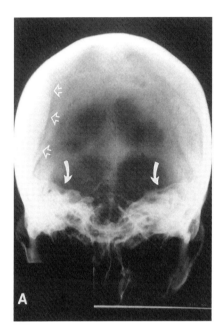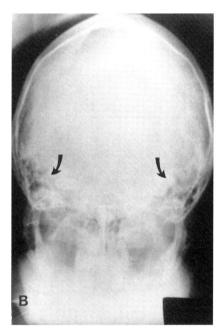

Figure 8-14   A: post-mortem and **B**: ante-mortem Townes view of the skull were submitted for possible identification. This clearly is a non-match. Note the difference in mastoid air cell development and distribution (arrows). Also, the post-mortem skull has an unusual feature, an old calcified subdural hematoma (open arrows) on the right.

Sella Tursica

Voluter[22] suggested comparison of size and configuration of the sella tursica for purposes of identification, pointing out that its protected central position in the skull base often preserved it even in the face of extreme trauma, incineration, or decomposition. Actually, Singleton[23] had anticipated Volunter by using radiological comparison of the sella tursica in victims of the *Noronic* disaster.

These major features of the skull, the *frontal sinuses, mastoids,* and *sella tursica* are equally useful in disproving a presumed identification, and this often is possible without the fine radiographic detail required for a positive identification (Figure 8-15).

Other Identifying Features in the Skull

The general configuration of the skull, protuberances such as the brow ridge and the inion, vascular grooves,[24] surgical lesions,[25] cranial sutures,[26] trauma, hyperostosis interna frontalis,[6] and disease states may prove useful in any given case of identification through comparison of skull images (Figures 8-16, 8-17, 8-18, and 8-19). The mandible may contribute features. Also, the upper segments of the cervical spine usually are included in lateral views of the skull. Note the non-match of the upper cervical segment in Figure 8-15A and B.

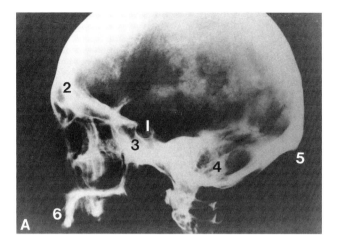

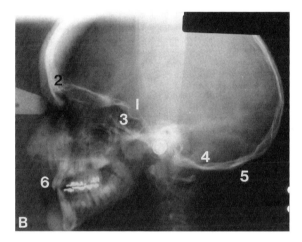

Figure 8-15   A 16-year-old girl disappeared from her home in Mississippi. She had had an orthometric skull examination a year earlier. Two years after her disappearance, skull roentgenograms from an unidentified young female body were sent for comparison. **A**: post-mortem study. **B**: ante-mortem x-ray. There is no match. Note differences in the sella tursion (1), frontal (2) and sphenoid (3) sinuses, and general configuration of the bony calvaria, brow slope, depth of posterior fossa (4), inion (5), and angle of maxillary incisors (6).

Chest

Since the chest is the area of the body most often examined radiologically, it frequently affords positive comparative radiological identification.

The pattern of costal cartilage ossification may be unique. Murphy found it most useful.[6] Martel and co-workers,[27] in a prospective study, believed they found unmistakable costal cartilage markers. However, they divided their test cases by sex and may have fallen into the same trap as Vastine et al.[28] who believed identical twins had identical costal cartilage ossification patterns. The similarities of pattern may have been sexually determined rather than individually unique. Ossification of costal cartilage is a dynamic progressive process and attempts to match patterns over time lapses are fraught with difficulty.

Calcification within the lungs or pleura may be shape, size, and/or location specific but tend to be displaced on post-mortem radiographs as the lung collapses.

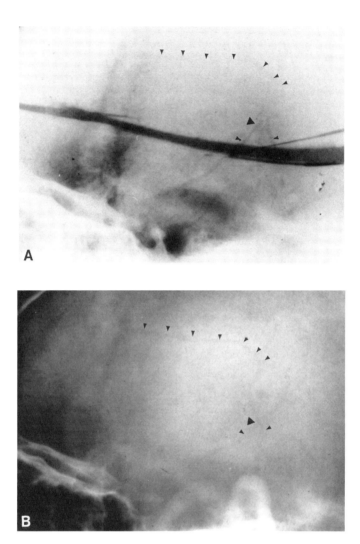

Figure 8-16   This body lay in the morgue for two years before ante-mortem films from a likely "missing person" became available. **A**: a close-up lateral view of the post-mortem, post-autopsy skull could be matched with **B**: the ante-mortem study, by comparing vascular grooves. This person also had an unusual "pig-tail" wire suture in his jaw as an additional matching feature. **C**: post-mortem, **D**: ante-mortem.

Anomalies, diseases, tumors, and traumatic lesions of the ribs may contribute to identifying matches.

Sternal configuration on lateral views has contributed to identification of unknown remains in at least two cases.[29,30] A cross-table lateral view of the body is required to compare with an ante-mortem lateral view of the chest (see Chapter 23).

Scapular configuration in post-mortem and ante-mortem radiographic studies allowed Ubelaker[31] to make a positive identification (Figure 8-20).

The vertebral segments of the thoracic spine and the costovertebral joints usually are obscured on chest radiographs by the heart and mediastinum, although special techniques may bring them into view.[8] However, the cervicothoracic junction of the vertebrae and upper ribs is seen fairly well on most chest radiographs and may serve for comparison

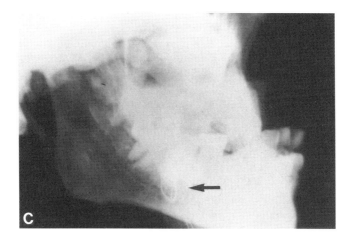

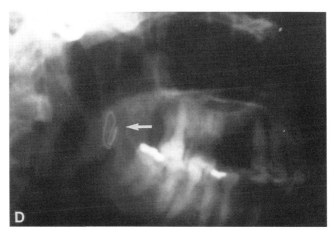

Figure 8-16 (Continued)

identification.[32,33] The positioning of patients for the ubiquitous posteroanterior view of the chest is highly standardized nationwide, and anatomic structures at the thoracic inlet and in the pectoral girdles are quite reproducible (Figures 8-21, 8-22, and 8-23). Sanders et al.[34] used a variant configuration of the medial end of a single clavicle to effect radiological identification.

   However, there is a serious recurring problem in comparing features in post-mortem and ante-mortem chest radiographs. The most common ante-mortem chest radiograph, by far, is obtained in the posteroanterior position with the patient erect or standing with the shoulders thrust forward against the film holder and the arms akimbo (Figure 8-24A). The usual post-mortem chest radiograph is obtained with the body supine, the shoulders back, and the arms alongside the body (Figure 8-24B). The result is a quite different, often incomparable, distortion and projection of the cervicothoracic bony structures and the bony components of the pectoral girdle (see Chapter 23 for methods of avoiding this problem). If the ante-mortem chest examination was performed with the patient supine, the problem is obviated, of course. When ante-mortem radiographs are not available before disposal or disposition of the body, it is wise to get post-mortem radiographs comparable to both erect posteroantero and supine anteroposterior views.

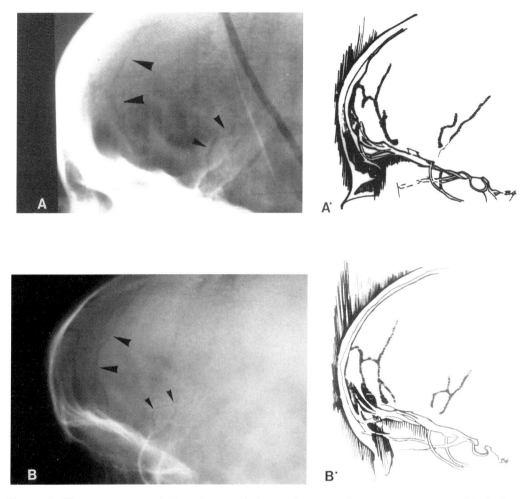

Figure 8-17   Messmer and Fierro's case [24] shows that vascular grooves, once established in the skull, undergo little change with growth and development. **A**: skull radiograph of decomposed remains of a 13-year-old female found 3 months after her disappearance. **B**: skull radiographs from an ante-mortem examination at age six. The pattern of vascular grooves (arrowheads) is identical. **A**[1] and **B**[1]: tracings to assist the viewer. (From Messmer, J. M. and Fierro, A. F., *Am. J. Forensic Med. Pathol.*, 7, 159, 1986. With permission.)

Finally, the proliferation of open heart surgery presents another feature for radiological identification. Wire sutures used to close median sternotomies and vascular clips offer opportunity for ante-mortem and post-mortem matches, and in this case the ante-mortem radiographs will most often have been made with the patient supine (Figure 8-25).

Abdomen and Pelvis

The abdomen and pelvis are the components of the human body most likely to survive catastrophe sufficiently intact to be useful for radiological identification. The retroperitoneal tissues, the lumbosacral spine, protected by surrounding heavy musculature and ligaments often remains articulated and easy to position and radiograph for comparison with ante-mortem studies.[6,35, 36]

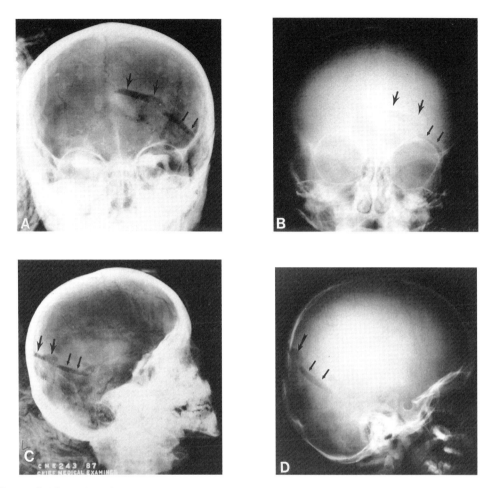

Figure 8-18 Identification of **A, C**, decomposed post-mortem remains by comparison with **B, D**, ante-mortem skull examination showing surgical defects from a lambdoid synostectomy. (From Hogge, J. P., Messmer, J. M., and Fierro, M. F., *J. Forensic Sci.*, 40, 688, 1995. Copyright ASTM, reprinted with permission.)

Since each lumbar vertebra develops from three primary and five secondary ossification centers, there is great variation in the eventual size and configuration of the individual components of each vertebra and between the different vertebra making up the spinal column (Figure 8-26). The spine also is subject to disease, trauma, tumor, and degeneration. A study of the lumbar spine in 936 healthy asymptomatic young men who were candidates for the Air Force Academy or Air Cadet training showed at least one roentgenologically identifiable abnormality in 60% of them[37] (Table 8-5). Consequently, identification by comparison of individual vertebral characteristics often is relatively simple.

Example Case 8-2 — A severely decomposed body (Figure 8-27A) was found in southern New Mexico. A chest radiograph (Figure 8-27B) revealed the probable cause of death. Law enforcement officers suggested a possible victim who had undergone an earlier GI series. Enough vertebral elements were unobscured by barium on a film from the GI series (Figure 8-27C) to permit a positive match with the post-mortem radiograph of the lumbar spine (Figure 8-27D).

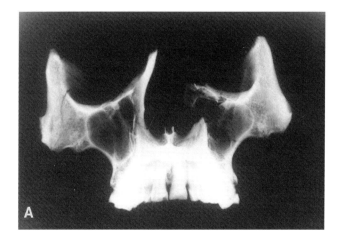

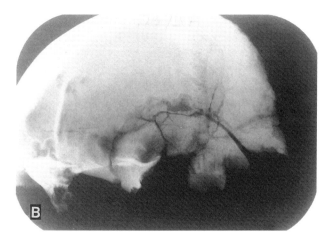

Figure 8-19   Professor Walter Bessler of Winterthur recently identified the exhumed remains of the Swiss hero, Jürg Jenatsch, from skull fragments shown **A**: in frontal view, and **B**: in slightly oblique lateral view with the frontal bone to the left. Jenatsch had freed the canton of Graubünder from foreign occupation. He was killed on 24 January, 1639 by the stroke of an axe (perhaps wielded by a former lover). The left side of the cranial vault and left orbit are destroyed and fissures are visible in both maxillary regions and the right zygoma. This led Professor Bessler to assume that Janatsch either received a blow to the left temporal region, then fell on his face, or was struck twice, the second blow to the left orbital region. (Original images courtesy Professor Dr. Walter Bessler, Winterthur, Switzerland, 1997.)

The pelvis also is an osseous survivor with many distinctive features for matching.[6,33] Figure 8-28 demonstrates a match on a "floater" from Elephant Butte Lake using a peculiar bony excrescence on the iliac crest. Congenital acetabular dysplasia with hip dislocation on a post-mortem roentgenogram led to identification of one case.[38]

Other Bones

Other bones have been used for radiological identification: the patella,[2] the elbow and assorted long bones in extremities,[33] and the hand and wrist.[21] (Greulich[39] studied radiographs of the hands and wrists of 70 pairs of same-sexed twins, of which 40 pairs were believed identical, and found all had individual distinguishing features.)

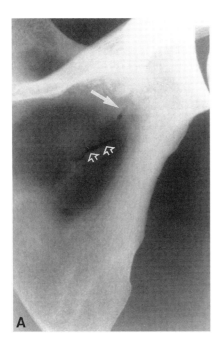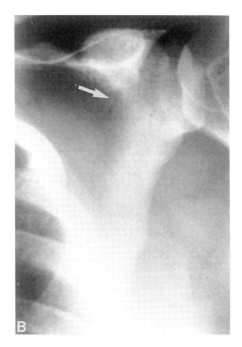

Figure 8-20 **A**: post-mortem and **B**: ante-mortem radiographs of the scapula. The morphology of the lateral border with its undulations is identical and was not matched when compared with 100 other scapulae from the Smithsonian collection. Not mentioned, but also contributing to the match, is a vascular channel (arrows) present in both images. There is a post-mortem fracture in **A** as well (open arrows). (From Ubelaker, D. H., *J. Forensic Sci.*, 35, 466, 1990. Copyright ASTM, reprinted with permission.)

Single Bone Identification

When dealing with unidentified human remains, any single bone is a potential matching identifier by radiological examination if the ante-mortem counterpart can be located, hence the recommendation that the entire body be radiographed before disposal or release.

Features leading to identification by matching radiographs or other images of individual bones can be classified as follows: (1) anomalous or unusual development; (2) disease or degeneration; (3) tumor; (4) trauma; (5) iatrogenic interference; and (6) vascular grooves and trabecular patterns.

In the happy instance when ante-mortem radiological studies of the presumed decedent are available while the body or bones are still at hand, then concentrated efforts to create exactly matching pairs of images is both practicable and rewarding. This may be done with trial and error positioning (and repositioning) of the remains or, if skeletonized, by using the shadow positioning technique of Fitzpatrick and Macaluso.[40] This involves making an underexposed duplicate of an ante-mortem film showing a promising bony feature. The outline of the skeletal part on the duplicate is used as a "mask" and placed on top of the film cassette. The x-ray tube is positioned at the same distance from the film as when the ante-mortem exposure was made. (This is usually 40 in. except for erect PA chest films at 72 in. and supine AP chest films at 36 to 40 in.) The skeletal part to be duplicated is held under the tube so that the positioning light casts the bone's shadow onto the cassette. Manual manipulation then can exactly superimpose the shadow onto the "mask" and an identical projection obtained — if there is, indeed, a match.

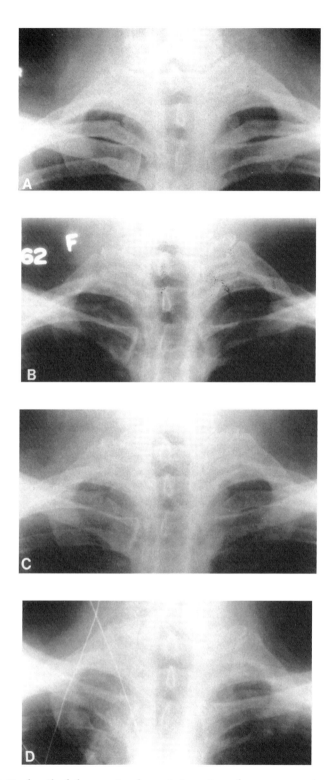

Figure 8-21 **A-D**: detail of the cervicothoracic junction of posteroanterior chest radiographs of the same person over a 50-year interval from 1944 to 1994. Note the identical configuration of the bony landmarks. (The first costochondral cartilage became ossified during this period of observation.)

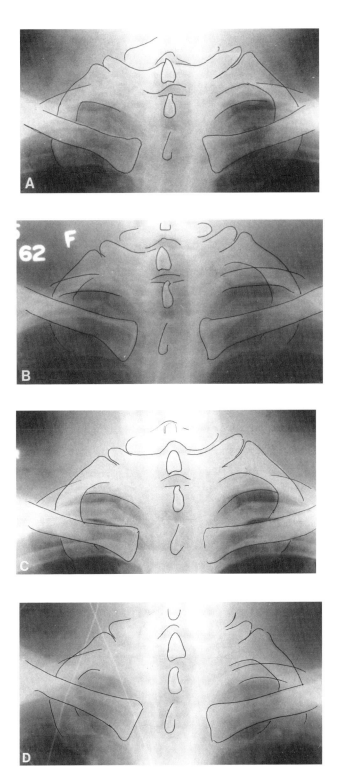

Figure 8-22 **A-D**: identical images as in Figure 8-21. Outlines of bony landmarks are traced in ink to assist inexperienced viewers in seeing similarities.

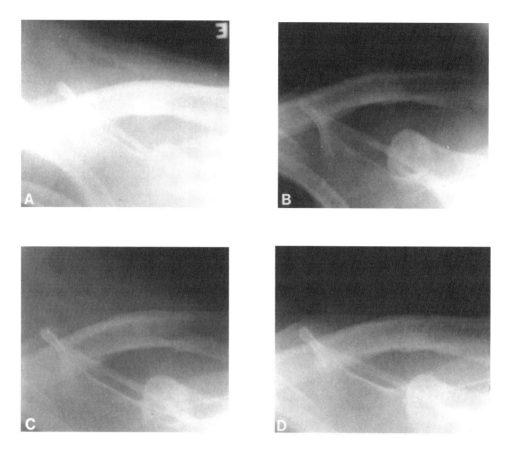

Figure 8-23 **A-D**: detail of the superior portion of the scapula and adjacent clavicle in same individual and same time interval as Figure 8-21. The matching features are obvious.

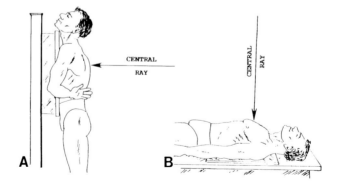

Figure 8-24 **A**: positioning for a posteroanterior erect view of the chest. **B**: positioning for an anteroposterior supine view of the chest. It is obvious that the position and projection of bony structures of the pectoral girdle and at the cervicothoracic junction will be quite different from one view to the other.

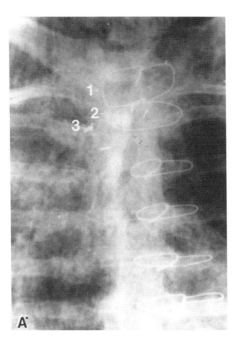
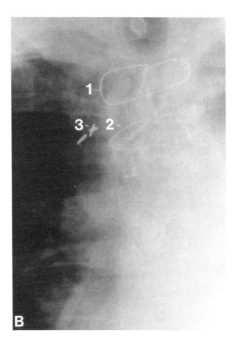

Figure 8-25   **A**: post-mortem and **B**: ante-mortem supine chest radiographs showing matching patterns of wire sutures in the sternum. (There is enough variation in angulation to shift the deeper clips so they do not match precisely. Others may move out of position with death and collapse of the thoracic viscera.)

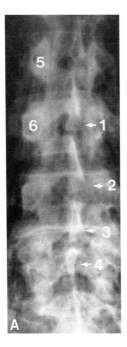
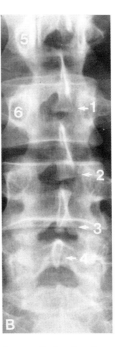

Figure 8-26   **A**: postmortem and **B**: ante-mortem frontal views of the lumbar spine. Highly individualistic configuration of the spinous processes enable an easy positive match. Other spinal elements can also be matched (see corresponding numbers).

TABLE 8-5   The "Normal" Lumbosacral Spine (936 Cases)

Entity	Number	Percent
Spina bifida occulta	334 total	35.7
Multiple	40	4.3
Previous Scheuermann's disease	194 total	20.7
With Schmorl's nodes	96	10.3
Scoliosis greater than 1 in.	5 total	0.5
Rudimentary ribs or ununited transverse process	60 total	6.4
Transitional vetebrae	108 total	11.5
Sacralization	31	3.3
Bilateral	20	2.1
Unilateral	11	1.2
Lumbarization	77	8.2
Bilateral	56	6.0
Unilateral	21	2.2
Spondylolysis	71 total	7.6
Bilateral	57	6.1
Unilateral	14	1.5
Spondylolisthesis	42 total	4.5
Limbus vertebrae	9	1.0
Hemangioma	4	0.4
None of above variations	376	40.2

(From Crow, N. E. and Brogdon, B. G., *Radiology*, 72, 97, 1959. With permission.)

Anomalous or Unusual Development

The dorsal defect of the patella (Example Case 8-1), the variations in vertebral configuration (Figure 8-26), and the rhomboid fossa of the clavicle in Sanders et al.[34] are examples of this category.

Disease or Degeneration

Judging from the literature, matching skeletal remains by lesions secondary to a disease process is rare. However degenerative changes are frequently helpful or definitive.

Example Case 8-3 — A body was found in early springtime beneath the loading dock of the feed store in a small Western town. Having frozen and thawed several times, and having suffered the depredations of a variety of varmints, the body was unrecognizable. Radiographs were obtained before burial at county expense. Finally, someone remembered that the town drunk hadn't been around much since the first blizzard of the previous winter. After some search, an ante-mortem view of the abdomen was found at the regional Veterans Administration Hospital, and matched perfectly with the post-mortem film (Figure 8-29).

Tumors

Bone tumors are relatively uncommon. In young persons, bone islands, nonossifying fibromata, or osteochondromata might sometime be found in a decedent. The tumefaction in Figure 8-28 would fit that category.

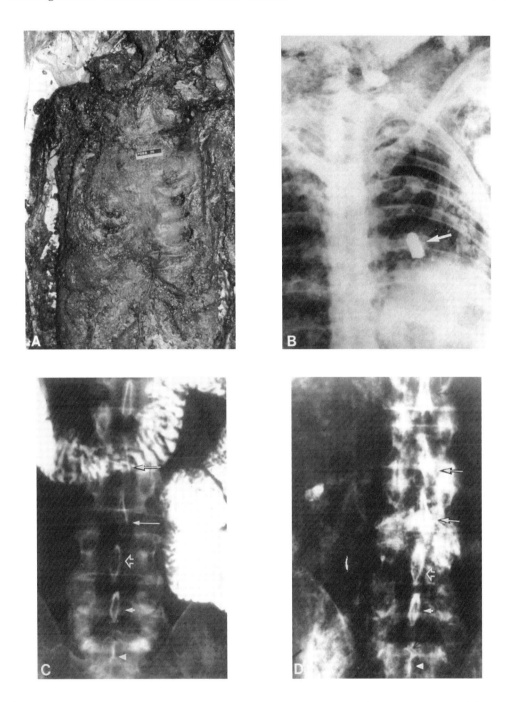

Figure 8-27 **A**: decomposed body. **B**: large caliber bullet in chest (arrow). **C**: abdominal roentgenogram from ante-mortem GI series reveals vertebral elements that can be matched with **D**: the post-mortem film. Note the two spinous processes slanted to viewer's right (arrows), the spinous process shaped like an exclamation point (open arrow), the elliptical process below (short arrow), and the vertebral bar on the first sacral segment (arrowhead).

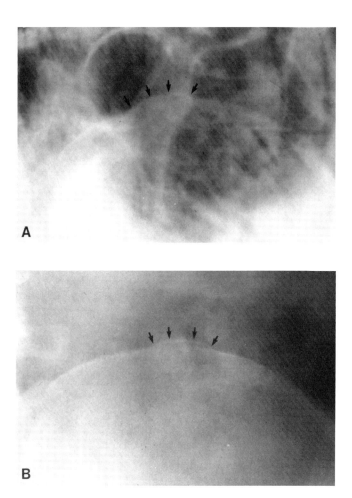

Figure 8-28   **A**: post-mortem and **B**: ante-mortem pelvic radiographs matched by an unusual bony excrescence on the left iliac crest (arrows).

Trauma

As predicted by d'Courmelles in 1898, traumatic lesions are helpful and fairly common features for identity matches.

Example Case 8-4 — A bag of bones was sent to Dr. Weston (see Preface) in hope that he could assist in the identification of this case (Figure 8-30A). The bones were those of a young adult male with no unusual features except for a healed fracture of the left clavicle with some residual deformity (Figure 8-30B). Law officers had a presumptive identification for the skeleton and found a radiograph of the left shoulder of that individual at age 14 with a fresh fracture of the left clavicle, but this only added to the *presumptive* identification. Finally, almost two years later, good investigative work turned up a chest film of the presumed decedent as an adult. High up in the corner of that film was a deformed left clavicle (Figure 8-30C). We were able to position the dried clavicle precisely enough (Figure 8-30D) to exactly reproduce the image of the clavicle on the chest film (Figure 8-30D), thus making a positive identification.

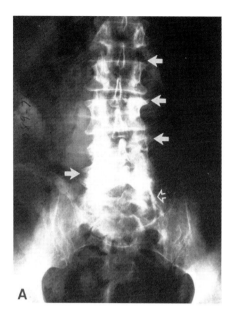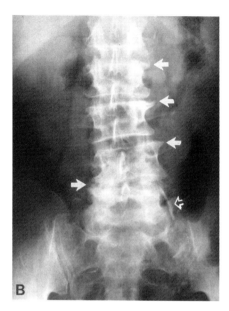

Figure 8-29   **A**: post-mortem and **B**: ante-mortem roentgenogram of the abdomen. Note the matching degenerative spurring and lipping of vertebral body margins (arrows). Additionally, the spinous processes match, and there is identical atherosclerotic calcification in the left common iliac artery (open arrows).

Iatrogenic Interference

Doctors and dentists leave their indisputable markers in some bodies and they are a godsend for identification purposes. Figures 4-2, 8-16C and D, and 8-25 are examples already shown. Figures 8-31 and 8-32 furnish additional examples of this category.

Vascular Grooves and Trabecular Pattern

Vascular foramina and grooves, and the pattern of bony trabeculae, are critical to the radiographic matching of some ante-mortem and post-mortem images, particularly if the residual skeletal material is fragmentary. Matching requires precise positioning of post-mortem specimens and excellent exposure technique. The detail required for identification purposes by direct inspection of radiographs often is difficult to reproduce in publications. We have demonstrated matching vascular patterns earlier (Figures 8-16, 8-17, and 8-20).

Kahana and Hiss[41] have reported a system of matching bony trabecular patterns using computerized densitometric line maps or densitographs. We believe going to these lengths are rarely if ever necessary, given good radiographic technique and position coupled with educated "eyeball" comparison. We have had good experience with direct trabecular comparisons, as has Murphy[6,33] and others.[21,27,34]

Example Case 8-5 — Skeletonized human remains were found in coastal wetlands. The skull was missing. The ends of the long bones were mostly destroyed. An innominate bone (hemipelvis) was the largest intact bone. The remains were identified as those of a young adult female. The Air Force had out a Missing Person report on a similar person. The usual pre-induction chest film had somehow been omitted, but a radiograph of the pelvis had been obtained during a bout of pelvic inflammatory disease. The innominate bone was

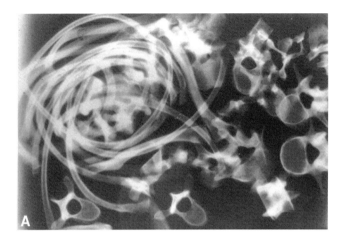

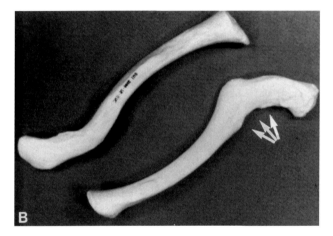

Figure 8-30   **A**: dried skeletal remains of a young adult male. **B**: slight deformity of the left clavicle from an old healed fracture of the lateral third. **C**: close-up of left clavicle in corner of ante-mortem chest radiograph. Note the irregular configuration and altered trabecular pattern related to the old healed fracture. **D**: with careful positioning of the dried clavicle a radiograph, **E**: reproduces the findings seen in the clavicle on the chest radiograph.

meticulously positioned to match the ante-mortem image and a perfect match of contour, vascular (nutrient) groove, and trabecular pattern was obtained (Figure 8-33).

Because of its mass, the innominate bone frequently escapes destruction and has many identifiable features. Moser and Wagner[42] have emphasized the importance of the nutrient canal as a forensic marker and describe three patterns: parallel (as in Case 8-5 above), V-shaped, and Y-shaped. The supra-acetabular, suprapubic portion of the innominate shows configurational variability and is rich with coarse trabecular patterns.

Example Case 8-6 — An almost totally skeletonized female body was retrieved from a pond near a home whose occupant had been missing for some months. The only ante-mortem radiograph of the missing woman was a pelvimetry study during an earlier pregnancy. A carefully positioned image of the right innominate bone exactly matched the counterpart structures on the pelvimetry study in both configuration and trabecular pattern (Figure 8-34).

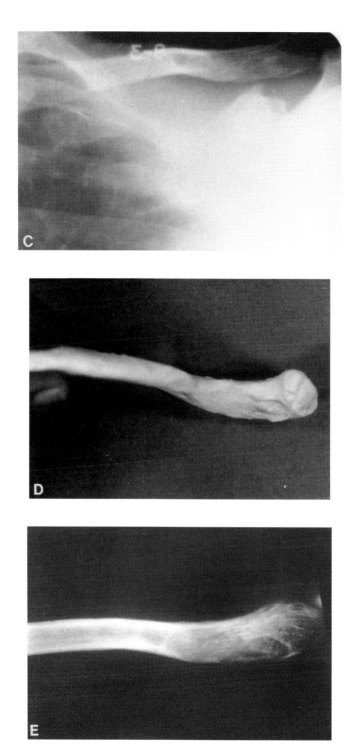

Figure 8-30 (Continued)

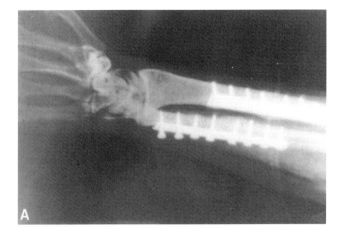

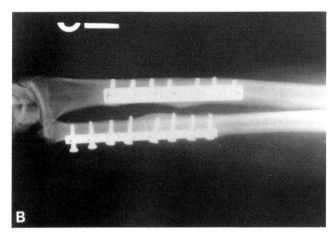

Figure 8-31   **A**: post-mortem and **B**: ante-mortem roentgenograms of the forearm of a air crash victim with "plate and screws" fixation devices in place.

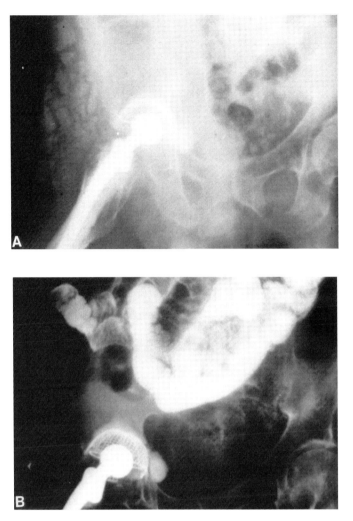

Figure 8-32   **A**: post-mortem and **B**: ante-mortem roentgenograms of an air crash victim who had undergone hip replacement surgery.

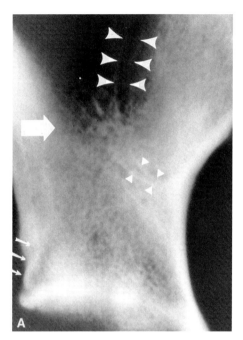 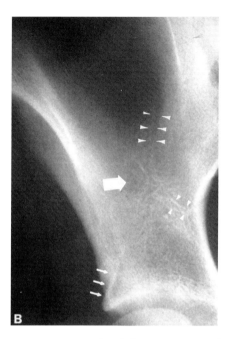

Figure 8-33   **A**: slightly enlarged detail of post-mortem x-ray study of the innominate bone. **B**: detail from ante-mortem pelvic radiograph. There are many matching features: general configuration, large vascular or nutrient groove (arrowheads), linear trabecular pattern (triangles), coarse trabecular pattern (large arrows), and focal contour feature (small arrows).

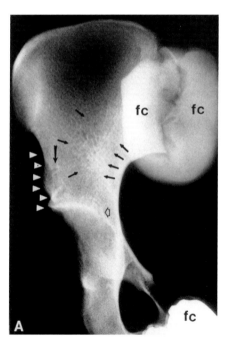 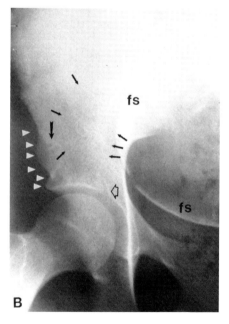

Figure 8-34   **A**: roentgenogram of innominate bone. **B**: detail of innominate bone included in earlier pelvimetry of the presumed decedent. There are matches in configuration (triangles), an acetabular notch (open arrow), and trabecular pattern (arrow); "fc" = florist's clay supports; "fs" = fetal skull.

References

1. Edlund, J. F., Some general considerations in the use of diagnostic imaging in forensic medicine, *Legal Medicine with Special Reference to Diagnostic Imaging*, James, A. E., Ed., Urban & Schwarzenberg, Baltimore, 1980, p. 244.

2. Riddick, L., Brogdon, B.G., Laswell-Hoff, J., and Delmar, B., Radiographic identification of charred human remains through use of the dorsal defect of the patella, *J. Forensic Sci.*, 28, 263, 1983.

3. Johnson, J. T. and Brogdon, B. G., Dorsal defect of the patella: incidence and distribution, *Am. J. Roentgenol.*,139, 339, 1982.

4. Brown, T. C., Delaney, R. J., and Robinson, W. L., Medical identification in the "Noronic" disaster, *J. Am. Med. Assoc.*, 148, 621, 1952.

5. Bass, W. M. and Driscoll, P. A., Summary of skeletal identification in Tennessee, 1971-1981, *J. Forensic Sci.*, 28, 159, 1983.

6. Murphy, W. A., Spruill, F. G., and Gantner, G. E., Radiologic identification of unknown human remains, *J. Forensic Sci.*, 25, 727, 1980.

7. Hogge, J. P., Messmer, J. M., and Quynh, N. D., Radiographic identification of unknown human remains and interpret experience level, *J. Forensic Sci.*, 39, 373, 1994.

8. Fitzpatrick, J. J., Shook, D. R., Kaufman, B. L., Wu, S.-J., Kirschner, R. J., MacMahon, H., Levine, K. J., Maples, W., and Charletta, D., Optical and digital techniques for enhancing radiographic anatomy for identification of human remains, *J. Forensic Sci.*, 41, 947, 1996.

9. Nye, P. J., Tytle, T. L., Jarman, R. N., and Eaton, B. G., The role of radiology in the Oklahoma City bombing, *Radiology*, 200, 541, 1996.

10. Snow, C. C. and Fitzpatrick, J., Human osteological remains from the Battle of the Little Big Horn, in *Archaeological Perspectives on the Battle of the Little Big Horn*, Scott, D., Ed., University of Oklahoma Press, Norman, OK, 1989, 243.

11. Sauer, N. J., Brantley, R. E., and Barondess, D. A., The effects of aging on the comparability of ante-mortem and post-mortem radiograph, *J. Forensic Sci.*, 33, 1223, 1988.

12. Holland, T. D., Use of the cranial base in the identification of fire victims, *J. Forensic Sci.*, 34, 458, 1989.

13. Kennedy, K. A. R., The wrong urn: commingling of remains in mortuary practice, *J. Forensic Sci.*, 41, 689, 1996.

14. Culbert, W. L. and Law, F. M., Identification by comparison of roentgenogram of nasal accessory sinuses and mastoid processes, *J. Am. Med. Assoc.*, 98, 1634, 1927.

15. Ubelaker, D. H., Positive identification from radiograph comparison of frontal sinus patterns, in *Human Identification*, Rathbun, T. A. and Buikstra, J., Eds., Charles C Thomas, Springfield, IL, 1984, chap. 29.

16. Asherson, N., *Identification by Frontal Sinus Prints*, H. K. Lewis, London, 1965.

17. Yoshino, M., Miyaraka, S., Sato, H., and Seta, B., Classification system of frontal sinus patterns by radiography. Its application to identification of unknown skeletal remains, *Forensic Sci. Int.*, 34, 289, 1987.

18. Krogman, W. M. and Iscan, M. Y., *The Human Skeleton in Forensic Medicine*, 2nd ed., Charles C Thomas, Springfield, IL, 1986, chap. 12.

19. Owsley, D. W., Identification of the fragmentary, burned remains of two U.S. journalists seven years after their disappearance in Guatemala, *J. Forensic Sci.*, 38, 1372, 1993.

20. Rhine, S., Radiographic identification by mastoid sinus and arterial pattern, *J. Forensic Sci.*, 36, 272, 1991.

21. Adkins, L. and Potsaid, M. S., Roentgenographic identification of human remains, *J. Am. Med. Assoc.*, 240, 2307, 1978.

22. Voluter, G., The "V" test, *Radiol. Clin.*, 28, 1, 1959.

23. Singleton, A. C., Roentgenological identification of victims of "Noronic" disaster, *Am. J. Roentgenol.*, 66, 375, 1951.

24. Messmer, J. M. and Fierro, A. F., Personal identification by radiographic comparison of vascular groove patterns of the calvarium, *Am. J. Forensic Med. Pathol.*, 7, 159, 1986.

25. Hogge, J. P., Messmer, J. M., and Fierro, M. F., Positive identification by postsurgical defects from unilateral lambdoid synostectomy: a case report, *J. Forensic Sci.*, 40, 688, 1995.

26. Sekharan, F. C., Identification of skull from its suture pattern, *Forensic Sci. Int.*, 27, 205, 1985.

27. Martel, W., Wicks, J. D., and Hendrix, R. C., The accuracy of radiological identification of humans using skeletal landmarks: a contribution to forensic pathology, *Radiology*, 124, 681, 1977.

28. Vastine, J. H., Vastine, M. E., and Orango, O., Genetic influence on osseous development with particular reference to the disposition of calcium in the costal cartilages, *Am. J. Roentgenol.*, 59, 213, 1948.

29. Tsunenari, S., Uchimura, Y., Yonemitsu, K., and Oshiro, S., Unusual personal identification with characteristic features in chest roentgenograms, *Am. J. Forensic Sci. Pathol.*, 3, 357, 1982.

30. Rougé, D., Telmon, N., Arrue, P., Larrouy, G., and Arbus, L., Radiographic identification of human remains through deformities and anomalies of postcranial bones: a report of two cases, *J. Forensic Sci.*, 38, 997, 1993.

31. Ubelaker, D. H., Positive identification of American Indian skeletal remains from radiographic comparison, *J. Forensic Sci.*, 35, 466, 1990.

32. Hyma, B. A. and Rao, V. J., Evaluation and identification of dismembered human remains, *Am. J. Forensic Med. Pathol.*, 12, 1991.

33. Murphy, W. A. and Gantner, G. E., Radiologic examination of anatomic parts and skeletonized remains, *J. Forensic Sci.*, 27, 9, 1982.

34. Sanders, I., Woesner, M. E., Ferguson, R. A., and Noguchi, T. T., A new application of forensic radiology: identification of deceased from a single clavicle, *Am. J. Roentgenol.*, 115, 619, 1972.

35. Owsley, D. W. and Mann, R. W., Positive personal identity of skeletonized remains using abdominal and pelvic radiographs, *J. Forensic Sci.*, 37, 332, 1992.

36. Ikeda, N., Umetsu, K., Harada, A., and Tsuneo, T., Radiological identification of skeletal remains: a case report, *Jpn. J. Legal Med.*, 41, 270, 1987.

37. Crow, N. E. and Brogdon, B. G., The "normal" lumbosacral spine, *Radiology*, 72, 97, 1959.

38. Varga, M. and Takács, P., Radiographic personal identification with characteristic feature in the hip joint, *Am. J. Forensic Med. Pathol.*, 12, 328, 1991.

39. Greulich, W. W., Skeletal features visible on the roentgenogram of the hand and wrist which can be used for establishing individual identification, *Am. J. Roentgenol.*, 83, 756, 1960.

40. Fitzpatrick, J. J. and Macaluso, J., Shadow positioning technique: a method for post-mortem identification, *J. Forensic Sci.*, 30, 1226, 1985.

41. Kahana, T. and Hiss, J., Positive identification by means of trabecular bone pattern comparison, *J. Forensic Sci.*, 39, 1325, 1994.

42. Moser, R. P., Jr. and Wagner, G. N., Nutrient groove of the ilium, a subtle but important forensic marker in the identification of victims of severe trauma, *Skeletal Radiol.*, 19, 15, 1990.

Radiology in Mass Casualty Situations

9

JOEL E. LICHTENSTEIN, M.D.

Contents

Introduction

Disasters of many kinds require processing and identification of multiple victims. Railroad and aircraft accidents, unfortunately, are common and come to mind immediately. Natural disasters such as earthquakes, floods, and hurricanes are recurrent problems. Collapse or fire in high-occupancy buildings such as hotels and factories provide other examples, such as the 1948 dockside explosion of fertilizer ships in Texas City, TX with 561 fatalities; the nuclear power plant accident at Chernobyl in the Ukraine in 1986; and the 1987 toxic chemical release at Bhopal in India, causing approximately 3000 deaths. The April 1955 bombing of the Federal Building in Oklahoma City is a recent example in which radiologists played a significant role.[1-3]

Mass casualties, by their nature, tend to involve unexpected emergencies. They are stressful situations in which even those with little prior interest or experience may be called upon to help. Radiology can be enormously helpful in the task of identifying victims. In an emergency, general radiologists may be asked to aid in a multidisciplinary team, usually headed by a forensic specialist. The basic principles of radiographic identification are the same as those applied to individual victims, but the circumstances and conditions are generally much different. Improvisation by inexperienced workers has usually led to the somewhat painful evolution of remarkably similar procedures and principles even in seemingly different circumstances. Hopefully, a recounting of the lessons learned from past events will provide a useful starting point for those called upon in the future and will minimize the need to keep "reinventing the wheel".

The most extensive experience to date is that gleaned by government agencies and is based largely on investigations of aviation accidents. The lessons learned, however, are applied readily to other mass disasters, as well as to smaller-scale events. The former Aviation Pathology Department (now the Armed Forces Medical Examiner) at the Armed Forces Institute of Pathology (AFIP) in Washington, D.C., aids in the investigation of all

U.S. military aviation fatalities and is a consultant to the National Transportation Safety Board. As part of a joint committee which coordinates all aviation pathology in the U.S., Canada, and the U.K., representative are participants or observers in most mass casualty aircraft accident investigations. Full-body radiography of victims is a routine part of the investigation of U.S. military aviation fatalities.

Identification of victims of mass casualties is important for a variety of reasons, some of which may not be immediately obvious. Usually it will be known that certain parties are among the victims of an event, but the degree of confusion as to precisely who is, or is not, included is often surprising. Passenger manifests and occupancy lists are notoriously inaccurate. Even in a closed population, where the names of all the victims are thought to be known, it is important to provide positive identification of individual remains if possible. Humanitarian and psychological motives drive efforts to release remains to grieving relatives rapidly, but with the assurance of accurate identification.[4,5] Legal and insurance requirements for accurate identification are clear. The scientific importance of accurate individual identification may be less obvious, but is vital as a source of data for safety engineering and accident prevention.

History

The first use of x-rays for the identification of multiple casualties was in the 1949 fire aboard the Great Lakes liner *Noronic* in Toronto, Canada.[6,7] Survey radiographs were obtained on 79 of 119 fatalities, and ante-mortem radiographs were obtained for 35 of these. Many additional radiographs were obtained as needed for comparison, and eventually 24 cases were positively identified by radiology alone (Figures 9-1 and 9-2). In many other cases x-rays were helpful in supporting or excluding identifications suggested by other techniques.

Figure 9-1   Arthur C. Singleton, M.D., 1900-1968. Dr. Singleton was a prominent Canadian radiologist who was Professor and Head of the Department of Radiology at the University of Toronto, and Past President of both the Canadian Association of Radiologists and the American College of Radiology. The Attorney General of Ontario asked him to conduct roentgenological examinations of the victims of the *Noronic* disaster in an attempt to assist in identification. Thus, Dr. Singleton became the father of mass casualty radiography. (From *Am. J. Roentgenol.*, 105, 1969. With permission.)

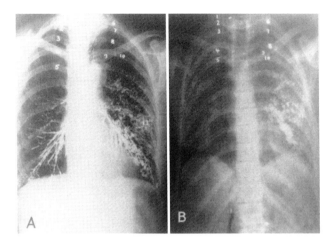

Figure 9-2   Perhaps the easiest of Dr. Singleton's identifications was the patient who had undergone a bronchogram, a procedure in which a contrast medium is instilled into the bronchial tree.[6] The opaque shadows in the lung are seen clearly on both **A**: ante-mortem and **B**: post-mortem radiographs. There were additional matching bony points. (From Singleton, A. C., *Am. J. Roentgenol.*, 66, 375, 1951. With permission..)

The largest application of radiology in a mass casualty involved the March 1977 crash of two 747 jumbo jets in the Canary Islands, resulting in 576 fatalities. An American plane on the ground was struck by a Dutch aircraft taking off. The majority of the 326 American victims were partially cremated, but there was relatively little fragmentation or commingling of remains. A team from the Armed Forces Institute of Pathology (AFIP) investigated the bodies after their return to a mortuary at Dover Air Force Base, Delaware. This government mortuary serves the eastern part of the U.S. as well as all of Europe and the Middle East. All remains were radiographed during initial processing and selected bodies later were studied further as required by the identification process.[8-10] Radiology provided the source of positive identification in 25 cases.

The 1979 crash of a wide-body jet at O'Hare Airport in Chicago resulted in 274 fatalities with more severe fragmentation. Similar techniques were employed, but a single radiologist, John J. Fitzpatrick, M.D., was called in relatively late in the investigation when 50 victims remained to be identified. Working mostly after hours and on weekends in addition to his normal duties on the teaching faculty at Cook County Medical Center, he was able to make 20 additional identifications.[10,11] This identification effort saw one of the first applications of digital computers to facilitate the tedious sorting and processing of massive amounts of ante- and post-mortem data.

A team from the AFIP also investigated the more than 900 victims of the November 1978 Jonestown, Guyana tragedy, although radiology played a relatively minor role.

A similar AFIP team identified all 256 victims of a military plane crash in Gander, Newfoundland in 1985, at which time the radiology facilities at Dover were expanded and upgraded.[12]

On June 23, 1985, Air India flight 162 (a Boeing 747) disintegrated at 31,000 feet as the result of a bomb explosion. There were 329 passengers aboard. Many were ejected from the aircraft, and 131 bodies were recovered from the sea off the coast of Cork, Ireland. The bodies were taken to the Cork Regional Hospital, a modern university teaching facility with 600 beds and an up-to-date full-service Department of Radiology. Total body radiography was carried out. Nearly all of the victims were Indians, most were young adults, 30 were children. Despite the massive radiological effort, all bodies were identified by nonradiological methods.[13,14]

Facilities

Mass disasters often require temporary morgues and improvised field x-ray operations. The details will depend upon the nature of the casualty and upon the number and condition of the victims. Usually it will be much more convenient to use preexisting, permanent radiology facilities in hospitals or in the medical examiner's offices, and the conventional teaching has been to try to do so whenever possible. The advantages of familiar surroundings, facilities, and personnel are difficult to overestimate. Clinical radiology departments may sometimes be used while avoiding normal patient traffic areas or by working at off-peak hours when practical. In larger-scale events, whole facilities may be commandeered.

In the 1990s the dogma regarding use of preexisting clinical facilities shifted somewhat because of public health and environmental issues. Concern over blood-borne pathogens has led to stringent regulations restricting access to disaster sites and to any material potentially containing human remains. Requirements include using isolation garments or decontamination suits and make it logistically difficult to bring remains into working clinical facilities. Such constraints may force a return to the use of field facilities and temporary morgues.

In any event, security and privacy should be major concerns. In that regard, some degree of isolation or the ability to cordon off facilities is a great advantage. Police or military personnel will be required to control the press and curious onlookers as well as grieving survivors.

The 1977 Canary Island crash provided a prototype for establishing an emergency investigative facility. A field x-ray department was set up in a warehouse area of the mortuary at Dover Air Force Base, Delaware. It was maintained for three weeks, during which all remains were radiographed. The location was chosen for its security capabilities as well as for its facilities and nearness to transportation (Figure 9-3).

Radiologists were part of a multidisciplinary team of over 130 military and federal civilian workers which included experts in fingerprinting, dental analysis, anthropology, blood chemistry, toxicology, medical photography, and personal effects investigators as well as forensic pathologists. An "assembly-line" system was established so that each group gathered whatever data were available in their discipline for each victim's body. Whenever possible, identifications were confirmed by multiple modalities. If one group, such as the FBI fingerprint team, made an apparent identification, all other modalities were cross-checked for consistency of their data. Radiological examination of all remains was an early step, so that films could be processed and reported prior to the pathologic examination which was performed near the end of the process. Thus, details which might be hidden on gross external examination, but which were revealed radiologically, could be sought and confirmed at autopsy (Figure 9-4).

When faced with an unexpected emergency, there is a tendency to adopt a "camp-out" mentality in which portable equipment and resources are assembled for use in field facilities. When morgues do not have fixed radiographic facilities, portable hospital x-ray units

Figure 9-3   **A**: the mortuary at Dover Air Force Base illustrating its obvious proximity to air transport, provision for security, and use of refrigerated vans (arrows) to temporarily augment the facility for preserving remains. Notice proximity to the runaway in the background. **B**: refrigerated vans are essential for storing remains at sites remote from adequate morgue facilities. Here they are used to store remains outside a hanger being used as temporary morgue during an aircraft investigation at O'Hare International Airport, Chicago.

with grid cassettes are commonly used. In an emergency, there is a temptation to take such units into the field (Figure 9-5). However, these machines have a limited working time on battery power and then must be recharged. They lack the power and the motorized scatter-reduction grids of fixed units, making it difficult to achieve consistent film quality. The use of grid cassettes requires careful alignment to prevent artifacts and the subject must be lifted and moved before and after each exposure.

During World War II, rugged, transportable field x-ray units were developed which could be powered from field generators or commercial power lines and which included built-in, under-table scatter-reduction grids (Figures 9-6 and 9-7). A smaller, collapsible portable unit with wheels was also produced (Figure 9-8A and B). These were still used in the early 1980s and may yet be available from military sources for emergency use. When contemplating use of unfamiliar equipment, sources of experienced technical assistance must be considered. Senior technologists or manufacturer's representatives may be most helpful.

The investigation of the Gander, Newfoundland crash used the same morgue at Dover AFB, and a similar team approach as that used for the Canary Island investigation. The

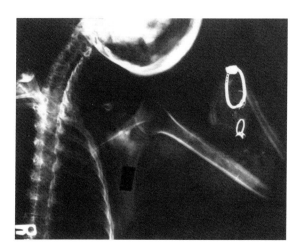

Figure 9-4   Radiograph of severely burned remains on which no personal effects were evident on external examination. A wristwatch and ring, clearly seen on the radiograph, were not found on initial autopsy. When recovered, both items were instrumental in identifying the victim, thus illustrating the value of obtaining radiographic data prior to pathologic examination. (From Lichenstein, J. E. and Madewell, J. E., *Der Radiologie*, 22, 352, 1982. With permission.)

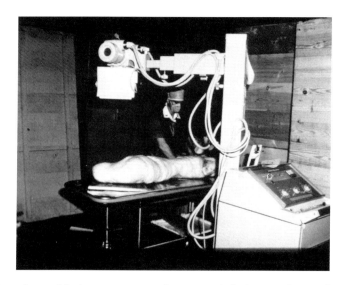

Figure 9-5   A rechargeable battery-powered x-ray unit being used to radiograph a wrapped casualty victim. A scatter-reduction grid cassette is positioned beneath the body and carefully aligned with the beam center to avoid artifacts. The body must be lifted and the cassette repositioned for each exposure. (From Lichenstein, J. E., Madewell, J. E., McKeekin, R. R., Feigin, D. S., and Wolcott, J. H., *Aviat. Space Environ. Med.*, 51, 1004, 1980. With permission.)

radiologists employed more modern, completely self-contained, air-transportable field x-ray facilities which included film processing capability, eliminating the need to transport cassettes (Figure 9-9).

The facilities at Dover were further expanded and modernized during the Persian Gulf conflict in 1992. Digital C-arm fluoroscopes (Figure 9-10) were obtained and roller-bearing conveyors were installed to ease handling of heavy remains (Figure 9-11). An innovation

Figure 9-6   A military field x-ray unit of the type developed during the Second World War is readily transported, can run off emergency generators or commercial power, and has a motorized scatter-reduction grid built into the table top, eliminating the need to move the subject between exposures. (Courtesy of Picker X-ray Corp., Highland Heights, OH.)

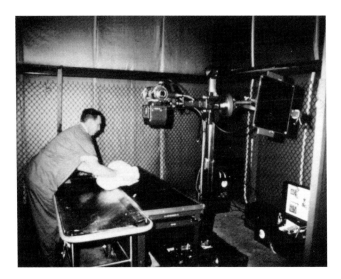

Figure 9-7   An old field x-ray unit being used to radiograph a wrapped body part during a mass casualty identification effort. Note that the machine is situated in an outside corner of a metal structure. Portable lead shields have been assembled to separate the machine from adjacent work areas. (From Lichenstein, J. E. and Madewell, J. E., *Der Radiologie*, 22, 352, 1982. With permission.)

was the installation of baggage-scanning radiographic units for screening of arriving remains. Similar units were also installed in the Persian Gulf to permit screening remains for hidden live ammunition before shipment to Dover (Figure 9-12). They are also useful to rapidly screen large quantities of debris for any potentially human material or any other specific items that might have distinctive radiographic characteristics.

Darkrooms for handling and processing film, and the associated chemical and water supply issues, are major problems in field operations. In some cases preexisting fixed

Figure 9-8   World War II/Korean War era collapsible military portable x-ray unit. **A**: equipment packed in shipping container. **B**: unit assembled and ready for use. (Courtesy Picker X-ray Corp., Highland Heights, OH.)

Figure 9-9   External view of air-transportable self-contained field x-ray facilities expanded and in use with generator cables and air-conditioning hoses.

facilities in nearby hospitals have been used to load and unload cassettes which are then transported to and from the investigation site. In such cases great care must be taken to properly label individual films and collate film packages. A compulsive, reliable member of the team should be stationed at the processing facility to assure quality control. Many of these problems are avoided if the modern military field units can be made available. If not, smaller table-top processors may be acquired for small-scale operations (Figure 9-13). Some of these can be used without permanent plumbing for water supply. Sometimes, darkrooms have been "jury-rigged" and temporary plumbing installed. In the case of the DC-10 crash at O'Hare Field a darkroom was improvised inside a cargo compartment of a wide-bodied jet.

Figure 9-10   Digital C-arm fluoroscope of the type used by the military in processing Persian Gulf War remains. Its television monitor display is useful for initial screening and images can be stored on a hard disk for later analysis or print-out in a variety of formats.

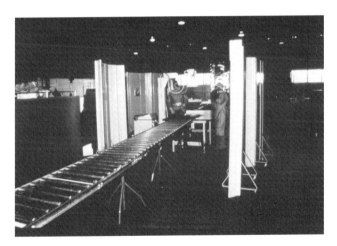

Figure 9-11   Roller-bearing conveyors arranged to aid in transporting heavy remains. Note the use of several individual x-ray shields arranged to provide radiation protection for other teams.

The radiologists should set up a temporary office at the morgue where they can supervise the radiography and interpret the films while maintaining immediate contact with other investigators. Almost any kind of viewing equipment can be used. However, the type which store films on plastic scrolls are particularly useful to permit comparison of large numbers of pre- and post-mortem images while minimizing repetitive film handling (Figure 9-14). A bright light is especially useful because technologists may have difficulty optimizing exposures and extremes of density range are likely.

It may be desirable to use standard full-size 14 × 17 in. (35.6 × 43.2 cm) film exclusively for ease of handling. Permanent metallic markers should always be used to label films at

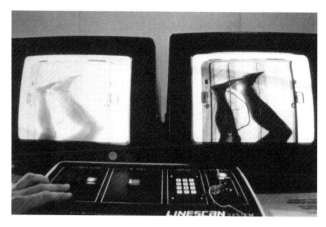

Figure 9-12   Linescan low-dose baggage scanning fluoroscope in use to screen remains still in body shipping caskets.

Figure 9-13   Example of small, self-contained, table-top film processor suitable for small-scale operations. (Courtesy of Kodak Corp., Rochester, NY.)

the time of exposure to eliminate any questions engendered by adhesive labels or hand-scrawled markings applied after processing.

Radiation exposure to team members may be minimized by placing the x-ray exposure facility physically separated from other team activities. An outside corner of a building may be used, with portable prefabricated lead shields erected around the radiographic units (Figure 9-15). In protracted operations, radiation protection specialists should be employed. Film badges should be issued to all workers in the immediate area and radiation levels monitored.

Routine methods of film reporting are usually impractical in a field environment. Arrangements for dictation, transcription, and secretarial support are likely to be cumbersome or entirely unavailable. A photocopier, however, is almost essential. A single-page, hand-written x-ray report is useful (Figure 9-16). A simple form can be duplicated and one copy attached to the outside of the x-ray package for easy reference, while another accompanies the body to permit its review by the pathologists at the time of the autopsy.

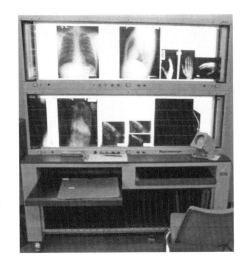

Figure 9-14 "Rotoscope" film viewer. The scroll system of mounting the films is especially useful for directly comparing large numbers of pre- and post-mortem images for potential matching. Note the bright-light (arrow) for viewing overexposed radiographs.

Figure 9-15 Portable lead-lined x-ray shield being assembled. Designed to protect an individual technologist, several of these may be combined to form a wall to provide radiation protection for nearby workers. (From Lichenstein, J. E., Madewell, J. E., McKeekin, R. R., Feigin, D. S., and Wolcott, J. H., *Aviat. Space Environ. Med.*, 51, 1004, 1980. With permission.)

Yet another copy may be included in a master folder. A simple diagram (Figure 9-17) to indicate portions of the body present or missing is helpful.

Identification

The main goal of the initial medical investigation of mass casualties is usually the rapid identification of the victims, rather than determining the mechanism of death. Classically, identification is accomplished by visual recognition, analysis of personal effects, fingerprints, and dental charting — roughly in increasing order of usefulness in increasingly difficult cases. When burning and mutilation preclude those methods, radiology may

```
┌─────────────────────────────────────────────────────────────────────────┐
│                        X-RAY REPORT              I.D. #_____           │
│                                                  NAME _____      │
│                                                                           │
│  GROSS FEATURES:                                                          │
│                                                                           │
│                                                                           │
│  APPROX. AGE:   Child                                                     │
│                                                                           │
│                 Teen                                                      │
│                 Adult                                                     │
│                     Without Degen. Changes                               │
│                     With Degen. Changes                                  │
│  BONE STRUCTURES:   Small      Large                                      │
│  POSSIBLE SEX:  Male ____    Female ____,    ? ____                       │
│  POTENTIALLY USEFUL IDENTIFYING FEATURES:                                 │
│     (1)  Foreign Bodies                                                   │
│     (2)  Personal Effects                                                 │
│     (3)  Appliances                                                       │
│     (4)  Surgical Changes                                                 │
│     (5)  Anomalies or Unique Skeletal Features                            │
│     (6)  Dental Structures:  Not Seen ____   Seen ____                    │
│     (7)  Sinuses:  Not Seen ____   Seen ____                              │
│  ADDITIONAL VIEWS SUGGESTED:                                              │
│                                                                           │
│                                                                           │
│                                                                           │
│  COMMENTS:                                                                │
└─────────────────────────────────────────────────────────────────────────┘
```

Figure 9-16   A simple one-page x-ray report form for field use when screening casualty victims. It can be duplicated and one copy attached to the outside of the x-ray package for easy reference while another accompanies the body and, if needed, yet another copy may be included in a master folder. (From Lichenstein, J. E., Madewell, J. E., McKeekin, R. R., Feigin, D. S., and Wolcott, J. H., *Aviat. Space Environ. Med.*, 51, 1004, 1980. With permission.)

become the primary (and often the only) means of positive identification. Even when teeth remain, forensic odontologists use x-rays as an extension of dental charting because radiographs provide almost unlimited points of identity. Matches may be based upon very tiny details of dental filling shapes and trabecular patterns in surrounding alveolar bone.

Ideally, all forensic autopsies should include preliminary radiographic screening. The help these data provide the pathologist may be an end in itself, but it also provides the first step in primary radiographic identification. Important clues may be demonstrated if the victims are radiographed initially with clothing and personal effects in place. Films should then be obtained in an as-near anatomic position as possible, following removal or artifacts and clothing. This provides a screening study for the pathologist by emphasizing dental and surgical artifacts, ante-mortem anatomical variations, and estimates of age, sex, and stature, as well as descriptions of observed personal effects and foreign bodies. Victims successfully identified by other means (e.g., dental anatomy, fingerprints, etc.) may receive no further radiographic investigation except to check for inconsistencies of data between the various techniques. Those bodies not identified by other means may then be reexamined in additional projections or by using more elaborate techniques for comparison and matching with available ante-mortem films (Figure 9-18).

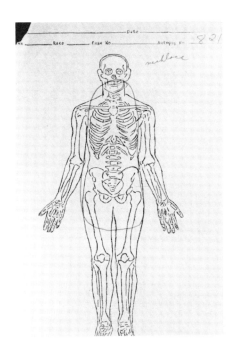

Figure 9-17   Another simple diagram to indicate the portions of a body present or absent. It may be used separately or included upon a single-sheet report form.

Sometimes, surgical changes, effects of old injury, or anomalies demonstrated by the preliminary radiographic data may be specific enough for identification based upon history alone. However, when dealing with many victims, the *sine qua non* is the availability of ante-mortem radiographs for direct comparison. In addition to physicians and dentists, local medical societies, employers, and practitioners such as chiropractors and podiatrists should be contacted as potential sources of ante-mortem x-rays.

The number of exactly matching features required for a positive identification depends upon the number of victims involved. Often, complex anatomic patterns found in ante- and post-mortem material can be superimposed radiographically to provide indisputable evidence of identity even from very small fragments. Potentially matching remains can be reexamined in various projections after clearing away soft tissue and debris to permit such superimposition (Figure 9-19). The spine and individual bones such as the clavicles are particularly amenable to this technique.[15]

Even when complete superimposition is impossible, x-ray data often will support or, by disclosing obvious mismatches, refute a tentative identification suggested by another technique. A basic principle is the requirement of confirmation by as many different techniques as possible, and the careful cross-checking of each technique for exclusionary data, before making a final certification of identity.

In the case of burning and mutilation, there are often some remains for which too few data are available for positive identification by the ordinary means of directly matching ante- and post-mortem features. Then reliance must sometimes be placed on a process of exclusion. When a small number of such bodies remain to be identified, they can be separated by gross exclusionary features such as sex, stature, and blood type, which would not by themselves be definitive. The computer can be a useful tool in handling multiple potentially identifying features among multiple bodies or parts (Figure 9-20). The inferences drawn from this process can lead to definitive identification, but only so long as it is known absolutely that each body must correspond to one of a known group of victims.[5]

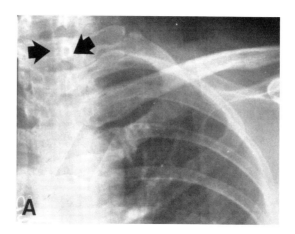

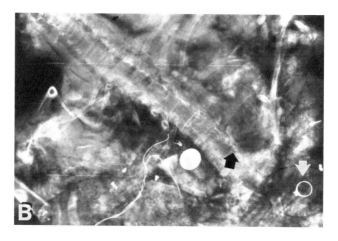

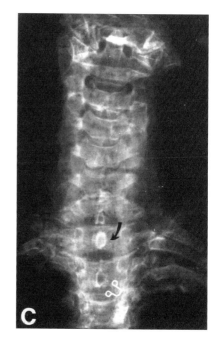

Figure 9-18   **A**: an ante-mortem film of a known victim of the Chicago DC-10 crash. Arrows indicate tracheal calcifications and a T-1 spinous process with a dense cortex relative to that of T-2. **B**: post-mortem film taken with remains in a body bag shows severe disruption of the skeleton and multiple foreign bodies including aircraft parts. A ring (white arrow) was noted and recovered. It was later identified as belonging to the victim seen in **A**. A black arrow points to calcified tracheal cartilages similar to those seen in **A**. **C**: the upper cervicothoracic portion of the skeleton was cleaned and radiographed in standard anatomical positions. Note the density of the T-1 spinous process (curved arrow) and the shape of the C-7 spine, findings that match those in the ante-mortem film **A**. (From Lichtenstein, J. E., et al., *Am. J. Roentgenol.*, 150, 751, 1988. With permission.)

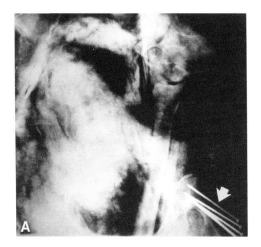
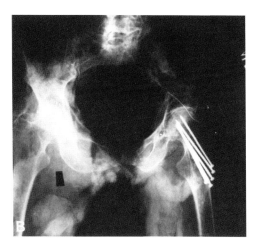
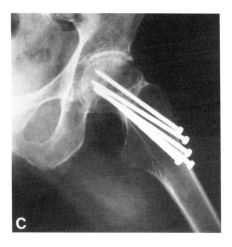

Figure 9-19 **A**: initial screening study of wrapped remains showing metallic screw fixation of a proximal femur fracture (arrow). **B**: note improvement achieved by reexamination in anatomic position after unwrapping. Superimposition with ante-mortem film (**C**) permitted positive radiographic identification. (From Lichtenstein, J. E., et al., *Am. J. Roentgenol.*, 150, 751, 1988. With permission.)

The technique was employed in the last stages of identifying 256 bodies from a 1985 military transport plane crash in Gander, Newfoundland in which it was thought that all the passengers and crew were known and that no other victims were involved.[12]

Injury Mechanism and Pattern Analysis

While identification itself is important for humanitarian and legal reasons, scientific interest lies in the need to identify victims to correlate their injury mechanisms with their relationship within the fatal environment.[16–26]

If the nature and cause of an event is to be analyzed, the detailed mechanisms of injury and death of the victims must be determined. That requires that the location and roles of individuals within the fatal environment be known. This, in turn, requires documentation of the site of discovery of the remains and their accurate identification as specific individuals. There is a special need to identify and analyze the remains of those in control of the environment, such as pilots or plant operators. Patterns of injury to hands and feet of aircrew members, for example, may establish the status of controls and suggest the position or actions of the victims. Such analysis is useful not only for investigation of specific events,

```
        NAME              SEX    RACE          AGE    HT   WT    HAIR CLR         *** F E A T U R E S ********************
   *                       M    WHITE          47     65  155    BROWN&RED        KNEE INJUR

        #  SEX  RACE          AGE        STATURE     WEIGHT      HAIR CLR
  25   955   M   WHITE      45 +- 10    66 +-  2    160 +- 10   BROWN&RED        POST/TEETH
  25  1013   M   WHITE      45 +- 10    67 +-  2    150 +- 15   BROWN&RED        MUSCULAR
  22   941   M   WHITE      28 +-  4    68 +-  3    155 +- 15   BROWN&RED        POST/TEETH
  22   988   M   WHITE      55 +- 10    66 +-  2    170 +- 15   BRN&GRYNG        CIRC
  22   994   M   WHITE      55 +- 10    67 +-  2    190 +- 10   BROWN&RED
  22  1031   M   WHITE      45 +- 10    68 +-  2    150 +- 20   BRN&GRYNG        FX/UP/EXTR
  22  1036   M   WHITE      40 +- 10    68 +-  4    170 +- 15   BROWN&RED        POST/TEETH
  22  1064   M   WHITE      33 +-  6    68 +-  3    165 +- 15   BROWN&RED        POST/TEETH  CIRC        FX/BACK
  21   792   M   WHITE      50 +- 10    71 +-  4    230 +- 30   BROWN&RED        HIRSUTE
  21  1025   M   WHITE      50 +- 15    72 +-  4    200 +- 20   BROWN&RED        MED. BLD


        NAME              SEX    RACE          AGE    HT   WT    HAIR CLR         *** F E A T U R E S ********************
   *                       M    WHITE          37     68  160    BROWN&RED

        #  SEX  RACE          AGE        STATURE     WEIGHT      HAIR CLR
  25   799   M   WHITE      40 +- 10    69 +-  3    160 +- 15   BROWN&RED        METALPLATE UNCIRC     HIRSUTE      LARGE/HEAD
  25   803   M   WHITE      35 +- 10    70 +-  3    170 +- 15   BROWN&RED        POST/TEETH
  25  1036   M   WHITE      40 +- 10    68 +-  4    170 +- 15   BROWN&RED        POST/TEETH  CIRC        FX/BACK
  25  1064   M   WHITE      33 +-  6    68 +-  3    165 +- 15   BROWN&RED
  23   910   M   WHITE      50 +- 10    67 +-  3    170 +- 20   BROWN&RED        POST/TEETH
  23   941   M   WHITE      28 +-  4    68 +-  3    155 +- 15   BROWN&RED        HIRSUTE    CIRC
  23   944   M   WHITE      35 +- 10    69 +-  3    165 +- 10   -                FX/UP/EXTR
  23  1031   M   WHITE      45 +- 10    68 +-  2    150 +- 10   BRN&GRYNG        CIRC
  22   988   M   WHITE      55 +- 10    66 +-  2    170 +- 15   BRN&GRYNG
  22   990   M   WHITE      45 +- 10    70 +-  4    150 +- 20   -
```

Figure 9-20   Example of computerized sorting for identifying features of multiple bodies in a mass casualty situation.

but more importantly to correlate patterns found in similar incidents in an attempt to prevent them in the future.

Events where forces are on the borderline of survivability are of particular interest. Important questions concern the factors determining why some survive, or do not, in potentially survivable situations. Head or lower-extremity injuries can explain failure to escape from otherwise survivable situations such as post-crash fires. Separating mechanical from thermal injury patterns and determining whether burning was the cause of death or occurred post-mortem after other debilitating injuries are important examples. These data are vital in studying patterns of mass casualties in order to improve engineering and safety procedures.

References

1. Anon., *ACR Bull.*, 6, 25, 1995.

2. Allen, E. W., Scenes from the Oklahoma City bombing, *J. Nucl. Med.*, 36, 30, 1995.

3. Nye, P. J., Tytle, T. L., Jarman, R. N., and Eaton, B. G., The role of radiology in the Oklahoma City bombing, *Radiology*, 200, 541, 1996.

4. Gross, E. M. and Blumberg, J. M., Identification and injuries of air-crash victims, *Arch. Environ. Health*, 13, 289, 1966.

5. Tarlton, S. W., Identification in aircraft accidents, in *Aerospace Pathology*, Mason, J. K. and Reals, W. J., Eds., College of American Pathologists Foundation, Chicago, 1973, 53.

6. Singleton, A. C., The roentgenological identification of victims of the "Noronic" disaster, *Am. J. Roentgenol.*, 66, 375, 1951.

7. Brown, T. C., Delaney, R. J., and Robinson, W. L., Medical identification in the "Noronic" disaster, *J. Am. Med. Assoc.*, 148, 621, 1952.

8. Lichtenstein, J. E., Madewell, J. E., McMeekin, R. R., Feigin, D. S., and Wolcott, J. H., The role of radiology in aviation accident investigation, *Aviat. Space Environ. Med.*, 51, 1004, 1980.

9. Lichtenstein, J. E. and Madewell, J. E., Role of radiology in the study and identification of casualty victims, *Der Radiologe*, 22, 352, 1982.

10. Lichtenstein J. E., Fitzpatrick, J. J., and Madewell, J. E., Role of Radiology in fatality investigations, *Am. J. Roentgenol.*, 150, 751, 1988.

11. Joyce, C. and Stover, E., *Witnesses from the Grave*, Little, Brown, Boston, 1991, 94.

12. Mulligan, M. E., McCarthy, M. J., Wippold, F. J., Lichtenstein, J. E., and Wagner, G. N., Radiologic evaluation of mass casualty victims: lessons from the Gander, Newfoundland accident, *Radiology*, 168, 229, 1988.

13. Hill, I. R., The Air India jet disaster Kalishna-injury analysis, *Uses of the Forensic Science*, Caddy, B., Ed., Scottish Academic Press, Edinburgh, 1986, 121.

14. Harbinson, J. F. A., Pathology organization and victim identification after the losses of Air India flight 182, 23/6/1985, *Can. Soc. Forensic Sci. J.*, 20, 16, 1987.

15. Sanders, I., Woesner, M. E., Ferguson, R. A., and Noguchi, T. T., A new application of forensic radiology: identification of deceased from a single clavicle, *Am. J. Roentgenol. Radium Ther. Nucl. Med.*, 115, 619, 1972.

16. Barrie, H. J. and Hodson-Walker, N., Incidence and pathogenesis of fractures of the lumbar transverse processes in air crashes, *Aerosp. Med.*, 41, 805, 1970.

17. Besant-Matthews, P. E., Photography and radiography in aircraft accident investigation, in *Aerospace Pathology*, Mason, J. K. and Reals, W. J., Eds., College of American Pathologists Foundation, Chicago, 1973, 177.

18. Dunne, M. J., Jr. and McMeekin, R. R., Medical investigation of fatalities from aircraft-accident burns, *Aviat. Space Environ. Med.*, 48, 964, 1977.

19. Fatteh, A. V. and Mann, G. T., The role of radiology in forensic pathology, *Med. Sci. Law*, 9, 27, 1969.

20. Gable, W. D., Pathology patterns in aircraft accident investigation, *Aerosp. Med.*, 39, 638, 1968.

21. Krefft, S., Estimation of pilot control at the time of crash, in *Aerospace Pathology*, Mason, J. K. and Reals, W. J., Eds., College of American Pathologists Foundation, Chicago, 1973, 96.

22. Kreft, S., Who was at the aircraft's controls when the fatal accident occurred?, *Aerosp. Med.*, 41, 785, 1970.

23. Mason, J. K., Passenger tie-down failure. Injuries and accident reconstruction, *Aerosp. Med.*, 41, 781, 1970.

24. McMeekin, R. R., An organizational concept for pathologic identification in mass disasters, *Aviat. Space Environ. Med.*, 51, 999, 1980.

25. Rhodes, R. S., Misleading injury patterns, *Aerosp. Med.*, 41, 794, 1970.

26. Simson, L. R., Jr., Roentgenography in the investigation of fatal aviation accidents, *Aerosp. Med.*, 43, 81, 1972.

SECTION III

Gunshot Wounds

Radiology of Gunshot Wounds

10

JAMES M. MESSMER, M.ED., M.D.

Contents

Introduction

Violence is an unfortunate fact of life in the U.S. Guns, and in particular handguns, make a major contribution to this ongoing national crisis.[1–3] There are about 65 murders per day in the U.S. (the highest homicide rate of any Western industrialized country).[1,4,5] About 70% of those murders are committed with firearms. After vehicular accidents, homicide is the second leading cause of juvenile injury-related deaths. Firearms are the instrument of 34,000 deaths and nearly a quarter-million nonfatal injuries annually in the U.S.[1,6,7]

The informed forensic radiologist has much to offer the forensic pathologist in the investigation of deaths by gunshot wounds.[8] This chapter will provide an overview of what information the radiologist should consider in such investigations. For more detailed information the reader is referred to the references at the end of the chapter.

Basic Radiological Information

The forensic pathologist uses x-rays in evaluating gunshot wounds in several ways.[9,10] First and foremost, the pathologist is interested in the *location of the bullet*. While this may seem straightforward from external inspection of the body, bullets will frequently end up in a site far distant from their entrance points, particularly if they have struck bone. The natural curvature of the ribs and the skull can cause bullets to change trajectory significantly. The availability of fluoroscopy in the autopsy suite is especially valuable for allowing the pathologist to scan the body for unsuspected bullets. Knowing the specific location of a bullet saves the pathologist much time and may avoid needless effort in searching for bullets that are inaccessible. Figure 10-1 demonstrates a case where only one bullet was easily accessible.

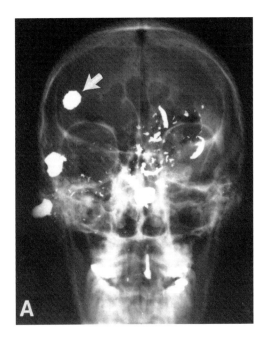

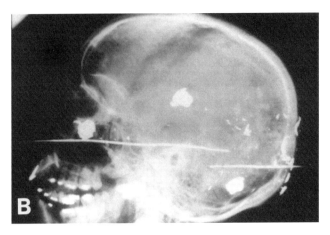

Figure 10-1 **A**: an execution-style murder resulted in five bullets, but only the bullet over-lying the right frontal sinus (arrow) was easily accessible. The remainder were lodged within the facial bones. **B**: shows the futility of probing for bullets. (From Messmer, J. M. and Fierro, M. F., *RadioGraphics*, 6, 457, 1986. With permission.)

X-rays will also reveal whether there are bullets of a different *caliber* present. This can be valuable in cases where multiple weapons are involved. The *number of bullets* is also important and must be correlated with the entrance and exit wounds. A discrepancy may lead to a search for bullets at the scene. More than one bullet may enter through a single entrance wound, particularly when automatic weapons are used.

X-rays may also reveal information about the *angle* and *direction of fire* (Figure 10-2). Small metallic fragments produced when a bullet strikes bone may lead directly to the bullet and clearly indicate the bullet's path. Correlating this information with the scene of

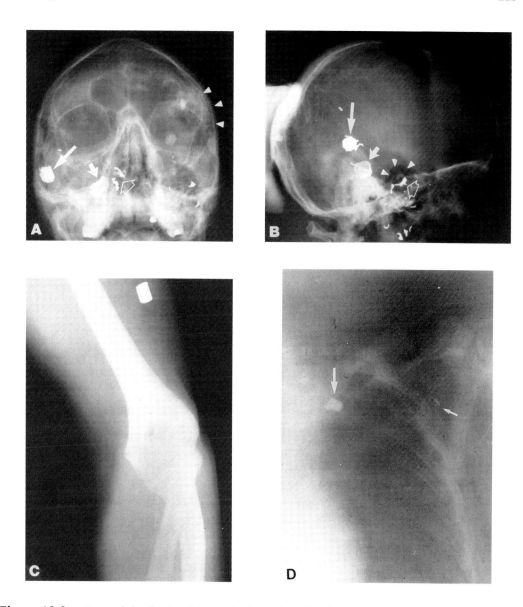

Figure 10-2   Case of the fleeing felon: a body with multiple short-range gunshot wounds was found beside the highway. The location of wounds suggested that the victim might have been in the right-hand seat of an automobile, his assailant in the driver's seat. Later, the driver was stopped for speeding in the blood-stained car, and confessed. The victim was a hitch-hiker, fleeing escape from prison, who unfortunately got picked up by an even meaner felon who robbed and killed him. **A**: frontal and **B**: lateral view of the skull show a left temporal wound of entry (arrowheads). There are scattered bone and bullet fragments throughout. The bullet bounced off the sella (open arrow). The jacket (short arrow) separated, and the bullet (long arrow) came to rest against the right parietal bone posteriorly. **C**: nonfatal gunshot to the left upper arm. **D**: nonfatal bullet wound, trajectory from left axilla (small arrow) to left mediastinal border (large arrow). A smaller-caliber bullet found radiographically in the left leg proved to be from a foiled robbery years earlier.

the crime helps recreate the relative positions of victim and assailant. While the type of weapon can frequently be determined by eyewitness reports or recovery of the weapon from the scene, the radiographs may reveal clues as to the *type of weapon*. For example, high-velocity hunting ammunition wounds can leave a characteristic "lead snowstorm" radiographic picture because of extensive fragmentation of the unjacketed bullet (Figure 10-3).

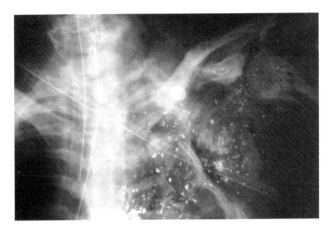

Figure 10-3   A high-velocity rifle wound to the chest left a typical "lead snowstorm" of fragments. The victim was accompanying her daughter who had just won a divorce. The enraged ex-husband shot and killed his ex-wife as she exited the courthouse, then killed his ex-mother-in-law as she cowered behind a car. (Note the spread of the "snowstorm" from superolateral to inferomedial.) The shooter was judged not guilty by reason of insanity in the first event, and guilty of murder in the second event. (This judicial result may be the first of its kind for two killings occurring within a matter of seconds.)

X-rays may be the first *indication that a crime has been committed* when decomposed bodies are discovered. The normal putrefaction that occurs, with its attendant bloating of the tissues and deformity of the body, can easily mask an entrance wound. (Figure 8-27A and B). Bodies partially destroyed by fire or skeletonized remains should always be radiographed to determine unsuspected foul play (Figure 3-21). Retrieval of the metallic fragments can even help in the identification of remains if there is a gunshot wound in the past history of the presumed decedent.

Weapon Ballistics

A general understanding of bullets, weapons, and the tissue damage bullets inflict is valuable in film interpretation. [2,11–15] The three general types of guns are handguns, rifles, and shotguns. The muzzle velocity of rifles is higher than that of handguns or shotguns. Table 10-1 gives a list of common weapons and their muzzle velocities. The bullets fired by handguns and rifles are similar, but are distinctly different from those fired from shotguns. Each type of weapon has characteristic wounding patterns. In general, higher-velocity bullets cause more damage than slower ones, but speed is not the only factor in tissue destruction. The weight of the bullet, its internal construction, and the amount of

TABLE 10-1 Some Common Weapons and Muzzle Velocities

Cartridge	Muzzle Velocity (ft/sec)
.22 Short HV	1125
.22 Long HV	1240
.30-.30 Winchester	2410
.357 Magnum	1550
.38 S & W	685
.44 Special	755
M-16	3250

pitch and yaw during the flight of the bullet also play an important role in the amount of damage.

Types of Bullets

The type of ammunition used for handguns and rifles is a cartridge which consists of a cartridge case (usually made of brass), primer, powder charge, and the bullet.[9] The caliber of a bullet is expressed as a decimal corresponding to the diameter in inches, or by the actual diameter in millimeters. Bullets of identical calibers may have different weights, and the forensic pathologist measures both weight and caliber to define the weapon more accurately.

Lead is the most common base metal used for making bullets. Antimony or tin is usually added to the lead to increase the hardness. The lead bullet can be fully or partially covered by other metals. Copper or copper alloys are frequently used in the production of such "full metal-jacketed" or "partially metal-jacketed" bullets. This coating, called gilding, both hardens and lubricates the bullet as well as prevents leading of the action and barrel, which can cause the weapon to jam. A partially metal-jacketed bullet exposes the lead tip, which can then be hollowed out to increase the mushrooming effect of the bullet as it enters tissue.

The barrels of rifles and handguns have grooves along their length to impart a rotational spin along the long axis of the bullet which stabilizes the flight and aids in the accuracy of the bullet. These grooves cause unique markings on either the lead or metal jacket of the bullets (Figure 10-4). These "class characteristics" may indicate the make and model of the weapon. More subtle imperfections in the barrel and grooves cause unique markings and are the basis for determining whether a particular weapon fired a particular bullet.

In the case of the partially metal-jacketed bullet, the metal jacket may separate from the lead portion of the bullet and can be readily identified radiographically by its lower radiodensity than the lead component (Figure 10-5). It is important to remember that in partially metal-jacketed bullets the ballistic markings are on the metal jacket and not the lead. Hence, it is the jacket that must be retrieved for testing.

Radiologists should always note the location of fragments of a sufficient size that might contain ballistic information. Accurate location of bullets can save the forensic pathologist significant time.

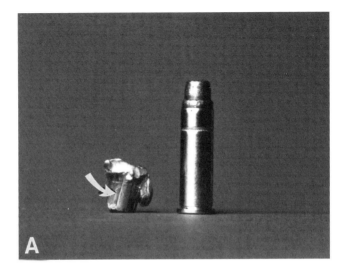

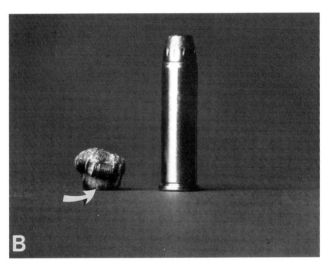

Figure 10-4   **A**: a solid lead bullet demonstrates the characteristic ballistic markings (arrowhead). **B**: in the partially jacketed bullet the crucial ballistic information is on the copper jacket rather than the lead component (arrowhead). (From Messmer, J. M. and Fierro, M. F., *Radio-Graphics*, 6, 457, 1986. With permission.)

Information about the type of bullet can be determined by its radiographic appearance. "Mushrooming", which is the characteristic flattening of one end of the bullet when it strikes flesh, indicates a solid lead or partially metal-jacketed bullet. A bullet with a unique appearance that was pulled from the market in 1993, but can occasionally be seen, is the Black Talon. The design of this bullet is a hollow-point tip with sharp metal points that unfold upon impact (Figure 10-6). The concept was that the sharp metal points would cause more damage than the simple mushroom effect of the plain lead bullet. In fact, despite the formidable appearance, the differences in wounding effect are negligible.[16] It is important, however, for the radiologist to be aware of this type of bullet and alert the forensic pathologist or surgeon to its presence since the sharp metallic tips can easily penetrate a rubber glove and injure the investigating physician.

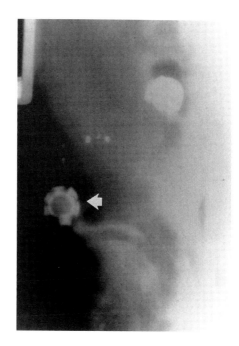

Figure 10-5 In this gunshot wound to the left hip, the lead and jacket components have become separated. The important ballistic information is on the jacket (arrow). (From Messmer, J. M. and Fierro, M. F., *RadioGraphics*, 6, 457, 1986. With permission.)

The Glaser safety slug is a bullet designed to impart all of its kinetic energy into the tissue. Consisting of multiple small lead pellets encased in a copper cup with a Teflon® plug at the tip, these bullets are designed to incompletely penetrate the victim, therefore eliminating the possibility of ricochet or injury to bystanders; hence the "safety" name. The radiographic appearance mimics that of a shotgun wound and tissue damage can be extensive, particularly at close range[17,18] (Figure 10-7). The copper cup may be visible radiographically, but the Teflon® plug is not.

Another handgun load with a radiographic "signature" is the Winchester Western .25 caliber centerfire cartridge introduced in 1981. It contains a copper-coated lead hollow-point bullet filled with a single No. 4 steel pellet.[19] The radiographic finding of a single small bullet accompanied by a single small shot is unique.

Bullets made of rubber or plastic are uncommon in the U.S. and are not visible radiographically.

Tissue Damage

The amount of tissue damage that occurs is proportional to the amount of the bullet's kinetic energy which is expended in the tissue. While the literature has emphasized the importance of bullet velocity in tissue damage, the weight of the bullet, internal composition and configuration, and yaw in the flight path are also contributing factors.[2,11–14] Yaw is the angle of the long axis of the bullet with its path of flight. A bullet entering tissue at 90° of yaw would present a significantly larger surface area and therefore cause more tissue damage. The rifling on the inside of the barrel imparts a spin to the bullet which stabilizes its flight. As the bullet exits the barrel the emerging gas may produce minimal yaw during the flight path, but once the bullet enters tissue it can rotate and cause greater damage.

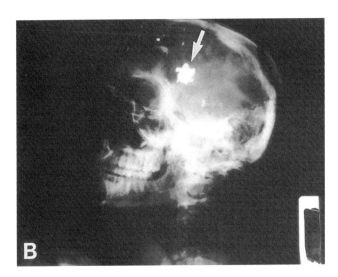

Figure 10-6 **A**: fired Black Talon demonstrates the characteristic sharp projections that are exposed as the bullet mushrooms. **B**: the radiograph of this homicide victim demonstrates the characteristic appearance of the Black Talon (arrow) and allows for a radiographic determination of the type of bullet. (It also warns the autopsy surgeon of a potential puncture wound.)

A bullet which expends all of its kinetic energy in a body imparts its maximum potential of stopping power. A bullet that passes completely through a body intact, retaining its kinetic energy, will cause less damage than a bullet which enters and fragments.

As noted above, the composition of the bullet is also important in determining the amount of tissue damage. The Hague Peace Conference of 1899 stipulated that bullets used in war should be protected against deformity by a copper jacket. Ironically, the bullets now frequently used in peacetime have more destructive potential than those used in war.[14]

Other factors which contribute to tissue damage are the elasticity of the tissue struck, the production of bone fragments, and temporary cavitation. Less-elastic tissue such as

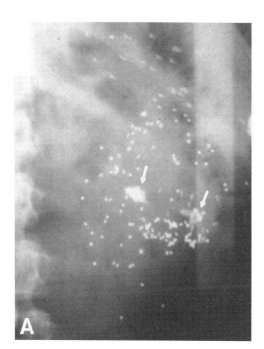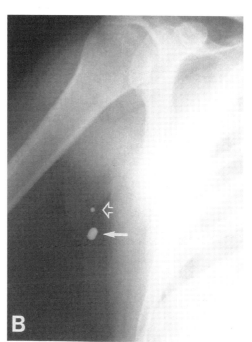

Figure 10-7   **A**: a fatal wound to the flank from a Glaser safety slug which mimics a shotgun wound radiographically. Extensive damage to the retroperitoneum and kidney resulted in a rapid death from exsanguination. Arrows indicate fragments of the cup. **B**: Winchester-Western .25 caliber centerfire handgun load consisting of a copper-coated lead hollow-point bullet (arrow) containing a single No. 4 steel birdshot pellet (open arrow). (Courtesy of Dr. James C. Downs.)

the brain, liver, or spleen will incur more damage than the more elastic muscle of the extremities. When a bullet strikes bone its path can be deflected and fragmentation can occur, producing bone fragments which act as additional small projectiles, thus increasing tissue damage.[20] As the bullet passes through the body it pushes tissue away from its path. In the first several microseconds a temporary cavity forms which can damage relatively unyielding tissue but has less effect on elastic tissue such as muscle.

Extensive skull fracturing occurs with higher-caliber gunshot wounds to the head (Figure 10-8). If the fracture lines extend across the intracranial vascular sinuses and the wound is open to the outside, the negative hydrostatic pressure draws air into the vascular system as the heart continues to beat. This air can occasionally be visualized radiographically in the vascular sinuses and the occipital veins (Figure 10-9). If the amount of air is sufficiently extensive, post-mortem views of the chest will show air in the great vessels, heart, and pulmonary outflow tract[21] (Figure 10-10). The presence of the air may be a causative factor in the eventual cessation of the heart beat.

Air embolism can be venous or arterial. Up to 100 cc of venous air can be handled by the body without fatality if the air is introduced slowly.[22] Arterial air emboli can occur when air enters the left side of the heart, usually through a patent foramen ovale or penetrating lung trauma.[23–28] Arterial air can be more deadly, with as little as 2 to 3 cc of air causing death experimentally in animals.[29,30] The explanation for the disparity in the

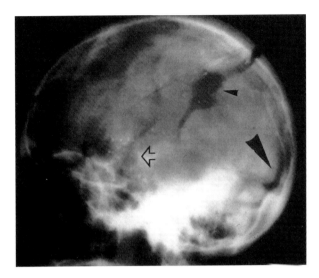

Figure 10-8   A lateral skull film with a large-caliber suicide gunshot wound demonstrates
the entrance wound (arrow) and the larger exit wound (arrowhead). Note the extensive fracturing.
There is also air within the sigmoid sinus (large arrowhead). (From Messmer, J. M. and Fierro,
M. F., *RadioGraphics*, 6, 457, 1986. With permission.)

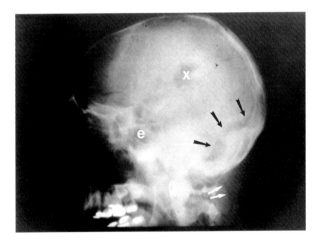

Figure 10-9   A self-inflicted .45 gunshot wound to the head with a through and through
injury (e = entrance, x = exit). Note the air in the sigmoid sinus (arrows) and occipital vein
(white arrows). (From Messmer, J. M. and Fierro, M. F., *RadioGraphics*, 6, 457, 1986. With
permission.)

clinical pictures is that arterial air can enter the coronary arteries, causing fatal arrhythmias,
or enter the cerebral arteries producing cerebral insufficiency. The presence of air
exclusively in the venous system differentiates if from the type of air pattern seen in the
normal putrefactive process, which is more extensive and involves the vascular system and
soft tissues.

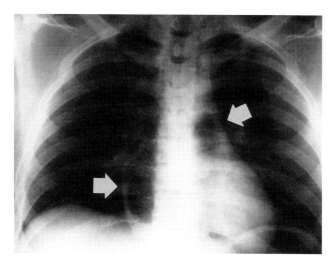

Figure 10-10   A post-mortem view of the chest in a patient with a .38 caliber suicide gunshot wound to the head. There is air in the right atrium and pulmonary outflow tract (arrows) which entered the vascular system through the intracranial sinuses. (From Messmer, J. M. and Fierro, M. F., *RadioGraphics*, 6, 457, 1986. With permission.)

Shotguns

Shotguns differ from handguns and rifles in that the inside of the barrel is smooth and the missile consists of a few to hundreds of metal spheres packed in a paper or plastic tube. The pellets, or shot, emerge from the barrel in a mass that disperses into a pattern determined by the range of fire, barrel length, and degree of "choke", which is partial constriction of the bore of the shotgun at its muzzle end to control the distribution of the shot. The spherical shape of shot adds to instability in flight. As a result of all these factors, the effective range for shotguns is usually measured in tens of meters, as opposed to rifles which have ranges of hundreds to thousands of meters.[14]

The caliber of shotguns is measured in gauges rather than hundredths or thousandths of inches as rifles and handguns are measured. The range of gauge is from 8 (largest) to .410 (smallest). (The latter designation is actually the caliber of the barrel measured in thousandths of an inch: there is also a 9-mm shotgun, named for its barrel diameter[2]). For the other gauges, the number represents the number of lead balls of a diameter equal to the diameter of the barrel that would weigh one pound.

There are two basic sizes of shot, birdshot and buckshot. The size of the individual shot is expressed by a number ranging from 12 (smallest) to 000 (largest). The total number of shot in any one shell depends on the size of the shot and the gauge of the shell. For example, more size 9 birdshot pellets will be contained in a 12-gauge shell than in a 20-gauge shell. The largest 00 and 000 buckshot have diameters of .33 and .36 in., respectively making them equivalent in size to handgun bullets.

Typically, wounds from shotguns are among the worst seen in civilian wounds.[15,31] At ranges of 1 to 2 yards the entrance wound is usually a single large, jagged-edged wound. As the range increases to 3 to 4 yards, and depending on the gauge of the weapon and the size of the pellets, there may be single pellet wounds around the periphery of the larger wound. At distances beyond 20 yards the full pattern has developed and there will be multiple small pellet wounds (Figure 10-11).

Suicide by Gunshot

Annually, the number of suicides exceeds the number of murders in the U.S., and firearms are involved in up to two-thirds of suicides. A general knowledge of the characteristics of suicide gunshot wounds can help avoid unwarranted conclusions.

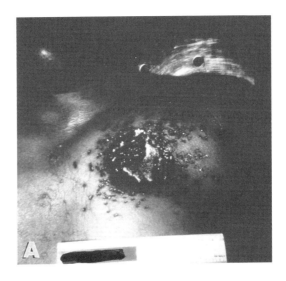

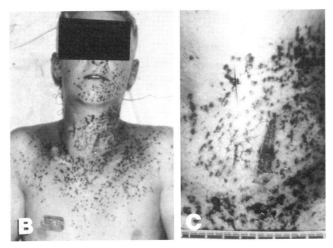

Figure 10-11   **A**: a fatal shotgun wound from several yards away shows that some of the pellets have begun to form the pattern, but the bulk have entered as a mass causing the larger wound centrally. **B**: a fatal shotgun wound to the upper chest and face shows multiple entry points indicating the weapon was fired from a distance of approximately 40 ft allowing the pattern to develop. **C**: close-up of neck with inch ruler at bottom showing shot spread distance. (From Messmer, J. M. and Fierro, M. F., *RadioGraphics*, 6, 457, 1986. With permission.)

The majority of suicide gunshot wounds are contact wounds, usually to the right side of the head since most people are right-handed. Therefore, wounds to the right temple are common and usually have a posterior and superior trajectory (Figure 10-12). However, the nondominant hand is used often enough that it cannot be considered exceptional or beyond the realm of the possible.[32] Suicide wounds to the top or back of the head have been reported. Suicide gunshot wounds in or near the eye are uncommon and raise the possibility of a homicide. Likewise, suicide wounds to the mouth generally do not involve the tongue. When the tongue is involved, the possibility of homicide is raised. The mechanism of action is proposed to be the victim's attempt to push the weapon from the mouth with the tongue.[10]

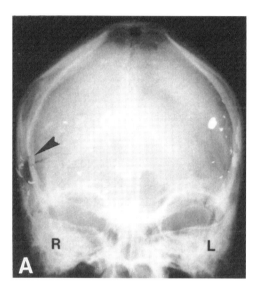

Figure 10-12 **A**: the frontal radiograph of the skull demonstrates the entrance wound (arrowhead) in the right temporal region with metallic fragments scattered throughout the brain tissue. The major fragment comes to rest inside the skull at a higher level than the entrance wound. **B**: the lateral radiograph shows the anterior to posterior distribution to the metallic fragments. A paper clip marks the entrance wound. Note also the minimal calvarial fracturing.

In suicide by gunshot — whether handgun, rifle, or shotgun — the favored targets are the head, chest, and abdomen, in that order.[32] In shotgun wounds to the head, the handedness of the suicidal person does not correlate as well as with the temple wound since one hand must hold the muzzle to the head while the other pulls the trigger. The unconscious selection of priorities for these tasks by the shooter is unpredictable. However, because of the contortion required to shoot oneself in the chest or abdomen with a long gun, "trigger-handedness" usually correlates with trajectory; downward and to the left for a right trigger hand, and downward and to the right for lefties.[32]

The presence of multiple gunshot wounds, or the radiological finding of several bullets, does not preclude suicide. The victim may have had previous nonfatal gunshot wounds, for instance. There are reports of nonfatal gunshot suicide attempts followed by success with poisoning or hanging.[32] About 2% of suicides involve multiple gunshot wounds. These remarkable cases can involve faulty ammunition, poor aim resulting in a nonfatal wound, fleeting survival or reflex action producing more firings, or the use of automatic weapons.[32–35] There are reports of up to four suicidal gunshot wounds to the head[33] and nine suicidal gunshot wounds to the chest.[35]

References

1. Collins, K. A. and Lantz, P. E., Interpretation of fatal, multiple, and exiting gunshot wounds by trauma specialists, *J. Forensic Sci.*, 39, 94, 1994.
2. Hollerman, J. J. and Fackler, M. L., Gunshot wounds: radiology and wound ballistics, *Emergency Radiol.*, 2, 171, 1995.
3. Kassirer, M. D., Firearms and the killing threshold, *N. Engl. J. Med.*, 325, 1647, 1991.
4. Federal Bureau of Investigation, Crime in the United States 1992, Uniform Crime Reports, U.S. Department of Justice, Washington, D.C., 1993.
5. Novello, A. C., Shosky, J., and Froehkle, R., From the Surgeon General for Health, U.S. Public Health Services, *J. Am. Med. Assoc.*, 267, 3007, 1992.
6. Mason, J., From the Assistant Secretary for Health, U.S. Public Health Service, *J. Am. Med. Assoc.*, 267, 3003, 1992.
7. Teret, S. P., Wintemute, G. J., and Beilenson, P. L., The firearm fatality reporting system, *J. Am. Med. Assoc.*, 267, 3073, 1992.
8. Messmer, J. M. and Fierro, M. F., Radiologic forensic investigation of fatal gunshot wounds, *RadioGraphics*, 6, 457, 1986.
9. Di Maio, V. J. M., *Gunshot Wounds. Practical Aspects of Firearms, Ballistics, and Forensic Techniques*, Elsevier, New York, 1985, chap. 11.
10. Fatteh, A. , *Medicolegal Investigation of Gunshot Wounds*, Lippincott, Philadelphia, 1976.
11. Fackler, M. L., Wound ballistics. A review of common misconceptions, *J. Am. Med. Assoc.*, 259, 2730, 1988.
12. Hollerman, J. J., Fackler, M. L., Coldwell, D. M., and Ben-Menachem, Y., Gunshot wounds. 1. Bullets, ballistics, and mechanisms of injury, *Am. J. Roentgenol.*, 155, 685, 1990.
13. Hollerman, J. J., Fackler, M. L., Coldwell, D. M., and Ben-Menachem, Y., Gunshot wounds. 2. Radiology, *Am. J. Roentgenol.*, 155, 691, 1990.
14. Swan, K. G. and Swan, R. C., Principles of ballistics applicable to the treatment of gunshot wounds, *Surg. Clin. North Am.*, 71, 221, 1991.

15. Wilson, J. M., Shotgun ballistics and shotgun injuries, *West. J. Med.*, 129, 149, 1978.

16. Wilbur, C. G., Letter to Editor, *J. Forensic Sci.*, 40, 722, 1995.

17. Leffers, B. and Jeanty, D., Handgun pellet ammunition ("snake shot") wounds: report of three cases, *J. Forensic Sci.*, 27, 433, 1982.

18. Jones, A. M., Reyna, M., Sperry, K., and Hock, D., Suicidal contact gunshot wounds to the head with .38 special Glaser safety slug ammunition, *J. Forensic Sci.*, 32, 1604, 1987.

19. Di Maio, V. J. M., *Gunshot Wounds. Practical Aspects of Firearms, Ballistics, and Forensic Techniques*, Elsevier, New York, 1985, chap. 15.

20. Fackler, M. L., Surinchak, J. S., Malinowski, J. A., and Bowen, R. E., Bullet fragmentation: a major cause of tissue disruption, *J. Trauma*, 24, 35, 1984.

21. Messmer, J. M., Massive head trauma as a cause of intravascular air, *J. Forensic Sci.*, 29, 418, 1984.

22. Erben, J. and Nadvornik, R., The quantitative determination of air embolus in certain cases of fatal trauma, *J. Forensic Med. Pathol.*, 10, 45, 1963.

23. Graham, J. M., Beall, A. C., Matlox, K. L., and Vaughan, G. D., Systemic air embolism following penetrating trauma to the lung, *Chest*, 27, 449, 1977.

24. Meier, G. H., Wood, W. J., and Symbas, P. N., Systemic air embolization from penetrating lung injury, *Ann. Thorac. Surg.*, 27, 161, 1979.

25. Smith, J. M., Richardson, J. D., Grover, F. L., Arom, K. V., Webb, G. E., and Trinkle, J. K., Fatal air embolism following gunshot wound to the lung, *J. Thorac. Cardiovasc. Surg.*, 72, 296, 1976.

26. Thomas, A. N. and Roe, B. B., Air embolism following penetrating lung injuries, *J. Thorac. Cardiovasc. Surg.*, 66, 533, 1973.

27. Thomas, A. N. and Stephens, B. G., Air embolism: a cause of morbidity and death after penetrating lung trauma, *J. Trauma*, 14, 633, 1974.

28. Westcott, J. L., Air embolism complicating percutaneous needle biopsy of the lung, *Chest*, 63, 108, 1973.

29. Durant, T. M., Oppenheimer, M. J., Webster, M. R., and Lang, J., Arterial air embolism, *Am. Heart J.*, 38, 481, 1949.

30. Rukstinat, G., Experimental air embolism of coronary arteries, *J. Am. Med. Assoc.*, 96, 26, 1931.

31. Froede, R. C., Pitt, M. J., and Bridgemon, R. R., Shotgun diagnosis: "it ought to be something else", *J. Forensic Sci.*, 27, 428, 1982.

32. Di Maio, V. J. M., *Gunshot Wounds. Practical Aspects of Firearms, Ballistics, and Forensic Techniques*, Elsevier, New York, 1985, chap. 14.

33. Introna, F. I., Jr. and Smialek, J. E., Suicide from multiple gunshot wounds, *Am. J. Forensic Med. Pathol.*, 10, 275, 1989.

34. Jacob, B., Barg, J., Haarhof, K., Sprick, C., Wörz, D., and Bonte, W., Multiple suicidal gunshot wounds to the head, *Am. J. Forensic Med. Pathol.*, 10, 289, 1989.

35. Habbe, D., Thomas, G. E., and Gould, J., Nine-gunshot suicide, *Am. J. Forensic Med. Pathol.*, 10, 335, 1989.

Pitfalls in the Radiology of Gunshot Wounds

11

JAMES M. MESSMER, M.ED., M.D.
B. G. BROGDON, M.D.

Contents

Introduction

In the radiological evaluation of gunshot wounds a number of pitfalls await the unwary, the overenthusiastic, or the inexperienced viewer. One must be careful not to exceed the limitation of the method. Some of the difficulties in evaluating suicide, or in discriminating between suicide and homicide, have been pointed out already. The radiologist should detect and demonstrate the evidence on the film; further speculation and assumption are the province of other members of the forensic team.

Size of the Missile

There is great temptation to estimate the caliber of a bullet or the size of shot by "eyeballing" a radiograph. It is a temptation to be resisted. Any missile radiographed within the body will be magnified to some degree, and only a small degree of magnification destroys any hope of "eyeball" accuracy (Figure 11-1).

A review of the characteristics of firearms involved in fatalities in Milwaukee during a 5-year period[1] showed that 26% involved either .22 or .25 caliber weapons in almost equal distributions, 67% involved weapons varying from .312 to .357 in. in diameter, and 7% were larger. It is obvious that the differences within the first two subgroups are minimal.

If there are two views taken at right angles of the bullet within the body, and accurate knowledge of the focal spot-to-bullet distance and the bullet-to-film distance, then the approximate caliber of the bullet can be calculated using the formula presented in

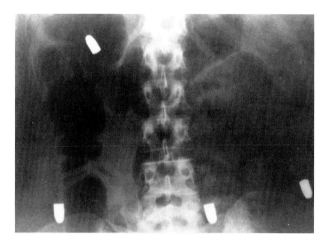

Figure 11-1   Effect of magnification. Bullets of .32 and .38 caliber were placed at different positions on a body and radiographed. Because of the variation in magnification due to different object-film distances, all of the bullets appear to be about the same size. (From Messmer, J. M. and Fierro, M. F., *RadioGraphics*, 6, 457, 1986. With permission.)

Figure 5-6. With this degree of accuracy one may distinguish an undeformed .22 caliber bullet from a .25 and a .38 from a .45.[2] A .38 caliber bullet (actually .357 in. in diameter) cannot be distinguished from a .357 or a 9 mm (.355 in.). The designations of caliber are misleading since a .38 is not really .38 in. in diameter and a .44 is really .4295 in. in diameter.[2,3]

A rather elaborate radiographic method of estimating caliber and weight of both deformed and undeformed bullets has been reported by Bixler et al.[4] Three orthogonal radiographs, fluoroscopically aligned, are used to determine the cross-sectional area of the bullet, and the weight determination is dependent on a data base derived from 48 bullets previously removed from humans. This technique was accepted for purposes of an internal police investigation but, when reported, had not yet been accepted in a U.S. court.

Apparently one federal court has admitted a quantitative method of bullet identification by means of the ratio of bullet diameter to length.[5]

Attempts have been made by Berryman et al.[6] to determine the caliber of a missing bullet. The entrance wounds in cranial bone were examined to investigate relationships between wound diameter and bullet caliber. They found so many variables affected the equation (large variety of bullets involved, variation in shape and surface, gyroscopic instability, intermediate targets, and tangential entries) that accurate caliber determination was undependable. They believe that this method could be improved sufficiently to allow elimination of suspect weapons, but not to identify a specific caliber.

An entrance wound in skin cannot be used to determine caliber. It may be even smaller than the diameter of the bullet or, if entering through a skin fold or crease, may even be slit-like in configuration.[7]

A bullet entering the body ordinarily will travel in a straight line until it comes to rest, strikes bone, or exits the body. Radiologic evaluation can be helpful in any of these instances, and in the exceptions to the rule.

Determination of entrance and exit are usually the province of the attending clinician or the autopsy surgeon. Collins and Lantz[8] found that even trauma specialists had difficulty interpreting entrance and exit wounds and number of projectiles: 74% of multiple gunshot wounds were interpreted incorrectly, and 37% of exiting single gunshot wounds were misclassified.

Determination of entrance and exit wounds in the skull by the rule of intersecting fractures has been described already in Chapter 3 (see Figure 3-7).[9] If a bullet strikes bone, its subsequent path may be indicated by metal and bone splinters (see Figure 3-5, where a fleeing burglar was shot in the back). Small lead particles show how the bullet was deflected around the curve of the rib before coming to rest in superficial soft tissue. Often, however, the scattered pattern of bone and metal fragments is so disorganized that the pathway is indeterminate.

Canadian investigators[10] hypothesized that a centerfire rifle projectile might produce a cone-shaped fragment pattern with the apex at the entry site, thus allowing interpretation of the trajectory from routine radiographs. This could be useful when entrance and exit wounds are altered or destroyed by decomposition or other causes. They found it difficult to accurately describe a three-dimensional cone from two-dimensional radiographs. An incorrect opinion of bullet direction was rendered 57% of the time when the entry site was unknown, and in 19% of the cases even when the location of wounds was known.

Gas or air may be introduced into the body of a gunshot victim from the outside or from the gastrointestinal tract or respiratory system, but will not mark the bullet pathway dependably. Rather, the air in solid tissues will tend to distribute along fascial planes or in body cavities by gravitational forces.

In the living, computed tomography (CT) is invaluable in analysis of gunshot wounds of the head and neck or body.[3] Foreign materials carried into the wound may simulate tissue densities; wood splinters may be confused with air shadows. CT of the abdomen ideally is performed before peritoneal lavage. Angiography may be required to evaluate possible damage to the cardiovascular system, and contrast studies of the esophagus are recommended in midline wounds of the neck or thorax. Remember that the digital scout film or topogram preliminary to a CT scan is useful in localization of missiles.

Large metallic fragments in the body may produce large "star patterns" which obscure detail on CT. Magnetic resonance imaging (MR) then may be particularly helpful in assessing injury to neural and vascular structures and to solid organs. However, if the metallic fragments are ferrous or paramagnetic (i.e., some forms of nickel, cobalt, or iron), MR artifacts also may obscure detail. Ferrous metals in the brain, spinal cord, or eye are contraindications to MR examination, as is the presence of a cardiac pacemaker.[2]

Steel shot, required by law when hunting waterfowl, are affected by large magnetic fields. Usually they can be differentiated radiographically from lead shot by their resistance to deformation (see below under "Pellet Problems").

Number of Bullets

Determination of the number of bullets expected or found within the body may be surprisingly difficult. There may be confusion between entrance and exit wounds. It is possible that a bullet will enter the same wound made by a round fired earlier in a sequence. Rarely, a bullet will lodge in the barrel of the weapon after firing; a second firing may propel both bullets out of the barrel. These "tandem bullets" can enter the body through the same entrance hole.[11]

Other metallic densities may be confused radiographically with a bullet (Figures 11-2 and 11-3). Further, not all projectiles shot from guns are bullets (Figure 11-4).

Example Case 11-1 — This young man was shot in the left chest and developed an pneumothorax which necessitated placing a pleural drainage tube. The tube appeared to be malfunctioning, and a frontal view of the chest showed a bullet-shaped density at the end of the chest tube (Figure 11-5A). The question was raised whether the bullet had become lodged in the chest tube. A frontal view of the abdomen revealed an apparent second bullet, although the victim claimed to have been shot only once. Figure 11-5B showed that the bullet-shaped density was an integral part of the tube tip, designed to facilitate insertion. The real bullet had slipped into the abdomen through a rent in the diaphragm.

More common, and more important, is the "missing" bullet. The bullet may be "missing" because some other injury is mistaken for a gunshot wound, or because an exit wound is overlooked or disguised. More often, the bullet is "missing" because it is not in its expected location due to migration or embolization.

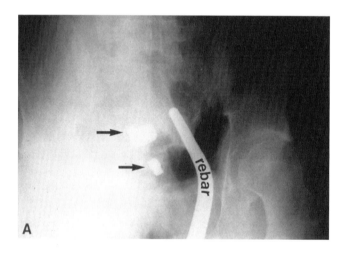

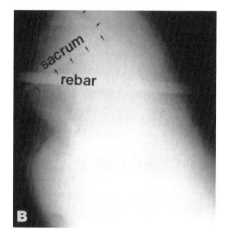

Figure 11-2 Articles of clothing can be confused with bullets. **A**: arrows point out a zipper pull and a waist fastener that could be confused with bullets. Actually, this biker crashed into a bridge under construction and impaled himself, **B**: on a length of rebar which was cut off and brought in with him. He survived. Deceased gunshot victims should be radiographed initially with their clothes on in order to detect any spent bullets lying loose in the clothing.

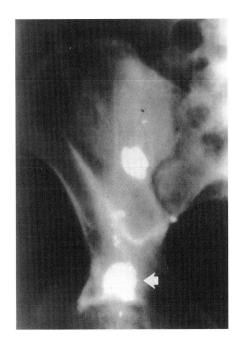

Figure 11-3   This is the same gunshot wound as shown in Figure 10-5. On this frontal view (which was taken first) the separated jacket (arrow) might be confused with a second bullet. (From Messmerr J. M. and Fierro, M. F., *Radio-Graphics*, 6, 457, 1986. With permission.)

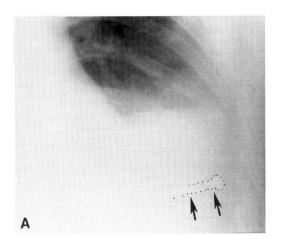

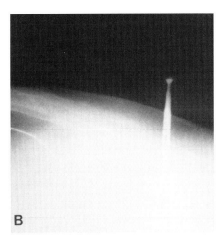

Figure 11-4   Wound from a stud gun. **A**: the missile (arrows) is barely seen within the density of the liver and blood or fluid in the left pleural space and is outlined for the reader's benefit. **B**: cross-table lateral view of chest. (head toward viewer's left). The stud has entered the chest at the level of the tip of the xiphisternum.

Migration of Missiles

Movement of foreign objects within the body can occur in tubular structures such as the vascular system, the bronchial tree, the alimentary canal, the urinary tract, and the neural canal. They can also travel within less confined spaces such as the pleural space or the peritoneal cavity. Because they are of metallic density, bullets and pellets are readily

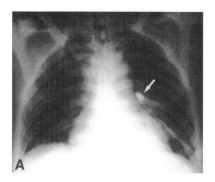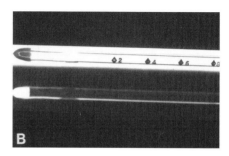

Figure 11-5   A: chest radiograph shows bullet-shaped density at tip of chest tube. **B**: photograph (top) and radiograph (bottom) show that the bullet-shaped density is an integral part of the tube. (From Messmer, J. M. and Fierro, M. F., *RadioGraphics*, 6, 457, 1986; Messmer, J. M. and Wadsworth, J. D., *J. Forensic Sci.*, 29, 340, 1984. With permission.)

visualized radiographically. Any missile not quickly located near its wound of entry or along an obvious tract requires radiological localization. In the dead, this can save time for the forensic pathologist in recovering essential evidence and information. In the living, rapid and accurate location of migrating missiles can be life saving as well as time saving.

Factors determining or modifying missile migration include force and direction of blood flow, gravity and position, pressure changes associated with the Valsalva maneuver, variation in vascular anatomy, the site of entry, and the weight of the projectile.[12,13]

Patients with missile migration may demonstrate absence of a projectile from the general area of an entrance wound, change in position or number of bullets or pellets (or fragments thereof), lack of an exit wound, and in some cases suggestive clinical findings such as signs of a distal vascular occlusion.[12] It must be remembered that a bullet found in a location inconsistent with the entry wound bullet path may not reflect either migration or embolization; one must investigate the possibility that it resides there as a result of an old gunshot wound in the remote part.[2]

Not infrequently, serial radiographic studies will be necessary to reveal movement of the bullet (Figure 11-6).

Bullets fired into the spine may lose velocity abruptly against the strong bone structure there and sink for surprising distances in the spinal subarachnoid space. Radiological examination offers the only rapid and easy way to locate such missiles, and will prevent laminectomy at the wrong level (Figures 11-7 and 11-8).

The urinary tract is a rare location for missile migration. Bullets or pellets can gain access through wounds in the kidney or bladder (Figure 11-9).

Wounds to the face can result in bullets being swallowed[13] (Figure 11-10). Projectiles fired into the chest or abdomen can be introduced directly into the alimentary canal[14] (Figure 11-11). The bullets usually will pass uneventfully in the stool, but the thoracic or abdominal cavities may be contaminated by a leakage from the perforated gut.

Example Case 11-2 — A young male was shot in the right chest just beneath the nipple. There was no exit wound. A chest radiograph (Figure 11-11A) showed pneumothorax but no intrathoracic bullet; however, a bullet (arrow) was seen in the right upper abdominal quadrant. Upon the assumption that the diaphragm had been penetrated, a laparotomy was performed, but the diaphragm and all abdominal organs were found to be intact and

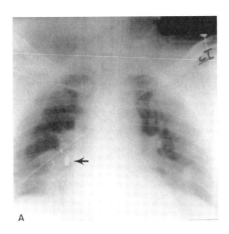
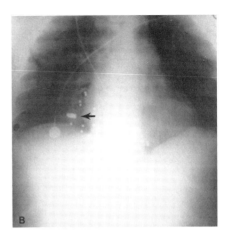

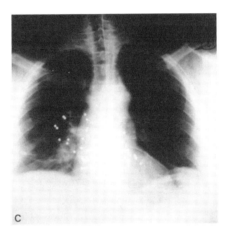

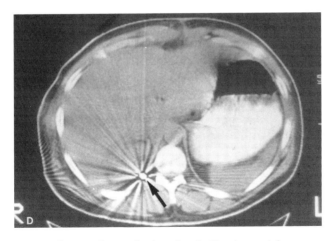

Figure 11-6   **A**: supine chest radiograph showing bullet (arrow) from acute gunshot wound. Small shot are from an old shotgun injury. It was not possible to do a lateral or erect view because of the patient's clinical condition. **B**: supine chest two days later. Bullet has rotated and moved — obviously in pleural space. **C**: two days later bullet disappears from chest radiograph. **D**: CT reveals bullet deep in posterior costophrenic sulcus (star pattern). Bullet obscured on routine chest film by density of full-thickness liver.

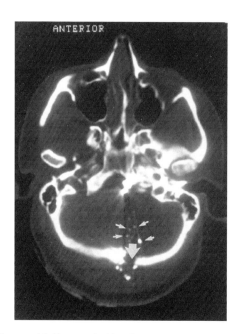 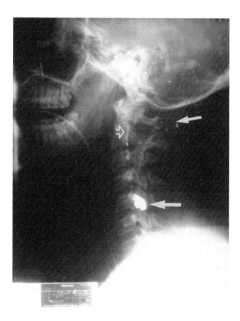

Figure 11-7   **A**: bullet fired into the base of the skull cut a groove in the occipital bone (large arrow) scattering fragments (small arrows) into the posterior fossa as shown on CT examination. **B**: lateral view of cervical spine shows the bullet traversed the posterior elements of the C-1 vertebra (small arrows), impacted on the posterior body of C-2 (open arrows), then dropped in the spinal canal before coming to rest at the C-5 level (large arrow).

normal. Five days later a CT was done to localize the bullet, now thought to be within the liver. Rather, the topogram (Figure 11-11B) showed the bullet in the right lower quadrant, and the CT scan (Figure 11-11C) localized it within the cecum. This prompted a contrast study of the esophagus (Figure 11-11D) which demonstrated a leak (arrow) at the bullet entry site. The bullet passed in the fecal stream.

We have also seen a case where shotgun pellets introduced directly into the stomach through an abdominal wound migrated into the esophagus by the mechanism of gastroesophageal reflux.

Missiles can enter the tracheobronchial tree by direct penetration or aspiration (Figure 11-12).

Once its energy is spent, a bullet can come to rest in one of the components of the cardiovascular system, or it may migrate to a distant site. The eventual resting place of a bullet which enters either the arterial or venous system depends closely upon its site of entry, the position of the victim, and the weight of the projectile. [15–23] Approximately 80% of vascular emboli are arterial and 20% are venous.[24] Vascular emboli are most often seen in adults, although there are reports in children.[25]

In general, bullet emboli are associated with small-caliber, low-velocity bullets. Heavier projectiles tend to "sink" and are more likely to be found in the dependent portions of the body (Figures 11-13 and 11-14). In a collective review of 36 cases of cardiac wounds associated with peripheral embolization, 75% involved embolization to the lower extremities and the remainder to the neck and visceral vessels.[26,27] Lighter projectiles such as shotgun pellets can be swept superiorly, against gravity, by arterial flow pressure. There are several case reports of intracerebral vascular accidents caused by migrating shotgun

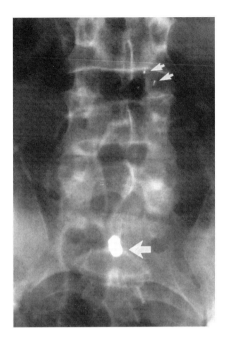
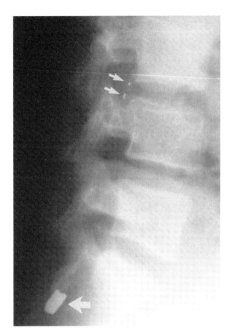
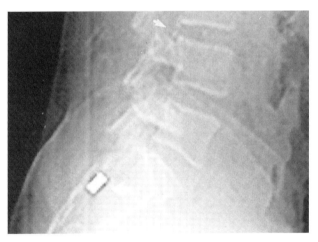

Figure 11-8   Gunshot wound to the back **A**: frontal and **B**: lateral views show the bullet struck the left inferior articular process of the L-3 vertebra, leaving two small metal fragments (small arrows), then dropped into the subarachnoid space, coming to rest in the caudal sac (arrow). **C**: note that the topogram or digital scout film for a subsequent CT is just as useful as the lateral radiograph.

pellets where the site of entry is usually either the neck or the chest.[28–32] We have personally seen only one such case.[33]

Example Case 11-3 — A young male was shot in the chest and abdomen with a shotgun. At surgery he was found to have four puncture wounds in the heart, hemopericardium, and multiple puncture wounds in the spleen, pancreas, colon, and small bowel. (Figure 11-15A shows the shot pattern over the heart postoperatively.) His postoperative progress was satisfactory for three days, then suddenly he developed dyspnea, chest pain, and cardiac

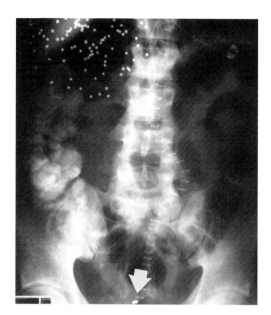

Figure 11-9   A shotgun wound to the back injured the right kidney. The two pellets overlying the lower pelvis entered the urinary bladder (arrow) after passing through the right ureter.

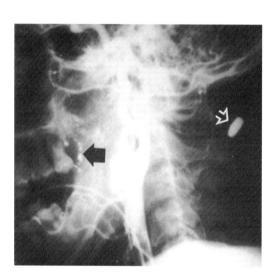 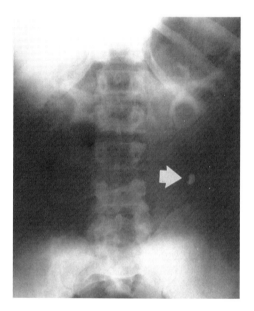

Figure 11-10   **A**: this victim was shot twice in the face with a .25 caliber handgun. A lateral view of the neck following injection of contrast into the common carotid artery shows one bullet in the soft tissues of the posterior neck (open arrow) and metallic fragments (arrow) over the coronoid process of the mandible. **B**: a supine view of the abdomen shows a bullet (arrow) in the left abdomen. This bullet had been swallowed and was eventually recovered in the stool. (From Messmer, J. M. and Fierro, M. F., *RadioGraphics*, 6, 457, 1986. With permission.)

collapse. Although resuscitated, he remained comatose and developed a dense left hemiplegia. A repeat chest radiograph (Figure 11-15B) showed that one of the bullets formerly overlying the heart shadow was gone. A carotid arteriogram (Figure 11-15C and D) showed that it had migrated to the right middle cerebral artery, which was totally occluded. The patient died, and the charge was changed from attempted murder to murder.

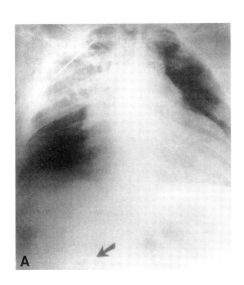

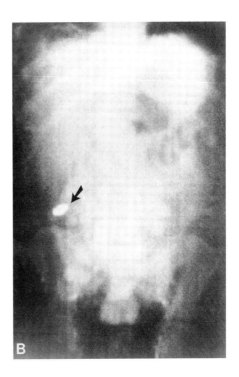

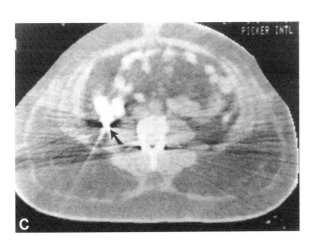

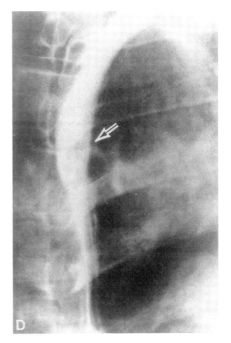

Figure 11-11   **A**: chest radiograph: no intrathoracic bullet, but one seen faintly beneath the diaphragm (arrow). **B**: digital scout film prior to CT shows bullet in RLQ (arrow). **C**: bullet creates star pattern in cecum on CT scan. **D**: wisp of water-soluble contrast medium escapes esophagus at site of bullet injury. (From Hughes, J. J., *J. Trauma*, 27, 1362, 1987. With permission.)

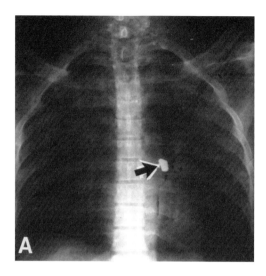

Figure 11-12   **A**: this victim suffered two gunshot wounds to the face. A radiograph of the head (not shown) demonstrated only one bullet. A frontal view of the chest demonstrates a bullet (arrow) overlying the left hilum. **B**: the autopsy findings showed the blackened bullet that had been aspirated within the left main stem bronchus (arrows).

Pellets and small bullets may be transported by venous flow, even against gravity, and cause great mischief (Figures 11-16, 11-17, and 11-18). Even large missiles occasionally follow venous flow[12] (Figure 11-19).

Missile penetration of a major vessel, even the aorta, may not lead to fatal or even serious exsanguination, but distal occlusion is virtually inevitable (Figure 11-20).

Example Case 11-4 — A young male was shot in the left flank with a handgun, but no bullet was present on the admission radiograph of the abdomen. Physical examination revealed no pulse in the left leg. A radiograph (Figure 11-20A) showed the bullet in Hunter's canal along the course of the superficial femoral artery. An aortogram (Figure 11-20B)

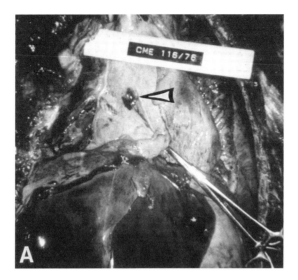

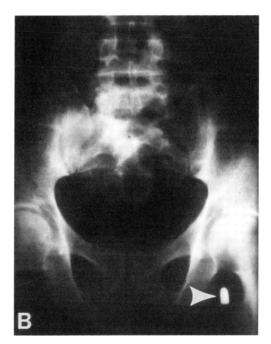

Figure 11-13 **A**: although the autopsy revealed a gunshot wound to the anterior surface of the heart (arrowhead), a frontal view of the chest had revealed no bullet. **B**: a radiograph of the pelvis showed a bullet overlying the left groin. Post-mortem dissection showed it to be in the left femoral artery. Forces of both gravity and flow probably effected this migration. (From Messmer, J. M. and Fierro, M. F., *RadioGraphics*, 6, 457, 1986. With permission.)

demonstrated a pseudoaneurysm originating on the posterior wall of the aorta, indicating the site of bullet entry.

In general, symptomatic missiles should be removed. Left atrial or ventricular missiles floating free should be removed prophylactically. Missiles floating in the right heart may be removed or watched. Embedded missiles in the heart are relatively safe. Bullets that

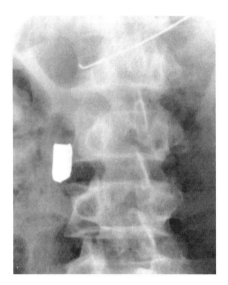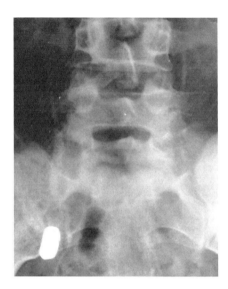

Figure 11-14   A: abdominal roentgenogram of a young male immediately after admission for a gunshot wound to the mid-abdomen shows the bullet just to the right of L-3. **B**: subsequent scout film prior to an excretory urogram shows the bullet has migrated from its initial position (consistent with the inferior vena cava) *against* venous flow to a location consistent with the right iliac vein.[12]

have traversed the bowel before embedding may be removed to prevent potential infection. Missiles next to major vessels may be removed to avoid risk of erosion into the vessel.[2,3] Cardiac neurosis from knowledge of a bullet within the heart may be a patient-management problem.[34]

To summarize the problems of missile migration, we would reiterate that radiographic detection of missile migration depends upon careful examination of serial studies and a knowledge of the manifestations of missile migration. These include a change in the number or positions of missile fragments, absence of a missile from the general area of the wound, or the development of signs of distal vascular occlusion. We recommend radiographic examination immediately prior to operation to confirm the anatomic location of missiles to be removed, since failure to find a missile at operation may require multiple intraoperative radiographs to survey the body for the final resting place of a bullet embolus.

Pellet Problems

Deformation

Except for the steel loads mandated for waterfowl hunting, shotgun pellets of all sizes are subject to deformation. Froede et. al. have pointed out that deformation of round pellets, particularly flattening, should be recognized as "a gross radiographic pitfall".[35] Large shot, in particular 0 or 00, upon flattening and/or fragmentation may bear no resemblance to shot and, rather, suggest large-caliber bullets or jackets. Lead shot will deform upon impacting firm body tissues, especially bone. Shot ricocheting off hard surfaces back into the body may be especially confusing. Radiography in more than one projection will help sort out these problems. In one case, lack of deformation of round shot was helpful in evaluating a death scene.

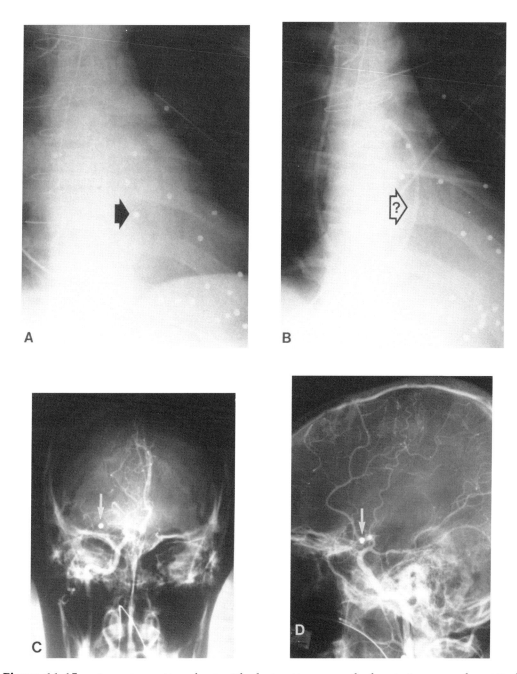

Figure 11-15   **A**: postoperative chest with shot pattern over the heart. Arrow marks critical shot, which is missing three days later, **B**: when the patient undergoes a sudden clinical crisis. **C** and **D**: right carotid arteriogram shows occlusion of the right middle cerebral artery by the pellet embolus (arrow). (Figure 11-15**C** and **D** from Kase, C. S., White, R. L., Vinson, T. L., and Eichelberger, R. P., *Neurology, 31, 458. W*ith permission.)

Example Case 11-5 — The partially clad, mostly decomposed body of a young male was found in southern New Mexico in the springtime. The remnants of clothing and, more importantly, ante-mortem and post-mortem roentgenographic matches of a previously fractured arm, enabled positive identification of the body. He was a young Navajo

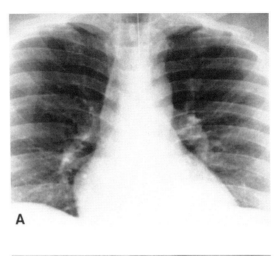

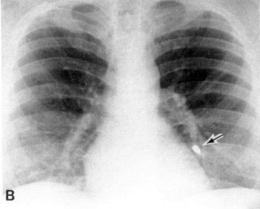

Figure 11-16 **A**: normal supine postoperative chest radiograph of young male following gunshot wound to abdomen. A tear in the inferior vena cava had been found at laparotomy. Several days later signs of pulmonary embolism developed. A repeat study, **B**: showed the bullet (arrow) embolized to a branch of the left pulmonary artery.[12]

sub-teenager who had run away from a Bureau of Indian Affairs boarding school during a blizzard the preceding winter — presumably to return to his home on an Arizona reservation. The problem was that the roentgenological studies of the body, as found, showed numerous very small shotgun pellets. Was he a homicide? It was noticed (Figure 11-21A) that *none* of the pellets were deformed, and that the shot pattern was unusual as compared to the usual shotgun victim's roentgenogram (Figure 11-21B). The body had been found in the periphery of the Sheriff's Posse Skeet and Trap Range which had been heavily used all winter. It is believed that the young lad died of exposure his first night out, and that spent shot from skeet loads had drifted down onto, and into, the decomposing body and its clothing throughout the long winter of his disappearance.

Pellet Pattern: Range of Fire

The spherical pellet fired from a nonrifled shotgun, is aerodynamically disadvantaged. It slows down rapidly in air or tissue. It is not a long-range missile. Pellets exiting a shotgun

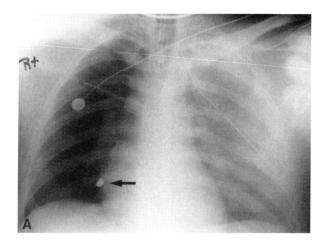

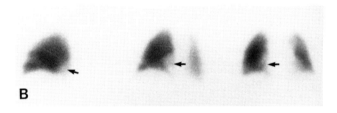

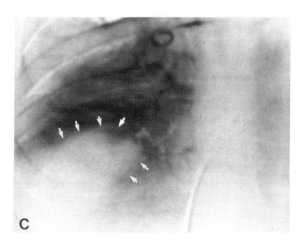

Figure 11-17   Another inferior vena cava to pulmonary artery embolus. **A**: chest radiograph.
B: positive radioisotope lung scan showing perfusion defect in the right lower lobe posteriorly
(arrows). **C**: pulmonary arteriogram. Contrast is reversed in this subtraction image so that
perfused lung is black, nonperfused lung is clear (arrows).

muzzle gradually spread out. There are many systems for determining the range of fire of
shotguns using information on gauge, shot size, choke, distance, etc. Most are relatively
inaccurate. The radiologist needs to know that the shot pattern is compacted at contact
or close range where other materials (wad, shot cup, plastic, cardboard) may appear in the
wound and on the radiograph, then spreads with increasing range or distance (see Figure

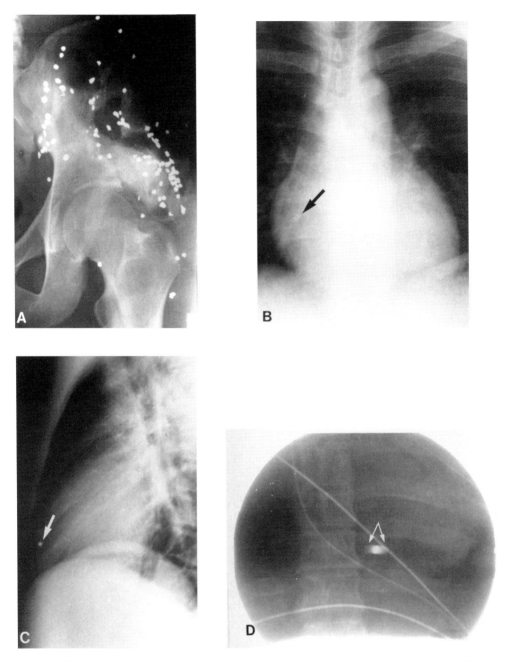

Figure 11-18   **A**: shotgun wound to the left hip. **B** and **C**: routine PA and lat. chest radiographs reveal a pellet lying within the heart. **D**: spot-film taken during fluoroscopy shows to-and-fro blurring of the shot as it moves with the heart beat. This means it is either in the wall of the right ventricle or trapped in the chordae tendineae inside the right ventricle. A shot moving freely in the ventricular cavity would describe a more circular motion.

10-11). There is a large pitfall in this generalization. Whereas making conclusions about the range of shotgun fire from external inspection of the wound is usually accurate, drawing conclusions from radiographs is another potential pitfall. Radiographically, the dispersal of pellets may suggest that the weapon was fired from a distance, when in actuality the

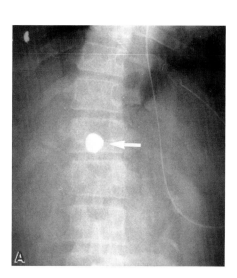
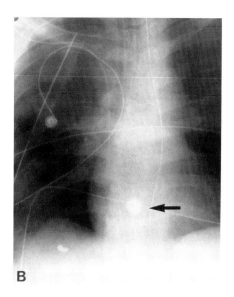

Figure 11-19 **A**: a .45 caliber handgun wound to the back introduced a large bullet into the inferior vena cava. **B**: serial film studies showed it moved slowly into the right ventricle (arrow) where it stayed until removed with a stone-basket introduced into the right ventricle via the jugular vein and superior vena cava.

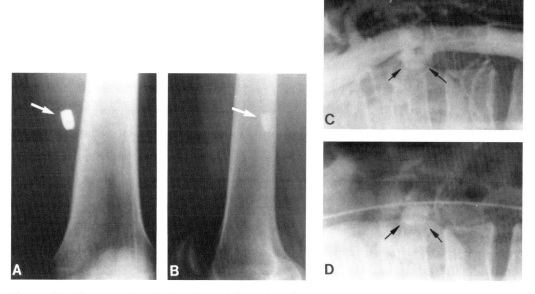

Figure 11-20 **A** and **B**: bullet (arrow) from left flank wound now lodged in the superficial femoral artery in the thigh. **C** and **D**: early and late films from a lateral aortogram show a pseudoaneurysm (arrows) arising from the posterior wall of the aorta.

weapon was fired from close range (Figure 11-22). The phenomenon responsible for this is known as the "billiard ball" effect (Figure 11-23). When a mass of shotgun pellets enters tissue, the first pellets which penetrate are slowed and struck from behind by the following

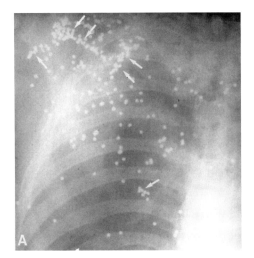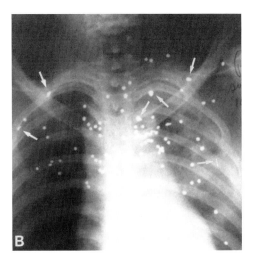

Figure 11-21   **A**: shot pattern over the body of a young Indian boy is unusual (see arrowed clusters) and NO pellets are deformed. **B**: typical shot pattern of a relatively long-range shotgun wound. Note the many deformed pellets (arrows).

pellets which can cause them to scatter through the tissue much like a cluster of billiard balls struck by the cue ball. The radiographic image must be correlated with the physical examination of the skin surface wound pattern in order to avoid incorrect range estimates.[2]

Bullet Wounds: Range of Fire

The range of fire assessments of bullet wounds may depend on the composition and relative amounts of residue found on the skin. Primer residue usually contains some combination of lead, antimony, or barium. Bullet residue from nonjacketed bullets is 70 to 90% lead. Coated bullets leave an admixture of lead and copper. Jacketed or semijacketed bullets produce the least amount of lead and only small amounts of copper-containing residue.[37]

Residue deposits on excised skin have been examined with soft x-rays generated by the Faxitron unit (see Chapter 22, Figure 22-6) for localization, then further studied by scanning electron microscopy and energy-dispersive analysis of x-rays.[36]

Clothing can redistribute gunshot residue and even prevent it from reaching the skin. Thus, examination of the clothing may be as important as examination of the body.[37] Clothing may be so blood-soaked as to render direct examination impossible. Again, Faxitron examination of the clothing can be extremely helpful in defining the location and distribution of gunshot residue, thus allowing further collection and analysis (Figure 11-24).

Final Comment

The forensic evaluation of gunshot wounds and weapon ballistics is complex and wide-ranging, and the typical radiologist has limited expertise in this area. The forensic pathologist seldom is reluctant to accept assistance from an interested and knowledgeable

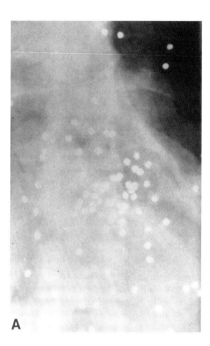 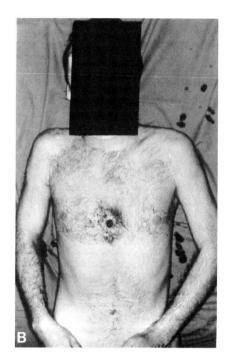

Figure 11-22 **A**: a post-mortem radiograph of the midbody area shows a spread out pattern of shotgun pellets suggesting that the weapon had been fired from a distance. **B**: the wound was, in fact, a contact suicide wound of the epigastrium. (From Messmer, J. M. and Fierro, M. F., *RadioGraphics*, 6, 457, 1986. With permission.)

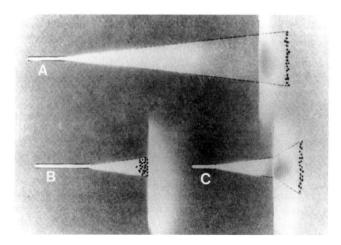

Figure 11-23 Schematic drawing illustrating the "billiard ball" effect. **A**: if a shotgun is fired at intermediate to long range, the pattern has a chance to form. The pellets enter the body through individual openings. A spread pattern of pellets will be seen on a radiograph. **B**: if the shotgun is fired at close range, the leading pellets are slowed as they enter the body and are struck by the trailing pellets. **C**: the colliding pellets ricochet to spread the shot pattern so that it may simulate the pattern of longer-range fire. This is known as the "billiard ball" effect. (Redrawn from Messmer, J. M. and Fierro, M. F., *RadioGraphics*, 6, 457, 1986. With permission.)

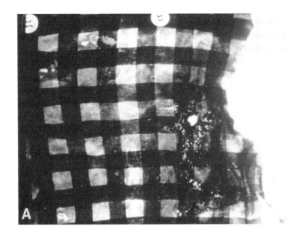

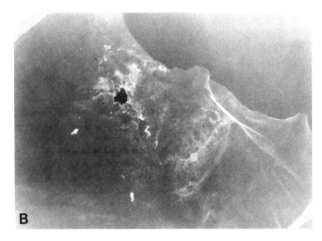

Figure 11-24 **A**: a blood-soaked red and black plaid flannel shirt is a difficult field to examine for gunshot residue. **B**: a low-energy radiograph with the Faxitron unit discloses the location and distribution of residue.

radiologist, but it is incumbent upon the radiologist to become informed, and to recognize the pitfalls and limitations of the specialty as it applies to the investigation of the gunshot victim.

References

1. Hargarten S. W., Karlson, T. A., O'Brien, M., Hancock, J., and Quebbeman, E., Characteristics of firearms involved in fatalities, *J. Am. Med. Assoc.*, 275, 42, 1996.

2. Hollerman, S. W. and Fackler, M. L., Gunshot wounds: radiology and wound ballistics, *Emergency Radiol.*, 2, 171, 1995.

3. Hollerman, S. W. and Fackler, M. L., Bullets, pellets, and wound ballistics, in *Radiologic Guide to Medical Devices and Foreign Bodies*, Hunter, T. B. and Bragg, D. B., Eds., C.V. Mosby, St. Louis, 1994, chap. 19.

4. Bixler, R. P., Ahrens, C. R., Rossi, R. P., and Thickman, D., Bullet identification with radiography, *Radiology*, 178, 563, 1991.

5. Molnar, S., Identification of bullet caliber from x-ray film, *Assoc. Firearm Tool Mark Examiners Newsl.*, 12, 45, 1971.

6. Berryman, H. E., Smith, O. C., and Symes, S. A., Diameter of cranial gunshot wounds as a function of bullet caliber, *J. Forensic Sci.*, 40, 751, 1995.

7. Di Maio, V. J. M, *Gunshot Wounds*, Elsevier, New York, 1985, chap. 4.

8. Collins, K. A. and Lantz, P. E., Interpretation of fatal, multiple and existing gunshot wounds by trauma specialists, *J. Forensic Sci.*, 39, 94, 1994.

9. Smith, O. C., Berryman, H. E., and Lahren, C. H., Cranial fracture patterns and estimate of direction from low velocity gunshot wounds, *J. Forensic Sci.*, 32, 1416, 1987.

10. Straathof, D., Bannach, B. G., and Dowling, G. P., Radiography of centrefire gunshot wounds, in Proc. Am. Acad. Forensic Sci. Annu. Mtg., New York, 1997, p. 138.

11. Di Maio, V. J. M., *Gunshot Wounds*, Elsevier, New York, 1985, chap. 10.

12. Hughes, J. J., Brogdon, B. G., and Eichelberger, R. P., Migrating missiles, *Ala. J. Med. Sci.*, 21, 416, 1984.

13. Messmer, J. M. and Fierro, M. F., Radiologic forensic investigation of fatal gunshot wounds, *RadioGraphics*, 6, 457, 1986.

14. Hughes, J. J., Bullet injury to the esophagus detected by intestinal migration, *J. Trauma*, 27, 1362, 1987.

15. Ledgerwood, A. M., The wandering bullet, *Surg. Clin. North Am.*, 57, 97, 1977.

16. Di Maio, V. J. and Di Maio, D. J., Bullet embolism: six cases and a review of the literature, *J. Forensic Sci.*, 17, 394, 1972.

17. Fatteh, A. and Shah, Z. A., Bullet embolus of the right profunda femoris artery, *J. Forensic Sci.*, 15, 139, 1968.

18. Kelley, J. L., A bullet embolus to the left femoral artery following a thoracic gunshot wound, *J. Thorac. Surg.*, 21, 608, 1951.

19. Morton, J. R., Reul, G. L., Arbegast N. R., Okies, J. E., and Beall, A. C., Bullet embolus to the right ventricle, *Am. J. Surg.*, 122, 584, 1971.

20. Padula, R. T., Sandlet, S. C., and Camishion, R. C., Delayed bullet embolization to the heart following abdominal gunshot wound, *Ann. Surg.*, 169, 599, 1969.

21. Saltzstein, E. C. and Freeark, R. J., Bullet embolism to the right axillary artery following gunshot wound of the heart, *Ann. Surg.*, 158, 65, 1963.

22. Sclafani, S. J. and Mitchell, W. G., Retrograde venous bullet embolism, *J. Trauma*, 21, 656, 1981.

23. Symbas, P. N., Hatcher, C. R., and Mansour, K. A., Projectile embolus of the lung, *J. Thorac. Cardiovasc. Surg.*, 5, 97, 1968.

24. Rich, N. M., Collins, G. J., Andersen, C. A., McDonald, P. T., Kozloff, L., and Ricotta, J. J., Missile emboli, *J. Trauma*, 18, 236, 1978.

25. Massad, M. and Slim, M. S., Intravascular missile embolization in childhood: report of a case, literature review, and recommendations for management, *J. Pediatr. Surg.*, 25, 1292, 1990.

26. Shannon, J. J., Vo, N. M., Stanton, P. E., and Dimler, M., Peripheral arterial embolization: a case report and 22 year literature review, *J. Vasc. Surg.*, 5, 773, 1987.

27. Ward, P. A. and Suzuki, A., Gunshot wound of the heart with peripheral embolization: a case report and review of literature, *J. Thorac. Cardiovasc. Surg.*, 68, 440, 1974.

28. VanGilder, J. C. and Coxe, W. S., Shotgun pellet embolus of the middle cerebral artery, *J. Neurosurg.*, 32, 711, 1970.

29. Dadsetan, M. R. and Jinkins, J. R., Peripheral vascular gunshot bullet embolus migration to the cerebral circulation: report and literature review, *Neuroradiology*, 32, 516, 1990.

30. Dada, M. A., Loftus, I. A., and Rutherford, G. S., Shotgun pellet embolism to the brain, *Am. J. Forensic Med. Pathol.*, 14, 58, 1993.

31. Oser, A. B., Moran, C. J., Cross, D. T., and Thompson, R. W., Shotgun pellet embolization to the intracranial internal carotid artery: report of a case and review of the literature, *J. Trauma*, 1, 200, 1994.

32. Jones, B. L. and Tomsick, T. A., Shotgun pellet embolism to the basilar artery, *Am. J. Roentgenol.*, 165, 744, 1995.

33. Kase, C. S., White, R. L., Vinson, T. L., and Eichelberger, R. P., Shotgun pellet embolus to the middle cerebral artery, *Neurology*, 31, 458, 1981.

34. Bland, E. F. and Beebe, G. W., Missiles in the heart, *N. Engl. J. Med.*, 274, 1039, 1966.

35. Froede, R. C., Pitt, M. J., and Bridgeman, R. R., Shotgun diagnosis: "it ought to be something else". *J. Forensic Sci.*, 27, 428, 1982.

36. Lang, P. E., Jerome, W. G., and Jaworski, J. A., Radiopaque deposits surrounding a contact small-caliber gunshot wound, *Am. J. Forensoc Med. Pathol.*, 15, 10, 1994.

37. Di Maio, V. J. M., *Gunshot Wounds*, Elsevier, New York, 1985, chap. 12.

SECTION IV

Radiology in Nonviolent Crimes

Excluding tort actions for personal injury and/or malpractice, the major thrust of forensic radiology has been the evaluation of violence and violent crime. It is used to evaluate missile injuries and other traumatic lesions. It has established the age, and thus sealed the fate, of convicted murderers. It discovers abuse. It seeks to explain accidental or unattended death. It is employed to identify remains that have been mutilated, incinerated, separated, commingled, decomposed, or dehydrated and are beyond recognition by more conventional means.

But as we have already seen in Chapter 2, the radiologic pioneers also applied Röntgen's rays to such relatively peaceable criminal pursuits as mail fraud, adulteration of foodstuff, and forgery of legal documents and other items.

In this section, three modern examples of the use of the x-ray in detecting nonviolent crimes are presented.

B.G.B.

Smuggling

12

B. G. BROGDON, M.D.

Contents

Introduction

As already mentioned in Chapter 2, as early as 1897 the French customs service (*la Douane*) was using fluoroscopic x-ray equipment to apprehend smugglers of contraband seemingly widely disparate in importance by today's standards, ranging from jewels to cigarettes and matches (which were monopolies of the government).[1]

The "Body Packer"

Beginning in the 1970s a new breed of smuggler began to be recognized and apprehended by the radiologic method.[2] This was the "body packer", a specialized type of "mule", who smuggled contraband drugs (mostly cocaine) across borders in specially devised packages secreted in the carrier's rectum, vagina, or alimentary canal.

Many of these smugglers were users or addicts earning the wherewithal to feed their own habit. A few were simply bringing in a supply for their own use. Others were commercial carriers in it for the money or the excitement.[3] The monetary rewards are not insubstantial. The value of Third World purchases can increase almost tenfold with successful (undetected) importation.[4] Whatever the motivation the purpose is the same — to transport concealed narcotics across borders and through customs without detection.

Packages stored for the "short haul" in the vagina or rectum are easily accessed and discovered by manual examination in a body search. This probably prompted the more common practice of swallowing the packages of contraband since no authority has immediate access to the gastrointestinal tract.[5] Body packing quickly became a worldwide problem.

Packaging

Cocaine, heroin, amphetamines, hashish, and marijuana have all been transported in the alimentary tract.[3,6–9] Typically the drug is wrapped in several layers of latex by using condoms, the fingers of surgical gloves, or even toy balloons. Sometimes inner layers of other materials such as carbon paper, cellophane, and plastic wrap are included. The ends of the packages are securely tied like a sausage and the resultant package is swallowed or secreted in the rectum. Up to 214 packages have been found in a single "mule".[10] The packages usually contain 3 to 7 g of narcotics.[11] They are round or oval in shape and most are only 1 to 2 cm in diameter.[5]

Diagnosis/Detection

Early cases of body packing were brought to official attention when the perpetrators became ill or died from an overdose of the transported drug (Figure 12-1). Other cases came to light because of obstruction of the alimentary canal. One inept smuggler succeeded in lodging the packet in the cervical esophagus, with total esophageal obstruction to the extent that he was unable to swallow his own saliva.[3] Thus, apprehension of the smuggler is important not only from the standpoint of law enforcement, but it may also save the life of the miscreant. A package that does not pass through the gastrointestinal tract may break open and cause death as long as ten days after ingestion.

Some condoms may act as semipermeable membranes. Once fluid from the gastrointestinal tract gains access to the package the law of Gibbs-Donnan equilibrium takes effect; cocaine hydrochloride, a salt, may diffuse out into the gut or may cause additional fluid to be drawn into the package to the point of rupture. In either event, cocaine toxicity can ensue rapidly.[12] Cases of clinical obstruction or drug overdose led to abdominal radiography, and this disclosed the classic radiologic finding in the body packer. During wrapping, air gets captured between the layers of packaging in the majority of cases. Gastrointestinal gas may pass into a deteriorating package. Gas may be generated inside the package by fermentation of plant material at body temperature as in the case of marijuana.[8,13]

Radiographically one looks for regularly shaped round or oval foreign bodies outlined by arcuate or encircling thin air shadows, sometimes in multiple layers (Figure 12-2). The entire package may be outlined by intramural gas in the gut. The bag form may taper

Figure 12-1   Latex-covered narcotic packages are shown in the opened stomach of a body packer who died of an overdose when one of the packages ruptured. (Courtesy of James M. Messmer, M.D.)

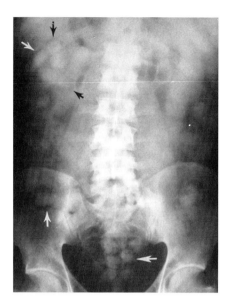

Figure 12-2   Abdominal radiograph of a body packer showing rounded and ovoid, slightly hyperdense packages, some of which are clearly surrounded by a halo of entrapped gas or air (some are marked with arrows). (Courtesy of Richard N. Aizupuru, M.D.)

slightly from its fundus to the neck, which may have a rosette form where it has been tied off.[14] The bags may be of variable density — hyperdense, hypodense, or isodense.

Advanced Packaging and Detection Techniques

Packaging has become more sophisticated as detection rates have increased. McCarron and Wood[11] have proposed a classification of cocaine packages. *Type I* is the common package of two to four layers of condoms, balloons, or glove fingers tied or taped for configuration and closure that usually appear as well-defined, slightly hyperdense, homogeneous shadows surrounded by complete or incomplete halos of air (inner layers of plastic or cellophane tend to break up the encircling air shadows). *Type II* bundles are covered with five to seven layers of tubular latex tightly and smoothly tied at each end; these are similar in density to soft tissues with a regular gas halo. *Type III* packages are composed of hardened cocaine parts wrapped first in aluminum foil, then overwrapped with three to five layers of tubular latex and securely tied at each end; these are smaller, very hard, irregularly shaped packages which may be missed on routine abdominal roentgenograms or mistaken for fecal collections.

Some of the more "modern" packages may be machine wrapped and very difficult or impossible to see if not outlined by intraluminal bowel gas.[15] Also, some packers are clever enough to reduce their bowel gas by medication or fasting.

Since many "mules" are also addicts and consequently are chronically constipated, their rounded compact stools may resemble drug packets.[12] This can lead to false positive interpretations of plain abdominal radiographs.

The increased sensitivity of computed tomography is useful in evaluating equivocal cases (Figure 12-3). Water-soluble iodinated contrast material has been given orally to confirm or exclude body packages and also is used to follow the elimination of drug packets in smugglers treated conservatively rather than with surgery.[16] Some authors suggest routine urine testing of suspects to diminish false negative or positive findings, and as an indication for the necessity of further radiologic studies.[12,16,17]

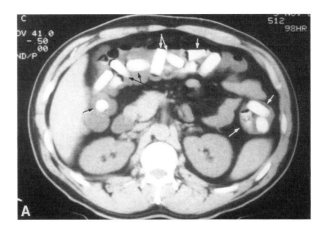

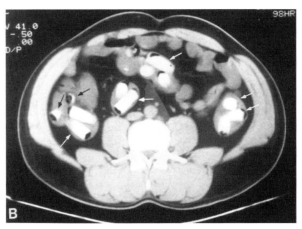

Figure 12-3   **A** and **B**: axial sectional CT images of a body packer shows multiple drug packages somewhat denser than the bowel, most of which contain entrapped air at the ends of the packages. (Courtesy of Richard N. Aizpuru, M.D.)

References

1. Collins, V. P., Origin of medico-legal and forensic roentgenology, in *Classic Descriptions in Diagnostic Radiology*, Vol. 2, Bruwer, A. J., Ed., Charles C Thomas, Springfield, IL, 1984, 1593.

2. Freed, T. A., Sweet, L. N., and Gauder, P. S., Balloon obturation bowel obstruction: a hazard of drug smuggling, *Am. J. Roentgenol.*, 127, 1033, 1976.

3. Dunne, J. W., Drug smuggling by internal body concealment, *Med. J. Aust.*, 2, 436, 1983.

4. Pinsky, M. F., Ducas, J., and Ruggere, M. D., Narcotic smuggling: the double condom sign, *J. Can. Assoc. Radiol.*, 29, 79, 1978.

5. Pamilo, M., Suoranta, H., and Suramo, I., Narcotic smuggling and radiography of the gastrointestinal tract, *Acta Radiol. Diagn.*, 27, 213, 1986.

6. Beerman, R., Nunez, D., Jr., and Weth, C.V., Radiographic evaluation off the cocaine smuggler, *Gastrointest. Radiol.*, 11, 351, 1986.

7. Suarez, C. A., Arango, A., and Lester, J. L., III, Cocaine-condom ingestion, *J. Am. Med. Assoc.*, 238, 1391, 1977.

8. Dassel, P. M. and Punjabi, E., Ingested marihuana-filled balloons, *Gastroenterology*, 76, 166, 1979.

9. Karhunen, P. J., Penttila, A., and Panula, A., Detection of heroin "body-packers" at Helsinki airport, *Lancet*, 1, 1265, 1987.

10. Gherardi, R. K., Baud, F. J., Leporc, P., Marc, B., Dupeyron, J.-P., and Diamant-Berger, O., Detection of drugs in the urine of body-packers, *Lancet*, 1, 1076, 1988.

11. McCarron, M. M. and Wood, J. D., The cocaine "body-packer" syndrome: diagnosis and treatment, *J. Am. Med. Assoc.*, 250, 1417, 1983.

12. Wetli, C. V. and Mittleman, R. E., The "body-packer" syndrome — toxicity following ingestion of ilicit drugs packaged for transportation, *J. Forensic Sci.*, 26, 492, 1981.

13. Karhunen, P. J., Suoranta, H., Panttila, A., and Pitkäranta, P., Pitfalls in the diagnosis of drug smuggler's abdomen, *J. Forensic Sci.*, 36, 397, 1991.

14. Sinner, W. N., The gastrointestinal tract as a vehicle for drug smuggling, *Gastrointest. Radiol.*, 6, 319, 1981.

15. Caruana, D. S., Weibach, B., Goerg, D., and Gardner, L. B., Cocaine-packet ingestion: diagnosis, management, and natural history, *Ann. Intern. Med.*, 100, 73, 1984.

16. Marc, B., Baud, F. J., Aelion, M. J., Gherardi, R., Diamant-Berger, O., Blery, M., and Bismuth, C., The cocaine body-packer syndrome: evaluation of a method of contrast study of the bowel, *J. Forensic Sci.*, 35, 345, 1990.

17. Gherardi, R., Marc, B., Alberti, X., Baud, F., and Diamant-Berger, O., A cocaine body packer with normal abdominal plain radiograms: value of drug detection in urine and contrast study of the bowel, *Am. J. Forensic Med. Pathol.*, 11, 154, 1990.

Larceny

13

B. G. BROGDON, M.D.

Contents

Larceny by Ingestion

In 1896, C. Thurston Holland (1863-1941) was a London physician who often assisted his friend, Sir Robert Jones, the famous pioneering orthopedist, in his free Saturday morning clinic. His introduction to radiology was quite accidental, having to do with a young patient who had a retained pellet from a shotgun wound in the hand. Nevertheless, Holland's interest was piqued by the novel experience, and he went on to become one of England's premier pioneers of radiology and well known throughout the scientific world. He became President of the First International Congress of Radiology in 1925 in London. He published a short memoir of the first year of radiology entitled, "X-rays in 1896" in *The Liverpool Medico-Chirurgical Journal*, 45, 61, 1937.[1]

In telling of the hysteria associated with the first news of Röntgen's discovery, Dr. Holland recounts several amusing examples, including the well-known advertisement for x-ray-proof underclothes for young ladies. He recalls that the *Strand Magazine* carried a series of stories (obviously fictional) illustrating "the Adventures of a Man of Science". In the July, 1896 issue a man suspected of having swallowed a diamond is lured by the "Scientist" into his laboratory where the culprit is undressed and carefully positioned so that the rays would pass through his body. "… my electrical battery worked well. The rays played admirably in the vacuum tube. I removed the cap from the CAMERA…". Get the idea? The climax, of course, was that the photographic plate clearly showed the diamond "just below the region of the ileo-caecal valve"! This undoubtedly is the first of many stories of *larceny by ingestion* thwarted by the x-ray.

Dr. Holland had noticed in a roentgenogram of a lady's hand that the diamonds in a large marquise ring did not "cast a shadow; the mounting appeared empty on the plate." So, on August 7, 1896 he exposed a diamond star and a paste brooch (Figure 13-1). The diamonds were radiolucent; the paste was densely opaque!

Despite Dr. Holland's finding, for a century now we have continued to be regaled periodically with sensational stories of "The Swallowed Diamond". Attempts to follow up on these press releases have been unsuccessful and puzzling. Either the radiographs seem never to have existed, or else they fail to show the ingested gem stones.

A case in point is illustrated in Figure 13-2. This newspaper clipping[2] has all the usual features of the genre: the distracted salesperson; the clumsy thief; the obligatory x-ray; the triumphant discovery, "He was x-rayed and there it was…"; the twist at the end of the tail — the poor rookie detective given the sordid task of retrieving the evidence; and, especially,

Figure 13-1   Holland's 1896 roentgenograph of a diamond star and a paste brooch. The diamond mountings appears empty, the paste "gems" are densely opaque. In 1896 this required a two-minute exposure. (From Bruwer, A. J., Ed., *Classic Descriptions in Diagnostic Radiology*, Charles C Thomas, Springfield, IL, 1984. With permission.)

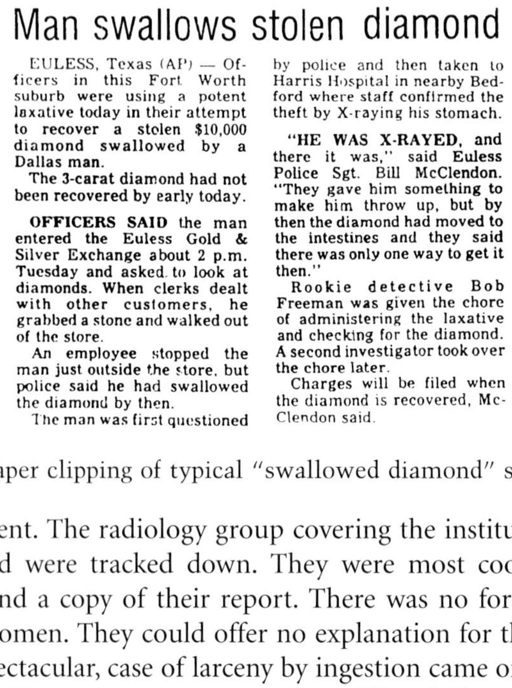

Man swallows stolen diamond

EULESS, Texas (AP) — Officers in this Fort Worth suburb were using a potent laxative today in their attempt to recover a stolen $10,000 diamond swallowed by a Dallas man.

The 3-carat diamond had not been recovered by early today.

OFFICERS SAID the man entered the Euless Gold & Silver Exchange about 2 p.m. Tuesday and asked to look at diamonds. When clerks dealt with other customers, he grabbed a stone and walked out of the store.

An employee stopped the man just outside the store, but police said he had swallowed the diamond by then.

The man was first questioned by police and then taken to Harris Hospital in nearby Bedford where staff confirmed the theft by X-raying his stomach.

"HE WAS X-RAYED, and there it was," said Euless Police Sgt. Bill McClendon. "They gave him something to make him throw up, but by then the diamond had moved to the intestines and they said there was only one way to get it then."

Rookie detective Bob Freeman was given the chore of administering the laxative and checking for the diamond. A second investigator took over the chore later.

Charges will be filed when the diamond is recovered, McClendon said.

Figure 13-2   Newspaper clipping of typical "swallowed diamond" story.

the missing denouement. The radiology group covering the institution where the examination was performed were tracked down. They were most cooperative and sent the original radiograph and a copy of their report. There was no foreign body of any kind visible within the abdomen. They could offer no explanation for the wire service story.

Another, more spectacular, case of larceny by ingestion came on the wire from Milan[3] (Figure 13-3). Think of it — 11,216 stones worth a million dollars! Perhaps the gems were outlined by air in the plastic bag? Dr. Leonardo Lovisatti, a friend who is a well-known radiologist in Northern Italy, was contacted. Some weeks later he replied, "… the police will not give any information… . I have been in touch with the heads of the most important Radiology Departments in Milan, but none of them can help. The Press Agencies have no lead on where the x-rays had been carried out."

Now if the thief swallows the mounting as well as the diamonds, the story is entirely different and credible (Figure 13-4).[4] Any metal used to mount precious stones will be apparent radiographically.

4A The Houston Post/Sun., January 18, 1987 ★

X-rays of woman's stomach
provide police sparkling results

MILAN, Italy (UPI) — A woman swallowed 10,999 diamonds and 217 emeralds in an attempt to smuggle them into Italy, but she was arrested after X-rays revealed the jewels in her stomach, police said Saturday.

Magdalena De Vree of Belgium flew into Milan's Linate Airport from Zurich, Switzerland "a few days ago," police said.

Customs police said the woman appeared nervous, but a search of her luggage turned up no contraband.

Smugglers, however, occasionally swallow drugs and other contraband, so police obtained a court order permitting them to take the suspect to a hospital for an X-ray examination.

The tests revealed the presence of two small plastic bags containing 10,999 diamonds and 217 emeralds in the woman's stomach. Police estimated the value of the jewels at about $1 million and arrested the woman.

Figure 13-3   Newspaper clipping of a spectacular story of grand larceny by ingestion.

Alabama's oldest newspaper
MOBILE REGISTER

May 12, 1994
Since 1813

THURSDAY

PORTLAND, Ore. — After waiting four days, deputies finally got the evidence in the disappearance of a diamond ring.

Steven Wade Hamilton produced the wedding band Tuesday, the sheriff's department said. He is accused of stealing it from a store Friday and then swallowing it, along with a less expensive ring.

Originally, the store estimated the value of the diamond ring at $2,300, but the $3,605 pricetag was still attached after deputies recovered the evidence at the Multnomah county jail.

On Sunday, Wade produced a ring valued at $160, plus two dimes and a nickel.

Hamilton, 32, faces robbery and criminal mischief charges.

—From wire reports

Figure 13-4   Newspaper clipping of thief whose taste ranged from diamond rings to small change.

Only one case is known to the author in which a positive radiograph was obtained after ingestion of an unmounted jewel. In that case Röntgen's rays betrayed not one crook, but two!

A woman who had been viewing a group of loose stones in a jewelry store was seen to put her hand to her mouth moments before abruptly arising from her seat to leave the store. She was detained by the proprietor who had her arrested. Subsequently, a radiograph of the abdomen was obtained and clearly showed an opaque foreign body in the typical shape of a brilliant-cut diamond (Figure 13-5). The charges against the woman were dropped, however, immediately after the radiologist pointed out to the arresting officers that real diamonds are not radiopaque and that the jeweler might be guilty of fraud!

Our experience and/or frustration with "swallowed diamond" stories led to the undertaking of a group of experimental radiographs. A couple of tissue-isodense plastic containers assembled like a "double-boiler" were set up so that specimens of real and *faux* gems could be suspended in 20 cm of water (Figure 13-6). This simple phantom reproduced the situation of a gem inside a fluid-filled viscus inside a reasonably trim body. Under those circumstances one can show that diamonds, emeralds, and rubies are not sufficiently

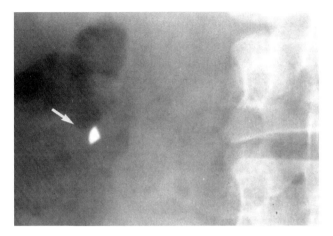

Figure 13-5   Radiograph of the abdomen of a suspected jewel thief. Note the dense object (arrow) in the shape of a brilliant cut diamond. (Courtesy of Robert R. Roper, M.D.)

Figure 13-6   Water-phantom for roentgenology of real and *faux* jewels. A ring (arrow) is positioned at middepth.

opaque to be visible inside the water-density structures of the human body by conventional roentgenology (Figure 13-7). While it is conceivable that their silhouettes might be apparent if suspended in an air-filled viscus, with routine positioning the gem would sink beneath any fluid present in even a partially aerated bowel. Many of the false gems were radiopaque. High-quality glass is quite dense. False pearls could be distinguished from real ones.

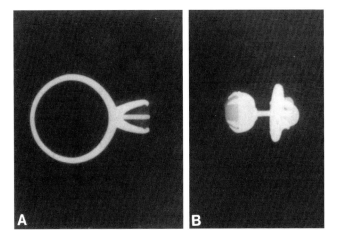

Figure 13-7   **A**: diamond solitaire ring, and **B**: fake solitaire tie-tack in 20 cm water-phantom.

Our conclusion is that conventional roentgenography or fluoroscopy is most unlikely to reveal swallowed precious stones. Negative findings in such cases do not preclude the presence of ingested gems. Demonstrated opaque "jewels" are likely semiprecious, at best.[5]

It is possible that computed tomography would offer greater sensitivity in the search for swallowed gemstones, but we know of no investigations along this line.

Radiology and Auto Theft

When Professor Röntgen opened to view the inner works, recesses, and loads in his prized shotgun with his new-found rays, he opened up a new field: *nondestructive testing*. The German and Austrian military were the first to employ this opportunity to examine armaments and other materials for quality control or defects without destroying the test object. Now nondestructive testing methods emphasizing a variety of radiant energy forms and sources are used widely in many industries. But industrial nondestructive testing is beyond the scope of this book.

Recently, however, the Israeli National Police have adapted the nondestructive testing method to the detection of the common nonviolent crimes of auto theft and auto forgery.[6]

Often a new identity is created for a stolen vehicle by one of three main methods: (1) simple alteration of documents; (2) obliteration and restamping of the engine and chassis vehicle identification number (VIN); or (3) transfer of key parts from a wrecked vehicle to a stolen one. In the latter instance, the part containing the VIN of the wrecked vehicle is cut out and welded onto the stolen vehicle. Ordinarily, the finish must be removed from the suspect vehicle in order to reveal the forgery. This is quite destructive, of course, and is quite undesirable, especially if no forgery is discovered.

The Israeli police have access to an industrial x-ray machine and have found that properly positioned radiographs readily display the tell-tale welding seams of the forged VIN on the stolen auto (Figure 13-8). The patterns of the original spot-welding and the secondary seam-welding with a filler rod are different (Figure 13-9).

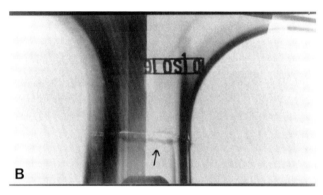

Figure 13-8   **A**: industrial x-ray tube in upper right corner of photo (arrow) is positioned to radiograph door post of suspected stolen and reidentified auto. **B**: positive print of radiograph shows a nonoriginal welding seam (arrow) on the door post below the number. (From Springer, E. and Bergman, P., *J. Forensic Sci.*, 39, 751, 1994. Copyright ASTM, reprinted with permission.)

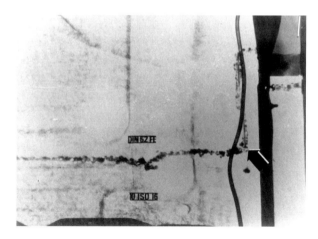

Figure 13-9   Positive print of a radiograph of flooring in the front passenger compartment showing nonoriginal welding. The arrow points to a common nail used as filler in the weld seam. (From Springer, E. and Bergman, P., *J. Forensic Sci.*, 39, 751, 1994. Copyright ASTM, reprinted with permission.)

References

1. Holland, C. T., X-rays in 1896, in *Classic Descriptions in Diagnostic Radiology*, Vol. 1, Bruwer, A. J., Ed., Charles C Thomas, Springfield, IL, 1984, 69.

2. **Anon.,** Associated Press release, *Mobile Press*, October 16, 1985, 34A.

3. **Anon.,** United Press International release, *Houston Post*, January 18, 1987, 4A.

4. **Anon.,** Wire report, *Mobile Register*, May 12, 1944, 2A.

5. Brogdon, B. G., Larceny by ingestion, Presented at the Annu. Meet. American Academy of Forensic Sciences, Cincinnati, February 23, 1990.

6. Springer, E. and Bergman, P., Applications of non-destructive testing (NDT) in vehicle forgery examinations, *J. Forensic Sci.*, 39, 751, 1994.

Radiology of Fakes and Forgery in Art

14

A. EVERETTE JAMES, JR., SC.M., J.D., M.D.

Contents

Introduction

The use of radiographic techniques to detect fraud and forgeries in the art world has great historical precedence. Within months of Röntgen's discovery, W. König of Frankfurt was using roentgen rays to examine oil paintings in order to detect alterations in them. More than 50 years ago Elliott published a 12-page article in the *American Journal of Roentgenology* on the use of roentgen rays and the scientific examinations of paintings (Figure 14-1). With the advance in digital imaging and other technologies, the opportunities to document both authenticity and fakery are enhanced. In this chapter we will use our personal experience with valuable paintings and antique waterfowl decoys as paradigms to illustrate basic principles and to provide some insight into approaches that have proven useful by illustrative vignettes.

Authentication of Antiques

The evidentiary nature of a visual image such as a radiograph, and the ability to produce an immediate permanent archive, are very compelling features as evidence. The same rules of evidence and documentation apply whether one is authenticating a $300,000 Elmer Crowell preening pintail decoy done at the turn of the century (Figure 14-2), a genre scene produced in the middle of the nineteenth century by John George Brown (Figure 14-3), the dental radiographs of Dr. Mengele, or the skull of *homo erectus*. This image process represents a unique method of documentation in which the final form provides any trier of fact an opportunity to visually examine the inner composition of the object at issue and is truly compelling legal evidence if properly introduced into the court and interpreted by an expert witness.

Antique waterfowl decoys represent a uniquely native North American art form. Since most of our cultural and artistic heritage is largely derivative, these objects are different as they are products of a true American heritage and tradition.

A   B

Figure 14-1   **A**: Elliott's example of a forgery after the style of Luca di Tommé. **B**: a roentgenogram shows the wooden panel was old and full of worm holes before the paint was applied. No artist would have painted a picture on a wormy piece of wood. Paint added after worm holes have appeared is a certain sign of forgery. (From Elliott, W. J., *Am. J. Roentgenol.*, 50, 779, 1943. With permission.)

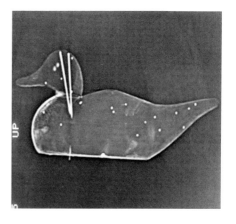

Figure 14-2   CT scout view or topogram of a pintail decoy by Elmer Crowell (*circa* 1910). There is shot in the body and head of the decoy. The neck has been fractured and shortened with pins inserted to strengthen this vulnerable area. The decoy is genuine but not pristine. An Elmer Crowell decoy brought $314,000 at auction. (Collection Ward Museum, gift of A. Everett James and Son.)

The first people to use decoys (a Dutch word for trap) were our Native Americans, who taught our colonial forebears to use them in luring waterfowl into close gunning range. Although the first decoys were fashioned from straw and earth, by the mid and late nineteenth century they were carved from wood. Later other materials were employed in their construction which can be used to "date" a decoy in questions of authenticity. After all, if the decoy was made of cork and Joe Lincoln of Accord, MA died before the use of cork — he did not make the decoy.

Decoys were carved according to certain species which varied in different geographic locations, and the materials and type of wood used reflected what was available in that area. The heads were carved separately from the bodies and were affixed with nails inserted

Figure 14-3 Painting attributed to John George Brown (*circa* 1850).

in an often characteristic pattern, or fitted with dowels. For example, Ned Burgess of Waterlilly, NC drove three nails in the base of the neck to affix the head. They were driven obliquely, two posterior and one anterior. If one is evaluating the authenticity of a "Ned Burgess" decoy and does not see this pattern, it is very likely not by the famous carver. Weights and ties were applied to the decoy to provide balance so that it would float properly in the water, and to secure the decoy when set out as part of a rig (large grouping of decoys placed on the water in a particular pattern to appear attractive to the waterfowl). Weights are often unique to a particular foundry and can be dated. Tie nails and patterns for fixation also are identifiable.

The wooden construction of a decoy is, indeed, a fortunate circumstance since with use certain characteristic changes due to aging and damage from weather conditions will be reflected by lines and fissures (checks) in the wood, and these can be seen on the radiograph. The hardware employed in the construction process also provides excellent data of an evidentiary nature as the same kind of nails were used during the same time period in cabinetry and building construction and can be quite accurately dated (Figure 14-4). As noted, weights were often produced in foundries near the waterfowl area where the decoy carvers lived. Thus, a weight made for the Ward brothers in Crisfield, MD will not be like that made for Joe Lincoln of Accord, MA, or Ned Burgess of Waterlilly, NC.

Just as one evaluates structural alterations due to aging and disease processes in human medicine, we can evaluate the *equivalent* changes in a decoy. These may be quite determinative in assessing its authenticity and value. Since it is no longer uncommon for individual decoys to sell for $25,000 (and a significant number have fetched over $100,000), the practice of "doctoring" and even faking decoys has become much more common. At these prices, it becomes "worth the effort" for the dishonest carver or fabricator.

While one can certainly carve a decoy body and apply a head that will present a form that upon visual inspection alone appears authentic (Figure 14-5), the internal structure of a 50-plus-year-old object composed of various materials is much more difficult. Nails from businesses that supply materials for restoration (usually furniture) will appear as

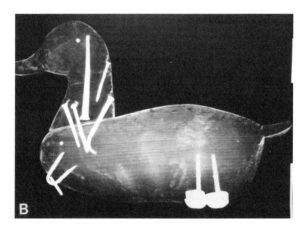

Figure 14-4   **A**: a Ruddy Duck decoy by Alvirah Wright (*circa* 1890). **B**: radiograph. The erect head, chubby body, and flat tail are characteristic of this rare and desirable carver. Note the extensive nail pattern to reinforce the neck due to n-use cracks. The density in the middle of the body is due to over-paint. The unique weight placement and tie line attest to the genuine nature of this decoy. Another member of this rig sold for $32,000 at auction, and many reheads or fakes have subsequently been fabricated. (James Collection.)

"vintage" nails. However, introducing these in such a manner that produces the "rust tracking" on the radiograph is another matter (Figure 14-6). Since decoys were used over long periods of time one would expect to see radiographic evidence of repositioning of the hardware, and if this is not present one should look for other signs of "newness" such as the lack of many layers of paint applied at different times. Decoys were used by guides, market gunners, and avid hunters for years, and they would be repainted to make them more visible.

In determining authenticity, one must appreciate that "authenticity" has several connotations. Many collectors will not accept a decoy that has had another head inserted (rehead), presumably due to damage of the original. The "rehead" can usually be detected by the difference in the grain pattern between the wood of the body and the inserted head, and the pattern of the nails to affix the head to the body (Figure 14-7). If the decoy was allegedly fashioned before the *Waterfowl and Migratory Game Acts* of 1914-1917, there often will be shot in the decoy; the legendary "market hunters", in an effort to be more

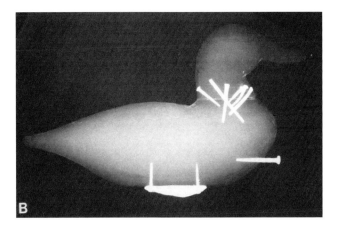

Figure 14-5 **A**: Ruddy Duck fashioned by an expert contemporary carver with aged wood, antique hardware, and style typical of a Knotts Island, Back Bay carver. The surface paint was applied in several coats and also aged. To visual inspection this has the appearance of a very desirable species which at auction might bring $15,000 to $25,000. **B**: roentgenogram reveals no reinsertion of hardware, age rust internally, true cracks and checks through the wood, or layering of the paint that would be expected if the decoy was truly from the 1900-1920 era.

efficient in their harvesting practices, shot the waterfowl while they were on the water in large groups. If one can detect shot in the body, then shot should also be present in the head (Figure 14-8).

"Pristine birds" are much more valuable than those that have been restored no matter how well the repair is done. Checks and cracks will often be filled in and paint applied over the area to conceal the repair. Fractures to the wood are most common in the midportion of the neck due to the hunter grasping this part of the decoy to set it out or to retrieve it after the hunt. Bills are often broken in use and storage because of their location where the wood is thin, making this a vulnerable area (Figure 14-9). No matter how skilled the deception, these repairs can be detected by radiographic studies.

Just as in almost all collectibles, authenticity and condition are the primary determinants of value. When the value reaches a certain level, the temptation of forgery and misrepresentation become compelling to some. While these attempts at perfidy may not initially be very sophisticated, and can readily be discovered, radiographic techniques may

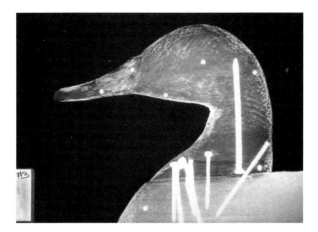

Figure 14-6   Decoy by Wilton Walker, Barca, NC (*circa* 1930). Note the faint halo of rust around the central nail used to strengthen the neck. The linear opacities on the neck represent paint in rasp marks, an old technique to create a nonreflective surface.

Figure 14-7   Radiograph of a decoy showing an antique body and a replaced head. There is an obvious difference in the paint layering and in the quality of the wood.

become the standard form of analysis to uncover and document the evidence that a crime of substantial money value has occurred. Astute collectors have come to rely upon radiographic studies as part of their standard evaluation practice prior to acquisition of a valuable decoy. After all, would it not be embarrassing to pay $30,000 for an Alvirah Wright that was not "right"? While the prices of collectable decoys have increased substantially, these pale by comparison with those of fine paintings. If one sits with a bidding paddle at a Sotheby's or Christie's auction and see many paintings selling for more than $1 million, one can understand that the temptation to produce a fake can be very compelling.

Analysis of Paintings

In discussing the radiographic analysis of paintings these remarks will deal primarily with oil paintings that are applied on canvas, as these are the most commonly encountered

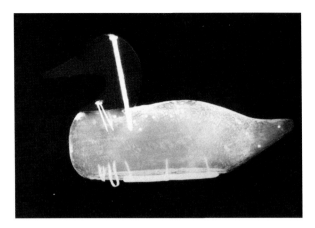

Figure 14-8   Another reheaded decoy. The new wood of the head and neck is almost entirely radiolucent. The aged paint and wood of the body is in sharp contrast. Note also the lead shot in the body but none in the head.

combination of medium and support. We will mention paintings applied to paper, board, panel, and masonite. While radiographic studies are most often used to assess the condition of a painting prior to acquisition or restoration, these diagnostic techniques apply to determining fakes and forgeries as well.

Oil paintings may contain as many as seven layers that have their own characteristic appearance during the aging process. The response to the external elements as well as internal changes over time give a painting its look or patina. Thus, the successful faker or forger must not only duplicate the compositional materials but the aging process as well. While it may be readily feasible to meet the challenge of a visual or raking and UV light inspection, the differential absorption of the x-rays by the compositional materials can provide powerful documentary evidence that a painting is not what it is purported to be.

As noted earlier, there is an aging process that should be expected with paintings, and particularly with certain types of compositional techniques and materials. As an example, the "visionary artists" such as Albert Pinkham Ryder and Ralph Blakelock are among the most "faked" artists. They painted at the end of the last century and the first decade of the present, producing dark, moody paintings composed of many layers of varnish and pigment. Their works will show abundant crackleur (crackle or simply cracks) that should penetrate to the support, whether linen fibers of canvas, board, or wooden panel. The application of many pigment layers characteristically makes these paintings unstable, and the radiograph will show the cracks and fissures (Figure 14-10). If this is not seen, then the chance that the work is a painting by one of the visionary group is almost nonexistent.

Pigment materials can be assessed very well by radiographic techniques. One should recall that with older works repairs may have been necessary, and these areas will have different composition materials than the original. Since the radiographic image most often will encompass the entire painting or at least a large area of the work, one can determine by attenuation of x-rays where to sample in order to evaluate the compositioned material (Figure 14-11). Blind multiple biopsies and sample selection for chemical or dating analysis can produce inaccurate results if the samples are unwittingly taken from an area of repair.

Once, we were called by a major American museum to examine a quite valuable painting because the restorer realized the surface appearance was changing. The work had never been properly cleaned and varnished since its acquisition in the 1920s. On raking

Figure 14-9   **A**: a broken Canvas Back decoy by Ben Ethridge of the North Carolina Outer Banks (*circa* 1920). **B**: an expert bill replacement was done which is undetectable, **C**: even by close visual inspection. **D**: radiography discloses the hairline fracture between the arrows. According to the tenants and strict criteria of decoy evaluation, this fracture reduces the importance of this decoy several-fold. Radiography was determinant in this evaluation process.

light examination, the surface was very uneven and there was specific crackleur at the apex of ridges that were not present in previous descriptions by curators during the 60 years the museum had owned the painting. Although we performed a CT to look at the individual pigment layers, plain radiography at different kilovoltage levels revealed the etiology of the changes — there was one, and possibly two, paintings underneath the one producing the external visual image (Figure 14-12). This led to a lively and enthusiastic discussion by the museum staff as how to "rescue" the images under the one they had (which was valued at above $1 million). Recognizing that neither our malpractice insurance nor emotional composition made it appropriate to be a party to this type of activity, we made a discreet exit and never attempted to find out what transpired as a result of the radiographic findings.

We were once requested by a museum and an auction house to evaluate a genre painting allegedly by a famous artist of the mid-nineteenth century, John George Brown (Figure 14-3). The painting had been consigned by the grandson of the artist. Upon inspection by the curator of the museum that might acquire it and the staff of the painting department

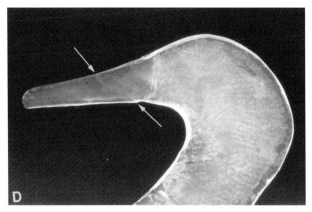

Figure 14-9 (Continued)

of the auction house, there was concern about the authenticity of the painting as to whether it had been significantly restored or in fact almost entirely inpainted, in which case it would not be a desirable example of the artist's work for public display.

As one obtains a relevant history in any type of examination and gleans whatever information is obtainable by visual inspection, the investigation of a painting should proceed in a like manner. On viewing the work, the right side of the painting containing a seated female figure was very competently rendered in the manner of John George Brown. This part of the canvas displayed the expected crackleur and patina of a mid-nineteenth century work using pigment containing some amount of lead. However, the left side of the painting contained a window through which one viewed a bright, almost garish landscape composed with little sense of perspective and completely out of concert with the excellent draftsmanship for which John George Brown was known. The museum and the auction house wanted to declare the entire work a fake, but we were intrigued by the provenance (pedigree) and the fact that only the left side of the painting had elements that were not the work of John George Brown.

We took the work to the New York Medical Center (Cornell) and persuaded our colleagues to allow us to do a scanning CT and plain radiography using different kilovoltage settings. We hoped to detect lead in the pigment composition, certainly in the right side of the work if not the left. The CT was obtained to see if the so-called Hounsfield numbers would identify lead.

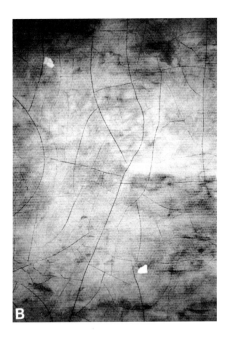

Figure 14-10 **A**: *Creek at New Bedford* by Ralph Blakelock. **B**: magnification radiograph discloses the typically abundant crackleur of this artist.

The radiograph (Figure 14-13) revealed quite strikingly that the right side of the composition pigment layer contained lead and that the left-side pigment was probably of acrylic, which was later confirmed by chemical analysis. This material was only available many decades after the death of John George Brown. Thus, the right side of the painting was stylistically characteristic of John George Brown and the pigment layer was composed of materials consistent with the middle of the nineteenth century, whereas the left side of the painting was obviously of fairly recent vintage and composed by a rather unskilled hand. The radiograph demonstrated that the left side was not painted over the original John George Brown as the pigment layer was entirely of the acrylic application. Further inquiry revealed the true cause of this diagnostic dilemma. We had thought the scenario probably was that the left side of the work had been severely damaged, with removal of

Figure 14-11   Detail radiograph of a Saracen painting, artist unknown, shows damage to the linen canvas repaired with a lead-based filler, consistent with an old repair.

Figure 14-12   Radiograph of a valuable painting revealing one, possibly two, paintings beneath the external visual image.

the pigment and repainting of the scene afterward. In fact, the painting had been inherited unfinished and was "completed" by another hand shortly before it was consigned to auction.

In the nineteenth and early twentieth centuries, smuggling of masterpieces from Europe became an all too common practice. One of the methods to escape detection was to paint an image over the Old Master and then remove it later. Radiographs, of course, would easily detect this deceitful practice today.

The ability to transform the images of art objects from the analog to the digital format opens up great possibilities in detection of frauds and forgeries. Digital radiography in this context is meant to describe any method of radiographic image production in which the

Figure 14-13 Radiograph of the John George Brown painting shown in Figure 14-3. The right-hand side of the picture shows a composition pigment layer containing lead, whereas the left-side pigment is acrylic. The early painting had been unfinished and was "completed" recently by another hand.

silver halide-based film is replaced by an electronic system to either produce or display an image. We have experimented with film-based, digital fluoroscopic, scanned projection, and scan point source systems.

Digital radiography opens up possibilities such as subtraction of various pigment layers or separation of the pigment layer image from the support upon which this layer rests. Digitalization may well allow more accurate characterization of the compositional materials to establish the authenticity, or lack thereof, of a particular work. In theory, the brush-stroke pattern of a particular artist might be characterized by the scanning digital technique. By studying a body of the artist's work in this manner one might develop a signature or profile of this technique. The technology utilized in crime labs and in determination of chromosome abnormalities, such as deletions, might be applied using digital imaging methodology.

In the detection of fakes and frauds as well as in the determination of composition of many art objects, a technique providing visible images that can be observed by the lay public and appropriately described and interpreted by experts provides unique and compelling data. The role of newer technologies, such as MRI, is yet to be explored. This discussion has centered upon the applications with which we have had personal experience, and biomedical imaging technology that is widely available. Hopefully, this has provided some insight into the possibilities of radiographic imaging taken in its largest context.

Acknowledgments

I am indebted to Felix Fleischner, who taught me to be inquisitive about what one does not presently know, and to Russ Morgan, who provided me the environment as a graduate student to learn the basics of imaging technology. To my colleagues in Radiological Sciences at Johns Hopkins and the Center for Medical Imaging Research at Vanderbilt, as well as coinvestigators such as Mitch Bush at the Smithsonian, I owe a great debt of gratitude. The Eastman Corporation has kindly allowed republication of several illustrations used in monograph Vol. 63, No. 1, *Medical Radiography and Photography*. Finally, I would like to note the inspiration of my mother, Pattie Royster James, age 94, and Aunt Geneva James Weaver, who taught me to appreciate beauty in many forms.

Bibliography

Bridgman, C. and Keck, S., The radiography of paintings, *Med. Radiogr. Photogr.*, 37, 3, 1961.

Elliott, W. J., The use of the roentgen ray in the scientific examination of paintings, *Am. J. Roentgenol.*, 50, 779, 1943.

Falke, T. H. M., Zweypfenning-Snijders, M. C., Zweypfenning, C. V. J., and James, A. E., Jr., Computed tomography of an ancient Egyptian cat, *J. Comput. Assist. Tomogr.*, 11, 745, 1987.

Glasser, O., *Wilhelm Conrad Röntgen and the Early History of the Roentgen Rays*, Charles C Thomas, Springfield, IL, 1934, chap. 18.

Held, J., Alteration and mutilation of works of art, *So. Alt. Q.*, 62, 1, 1983.

James, A. E., Jr. and Gibbs, S. J., Radiographic analysis of paintings, *Med. Radiogr. Photogr.*, 63, 1, 1987.

James, A. E., Jr., Gibbs, S. J., Sloan, M., Price, R. R., and Erickson, J. J., Digital radiography in the analysis of paintings: a new and promising technique, *J. Am. Inst. Conservation*, 22, 41, 1982.

James, A. E., Jr., An inside look at decoys, *Wildfowl Art*, 24, Summer 1987.

James, A. E., Jr. and Heller, R. M., Western Egyptian desert expedition, *Explorers*, September 1981.

James, A. E., Gibbs, S. J., Sloan, M., Erickson, J., and Diggs, J., Radiographic techniques to evaluate paintings, *Am. J. Roentgenol.*, 140, 215, 1983.

James, A. E., Jr., Waddill, W. B., and Feazell, G. L., The medical imaging technologies as evidence, *J. Contemporary Law*, University of Utah College of Law, 11(1), 1984.

James, A. E., Not every old canvas is down for the count, *Med. Econ.*, September 3, 1984.

James, A. E., Imaging the images, *Am. Med. News*, March 28, 1986.

James, A. E., Decoys yield up secrets to radiographic imaging, *Diagn. Imaging*, February 1985.

James, A. E., X-ray analysis of paintings, *Maine Antique Digest*, April 1987.

James, A. E., The use of x-ray imaging techniques in appraisal of paintings, *Valuation*, June 1985.

James, A. E., The healing of paintings, *South. Med. J.*, 84, 1231, 1991.

James, A. E., The radiography of art and artifacts, *Electromedica*, 44, 144, 1988.

James, A. E., The Radiographic Analysis of Decoys. Ward Foundation, Fall 1996.

James, A. E., Is your decoy real? *Decoy Hunter*, 1989.

Keck, C. K., *The Care of Paintings*, Watson-Guptill, New York, 1967.

Osterman, F. A., James, A. E., and Heshiki, A., Xeroradiography in veterinary radiography: a preliminary study, *J. Am. Vet. Radiol. Soc.*, 16, 143, 1975.

SECTION V

Radiology of Abuse

> Forensic Science is used to predict not the future
> but the past.
>
> **—Henry C. Lee**

Nowhere in forensic radiology is Dr. Lee's provocative aphorism less applicable than in the field of abuse. Here lies the opportunity to go beyond the limits of the necropsy "where death delights to help the living." The early identification and proper management of the victoms of abuse while they are still living cannot only predict, but also can modify, the future. Life can be preserved, even enhanced, and necropsy can be averted.

Child Abuse

15

B. G. BROGDON, M.D.

Contents

Historical Perspective

Virtually every application of radiology within the forensic sciences was initiated or predicted within one year of Röntgen's discovery. The conspicuous exception is perhaps radiology's greatest contribution to the forensic sciences. That it took 50 years and the reluctant conclusions of an observant pediatric radiologist to awaken public conscience and consciousness about one of its greatest evils is a sad commentary on humanity through the ages.

The very idea that there is such a thing as child abuse is a relatively modern concept arising from an ignoble history.[1] From biblical times through the Age of Industrialization, paternal power was absolute. A father could abandon a child, abuse it, sell it into slavery, put it to death, or cut it in half. The father's right to correct or discipline was limited only by his conscience, and this right extended *in loco parentis* to all adults involved in rearing or supervising the child, including teachers, trainers, masters of apprentices, workhouse bosses, factory foremen, and superintendents of children's "asylums".

The industrial revolution with its unceasing demand for cheap labor exacerbated the problem as poor couples learned that their best money crop was the fruits of their loins. The excesses attendant to child labor and the workhouses did stir the social consciousness of some influential writers, notably Dickens in England and America. Some societal response began to emerge. It is interesting to note that the first Society for the Prevention of Cruelty to Children had to be established under the aegis of the Society of the Prevention of Cruelty to Animals, but only after arguing successfully that children were members of the animal kingdom.[1] A few child labor laws were enacted. Thus children gradually came under the protection of the law, in public at least, but not necessarily at home.

In 1860, Ambriose Tardieu (1818-1879) was a French physician specializing in pathology, public health, and legal medicine (Figure 15-1). A year later he would become Professor of Legal Medicine at the University of Paris, a post he held until his death. But in 1860 Tardieu published an article (Figure 15-2) on the abuse and maltreatment of children; it was reprinted in a book on wounds (Figure 15-3) published a year after his death. Unfortunately, this treatise seems to have had a much greater impact on modern historians[1-3] of child abuse than on Tardieu's contemporaries: unfortunate because in his 32 cases Tardieu set forth all of the salient features of child abuse — sociologic, demographic, and medical — except for the radiologic. He recognized care givers as the perpetrators, described the typical injuries, and observed the emotional responses of the victims. Still, the abused child as a clinical entity was largely unrecognized until the essential elements of this syndrome, both clinical and radiographic, started to surface in the 1930s, notably in a few centers such as Babies Hospital in New York.[4,5]

Figure 15-1   Ambroise Tardieu, 1818-1879. (From Silverman, F. N., *Radiology,* 104, 337, 1972. With permission.)

John Caffey (1895-1978) received his M.D. degree from the University of Michigan in 1919, spent almost three years in postwar Eastern Europe, then returned for a career in pediatrics, eventually being appointed to the full-time staff of Babies Hospital in New York City.[3] When that hospital finally installed a "modern" radiographic and fluoroscopic unit in 1929, Dr. Caffey was placed in charge of it. With no formal training in radiology, but with the encouragement and support of Dr. Ross Golden (Chairman of Radiology at the College of Physicians and Surgeons of Columbia University), Dr. Caffey became the father of Pediatric Radiology, the first recognized subspecialty in diagnostic radiology (Figure 15-4). Dr. Caffey had a very long and active career at Babies Hospital and, after his retirement there, at the Children's Hospital of the University of Pittsburgh. He made many contributions, but perhaps his most celebrated one had its genesis in an article published

MÉDECINE LÉGALE.

ÉTUDE MÉDICO-LÉGALE

SUR LES

SÉVICES ET MAUVAIS TRAITEMENTS

EXERCÉS SUR DES ENFANTS,

Par le Dr Ambroise TARDIEU,

Professeur agrégé de médecine légale à la Faculté de médecine.

Parmi les faits si nombreux et de nature si diverse dont se compose l'histoire médico-légale des coups et blessures, il en est qui forment un groupe tout à fait à part, et qui, laissés jusqu'ici dans l'ombre la plus complète, méritent à plus d'un titre d'être mis en lumière. Je veux parler de ces faits qualifiés sévices et mauvais traitements, et dont les enfants sont plus particulièrement victimes de la part de leurs parents, de leurs maîtres, de ceux en un mot qui exercent sur eux une autorité plus ou moins directe.

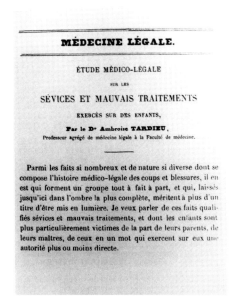

Figure 15-2 First page of Tardieu's 1860 paper on child abuse. (From Silverman, F. N., *Radiology*, 104, 337, 1972. With permission.)

ÉTUDE MÉDICO-LÉGALE

SUR

LES BLESSURES

COMPRENANT

LES BLESSURES EN GÉNÉRAL

ET

LES BLESSURES PAR IMPRUDENCE

LES COUPS ET L'HOMICIDE INVOLONTAIRES

PAR

AMBROISE TARDIEU

Professeur de médecine légale à la Faculté de médecine de Paris.

PARIS

LIBRAIRIE J.-B. BAILLIÈRE ET FILS

19, RUE HAUTEFEUILLE, 19

1879

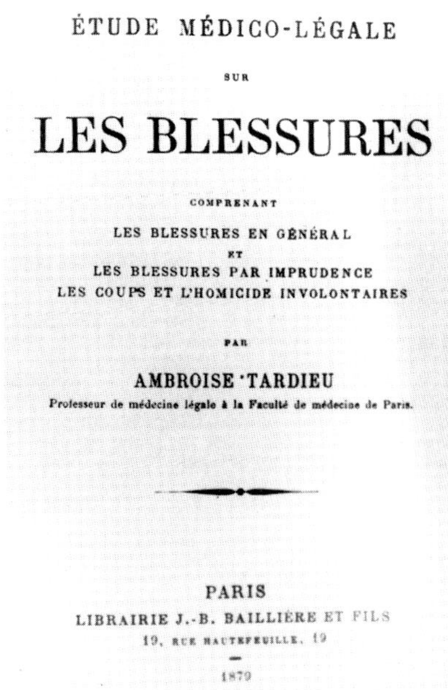

Figure 15-3 Title page of Tardieu's 1879 book on wounds, which included a reprint of his 1860 article on child abuse. (From Silverman, F. N., *Radiology*, 104, 337, 1972. With permission.)

in 1946.[6] This landmark paper described a peculiar association of multiple fractures of the long bones of children suffering from chronic subdural hematoma.

To digress for a moment, the history of subdural hematoma is one of interesting paradox. Both Paré and Vesalius recognized the traumatic basis of subdural hematoma in the case of Henry II of France who died after being injured in a tournament celebrating the marriage of his daughter to Phillip II of Spain.[1] However, in 1856 Virchow suggested an infectious cause for the condition. Since Virchow was an unarguable authority, his opinion prevailed for the next 70 years, and the condition was most commonly spoken of as "pachymeningitis interna hemorrhagica". However, Sherwood in his classic 40-page

Figure 15-4   John Caffey, the Father of Pediatric Radiology. (Reprinted with permission of the Center for American History of Radiology, Reston, VA.)

paper in 1930[7] reemphasized the likelihood of traumatic origin, but even so, in his conclusion he stated, "… the etiology is obscure. It was unusual to find that in 5 of the 9 cases described the patients were cared for in institutions or by foster mothers. Trauma due to injury at birth or other means is a possible factor, although not proved in the series of cases reported." In 1939, Ingraham and Heyl[8] reported that subdural hematoma appears more frequently in undernourished children and, in the majority of instances, there is a history of trauma.

To return to Caffey, in 1946 he described patients with subdural hematomas who also had multiple fractures in long bones. The bony lesions were somewhat unusual with metaphyseal fragmentation (Figure 15-5) and formation of what he called large involucrums (because they resembled that manifestation of chronic osteomyelitis, but which really is calcification in subperiosteal hemorrhages) (Figure 15-6). He also noticed a pattern of fractures in different stages of healing (Figure 15-7).

Some of Dr. Caffey's puzzlement shines through as he says,

> "For many years we have been puzzled by the roentgen disclosure of fresh, healing and healed multiple fractures of long bones of infants whose principle disease was chronic subdural hematoma. In not a single case was there a history of injury to which a skeletal lesions could reasonably be attributed. No predisposing generalized or localized disease for pathologic fracture was present. … the fractures appear to be of traumatic origin but the traumatic episodes and the causal mechanism remain obscure."

Nevertheless, the essential roentgen science of child abuse had been documented. Dr. Caffey confirmed his earlier findings in a distinguished lectureship in 1957[9] and illustrated some new radiographic features: traumatic bowing of the ends of the diaphyses due to metaphyseal infraction (Figure 15-8), metaphyseal cupping, and ectopic ossification centers (Figure 15-9) — all associated with the previous findings of involucrum formation,

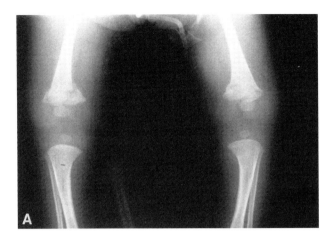

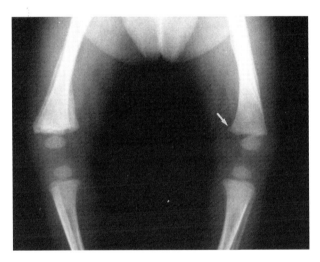

Figure 15-5   **A**: severe bilateral metaphyseal fragmentation in the distal femora. The "corner fractures fragments" are larger than usual. **B**: small "corner fracture" on left; "involucrum" on right.

metaphyseal fragmentation, and fractures of differing duration. The description was now more complete.

In a third communication in 1965,[10] Dr. Caffey spoke of the relative diagnostic values of the history, physical examination, laboratory tests, biopsy findings, and radiographic observations. Caffey noted that the history of trauma frequently was withheld. Giving the benefit of doubt, he opined that the history of trauma was sometimes unknown to the family. He concluded that, "the radiographic changes are pathognomonic of trauma, but they never identify the perpetrator of the trauma or his motive." He still believed that "the great majority of simple, even serious traumatic episodes to children … are accidents for which no one is responsible."

There still were careful disclaimers in excluding underlying processes such as infection, malnutrition, avitaminosis, metabolic bone disease, and the like as contributory factors. Dr. E. B. D. Neuhauser, Radiologist to the Children's Hospital in Boston, noted, "every case … has been an example of needless expense to the hospital or to the patient in our

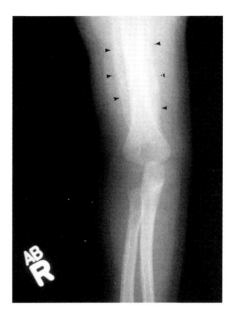

Figure 15-6 Large "involucrum" (actually a calcified subperiosteal hematoma) around the shaft of the humerus.

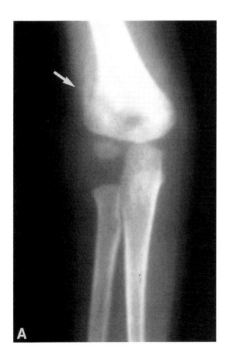

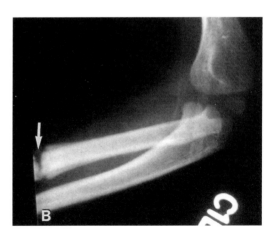

Figure 15-7 This is the initial presentation of the child whose terminal radiograph is shown in Figure 3-3. She first presented at age one with **A**: an acute fracture of the distal metaphysis of the humerus (arrow). **B**: on the edge of the lateral view a second fracture, a nonunion of the radius was seen (arrow). The child was removed from the home. The mother and father divorced. The father remarried and got the child back. The stepmother killed her with a fist to the epigastrium at age two.

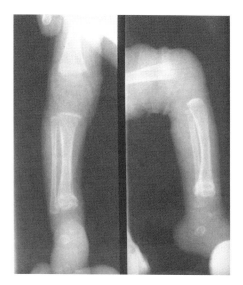

Figure 15-8   Example of what Caffey called "traumatic bowing".[6]

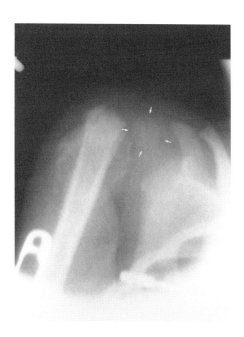

Figure 15-9   Example of what Caffey called "ectopic ossification centers".[6] The proximal humeral epiphysis (arrows) is widely separated from the metaphysis, which shows a large calcifying subperiosteal hemorrhage. The glenohumeral joint is wide but not dislocated.

hospital, with endless blood cultures, many studies, search of old films to see if it didn't really resemble scurvy and the roentgen department has forgotten what scurvy looks like, not having seen a case for some months …".[11]

Disciples of Caffey in Pittsburgh and Cincinnati further studied the problem, and Silverman's paper of 1953[12] can be credited with finally focusing the attention of the radiological community on the entity.

Still, a variety of somewhat euphemistic names were applied to the syndrome — mostly suggesting undetected trauma of some kind such as hidden, concealed, denied, unsuspected, unrecognized, or clandestine. Caffey suggested *parent infant trauma stress syndrome*

(PITS) long before the expression "it's the pits" existed.[2] Galdston[14] in 1965 offered the phrase *Parental Dysfunction* which causes no antiparent bias and suggests the psycho-emotional storms which paralyze parental self control. Several eponymic designations were proposed without general adoption: "Le Syndrome de Silverman" in France, "Le Syndrome de Caffey", "Caffey's Third Syndrome" and "The Syndrome of Ambroise Tardieu".[1] Finally, in 1962, Kempe[13,14] intentionally coined the name *Battered Child Syndrome* to attract attention to this neglected clinical and social problem. This provocative and anger-producing term was successful in gaining wide-spread public attention. This was enhanced by a science writers forum on the subject sponsored by the American College of Radiology in 1962, featuring a radiologist, a pediatrician, and a distinguished jurist on the panel.

Bert Girdany, who went to Pittsburgh following his residency with Dr. Caffey at Babies Hospital, recognized the inadequacy of the single physician in dealing with the problem and organized a trauma team made up of a pediatrician, pediatric psychiatrist, pediatric radiologist, and social worker. The value and results of this team approach were reported in Elizabeth Elmer's book, *Children in Jeopardy*.[15]

All of the pertinent findings finally had been established with the addition of another factor, that is, injury inappropriate in view of the history, circumstances, or stage of development of the involved child.[16]

Overview

It is recognized now that child abuse is an umbrella term covering a broad spectrum of intentional harmful interference with health, happiness, and the development of an infant or child. There are at least six forms of child abuse.

Spectrum of Child Abuse

For those who would want a much more thorough, in-depth account of child abuse than is possible within the limitation of a single chapter, the books by Kleinman[17] and Reece[18] are recommended.

Physical abuse — Abuse resulting in physical injury was the first form recognized, and the most deadly. Radiological findings are central to the diagnosis of the condition and to the prosecution of the perpetrators in the majority of the cases. Physical abuse is the principal concern of this chapter and will be discussed in some detail further on.

Nutritional deprivation — Radiographically, one may see osteoporosis of bone and diminished body fat in children who are starved. These are subtle findings and are likely to be unremarked unless there is stimulus from the history or other findings to search for them. Occasionally, infants are placed on faddist diets or are overmedicated at home. One can see evidence of hypervitaminosis or hypovitaminosis (i.e., vitamin A intoxication or rickets).

Emotional abuse — There is a clinical entity variously known as maternal deprivation syndrome, psychosocial dwarfism, deprivation dwarfism, abuse dwarfism, or Kaspar-Hauser syndrome.[19] Those afflicted may show growth retardation, retarded bone age, and osteopenia. Treatment will result in reversal of these findings, and there may even be spreading of cranial sutures from rapid brain growth.

Neglect of medical care or safety — This can result in all forms of trauma which are literally unintentional, but are actually due to neglect (i.e., massive injuries resulting from a vehicular accident in which the child is not secured in an approved seat).

Intentional drugging or poisoning — There are no specific radiographic findings. Arsenic has been seen in the stomachs of poisoned adults, but no examples in children are known. Children may be given drugs by parents or others. Prenatal drugging of infants is an increasing problem. Somewhat akin to poisoning is the abusive introduction of foreign objects into the esophagus of infants or children. Nolte[20] reviews the subject and reports instances of coins, beans, a cooking spatula, a teething ring, and broken glass being fed or forced-fed to the victims by adults or other children.

Sexual abuse — Sexual abuse does not come to the radiologist's attention unless there is massive injury such as colorectal or vaginal laceration with or without pneumoperitoneum.

Incidence of Child Abuse[21]

It is estimated that five children die every day in the U.S. from abuse or neglect by parents or care givers. This amounts to some 2000 deaths per year, of whom the vast majority are younger than 4 years old. Most are less than 2 years of age; 40% of the children who die from abuse and neglect are under 1 year of age. About 10 times as many children survive abuse as die from it. An estimated 18,000 children per year are permanently disabled by abuse or neglect. Actually, it is not known how many disabled persons have been made so by abuse. For instance, there are 90,000 Americans with brain damage from head injuries; no one knows how many were the victims of intentional childhood trauma.

Most physical abuse comes from the father or male care giver (stepfathers, boyfriends, close friends, brothers, cousins), not from the mother as would be the conventional wisdom. It is the enraged, stressed male who is most likely to beat the child, shake it, or suffocate it — most often to stop the infant from crying. Mothers are more likely to be responsible for child neglect deaths from drowning, fires started by unsupervised children, or dehydration and starvation. Most babies cry about 30% of the time and physical abuse to stop the crying becomes almost self-perpetuating since the battered, dazed, or brain-damaged child is indeed quite likely to stop crying for a while after the assault.

Radiology of Physical Abuse

Abusive head trauma is the leading cause of death from child abuse, or of all trauma-related deaths of children.[22] Skeletal injuries, particularly of the appendicular, are most likely to bring abuse to our attention and to document the problem. However, musculo-skeletal injuries are rarely fatal. Injuries to the rib cage are quite common (perhaps up to 25% of all skeletal fractures[23]) but frequently are missed on routine radiography if acute or fresh. Spinal fractures are rare but may have serious consequences. Fractures in the shoulder girdle are highly suspicious of abuse. Skull fractures are not necessarily an indication of abuse unless associated with intracranial damage and/or neurologic findings. Intentional trauma to the abdomen or thorax of the infant or child is less common than skeletal trauma but carries a 40 to 50% mortality rate.[21]

Protocols for Examination

There is no universal agreement on the proper system of examination of an infant or child suspected of being physically abused. Table 15-1 reproduces the American College of Radiology Appropriateness Criteria for examination of infants and children who are suspected of receiving physical abuse. These are categorized under four variant clinical conditions. The appropriateness criteria are intended as guides and are not to be construed as having any other weight.

Levitt et al. suggest in Reece's book[22] that in demonstrating lesions of abusive head injury CT is preferable for subarachnoid hemorrhage; MR is preferable for subdural hematoma, concussive injury, and shear injury; and CT and MR are equal in their efficacy for demonstrating epidural hematoma. CT is preferable for fracture detection.

Sty has been a long-time advocate of bone scintigraphy in evaluation of the suspected abused child, and has cogent arguments.[24,25] Kleinman has compared skeletal surveys with bone scintigraphy (Table 15-2) and shows that there are certain trade-offs.[26] There is no question that bone scans are more sensitive than radiographic surveys in detecting skeletal lesions. About 10% of fractures are seen only on scintigraphy. The exception is the skull fracture, which is more readily seen by radiography. Radiography has more specificity in that certain fracture patterns are virtually diagnostic of abuse. Further, the normally high uptake in the growing ends of the bones of infants and children, where many abuse lesions are found, is a distinct problem, especially if there are bilateral injuries. Scintigraphy demands good positioning and, consequently, sedation. The whole-body radiation dose is 2.5 times higher with scintiscanning, the examination is more expensive than routine radiography, and it takes much longer to get the results. Further, throughout the land it is relatively easy to obtain radiographs at any hour of the day or night with reasonably competent personnel to perform them. While this is true of scintigraphy in certain institutions, it is by no means universally available. Consequently, in most areas of the U.S., radiography is the examination of choice for injuries of the musculoskeletal system including the skull, with supplemental CT or MRI as indicated for head injuries. In institutions where radiography and scintigraphy are equally available, then the choice of modality rests entirely with the radiologist in charge, as it should with all other similar diagnostic decisions.

Follow-up or repeat skeletal surveys two weeks after suspicious findings on an initial skeletal survey, other imaging studies, history or physical examination, are strongly advocated by Kleinman and associates.[27] They found that follow-up studies increase the number of definite fractures by 27%.

CT is of inestimable value in evaluating trauma to the thoracic and abdominal viscera and is readily available almost everywhere now. CT is also excellent in disclosing rib fractures hard to see on routine radiography.

The relative advantages of CT and MR in the evaluation of brain injuries have already been mentioned. In the rare case of spinal injury in a child, MR is an ideal supplementary or complimentary examination to evaluate spinal cord damage.

Table 15-1 American College of Radiology Appropriateness Criteria

Radiologic Exam Procedure	Appropriateness Rating	Comments

Clinical Condition: Suspected physical abuse, child 2 yrs. or less
Variant 1: No focal signs or symptoms

Plain x-ray - skeletal survey	9	
Plain x-ray - skull film	9	
Ultrasound - abdomen	2	
MRI - brain	2	
CT - brain	No consensus	
Nuclear medicine - bone scan	No consensus	

Clinical Condition: Suspected physical abuse, child 2 yrs. or less
Variant 2: Head trauma by history, no focal findings, no neurological abnormality

Plain x-ray - skeletal survey	9	This includes two views of the skull.
CT - Brain	8	
MRI - brain	4	If necessary for added documentation.
Ultrasound - abdomen	2	
Plain x-ray - skull film	No consensus	Necessary if the two views in the skeletal survey and the CT do not show fracture.
Nuclear medicine - bone scan	No consensus	Indicated when a clinical suspicion of abuse remains high and documentation still necessary.

Clinical Condition: Suspected physical abuse, up to age 5
Variant 3: Neurological signs and symptoms, with or without physical findings

Plain x-ray - skeletal survey	9	This includes two views of the skull.
CT - Cranial without contrast	9	
Ultrasound - Cranial	2	
CT - Cranial with contrast	2	
Plain x-ray - skull film	No consensus	Necessary if the two views in the skeletal survey and the CT do not show fracture.
Nuclear medicine - bone scan	No consensus	Indicated when a clinical suspicion of abuse remains high and documentation still necessary.
MRI - brain	No consensus	If the CT is normal and documentation is necessary to prove abuse.

Clinical Condition: Any age child, visceral injuries, discrepancy with history
Variant 4: Physical and laboratory examinations inconclusive

Plain x-ray - skeletal survey	9	
CT - CECT abdomen + pelvis	9	
Ultrasound - abdomen + pelvis	2	
MRI - abdomen + pelvis	2	
CT - abdomen + pelvis	2	
CT - cranial with or without contrast	2	
MRI - cranial	2	

Note: An ACR Task Force on Appropriateness Criteria and its expert panels have developed criteria for determining appropriate imaging examinations for diagnosis and treatment of specified medical condition(s). These criteria are intended to guide radiologists and referring physicians in making decisions regarding radiologic imaging and treatment. Generally, the complexity and severity of a patient's clinical condition should dictate the selection of appropriate imaging procedures or treatments. Only those exams generally used for evaluation of the patient's condition are ranked. Other imaging studies necessary to evaluate other co-existent diseases or other medical consequences of this condition are not considered in this document. The availability of equipment or personnel may influence the selection of appropriate imaging procedures or treatments. Imaging techniques classified at investigational by the FDA have not been considered in developing these criteria; however, study of new equipment and applications should be encouraged. The ultimate decision regarding the appropriateness of any specific radiologic examination or treatment must be made by the referring physician and radiologist in light of all the circumstances presented in and individual examination. ACR appropriateness criteria are not designed as a guide for third-party reimbursement. Reprinted with permission of the American College of Radiology.

Appropriateness criteria scale: 1 2 3 4 5 6 7 8 9, 1 = least appropriate, 9 = most appropriate.

Table 15-2 Comparison of Skeletal Surveys and Bone Scintigraphy

	Skeletal Survey	Bone Scintigraphy
Sensitivity	Moderate	High
Specificity	High	Low
Sedation	Rare	Common
Dose		
Gonodal	Very low	Low
Metaphyseal	Very low	Moderate
Availability	High	Varies
Need for additional studies	Occasionally	Always
Cost	Low	70–300% higher
Technical factor dependency	Moderate	High
Interpreter dependency	Moderate	High

From Kleinman, P. K., *Diagnostic Imaging of Child Abuse*, Williams & Wilkins, Baltimore, 1987, p. 25. With permission.

Ultrasonography is of value in studying abdominal and retroperitoneal visceral injuries and has had some limited applications in the musculoskeletal system (Figure 15-10).[28]

MR is useful, of course, in evaluating fractures and other injuries in and around joints. It is not a convenient screening procedure, however, and will be mostly used in follow-up and in complementary studies.

Optimally, the radiologist should tailor each examination protocol to fit the demands of the clinical problem as it is presented, allowing for the parts of the body or organ systems affected or suspected of injury. If a "routine" skeletal survey by x-ray is needed, it should include AP supine and lateral chest, AP views of the upper extremities with PA hands, AP lumbar spine and pelvis, AP views of the lower extremities, AP feet, and frontal and lateral skull.[26,29] High-detail radiographs with good collimation are required. The all-inclusive "babygram" is to be avoided. If there are positive or suspicious findings for child abuse, a brain CT or MRI is advisable.

Skeletal Injuries

The frequency of skeletal injury in cases of child abuse varies widely in the literature, ranging from 11 to 55%.[30] The vast majority of fractures occur in patients under 3 years of age, and half of them are in infants. The extremities are convenient "handles" by which the child can be grabbed, swung, shaken, or pulled. Hence, extremity fractures are most common. Certain fractures and other skeletal injuries are particularly suggestive of intentional trauma.

Metaphyseal injuries — The metaphyseal lesion of child abuse, first described by Caffey, is virtually pathognomonic. This fracture extends transversely across the extreme end of the metaphysis separating a disc of bone from the primary spongiosa of the metaphyses and the zone of provisional calcification of the physis. This disc is usually thicker in its periphery than in its centrum and, according to the projection, may appear as a transverse fracture line, as metaphyseal chip fractures, or as a so-called bucket-handle fracture[30] (Figure 15-11). This metaphyseal injury is rarely accompanied by periosteal reaction; vascular injury and interference with growth may cause bowing of the extremity as

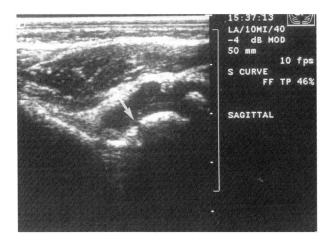

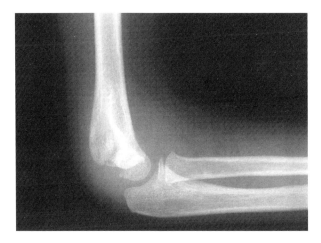

Figure 15-10   **A**: a supracondylar fracture of the distal humerus demonstrated by ultrasonography (arrow). **B**: confirmatory radiograph.

described in Caffey's second paper.[9] Metaphyseal injuries are ordinarily seen in children who don't yet walk and are not associated with normal handling, rough play, or accidental falls. The most common locations for these metaphyseal injuries are the knee, ankle, and distal humerus.[31]

Periosteal new bone — The periosteum is loosely attached to the underlying bone in infants and children and is easily separated by twisting and pulling. This results in subperiosteal hemorrhage which will calcify. These lesions are usually silent lesions but, if the bleeding is massive there may be palpable swelling and pain. This finding was referred to as involucrum in Caffey's original paper.[6] The subperiosteal calcification can be only a subtle thin line or may be of massive proportions. Shopfner[32] was first to point out that a single thin line of periosteal calcification can exist normally in infants 1 to 4 months of age, is invariably bilateral, and by itself is not diagnostic of abuse (Figure 15-12).

Diaphyseal spiral fractures — Oblique long bone fractures were found in 15% of children radiographed for suspected abuse in Hilton's experience,[31] but only 5% in the series of

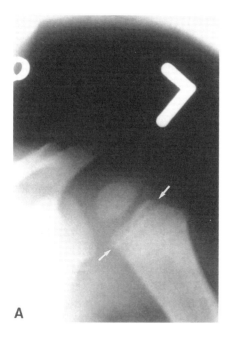

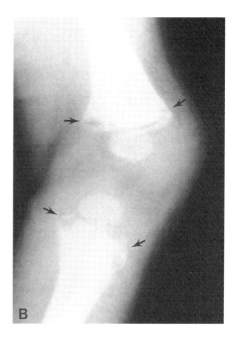

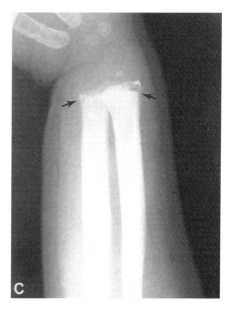

Figure 15-11 **A**: unusually good view of a classic metaphyseal lesion with the central ray exactly in the plane of the fracture (see text). **B**: infant knee shows classic "bucket-handle" fracture of the distal femur and "corner fractures" of the proximal tibia (arrows). Both fractures would look like **A** if the bones were not tilted relative to the central ray of the x-ray beam. **C**: "corner fracture" of the distal radius and ulna.

Klineman et al.[33] They are highly suggestive of abuse, particularly in the nonambulatory child (see Figure 3-6B). Like the "toddler's fracture" (see Figure 3-6A) they may be difficult to see when fresh and only become apparent when there is associated periosteal reaction. There may be extensive associated periostitis if treatment and immobilization is delayed[31] (Figure 15-13). These fractures apparently result from twisting or torsion forces.

Transverse long bone fractures — We have found these have a high specificity for child abuse in the nonambulatory child especially, and are a fairly common finding. They seem to be related to abusive grabbing and swinging forces which cleanly snap the bone (Figure 15-14).

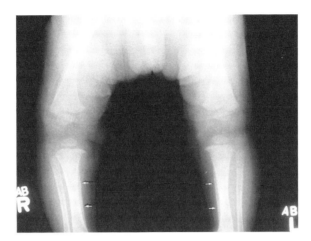

Figure 15-12   Physiological periosteal elevation in a 4-month-old infant. It is unilamellar, thin, and bilaterally symmetric (arrows). There are similar changes, less well seen, on the lateral aspects of the femoral diaphyses.

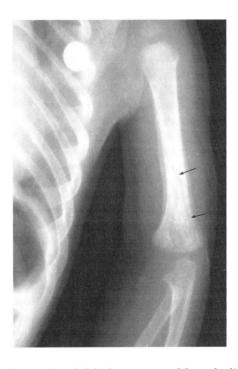

Figure 15-13   Healing spiral fracture of the humeral diaphysis extending into the metaphysis. The periosteal reaction suggests the injury probably is about 3 to 4 weeks old.

Dislocations — True joint dislocations are rarely seen in child abuse cases although dislocation of a secondary ossification center is not unusual. When dislocations are seen, they are usually associated with massive trauma and there should be a good explanatory history.

Rib fractures — Klineman et al. found rib fractures to be even more common than fractures of the long bones[33] (Figure 15-15). When fresh they may be very difficult to see, but usually heal with abundant callous and become quite obvious on delayed studies. Posterior rib fractures are particularly suggestive of child abuse and are thought to result from

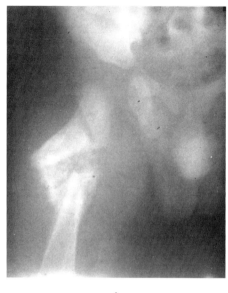

A

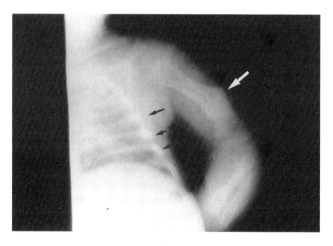

B

Figure 15-14   **A**: deformed healing transverse fracture of the femur in a 4-month-old abused infant. **B**: almost completely healed transverse fractures of the humerus with residual angulation (large arrow). There are lateral rib fractures as well (small arrows).

grasping the child with anterior compression of the chest. Applying force from front to back may cause fractures more laterally situated. Rib fractures are practically never seen after resuscitative efforts in children. Fractures of the first rib are highly suggestive of abuse. Scintiscans are ideal for detecting rib fractures (Figure 15-16).

Hand fractures — Except for fractures of the distal phalanx of the fingers from closing doors, hand and feet fractures are quite rare in infants and children and highly suspicious for abuse[31] (Figure 15-17). They were found in 4% of the series of Klineman et al.[33]

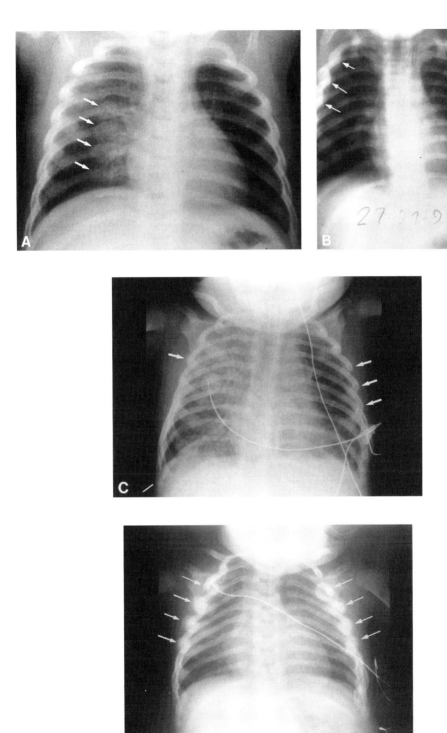

Figure 15-15   Rib fractures. **A**: typical healed posterior fracture from AP compression. **B**: healed lateral rib fractures. **C**: acute rib fractures (arrow) were missed and the baby sent home, then returned, **D**: with multiple bilateral healing fractures (note hazy callus surrounding ribs). At this time the infant also had a skull fracture. (**C** and **D** courtesy of Dr. Damien Grattan-Smith.)

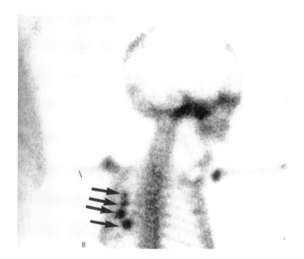

Figure 15-16   Nuclear bone scan is ideal for early detection of rib fractures (arrows). Note normal high uptake at growth plate in the shoulder. Symmetrical, bilateral metaphyseal injuries would be difficult to appreciate here. The infant is slightly rotated so the proximal humeral uptake is slightly asymmetrical. (Courtesy of Dr. Damien Grattan-Smith.)

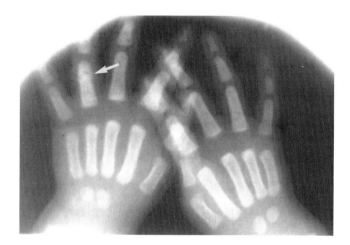

Figure 15-17   This 22-month-old Navajo is the same patient as seen in Figures 15-9 and 15-11A. The broken proximal phalanx (arrow) is further evidence of abuse. When social workers went to the home, they found a brain-damaged abused sibling.

Clavicle fractures — Clavicular fractures are the most common perinatal fracture, occurring typically in the midshaft. Such fractures are practically never seen in child abuse although injuries to the lateral end of the clavicle may be seen as a component of shaking.[34]

Scapular fractures — Fractures of the scapula are highly suspicious for child abuse and usually involve either the blade of the scapula or, more commonly, the acromion. Care must be taken to differentiate a true fracture from an ununited apophysis (Figure 15-18).

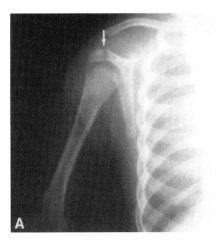

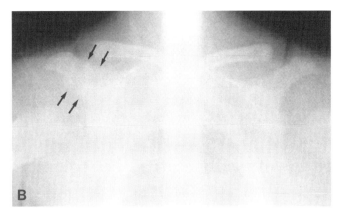

Figure 15-18   **A**: acute fracture of the acromial process of the scapula. **B**: healed fracture of the right acromion and normal opposite side.

Other rare fractures — A high specificity for child abuse is found in fractures of the sternum and the spinous processes of the spine.[30] Vertebral body fractures or subluxations are rare. This author has seen only one instance of lateral spine subluxation in 45 years of practice and that resulted from the child being swung against a wall (Figure 15-19). Cervical injuries are slightly more common.

Multiple fractures and fractures of different ages — Again, first mentioned by Caffey,[9] multiple fractures and fractures in various stages of healing have a high specificity for child abuse if there is an absent or inconsistent history of trauma (Figures 15-20 and 15-21). In a study of 165 fractures in 31 infants who died of child abuse,[33] all but 2 had at least 1 healing fracture present; 36 fractures were acute and 13 were of indeterminate age.

Skull fractures — Linear skull fractures are not highly suggestive of child abuse but the level of suspicion should increase with complex skull fractures. Skull fractures will be discussed under the general topic of head injuries.

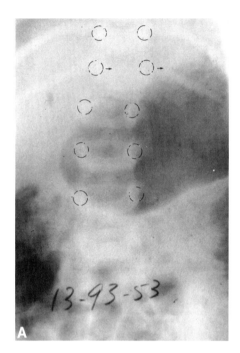 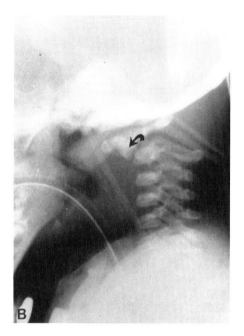

Figure 15-19   **A**: there is a lateral dislocation of T-12 on L-1. The pedicles are marked so the malalignment can be better appreciated on this low-contrast radiograph. This 2-year-old was brought in because she wouldn't "pass her water". She also had a skull fracture. She had been slammed against a wall. **B**: another infant who was hit in the back of the head with a blunt weapon, and sustained a separation of the odontoid process from the body of C-2 with anterior subluxation of C-1. Note separation of the spinous processes at the level of injury.

Confusing bone lesions of nontraumatic origin — A number of disease processes may simulate to some extent the bony injuries due to intentional trauma.[31,35] They will be familiar to most pediatric radiologists. Any radiologist serving as an expert in a court case involving child abuse should study them because opposing attorneys are likely to throw them up as substitutes for abuse. The most popular entity for this purpose is osteogenesis imperfecta. Others include congenital syphilis, ricketic conditions, Caffey's disease, leukemia, prostaglandin E therapy to keep the ductus open in congenital heart disease, Menkes' syndrome (kinky-hair disease), neuroblastoma, metastases, vitamin A intoxication, scurvy, osteomyelitis, methotrexate therapy (uncommon now), myelodysplasia, congenital indifference to pain (very rare), Schmid-like metaphyseal chondrodysplasia, Dilantin® therapy, and normal variants. We have already spoken of physiologic periosteal new bone. One may also see some spurring and cupping of metaphyses in healthy infants during the early months of life. Fractures of the extremities during childbirth, especially breech deliveries, may simulate the fractures of child abuse but rarely are seen in these days of high Caesarian rates.

Head Injuries

The most common cause of death from child abuse is trauma to the head.[22] Accidental trauma to the head in children is not often serious. Falls from baby chairs or tables, sofas, and beds rarely cause a linear fracture and this is usually not associated with intracranial damage. There is an extensive literature on the results and significance of falls from various

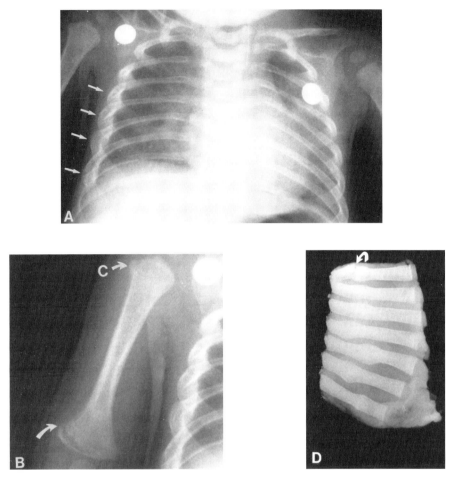

Figure 15-20   Multiple injuries in various stages of healing. A single "babygram" film showed **A**: old rib fractures (arrows), **B**: new "bucket-handle" fractures of distal right humerus, and **C**: "corner fracture" of the proximal right humerus (long arrow). The left arm is shown in Figure 15-13. **D**: post-mortem Faxitron study of a chest wall preparation shows a new rib fracture (arrow) through one of the old, healed fractures. (Courtesy of Dr. James C. Downs.)

heights onto different surfaces.[22, 36–41] Again, experts going to court with child abuse cases should familiarize themselves with this literature since it is almost always brought up if there is any head injury involved. If one can draw a generalization from the various reports it would be that head injuries resulting from falls from beds or sofas or down stairs yield a rare skull fracture and relatively minor trauma. Falls from extreme heights, falls onto extremely hard surfaces, or high-velocity impact injury provide the opportunity for serious injury and usually have a corroborative history. Children who fall from heights from 10 ft to up to 5 to 7 stories rarely die from those falls and, in fact, rarely sustain life-threatening injuries. Consequently, serious intracranial injuries and complex fractures of the skull resulting from "short falls" strongly suggest intentional trauma (Figure 15-22).

Intracranial Injuries

Intracranial injury is frequently associated with abusive head trauma and includes both subarachnoid and subdural hemorrhage, intracerebral and intracerebullar hemorrhage,

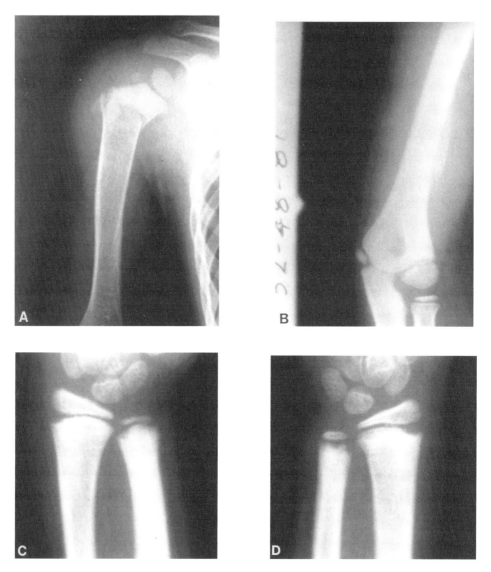

Figure 15-21   Multiple injuries in a 7-year-old girl who said her father beats her when he gets drunk. **A**: old Salter 2 fracture of the proximal humerus. **B**: myositis ossificans in left arm. **C** and **D**: bilateral epiphyseal injuries of the radius and ulna at the wrist with resorption of bone.

and massive edema (Figure 15-23). Combinations may exist, of course. Klineman[36] suggests that any case involving a complex skull fracture or a neurologic finding occurring in an infant or child after a fall from a height reported to be 90 cm (2.9 ft) or less should be regarded as possible abuse.

Radiographically demonstrated severe or complex skull fracture should be followed up with CT or MRI immediately (Figures 15-24 and 15-25). Even without skull fracture, CT or MRI is recommended when child abuse is strongly suspected from other findings.

Shaking Injuries

Guthkelch is credited with first linking subdural hematoma to shaking forces — a situation we now recognize as the "Shaken Baby Syndrome".[31,42] However, that claim of primacy may belong to Weston, who described three instances of subdural hematoma in infants who had been violently shaken.[30,43]

The head of the infant or child is large and heavy relative to the rest of its body, and sits at the end of a relatively long, narrow, and weak neck. When the baby is grasped by the chest, shoulders, or arms and shaken, the head can reach high levels of translational and rotational velocity. The brain inside the calvaria will move at a different speed and become asynchronous with the bony envelope (Figure 15-24). Tearing of bridging vessels can ensue, producing subdural hemorrhage. It has been shown that the rotational velocity or acceleration is causative. Translational motion alone (as in a woodpecker) will not produce the injury. Thus one can see massive intracranial hemorrhage and brain swelling with spreading of the intracranial suture, unassociated with skull fracture or soft tissue bruising (Figure 15-25). However, shaking is also frequently associated with direct injury to the head along with the shaking. There has been controversy as to whether the intracranial injuries can be accounted for by shaking alone, without a direct impact blow to the head, but this possibility is accepted by most authorities at the present time.[22,44,45]

Visceral Trauma

Thorax

Although the thoracic bony cage is one of the most frequent sites of abusive injuries, the thoracic viscera are rarely reported as being involved. Occasionally one sees some pleural fluid or blood associated with rib fractures. Pulmonary contusions are rarely reported. Injuries to the heart and mediastinum from blunt force are extremely rare as a manifestation of child abuse.[46]

Abdomen

On the other hand, the abdomen is a fairly frequent site of abusive trauma, particularly after children become ambulatory. Blunt force in the form of a fist or knee can cause severe damage to intraabdominal viscera and is associated with a high mortality rate. External physical evidence of trauma usually is lacking.[47] In the absence of history of a major traumatic episode, such as a vehicular accident, abuse should be suspected when these injuries are seen in young children.

Intramural hematoma of the duodenum is the most common of these injuries from child abuse.[46] Frequently the child will be brought in with vomiting as the duodenum becomes obstructed. The blow to the epigastrium compresses the retroperitoneal portion of the duodenum against the spine to produce the injury. The radiographic findings are typical on GI series or CT (Figures 15-26 and 15-27) . There may be associated injuries in other areas or organ systems.

Lacerations of the liver and pancreas may result from similar trauma. Lacerations of these organs have already been shown in Chapter 3, Figure 3-3. A pseudocyst may develop in the traumatized pancreas and can be demonstrated by GI series, ultrasound, or CT[46,47] (Figures 15-28 and 15-29).

Perforation of the small bowel, stomach, or colon can result from abusive blunt force of the abdomen although this is not quite as common as the preceding entities[47,48] (Figure 15-30).

Despite its vulnerability in other settings, the spleen is not often injured in child abuse. The kidneys, ureters, and bladder also are usually spared.[46]

Soft Tissues

Often, children with radiographically demonstrable injuries of child abuse will have associated soft tissue findings, particularly bruises and burns. These usually are not demonstrable radiographically, of course, but may be apparent to the radiographer who should alert the radiologist to the finding (Figure 15-31).

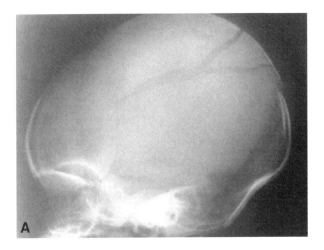

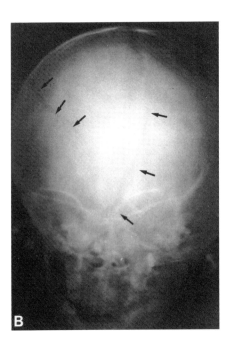
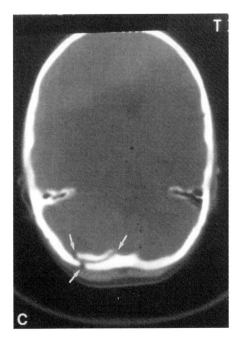

Figure 15-22   Skull fracture. **A**: complex skull fractures (same case as Figure 15-15C and D),. **B**, **C**, and **D**: complex skull fractures (boyfriend claimed he accidentally banged the baby's head against a door frame as he carried it from one room to another). **E**: same baby with fatal brain hemorrhage.

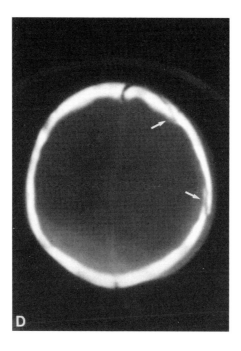

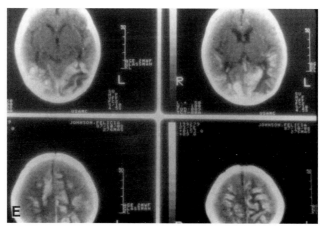

Fgure 15-22 (Continued)

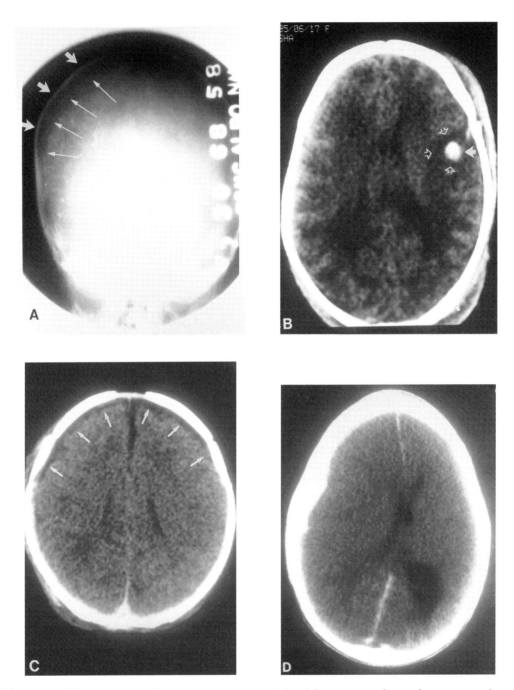

Figure 15-23 Intracranial Injuries. **A**: acute subdural hematoma shown by angiography as the dark space between the bony calvaria (short arrows) and the vascularized cortex (long arrows). **B**: hemorrhagic contusion (arrow) with surrounding edema (open arrows) on unenhanced CT. **C**: subdural hematoma around frontal lobe (arrows) on unenhanced CT. **D**: unenhanced CT shows blood in interhemispheric sulcus, extraapical blood on left, massive edema of right hemisphere with shift to the left, obstruction of left lateral ventricle at the foramen of Munro, and cisterns. **E** and **F**: MRI shows subdural blood around the cerebellum and temporal, frontal, and occipital lobes.

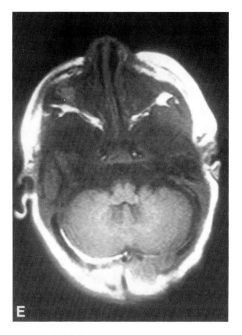 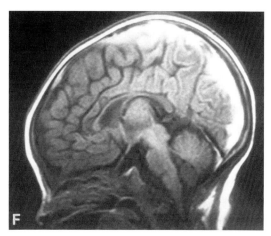

Figure 15-23 (Continued)

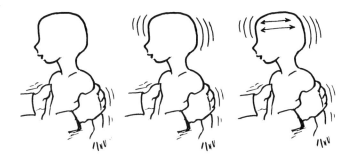

Figure 15-24   Shaken baby. Head and brain eventually oscillate asynchronously with both translational and rotational motion, shearing vessels and causing intracranial bleeding.

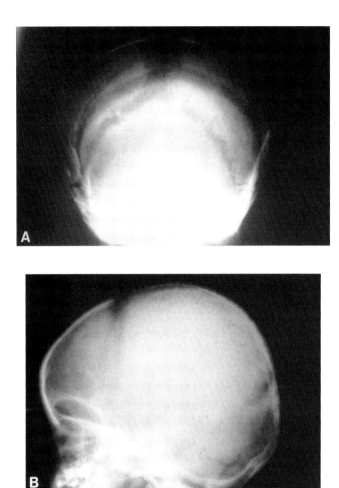

Figure 15-25   Shaken baby syndrome. No fractures, but marked sutural spreading from sub-dural hematoma and cerebral edema. This baby died within minutes of admission to hospital.

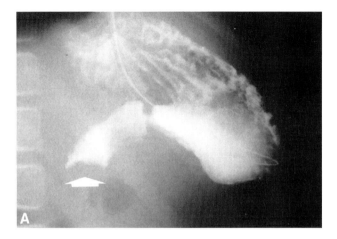

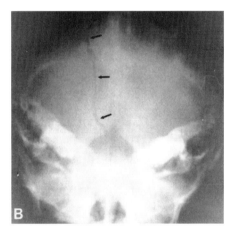

Figure 15-26   **A**: GI series shows obstruction of barium (broad arrow) at the second portion of the duodenum by intramural duodenal hematoma. "Pad sign" on stomach suggests pancreatic edema or hemorrhage. **B**: child also had an occipital skull fracture.

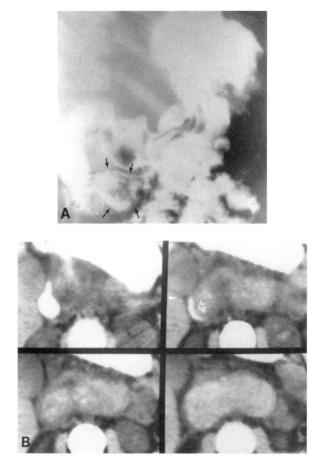

Figure 15-27 **A**: GI series shows widening and incomplete filling of the third portion of the duodenum (arrows) due to intramural hematoma. **B**: CT scans showed mottled densities of blood and contrast material in duodenum. Open arrow shows narrow channel remaining open for flow of contrast medium. (From Hughes, J. J. and Brogdon, B. G., *J. Comput. Tomogr.*, 10, 231, 1986. With permission.)

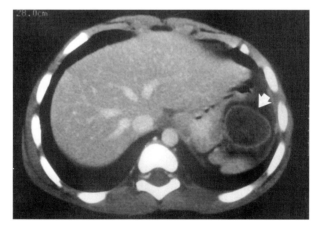

Figure 15-28 Enhanced abdominal CT shows pseudocyst in tail of pancreas (arrow) from abusive trauma to abdomen. (Courtesy of Dr. Damien Grattan-Smith.)

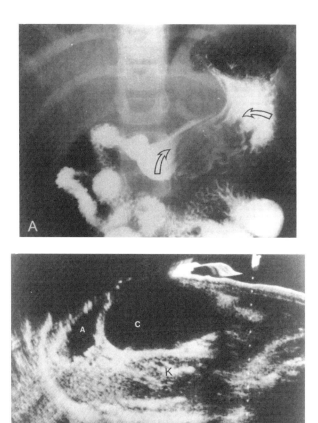

Figure 15-29   **A**: GI series shows impression on stomach (arrows) from pancreatic pseudocyst in a vomiting 4½-year-old child. **B**: ultrasonography shows anechoic mass (C) anterior to left kidney (K) and ascites (A). (From Kleinman P. K., Raptopoulos V. D., and Brill, P. W., *Radiology*, 141, 393, 1981. With permission.)

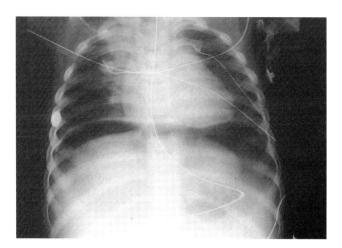

Figure 15-30   Free intraperitoneal air under diaphragm from traumatic gastric rupture. (Courtesy of Dr. Damien Grattan-Smith.)

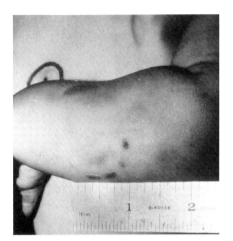
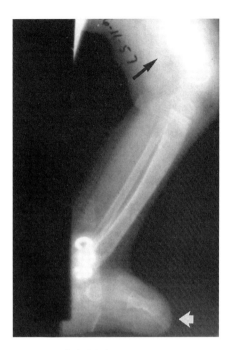

Figure 15-31   A: bruises and burns on the upper extremity of child shown in Figures 15-22B–E. **B**: 11-month-old girl from hippie commune. Fracture of distal femur is evident (black arrow). She literally had her feet held to the fire, and many of her toes were burned off (white arrow).

References

1. Silverman, F. N., Unrecognized trauma in infants, the battered child syndrome, and the syndrome of Ambriose Tardieu: Rigler Lecture, *Radiology*, 104, 337, 1972.

2. Caffey, J., The parent-infant traumatic stress syndrome: (Caffey-Kempe syndrome), (battered baby syndrome), *Am. J. Roentgenol.*, 114, 217, 1972.

3. Merten, D. F., Cooperman, D. R., and Thompson, G. H., Skeletal manifestations of child abuse, in *Child Abuse: Medical Diagnosis and Management*, Reece, R. M., Ed., Lea & Febiger, Philadelphia, 1994, chap. 2.

4. Evans, K. T. and Knight, B., Forensic radiology, *Br. J. Hosp. Med.*, 17, June, 1986, p. 17.

5. Silverman, F. N., Presentation of the John Howland Medal and Award of the American Pediatric Society to Dr. John Caffey, *J. Pediatr.*, 67, 1000, 1965.

6. Caffey, J., Multiple fractures in long bones of children suffering from chronic subdural hematoma, *Am. J. Roentgenol.*, 56, 163, 1946.

7. Sherwood, P., Chronic subdural hematomas in infants, *Am. J. Dis. Child.*, 39, 980, 1930.

8. Ingraham, F. D. and Heyl, H. L., Subdural hematoma in infants and childhood, *J. Am. Med. Assoc.*, 112, 198, 1939.

9. Caffey, J., Some traumatic lesions in growing bones other than fractures and dislocations, clinical and radiological features. The Mackenzie Davidson Memorial Lecture, *Br. J. Radiol.*, 30, 225, 1957.

10. Caffey, J., Significance of the history in the diagnosis of traumatic injury to children. Howland Award Address, *J. Pediatr.*, 68, 1008, 1965.

11. Neuhauser, E. B. D., Discussion of paper by F. N. Silverman, *Am. J. Roentgenol.*, 69, 413, 1953.

12. Silverman, F. N., The roentgen manifestations of skeletal trauma, *Am. J. Roentgenol.*, 69, 413, 1953.

13. Kempe, C. H., Silverman, F. N., Steele, B. F., Droegemueller, W., and Silver, H. K., The battered child syndrome, *J. Am. Med. Assoc.*, 181, 105, 1962.

14. Kempe, C. H., Pediatric implications of the battered baby syndrome. Windermere Lecture, *Arch. Dis. Child.*, 46, 28, 1971.

15. Elmer, E., *Children in Jeopardy*, University of Pittsburgh Press, Pittsburgh, 1967.

16. Brogdon, B. G., Child abuse: the radiologists' role, *Pathologist*, 31, 134, 1977.

17. Kleinman, P. K., *Diagnostic Imaging of Child Abuse*, Williams & Wilkins, Baltimore, 1987.

18. Reece, R. M., *Child Abuse: Medical Diagnosis and Management*, Lea & Febiger, Philadelphia, 1994.

19. Kleinman, P. K., *Diagnostic Imaging of Child Abuse*, Williams & Wilkins, Baltimore, 1987, chap. 9.

20. Nolte, K. B., Esophageal foreign bodies as child abuse, *Am. J. Forensic Med. Pathol.*, 14, 323, 1993.

21. Report of the U.S. Advisory Board on Child Abuse and Neglect, A Nation's Shame: Fatal Child Abuse and Neglect in the United States, U. S. Department of Health and Human Services, Washington, D.C., 1995.

22. Reece, R. M., *Child Abuse: Medical Diagnosis and Management*, Lea & Febiger, Philadelphia, 1994, chap. 1.

23. Kleinman, P. K., *Diagnostic Imaging of Child Abuse*, Williams & Wilkins, Baltimore, 1987, chap. 4.

24. Sty, J. R. and Starsbuk, R. J., The role of bone scintigraphy in the evaluation of the suspected abused child, *Radiology*, 146, 369, 1983.

25. Sty, J. R., Radiological imaging applications in forensic medicine, workshop at the Annu. Meet. Am. Acad. Forensic Sci., New Orleans, Feb. 14, 1994.

26. Kleinman, P. K., *Diagnostic Imaging of Child Abuse*, Williams & Wilkins, Baltimore, 1987, chap. 1.

27. Kleinman, P. K., Nimkin, K., Sprivak, M. R., Rayder, S. M., Madansky, D. L., Shelton, Y. A., and Patterson, M. M., Follow-up skeletal surveys in suspected child abuse, *Am. J. Roentgenol.*, 167, 893, 1996.

28. Nimken, K., Kleinman, P. K., Teeger, S., and Spevak, M. R., Distal humeral physeal injuries in child abuse: MR imaging and ultrasonography findings, *Pediatr. Radiol.*, 25, 562, 1995.

29. Kleinman, P. K., Refresher course on child abuse, Annu. Meet. Int. Skeletal Soc., New Orleans, Oct. 21, 1995.

30. Kleinman, P. K., *Diagnostic Imaging of Child Abuse*, William & Wilkins, Baltimore, 1987, chap. 2.

31. Hilton, S. V. W., Differentiating the accidentally injured from the physically abused child, in *Practical Pediatric Radiology*, Hilton, S. V. W. and Edwards, D. K., III, Eds., W. B. Saunders, Philadephia, 1994, chap. 14.

32. Shopfner, C. F., Periosteal bone growth in normal infants: a preliminary report, *Am. J. Roentgenol.*, 97, 154, 1966.

33. Kleinman, P. K., Marler, S. C., Jr., Richmond, J. M., and Blackbourne, B. D., Inflicted skeletal injury: a postmortem radiologic-histopathologic study in 31 infants, *Am. J. Roentgenol.*, 165, 647, 1995.

34. Kogutt, M. S., Swischuk, L. E., and Fagan, C. J., Patterns of injury and significance of uncommon fractures in the battered child syndrome, *Am. J. Roentgenol.*, 121, 143, 1974.

35. Brill, P. W. and Winchester, P., Differential diagnosis of child abuse, in *Diagnostic Imaging in Child Abuse*, Kleinman, P. K., Ed., William & Wilkins, Baltimore, 1987, chap. 11.

36. Kleinman, P. K., in *Diagnostic Imaging in Child Abuse*, Williams & Wilkins, Baltimore, 1987, chap. 8.

37. Helfer, R. E., Slovis, T. L., and Black, M., Injuries resulting when small children fall out of bed, *Pediatrics*, 60, 533, 1977.

38. Reiber, G. D., Fatal falls in childhood: how far must children fall to sustain fatal head injury? Report of cases and review of the literature, *Am. J. Forensic Med. Pathol.*, 14, 201, 1993.

39. Root, I., Head injuries from short distance falls, *Am. J. Forensic Med. Pathol.*, 13, 85, 1992.

40. Weber, W., Experimentelle untersuchungen zu schädelbruchverletzungen des säuglings, *Reichsmedizin*, 92, 87, 1984.

41. Nimityongskul, P. and Anderson, L. D., The liklihood of injuries when children fall out of bed, *J. Pediatr. Orthoped.*, 7, 184, 1987.

42. Guthkelch, A. N., Infantile subdural hematoma and its relationship to whiplash injuries, *Br. Med. J.*, 2, 430, 1971.

43. Weston, J. T., The pathology of child abuse, in *The Battered Child*, 3rd ed., Kempe, C. H. and Helfer, R. E., Eds., University of Chicago Press, Chicago, 1968, 77.

44. Gilliland, M. G. F. and Folberg, R., Shaken babies — some have no impact injuries, *J. Forensic Sci.*, 41, 114, 1996.

45. Collins, K. A. and Nichols, C. A., Pediatric homicide by shaking: a ten-year prospective study, Proc. Annu. Meet. Am. Acad. Forensic Sci., Washington, D.C., Feb. 21, 1997, p. 139.

46. Kleinman, P. K., Visceral trauma, in *Diagnostic Imaging of Child Abuse*, William & Wilkins, Baltimore, 1978, chap. 7.

47. Kleinman, P. K., Raptopoulos, V. D., and Brill, P. W., Occult non-skeletal trauma in the battered child syndrome, *Radiology*, 14, 393, 1981.

48. Fossum, R. M. and Descheneaux, K. A., Blunt trauma of the abdomen in children, *J. Forensic Sci.*, 36, 47, 1991.

Spousal Abuse and Abuse of the Elderly — An Overview

16

JOHN D. MCDOWELL, D.D.S., M.S.
B. G. BROGDON, M.D.

Contents

Introduction

Domestic violence in all of its forms — child abuse, spousal abuse, and elder abuse — is pervasive in Western society. Many persons have learned from within the family that violence is a means by which long- or short-term goals may be accomplished. In Western society, the family is the single most common locus of violence. It is impossible to separate one form of domestic violence from another. Abused children are likely to have abused mothers. Both men and women in a dysfunctional relationship may abuse each other. Spousal abuse does not magically begin or end at age 65.

Violence, while not uniquely American, is a learned behavior that is intergenerationally transmitted. Recent high-profile cases involving American public figures have sensitized most of us to the potential morbidity and mortality associated with dysfunctional family relationships. Americans are more likely to suffer injuries from domestic violence than they are likely to be injured by a person outside the home.[1,2] Prevalence estimates of domestic violence in the U.S. indicate that as many as 50% of all families have experienced some form of intrafamily violence,[1,3–5] and 25% of couples interviewed report at least one incident of physical abuse involving a family member. Despite this large number of suspected domestic violence cases, adequate surveillance of domestic violence does not exist.[6,7] Estimates of domestic violence based on reported cases might significantly underestimate the true prevalence rate.[8] A Lewis Harris Association poll of 1793 randomly surveyed women in Kentucky showed that 21% reported being physically abused by her partner, and nearly two-thirds of divorced or separated women reported being the recipient of nonaccidental trauma. Szihovacz[9] found that one in four surveyed women in Pennsylvania reported being assaulted by her intimate male partner.

National Crime Survey estimates indicate that between 5 and 6 million children, spouses, and elderly persons are physically abused every year in the U.S. Family violence causes in excess of 20,000 hospitalizations and uses nearly 100,000 hospital days, 30,000 emergency department visits, and nearly 40,000 physician visits each year. There are 175,000 days missed from paid work because of domestic violence. The total estimated annual medical cost incurred because of domestic violence exceeds $44 million.[10]

Within the dysfunctional and violent family, husbands, wives, children, and parents are all at risk for nonaccidental trauma. Whereas the family has traditionally been thought to be a shelter from harm, there is extensive evidence that the nuclear and extended family is anything but safe. It is not possible to separate the most common group of domestic violence victims — battered women and abused elders — from the other groups. Battered women and abused elders must be examined in the global context of dysfunctional relationships.

There is a strong relationship between spousal abuse and child abuse.[8,11] Studies have shown that between one-third and one-half of the families in which women have been battered also have children present who have been physically and/or sexually abused.[8,12,13] Physical abuse during pregnancy is not uncommon. Both the pregnant women and her unborn child are potential victims of intentional trauma.

Whereas battering in the nonpregnant female is more commonly directed against the head and neck,[14,15] abuse during pregnancy is frequently directed toward the breasts and abdomen.[3,16–18] The aggressive behavior directed against the abdomen of pregnant women with its potentially harmful effect on the fetus has engendered the term "prenatal child abuse". There is reportedly an increased rate of abortions and premature births found in women who give a positive history of physical abuse.

Cate et. al. first used the term "premarital abuse" to describe the physical violence associated with dating and courtship.[19,20] Their study reported that 22% of the respondents had been the victims of premarital violence or had been violent toward a premarital partner.

Spousal Abuse — Battered Women

The term "battered women" was first used in 1974 by Pizzey to describe the female victim of violence within marriage or cohabitation.[21] A commonly accepted definition of the term "battered women" is a woman who has received "deliberate, severe, repeated, demonstrable, physical injury from her partner".[12] In general terms an abused or battered woman is one who is subjected to serious and/or repeated physical injury as a result of intentional, deliberate assaults by her male companion.[2]

Physically dominating one's wife (including "wife beating") has had, until relatively recent times, both legal and social sanctions. The husband's authority to chastise his wife was explicitly written into the laws of church and state and later incorporated into English common law, which American law generally follows.[3,8] The husband's right to hit his wife was written into the law of the U.S. in 1824 with one limitation — that he was restricted from using a switch larger in diameter than his thumb.[22] This law was overturned in 1874, but the ruling was qualified with the statement that if no permanent injury had been inflicted, nor malice, cruelty, nor dangerous violence had been shown, that it is better to leave the parties to forgive and forget.

It is only within the last few decades that assault in the home has been recognized and prosecuted as criminal behavior. Contemporary American society began examining the issue of violence within the family in the mid-1960s when a national survey showed that 20% of all Americans approved of slapping one's wife.[23] Surprisingly, approval for physically striking one's mate increased with income level and education; 25% of college-educated men believed striking one's mate was acceptable behavior.

Most states presently have enacted and are enforcing legislation protecting persons abused by family or household members.[24,25] While there continues to be a positive trend toward actions taken on behalf of the abused/neglected child, legislators and health care providers have not responded as effectively on behalf of adult victims of domestic violence. While child abuse has been described as a major health problem that requires the highest priority, population-based estimates indicate that battered women are far more common than abused children.[25,26] Abuse is the single most common etiology for injury presented by women, accounting for more injury episodes than motor vehicle accidents, muggings, and rapes combined.[2,27]

Problems Identifying and Treating Victims of Domestic Violence

The recognition and reporting rate of adult domestic violence victims is quite low when compared to the actual prevalence. The reporting rate for battered women may be as low as 2% in large metropolitan emergency departments.[28] Also, some health care providers blame the victims for provoking the violence and hold them responsible for their own injuries.[29]

Recognizing and treating the domestic violence victim is the important first step toward intervention on behalf of the victim.

Associating Fractures with Domestic Violence

Radiographic examinations can provide evidence of intentional trauma in battered women. The majority of assaults in nonpregnant battered women are directed at the head, neck, and face. Ellis et al.[30] reviewed mandibular fractures occurring in Glasgow, Scotland from 1974 to 1983 and found that alleged assaults were the most common cause of fractures in males and females and that greater than 60% of the assaults of females occurred at home. A second 10-year review of fractures of the zygomatico-orbital complex showed that, in females, most (54%) assaults occurred at home, although women may give conflicting histories.[31]

Injury Patterns

The two most common causes of facial trauma in adults are motor vehicle accidents and domestic violence. The senior author analyzed hospital records of adult women to determine if any patterns specific to domestic violence could be determined and used to identify the battered women presenting for care of maxillofacial trauma (facial fractures).[32]

Certain variables were solely observed in one of the two study groups. LeFort 1 and LeFort 2 fractures were seen *only* in victims of motor vehicle accidents. Fractures of the mandibular ramus and fractures of the mandibular body/ipsilateral angle were seen only in battered women (Figure 16-1). Previous emergency department visitation and prior facial fracture (by patient history or radiographic report) were seen only in battered women[33] (Figure 16-2).

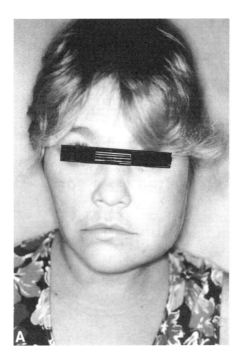

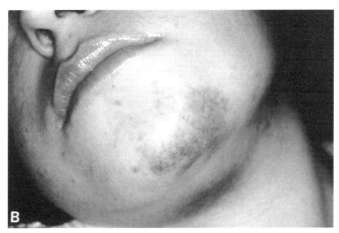

Figure 16-1   **A**: woman, 43, hit with husband's fists, has massive swelling over left jaw. **B**: bruise and abrasions to chin. **C**: separation of teeth at fracture site. **D**: panorex study shows fractures through the left mandibular angle and right mentalis.

Fractures

A total of 175 facial fractures were seen in the 114 records reviewed (the total number of fractures exceeds the number of records because some patients had more than one fracture associated with their presenting injuries): 89 fractures were found in the 58 victims of motor vehicle accidents and 86 fractures were found in the 56 battered women.

There were 117 cases of mandibular fractures (single and multiple sites), representing 66.86% of the total of 175 facial fractures. Of the mandibular fractures (single and multiple sites), 69 (58.97%) were seen in battered women.

In this study, fractures involving both the mandibular body and angle were the most common facial fractures, representing 33.71% (59/175) of all facial fractures. Fractures of the mandibular body and angles were seen much more frequently in battered women than in motor vehicle accident victims. Of the mandibular fractures involving the body and angle, 71.18% (42/59) were seen in battered women. Battered women presented with 73.53% (25/34) of the fractures involving the mandibular angle.

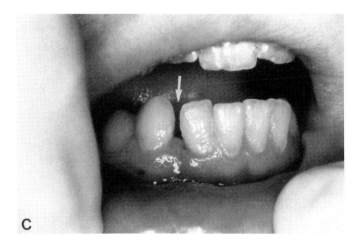

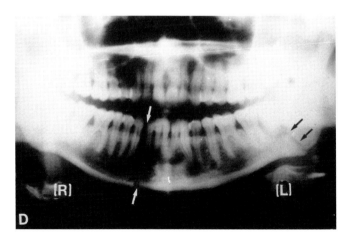

Figure 16-1 (Continued)

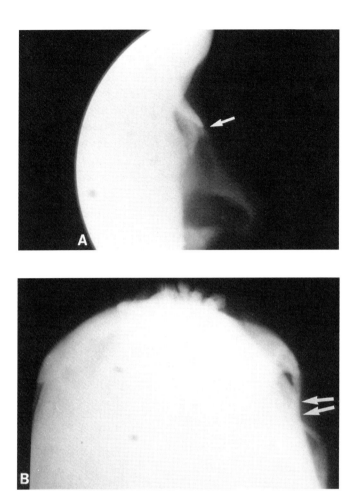

Figure 16-2   **A**: fractured nasal bone (arrow). **B**: depressed fracture of the left zygomatic arch (arrows).

Besides other facial fractures in battered women (zygomatico-facial, nasal bones, orbital fractures, etc.) injuries at other sites may be seen, of course. Defensive injuries (fending fractures of the hands and forearms) are not uncommon. Soft tissue injuries may be striking (Figure 16-3). Blows to the chest are frequent but, in our experience, rib fractures are not common. Abdominal injuries require more sophisticated studies (i.e., CT).

Delayed Presentation for Care

As previously described in the literature, victims of intentional trauma frequently report for care on a delayed basis — 57% of battered women presented for care more than 24 hours after their injuries were reportedly inflicted. Only 14% of women victims of motor vehicle accidents presented for care more than 24 hours after their injury.

Zachariades and co-authors[34] examined the medical records of battered women to determine the weapon and location of facial trauma associated with domestic violence. In over 70% of the facial injuries, the weapon was the husband's or boyfriend's hand. Mandibular fractures were the most common presenting facial injury, representing 39% of all facial injuries in women assaulted by their husbands or boyfriends.

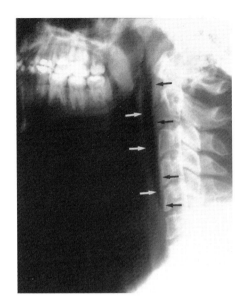

Figure 16-3   Young woman, hit in the throat by her boyfriend, sustained a rupture of the larynx with dissection of air into the prevertebral space (arrows).

Abuse of the Elderly

The elderly are the fastest growing age group in the U.S. It is estimated that by the year 2000 nearly 1 of every 5 Americans will be age 65 or older. More than 2 million Americans exceed the age of 85. The quality of life enjoyed by many of these older persons has been unequaled in previous decades. As individuals age, they can develop chronic diseases and disabilities that impair their ability to function independently and will eventually become dependent on the care of others. More than 60% of dependent persons will live with family members. Most of these family members will provide adequately for the elderly person. However, care givers might be persons who are reluctant, ill prepared, or incapable of providing necessary care. These living conditions may lead to circumstances in which the aged individual can become a victim, suffering neglect and abuse at the hands of the care givers.[35]

It is only in the last two decades that abuse of the elderly has attracted the attention of the public and the medical establishment, as if it were a new phenomenon. It is not a new phenomenon, but it has been unremarked and undetected. The first report of abuse of the elderly in the literature was Burston's letter to the *British Medical Journal* on "granny-battering".[36] This was followed closely by Butler's book, "*Why Survive?: Growing Old in America*".[37] Considerable interest in the problem has been stimulated, and all 50 states have some form of elder abuse law.[38]

Elderly abuse is almost as common as child abuse, affecting as many as 10% of the elderly in some form and about 2% with physical abuse. Those numbers are "soft" because large epidemiological studies are lacking, and both the victim and the perpetrators tend to deny its existence or belittle its seriousness.[39]

The elderly, like children, are at risk for several types of abuse. These have been variously categorized but would include: (1) physical abuse; (2) mental, emotional, or psychological abuse; (3) neglect; and (4) economic abuse such as theft or misuse of the elder's assets.[38] Some would include self-abuse or self-neglect, mostly involving the reclusive, sometimes incompetent, older person usually living alone.

Physical abuse of the elderly is usually received from the victim's spouse (50%), less often from the victim's child or children (23%) and, contrary to popular opinion, only in 17% of cases is the physical violence at the hand of nonfamily care givers.[40] While the reported incidence of physical abuse is almost gender neutral, abuse is proportionally higher in males because fewer males live alone.

The actual act of physical violence can range from a push or a shake to assault with a deadly weapon. In the Boston survey,[38] the most common act of physical violence was pushing, grabbing, or shoving (63%), followed by having something thrown at the victim (46%); slapping was involved in 42% of incidents; 10% of the physically abused elderly in this series had been hit with a fist, kicked, or bitten.[40]

The injuries sustained are nonspecific but, again, maxillofacial injuries rank high[35] as do defense injuries and those related to grasping, squeezing, or forcible restraint (Figures 16-4 and 16-5).

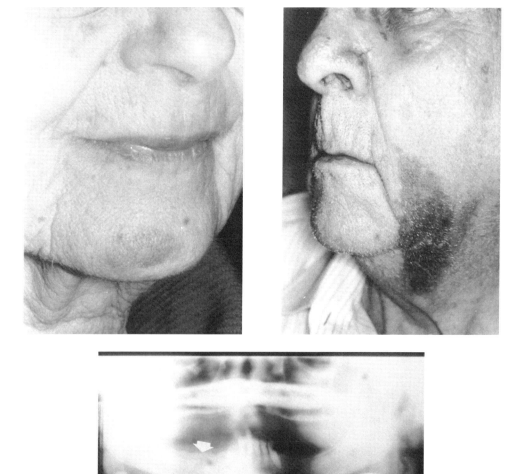

Figure 16-4   Elderly woman with **A** and **B**: bruises to both sides of jaw. Note also black eye at edge of **B**. Panorex, **C**, shows fracture at the level of the mental foramen on the right. A left mandibular angle fracture was demonstrated on another film (not shown).

One must be cautious. The mere presence of injury in an elderly person receiving home care or domiciled in a nursing facility is not proof of abuse. The elderly person with chronic disease, malnutrition, senile osteoporosis, and disuse atrophy can be extremely fragile. Handling injuries (fractures) can occur here just as they do in the premature nursery (Figure 16-6). One must be watchful for other signs of abuse or neglect, be alert to injuries inappropriate to the patient's level of activity, and one must be inquisitive. If possible, the

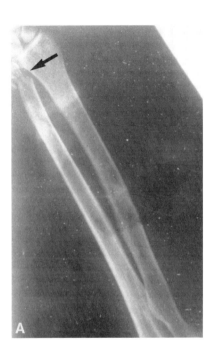

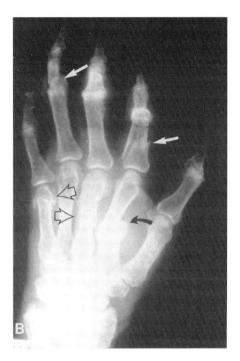

Figure 16-5   Bedfast octogenarian female with signs of abuse (injuries inappropriate to her level of activity, multiple injuries in various stages of healing). **A**: forearm with marked osteoporosis of bone and with displaced fending fracture of distal ulna at edge of film (arrow). **B** and **C**: both hands showing new (arrows), healing (open arrows), and healed (curved arrows) fractures with residual deformity, and dislocation (triangle). The fending fracture of the ulna is seen again (open curved arrow). (Courtesy of Dr. M. G. F. Gilliland.)

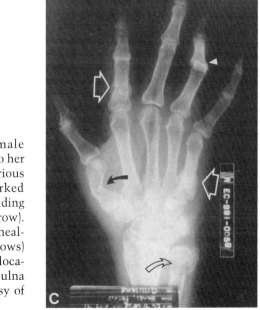

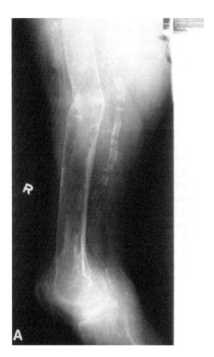 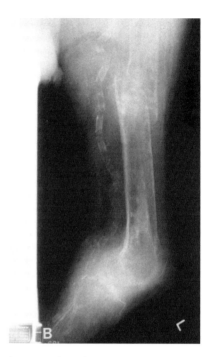

Figure 16-6   Elderly male diabetic with kidney failure, profound osteoporosis, and bilateral below-the-knee amputations making him difficult to lift or move. **A**: he sustained a fracture of the femur while being cared for at home. **B**: while being lifted and transported to the hospital by trained E. M. S. personnel, the other femur was broken. Impression: no abuse. (Courtesy of Dr. James C. Downs.)

suspected victim should be gently interrogated alone or where he is free of fear of retaliation or vengeance. The victim often is embarrassed by his situation and also afraid that a complaint may result in being torn from the abusive home situation to be thrown into a worse situation in the care of strangers.

Summary

Domestic violence is a serious public health problem with a potentially fatal outcome. Battered women, children, and elderly persons occur in all segments of society. Without intervention the frequency and severity of assaults tends to increase. Physicians, dentists, and other health care providers can learn to recognize the signs and symptoms of non-accidental trauma. Once recognized, the victims of nonaccidental trauma can be made aware of their rights under the law.

Every health care provider should be sensitized to the possibility that the patient may be a victim of intentional trauma. Competent clinicians would not consider discharging a patient presenting with a life-threatening condition, yet many battered women and elderly persons are discharged from the emergency department without any arrangement being made for their safety.[3,28] Treating the physical injuries without offering essential support to a domestic violence victim has been described as being "simply bad medicine".[24]

References

1. Staus, M. A., Gelles, R. J., and Steinmetz, S. K., *Behind Closed Doors: Violence in the American Family*, Sage Publications, Newbury Park, CA, 1988.

2. Stark, E. and Flitcraft, A., *Spouse Abuse in Surgeon General's Workshop on Violence and Public Health: Source Book*, Centers for Disease Control, Leesburg, VA, 1985, p. SA1.

3. Hilberman, E., Overview: "The wife-beater's wife" reconsidered, *Am. J. Psychia.*, 137, 1336, 1980.

4. Gelles, R., *The Violent Home: A Study of Physical Aggression Between Husbands and Wives*, Sage Publications, Beverly Hill, CA, 1974.

5. Dobash, R. E. and Dobash, R. P., The case of wife beating, *J. Fam. Issues*, 2, 439, 1981.

6. Krugman, R. D., Advances and retreats in the protection of children, *N. Engl. J. Med.*, 320, 531, 1989.

7. Centers for Disease and Control, Education about adult domestic violence in U.S. and Canadian medical schools 1987-1988, *Morbidity and Mortality Weekly Report*, 32, 17, 1989.

8. Walker, L. E., *The Battered Woman Syndrome*, Springer-Verlag, New York, 1984.

9. Szihovacz, M. E., Using couple data as a methodologic tool: the cases of marital violence, *J. Marriage Fam.*, 45, 633, 1983.

10. National Crime Surveys, *Am. J. Publ. Health*, 70, 65, 1989.

11. ACOG, The battered woman, *Am. Coll. Obstet. Gynecol. Tech. Bull.*, 124, 1, 1989.

12. Gayford, J. J., Battered wives, *Med. Sci. Law*, 15, 237, 1975.

13. Chez, R. A., Woman battering, *Am. J. Obstet. Gynecol.*, 158, 1, 1988.

14. Berrios, D. C. and Grady, D., Domestic violence: risk factors and outcomes, *West. J. Med.*, 155, 133, 1991.

15. Shepherd, J., Gayford, J., Leslie, I., and Scully, C., Female victims of assault, a story of hospital attenders, *J. Cranio-Maxillofac. Surg.*, 16, 233, 1988.

16. Schei, B. and Bakketeig, L., Gynaecological impact of sexual and physical abuse by spouse. A study of a random sample of Norwegian women, *Br. J. Obstet. Gynaecol.*, 96, 1379, 1989.

17. Sampselle, C. M., The role of nursing in preventing violence against women, *J. Obstet. Gynecol. Neonatal Nursing*, 20, 481, 1991.

18. Bewley, C. and Gibbs, A., Violence in pregnancy, *Midwifery*, 7, 107, 1991.

19. Makepeace, J. M., Courtship violence among college students, *Fam. Relat.*, 30, 97, 1981.

20. Cate, R. M., Henton, J. M., Koval, J., Chistopher, F. S., and Lloyd, S., Premarital abuse, a social psychological perspective, *J. Fam. Issues*, 3, 79, 1982.

21. Pizzey, E., *Scream Quietly or the Neighbors Will Hear*, R. Enslow Publishers, Short Hills, NJ, 1977.

22. Swanson, R., Battered wife syndrome, *Can. Med. Assoc. J.*, 130, 709, 1984.

23. Stark, R. and McEvoy, J., Middle-class violence, in *Change, Readings in Societal and Human Behavior*, CRM Books, Del Mar, CA, 1972, p. 272.

24. McLeer, S. V. and Anwar, R. A., Education is not enough, a systems failure in protecting battered women, *Ann. Emerg. Med.*, 18, 651, 1989.

25. Dewsbury, A. R., Battered wives. Family violence seen in general practice, *R. R. Soc. Health*, 95, 290, 1975.

26. Collier, J., When you suspect your patient is a battered wife, *RN*, 50, 22, 1987.

27. Drossman, D. A., Leserman, J., Nachman, G., Li, Z. M., Gluck, H., Toomey, T. C., and Mitchell, C., Sexual and physical abuse in women with functional or organic gastrointestinal disorders, *Ann. Int. Med.,* 113, 828, 1990.

28. Greany, G. D., Is she a battered woman? A guide for emergency response, *Am. J. Nursing,* 84, 724, 1984.

29. Ghent, W., DaSylva, N., and Farren, M., Family violence: Guidelines for recognition and management, *Can. Med. Assoc. J.,* 132, 541, 1985.

30. Ellis, E., Moos, K., and El-Attar, A., Ten years of mandibular fractures: An analysis of 2,137 cases, *Oral Surg. Oral Med. Oral Pathol.,* 43, 120, 1985.

31. Ellis, E., El-Attar, A., and Moos, K., An Analysis of 2,067 cases of zygomatico-orbital fractures, *J. Oral Maxillofac. Surg.,* 43, 417, 1985.

32. McDowell, J. D., A Comparison of Facial Fractures in Women Victims of Motor Vehicle Accidents and Battered Women, Published thesis, University of Texas Graduate School of Biomedical Sciences, San Antonio, Texas, 1993.

33. McDowell, J. D., Kassebaum, D. K., and Stromboe, S. E., Recognizing and reporting victims of domestic violence, *J. Am. Dent. Assoc.,* 123, 44, 1992.

34. Zachariades, N., Koumoura, F., and Konsolaki-Agouridaki, E., Facial trauma in women resulting from violence by men, *J. Oral Maxillofac. Surg.,* 48, 1250, 1990.

35. McDowell, J. D., Elder abuse, the presenting signs and symptoms in the dental practice, *Texas Dent. J.,* 107(2), 29, 1990.

36. Burston, G. R., Granny-battering, *Br. Med. J.,* 3, 592, 1975.

37. Butler, R. N., *Why Survive?: Growing Old in America,* Harper & Row, New York, 1975.

38. Wolf, R. S., Elder abuse: ten years later, *J. Am. Geriatr. Soc.,* 36, 758, 1988.

39. A. M. A., Council on Scientific Affairs Report: Elder abuse and neglect, *J. Am. Med. Assoc.,* 257, 966, 1987.

40. Pillemer, K. and Finkelhor, D., The prevalence of elder abuse. A random sample survey, *Gerontologist,* 28, 51, 1988.

Human Rights Abuse, Torture, and Terrorism

17

B. G. BROGDON, M.D.
ERIC W. LAWSON, M.D.

Contents

Role and Purpose of Radiology

The application of radiology in the forensic investigation of human rights abuse, torture, and acts of terrorism is not remarkably different from its role in other forensic areas. Dr. John J. Fitzpatrick, probably the most experienced American radiologist in this field, has described eight goals of radiological involvement:

1. To discover evidence of occult trauma;
2. To locate and evaluate foreign bodies accompanying, or imbedded within, human remains;
3. Identification of remains;
4. Bringing comfort and closure to survivors through identification of remains and determination of preterminal and terminal events;
5. Support applicants for refugee asylum by confirming or documenting evidence of occult trauma;
6. Setting the historical record straight;
7. Bringing perpetrators to justice;
8. Bringing an end to abuse in any form as an instrument of political or religious policy.[1,2]

Dr. Fitzpatrick, anthropologist Clyde C. Snow, and odontologist Lowell Levine were the core American members of an international team of forensic scientists organized in 1978 who are dedicated to (1) developing forensic evidence for use against perpetrators of human rights abuse, and (2) educating and supporting similar teams in other countries. This has resulted in courses and/or field operations in several overseas venues including

Argentina, Guatemala, Costa Rica, El Salvador, Bolivia, Kurdistan, and fragments of the former Yugoslavia. Radiological techniques for these activities are not unique, but conditions often are somewhat primitive and may require considerable on-site innovation.

The team has been able to find evidence of death from massive blunt head trauma as from clubs or gunstocks, cut marks (probably machete) to the head, and massive and multiple gunshot wounds from weapons of a type used only by government forces.

Torture

The World Medical Association Tokyo Declaration of 1975 defined torture as deliberate, systematic, or wanton infliction of physical or mental suffering by one or more persons acting alone or on the orders or any authority, to force another person to yield information, to make a confession, or for any other reason.[3]

Article 5 of the *Universal Declaration Of Human Rights* states "No one shall be subjected to torture, or to cruel, inhuman, or degrading treatment or punishment."[4]

Despite high ideals and declarations, torture, both individualized and organized, has existed throughout history and continues to be practiced in more than half of the countries in the world today; it had been documented to occur in 98 countries worldwide in 1988.[5–7] There are more than 20 million displaced persons throughout the world, more than a million have been settled in the U.S. Many have experienced war trauma, including torture, and have fled countries where torture is widely practiced.

Torture has evolved through the ages to become more sophisticated, is usually carried out in a clandestine fashion, and is often accompanied with deliberate attempts to reduce any physical evidence of its practice. Therefore, the documentation of abuse is difficult and often based on historical accounts, since physical findings at the time of examination usually are absent. Most torture is carried out in the early stages of arrest and incarceration. If not initially fatal, the physical signs of torture are usually healed by the time the victim can be examined by sympathetic authorities or human rights groups. The most common physical findings are scars on the skin and bone dislocations and fractures.[7]

Studies of victims show that the most common types of torture reported by survivors in six investigations accomplished between 1979 and 1985[6] were (1) beating, kicking, and striking with objects to the torso and/or genitalia and/or head; (2) threats or humiliation; (3) application of electricity; (4) blindfolding; (5) mock execution; (6) made to witness others being tortured; (7) "submarino" — submersion of the head in water; (8) isolation; (9) starvation; and (10) sleep deprivation. Most of these, of course, leave no direct or long-standing physical evidence. In the studies described above, very few radiographs were obtained to disclose healed or occult fractures. Apparently many of the fractures were so deformed that they could be diagnosed by palpation.

Radiologic documentation of torture employs similar procedures, techniques, and modalities as are employed in the study of child abuse and include roentgenograms, contrast studies, ultrasonography, scintigraphy, computed tomography, and magnetic resonance imaging.[8]

Radiologic Implications of Specific Tortures

A specific type of physical torture, especially common in the Middle East, is *falanga*, the application of repeated blows to the feet.[9-11] Routine roentgenograms and CT have documented foot fractures and extensive soft tissue edema of the feet and legs from falanga. Aseptic necrosis of bone as a sequela has also been reported. More recently, scintigraphy or radioactive bone scans have proved a useful modality to document soft tissue injury, which may persist as a positive finding in this procedure for some months after the injury. Bone scintigraphy also may reveal small fractures missed on plain films.

In some countries, beating, caning, or lashing is used as an authorized form of punishment, but it is considered inhumane in other parts of the world. The senior author has been shown an MRI study showing massive edema and hemorrhage in the soft tissues of the back over the thorax, reported to be the result of a legalized beating.

On the CBS television show, *Sixty Minutes*, of Sunday May 25, 1997, a segment was devoted to interrogation practices of Israeli authorities in dealing with terrorists or suspect terrorists. It was admitted that some of the suspects are violently shaken while being grasped by the shoulders or upper clothing. It was claimed that shaking had resulted in death from intracranial bleeding on at least one occasion. It is presumed that the injuries incurred, and the results as demonstrated by CT or MRI, would be virtually identical to those seen in the Shaken Baby Syndrome.

Terrorism

Radiologists have been involved in the evaluation of victims of terrorist activities eventuating in the bombing of buildings or aircraft. The only special consideration here is the examination of bodies (both dead and alive), not only for descriptions of injuries or for purposes of identification, but also to identify foreign objects which might lead to identification of the device employed and ultimately to the apprehension of the perpetrators.

Involvement of Physicians

While the majority of the physicians are devoted to preserving and defending human rights, unfortunately, and seemingly inevitably, some physicians become involved with abuse, torture, and other abridgements of human rights. In modern times this extends from Germany in the Third Reich where 45% of German physicians (a higher percentage than for any other profession)[12] were members of the Nazi Party and a number of whom were convicted as war criminals at Nuremberg,[13,14] to present-day Turkey where allegations of involvement in torture have been brought against 70 physicians and where 76% of physicians responding to a questionnaire did not consider beatings alone to constitute torture.[5]

Unquestionably, in regimes that countenance torture and other infringements of human rights, the medical community is under great pressures and coercion to look the other way, or to go along with the policy. In a retrospective case study of 200 alleged survivors of torture from 18 different countries, the Danish Medical Group of Amnesty

International documented that 20% of those victims reported that medical personnel were involved in their torture.[10] Undoubtedly many of those were unwilling but silent accomplices. Physicians throughout the world have played an important role in opposition to torture and infringement of human rights, but this often has required great courage and the risk of professional and physical punishment. Physicians groups and national medical societies must be constantly alert against any threat to human rights, particularly of a physical nature, and provide immediate and outspoken opposition before such practices and policies can take root.

References

1. Fitzpatrick, J. J., Role of radiology in human rights abuse, *Am. J. Forensic Med. Pathol.*, 5, 321, 1984.

2. Fitzpatrick, J. J., Human rights abuse, in *A History of the Radiological Sciences: Diagnosis*, Gagliardi, R. A. and McClennan, B. I., Eds., Radiology Centennial, Inc., Reston, VA, 1996, p.596.

3. World Medical Association, The declaration of Toyko, 1945, in *Ethical Codes and Declarations Relevant to the Health Professions*, Amnesty International, New York, 1994, p. 9.

4. Universal Declaration of Human Rights, 1948, in *Twenty-Five Human Rights Documents*, Columbia University Press, New York, 1994, p. 6.

5. Iacopino, V., Heiser, M., Pishever, S., and Kirschner, R. H., Physician complicity in misrepresentation and omission of evidence of torture in postdetention medical examinations in Turkey, *J. Am. Med. Assoc.*, 276, 396, 1996.

6. Goldfeld, A. E., Mollica, R. F., Pasavento, B. H., and Faraone, S. V., The physical and psychological sequelae of torture: symptomatology and diagnosis, *J. Am. Med. Assoc.,* 259, 2725, 1988.

7. **Anon.,** Editorial: Compromise, complicity and torture, *J. Am. Med. Assoc.*, 276, 416, 1996.

8. Cathcart, L. M., Berger, P., and Knazan, B., Medical examination of torture victims applying for refugee status, *Can. Med. Assoc. J.*, 121, 179, 1979.

9. Rasmussen, O. V., Medical aspects of torture, *Dan. Med. Bull.*, 37, 1, 1990.

10. Bro-Rasmussen, F., Henriksen, O. B., Rasmussen, O., et al., Aseptic necrosis of bone following falanga torture, *Ugeskr. Laeg.*, 144, 1165, 1982.

11. Lok, V., Tunca, M., Kumanlioglu, K., Kapkin, E., and Dirik, G., Bone scintigraphy as clue to previous torture, *Lancet*, 337, 846, 1991.

12. Sidel, V. W., Commentary: The social responsibilities of health professionals: lessons from their role in Nazi Germany, *J. Am. Med. Assoc.*, 276, 1679, 1996.

13. Grodin, M. A., Legacies of Nuremberg: medical ethics and human rights, *J. Am. Med. Assoc.,* 276, 1682, 1996.

14. Lifton, R. J., *The Nazi Doctors: Medical Killing and the Psychology of Genocide*, Basic Books, New York, 1986.

SECTION VI

Research and the New Modalities

Research and Applications of the New Modalities

18

B. G. BROGDON, M.D.

Contents

Introduction

As recounted earlier, most of the seminal investigations of the potential applications of the roentgen ray took place within the first year or two following Röntgen's discovery. In subsequent decades most of the literature in the field of forensic radiology was made up of case reports or very small retrospective studies. A few large retrospective investigations provided information on incidence and distribution of certain findings and propagated some standards, for instance in the field of skeletal development and maturation. The recognition that these early standards were not universally applicable has led to a spate of standards development for different countries and population groups in recent years.

Early Forensic Research

In the modern era some of the early forensic research has had to do with accident investigation. In 1944 Hass used radiography extensively in studying relations between force, injuries, and aircraft structure.[1] Simson showed the value of the aircraft accident necropsy 25 years ago in a clever reconstruction of a fatal accident from radiographic evidence.[2] He also showed that cervical spine fracture patterns were related to impact velocities. An innovative prospective approach to impact injuries was the work done by Jones and associates using fresh cadavers and the then-famous sled facility at Holloman Air Force Base,[3] again relating fracture and dislocation patterns to impact forces. One of the earlier accident investigation studies with forensic applications in the radiologic literature involved post-mortem radiology of head and neck injuries, which revealed a high incidence of cervical spine injuries and both intravascular and intracardiac air which might be missed by the unforewarned autopsy surgeon[4] (Table 18-1) (Figure 18-1). Other investigators have looked at the usefulness of radiography in studying injuries to the neck and skull in motor vehicle injuries.[5–7]

Table 18-1   Incidence of Head and Neck Injuries in 146 Victims of Fatal Traffic Accidents

Craniocervical trauma			82 (56.2%)
Skull fractures only	51 (34.9%)		
Skull and cervical injury	10 (6.8%)	61 (41.7%)	
		31 (21.2%)	
Cervical injury only	21 (14.3%)		
No craniocervical trauma			64 (43.8%)
Total			146 (100%)

From Aker, G. J., Oh, Y. S., Leslie, E. V., et al., *Radiology*, 114, 611, 1975. With permission.

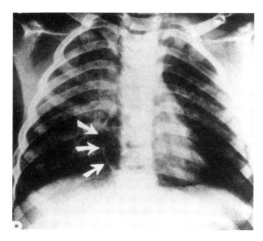

Figure 18-1   Example of air in the heart of a person suffering fatal massive injuries in a vehicular accident. (From Akers, G. J., Jr., Oh, Y. S., Leslie, E. V., Lehotay, J., Panaro, V. A., and Eschner, E. G., *Radiology*, 114, 611, 1975. With permission.)

Technical Advances and New Modalities

As technical advances have appeared in radiology, they have been embraced and modified by the forensic science community. Examples would include Vanezi's contrast techniques for study of cadaver vertebral artery systems,[8] the use of solidifying silicone rubber with lead oxide in autopsy studies of vascular structures,[9] and similar applications for the demonstration of esophageal, tracheal, and aortic fistulae.[10]

Physical anthropologists and forensic pathologists have been quick to see the potential usefulness of computed tomography as it has burgeoned in clinical use. Examples are Haglund's use of a toposcan for identification by comparison of frontal sinuses[11] and identification by comparative CT studies of the lumbar spine in Germany[12] (Figure 18-2). Rougé et al. compared CT scan images to exclude a possible indentification.[13]

Recently, Oliver et al. used an innovative comparison of computed radiographs and radiographs taken at autopsy to generate a three-dimensional reconstruction of a bullet path — a powerful forensic exhibit for the courtroom or the laboratory[14] (Figure 18-3).

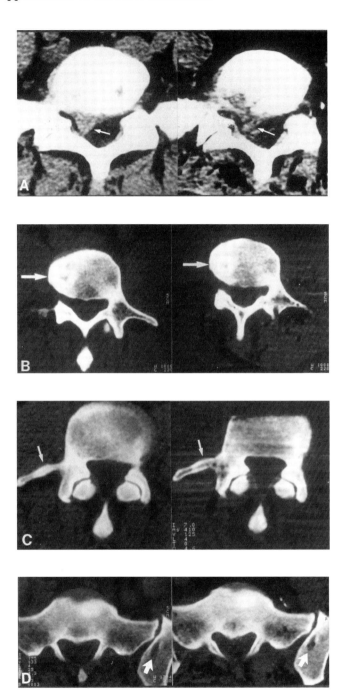

Figure 18-2 Identification through comparison of ante-mortem and post-mortem computed tomography. The ante-mortem study is on the viewer's left in each instance. **A**: shows a posterolateral disc herniation at L5-S1. **B**: shows a Schmorl's node in the inferior end-plate of L4. **C**: shows a peculiar thickening of the right transverse process of L4. **D**: shows identical lucencies in the left ilium at the sacroiliac joint. (Original images courtesy the authors, copyright ASTM, reprinted with permission.)

Modern CT scans can be computer-processed to select tissues for solitary display. Thus, a body part that had undergone CT scanning might be reprocessed for comparison with skeletonized remains (Figure 18-4).

Computed tomography units have become quite widespread and somewhat cheaper, hence they are more readily available for forensic research. Magnetic resonance imaging, on the other hand, is still quite expensive and machine time is at a premium in most locales. Although we have not seen such a case reported, it would be quite possible to match ante-mortem MR images with post-mortem radiographs (Figures 18-5 and 18-6).

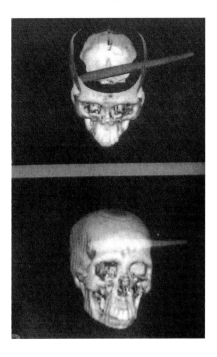

Figure 18-3 Two views of a reconstructed bullet path utilizing advanced computer techniques and stock CT data. The beam narrows from the entrance through the exit due to modeling of the radiation attenuation. (Images courtesy of the authors, copyright ASTM, reprinted with permission.)

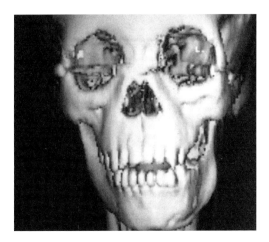

Figure 18-4 Example of a reconstructed three-dimensional image of a skull from the CT of the head of a living patient. This image can be manipulated upon any axis to match post-mortem x-rays or defleshed skull.

Problems and Promise of Interdisciplinary Effort

A rather sad commentary on the research examples cited and, indeed, on most forensic research employing radiologic methods and modalities, is that the overwhelming majority of investigators have been nonradiologists. Often they must struggle with substandard equipment and in ignorance of well-known radiologic tenets not published in their literature. On the other hand, most radiologists have little connection with the forensic sciences and are

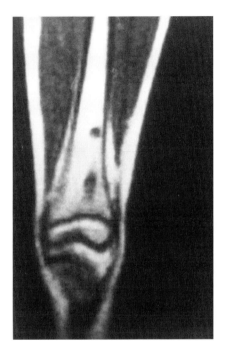 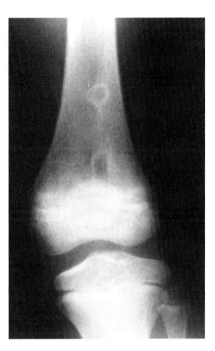

Figure 18-5   Comparison of **A**: MR, and **B**: radiographic images of an adolescent distal femur containing two fibrous cortical defects.

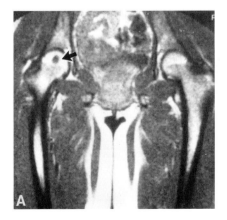 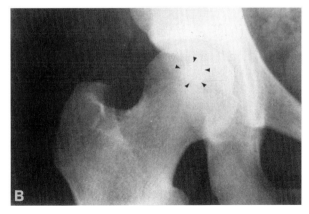

Figure 18-6   Comparison of **A**: MR, and **B**: radiograph images including the right femoral head which contains a bone island. In the T1 weighted image shown, the dense calcification is registered as a signal void. Still, the match is not difficult.

unaware of the research possibilities in that field, or of the problems that need solution. It is believed that forensic scientists in other disciplines would find radiologists in their area interested in cooperative efforts. Sharing of interdisciplinary skills and knowledge would improve the economy and effectiveness of investigative efforts, prevent some false starts and/or reinventions of well-worn wheels, and most important, expand scientific horizons.

The two short chapters following are examples of modern applications of new radiologic modalities in forensic investigations. One uses our most exciting new modality, magnetic resonance imaging, in post-mortem studies and promises to be of great help to the forensic pathologist, the other is an example of the adoption of an industrial technique for application in the fields of forensic sciences and clinical medicine.

References

1. Hass, G. M., Relations between force, major injuries and aircraft structure in design of aircraft, *Aviat. Med.,* 15, 395, 1944.

2. Simson, L. R., Jr., Roentgenography in the human factors of fatal aviation accidents, *Aerosp. Med.,* 43, 81, 1972.

3. Jones, A. M., Bean, S. P., and Sweeney, B. G., Injuries to cadavers resulting from experimental rear impact, *J. Forensic Sci.,* 23, 730, 1978.

4. Akers, G. J., Jr., Oh, Y. S., Leslie, E. V., Lehotay, J., Panaro, V. A., and Eschner, E. G., Postmortem radiology of head and neck injuries in fatal traffic accidents, *Radiology,* 114, 611, 1975.

5. Shkrum, M. J., Green, R. N., and Nowak, E. S., Upper cervical trauma in motor vehicle collisions, *Am. J. Forensic Sci.,* 34, 381, 1989.

6. Cain, C. M. J., Simpson, D. A., Ryan, G. A., Manock, C. H., and James, R. A., Road crash cervical injuries: a radiological study of fatalities, *Am. J. Forensic Med. Pathol.,* 10, 193, 1989.

7. Shkrum, M. J., Green, R. J., McClafferty, K. J., and Nowak, E. S., Skull fractures in fatalities due to motor vehicle accidents, *J. Forensic Sci.,* 39, 107, 1994.

8. Vanezi, P., Techniques used in the evaluation of vertebral artery trauma at postmortem, *Forensic Sci. Int.,* 13, 159, 1979.

9. Karhunen, P. J., Männikko, A., Penttilä, A., and Liastro, K., Diagnostic angiography in postoperative autopsies, *Am. J. Forensic Med. Pathol.,* 14, 303, 1989.

10. Karhunen, P. J. and Lalu, K., Radiographic demonstration of esophageal and tracheal fistulas at autopsy using a contrasting medium that vulcanizes at room temperature, *J. Forensic Sci.,* 36, 1129, 1991.

11. Haglund, W. D. and Fligner, C. L., Confirmation of human identification using computerized tomography (CT), *J. Forensic Sci.,* 38, 708, 1993.

12. Riepert, T., Rittner, C., Ulmcke, D., Oghuihi, S., and Scheveden, F., Identification of a unknown corpse by means of computed tomography (CT) of the lumbar spine, *J. Forensic Sci.,* 40, 126, 1995.

13. Rougé, D., Telmon, N., Arrue, P., Larrouy, G., and Arbur, L., Radiographic identification of human remains through deformities and anomalies of post-cranial bones: a report of two cases, *Am. J. Forensic Sci.,* 38, 997, 1993.

14. Oliver, W. R., Chancellor, A. S., Soltys, M., Symon, J., Cullip, T., Rosensman, J., Hellman, R., Boxwala, A., and Gormley, W., Three-dimensional reconstruction of a bullet path: validation by computed radiography, *J. Forensic Sci.,* 40, 321, 1995.

Use of Post-Mortem Cranial MRI in Evaluation of Suspected Child Abuse

19

BLAINE L. HART, M.D.

Contents

Introduction

Imaging techniques have performed an important function in the evaluation of child abuse since the syndrome was first defined.[1,2] In view of the well-documented sensitivity of MRI for intracranial injuries, the use of cranial MRI to complement autopsy in cases of suspected child abuse has been investigated.[3,4] This experience has confirmed the utility of this combined approach, and has defined strengths and weaknesses of MRI compared to autopsy alone.

Study Methods

During a 33-month period from 1990 to 1993, 11 cases of unexplained death or suspected child abuse in children 2 years of age or younger were evaluated. All were autopsied at the Office of the Medical Investigator in Albuquerque, NM. Population selection criteria were that the body was received at the medical investigator's facility within 24 hours of death and that MRI could be obtained within 24 hours of death, prior to autopsy. The age range of the study group was from 3 months to 26 months, with a mean of 13.4 months. There were 7 boys and 4 girls; 3 of the 11 children became unresponsive and were dead on arrival at a hospital despite attempts at resuscitation. The cause of death was not immediately apparent in any of these three. The other 8 had clinically apparent head injuries and had survived in the hospital from 11 hours to 5 days.

Post-mortem, preautopsy MRI of the head was performed on a 1.5-tesla clinical imaging system (GE Signa, General Electric, Milwaukee, WI). The imaging techniques varied with software changes over the period of study, but all examinations included sagittal T1-weighted and axial dual-echo intermediate and T2-weighted spin-echo images. Coronal spin-echo images were also obtained in all 11 cases: T1-weighted images in 3, T2-weighted images in 2, and both T1- and T2-weighted images in 6. Gradient-echo sequences were additionally used in three cases. Examinations were performed with a standard quadrature head coil. The mean post-mortem interval to MRI scan was 15.5 hours, with a range of 5 to 21 hours. Each study was read by a neuroradiologist prior to autopsy. The reader was aware of the suspicion of child abuse but not of the clinical details.

Autopsies were performed by forensic pathologists using standard protocol. The results of the MRI scan were available at the time of the autopsy and brain cutting. The final diagnosis in each case was made using all available information, including autopsy findings, MRI findings, skeletal survey, and investigation of circumstances surrounding the death.

Study Results

The cause of death was determined to be head injury in eight cases. There was no evidence of head injury in the other three children. (One death was due to accidental poisoning, one was considered the result of a seizure disorder, and the cause of one was undetermined.) In all three cases ultimately determined not to be due to child abuse, no cerebral abnormalities were detected on MRI.

Abnormalities detected with MRI and at autopsy in the 11 cases were categorized as follows: scalp or subgaleal hemorrhage, subdural hemorrhage, subarachnoid hemorrhage, brain contusion, cerebral edema, retinal hemorrhage, optic nerve hemorrhage, suture separation, mastoid fluid, hypoxic injury, herniation, and axonal shearing injuries (Table 19-1). No skull fractures were identified. Although both MRI and autopsy revealed these injuries, there were areas of significant difference as well as overlap in sensitivity of the two techniques (Table 19-2).

Brain contusion and edema, herniation, hypoxic injury, scalp hemorrhage, subdural hemorrhage, and vitreous hemorrhage were detected with both MRI and autopsy. Subarachnoid hemorrhage, optic nerve sheath hemorrhage, and suture separation were evident only by autopsy. The use of MRI demonstrated mastoid fluid readily, and in some cases MRI was clearly more sensitive for focal cortical injuries and for areas of shearing injury. A summary comparison is presented in Table 19-3, with extraaxial and intraaxial lesions compared. More lesions, as defined above, were identified by autopsy (66 in the 11 patients) than by MRI (27 lesions). The difference was greater with extraaxial lesions. MRI was more sensitive for the detection of intraaxial lesions (12 detected by autopsy and 13 by MRI); 7 lesions were detected only by MRI and 32 were detected only by autopsy. Many of the abnormalities detected by autopsy and not by MRI were scalp or subgaleal hematomas. Although useful information is revealed by comparison of the two techniques for detection of cranial injuries, it is important to consider the combination. In four of the eight cases of child abuse, the combination of MRI and autopsy was more sensitive than results likely to have been obtained from autopsy alone.

MRI was helpful at the time of brain cutting by calling attention to areas of abnormality. Coronal images facilitated correlation with the pathologic specimen. On occasion, multiple sections were obtained for microscopic study based on the MRI findings. For example, a tear in the body of the corpus callosum was present on both MRI and autopsy in one case

TABLE 19-1 Comparison of Features Detected by MRI and Autopsy in Eleven Cases of Suspected Child Abuse

	Patient Number																					
	1		2		3		4		5		6		7		8		9		10		11	
	M	A	M	A	M	A	M	A	M	A	M	A	M	A	M	A	M	A	M	A	M	A
Subscalp hematoma	–	+	–	+	+	+	–	+	–	+	–	–	–	+	–	–	–	–	+	+	–	+
Suture separation	–	–	–	+	–	–	–	–	–	+	–	–	–	–	–	–	–	–	–	–	–	–
Mastoid fluid	+	–	–	–	–	–	–	–	+	–	–	–	+	–	–	–	+	–	–	–	+	–
Retinal hemorrhage	–	++	–	++	–	++	–	++	++	++	–	–	–	+	–	–	–	–	–	–	–	+
Optic nerve sheath hemorrhage	–	++	–	++	–	++	–	++	–	++	–	–	–	–	–	–	–	–	–	–	–	++
Subdural hematoma	–	++	–	++	++	+++	++	+++	–	++	–	–	+	++	–	–	–	–	–	–	–	+
Subarachnoid hemorrhage	+	+	–	+	–	+	–	+	–	+	–	–	+	+	–	–	–	–	+	+	–	+
Diffuse edema	+	+	+	+	+	+	–	–	+	+	–	–	+	+	–	–	–	–	–	–	+	+
Subfalcine herniation	–	–	–	–	–	–	–	–	–	–	–	–	–	–	–	–	–	–	–	–	+	+
Hypoxic injury	–	–	–	–	–	–	–	–	–	–	–	–	–	–	–	–	–	–	–	–	+	+
Contusion or focal ischemia	–	–	–	–	+	–*	+	+*	–	–	–	–	–	–	–	–	–	–	–	–	+	+
Shearing injury	+	+*	–	–	–	–	–	–	–	–	–	–	–	–	–	–	–	–	–	–	–	–*

Notes: M, MRI; A, autopsy; –, no finding identified on respective modality; +, finding identified with MRI or autopsy; ++, bilateral finding (for subdural hematoma or retinal or optic nerve sheath hemorrhage); *, MRI finding that guided autopsy to abnormality or that could not be identified on autopsy.

Table 19-2 Sensitivity of MRI and Autopsy

Type of lesion	MRI + Aut +	MRI + Aut −	MRI − Aut +	MRI − Aut −	Total lesions M	Total lesions A	Total patients abnormal M	Total patients abnormal A
Subscalp or subgaleal hematoma	2	0	6	3	2	25	2	6
Suture separation	0	0	2	9	0	2	0	2
Mastoid fluid	0	5	0	6	7	0	5	0
Retinal hemorrhage	1	0	6	4	2	12	2	7
Optic nerve sheath hemorrhage	0	0	6	5	0	12	0	6
Subdural hematoma	3	0	4	4	5	13	3	7
Subarachnoid hemorrhage	0	0	7	4	0	7	0	7
Diffuse edema	6	0	1	4	6	7	6	7
Subfalcine herniation	1	0	0	10	1	1	1	1
Hypoxic injury	1	0	0	10	1	1	1	1
Contusion or focal ischemia	2	1	0	8	6	4	3	3
Shearing injury	1	1	0	9	2	1	2	1

Note: M = MRI; A = autopsy.

TABLE 19-3 Summary of MRI/Autopsy Correlation

Total # of MRI abnormalities	27
Total # of autopsy abnormalities	66
Total # of MRI abnormalities, extraaxial	14
Total # of autopsy abnormalities, extraaxial	54
Total # of MRI abnormalities, intraaxial	13
Total # of autopsy abnormalities, intraaxial	12
Lesions MRI +, autopsy −	7
Lesions MRI −, autopsy +	32

(Figure 19-1). The area that might have been considered an artifact of brain cutting, especially since little hemorrhage was present in the region, was clearly present on the MRI. In another case, a shearing injury in the splenium of the corpus callosum was demonstrated on MRI. The lesion was confirmed with careful sectioning of a soft "respirator" brain that would otherwise have been very difficult to examine. A subacute cortical contusion that represented an injury several weeks old was clearly shown on MRI. Different ages of subdural hematomas were strikingly demonstrated with MRI.

All cases of severe brain edema and brain death had a distinctive appearance on MRI. Severe swelling of the brain was present, and the subarachnoid cisterns were obliterated (Figure 19-2A). This did not represent a post-mortem change, since the three cases not due to head injury presented normal MRI findings (Figure 19-2B). In fact, the MRI studies generally appeared very similar to routine clinical studies, other than the condition of static rather than flowing blood.

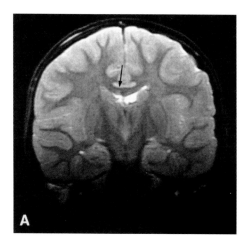

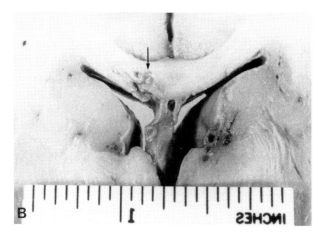

Figure 19-1 This 19-month-old boy had suffered cardiopulmonary arrest during transport to the hospital after reportedly being beaten. **A**: a coronal T2-weighted image from post-mortem MRI shows a small focus of increased signal intensity in the body of the corpus callosum (arrow). **B**: careful sectioning of the brain at the corresponding location disclosed the tear (arrow). (The photograph has been reversed to correspond with radiographic convention used in MRI.) (From Hart, B. L., Dudley, M. H., and Zumwalt, R. E., Post-Mortem Cranial MRI and Autopsy Correlation in Suspected Child Abuse, poster presentation at 1994 RSNA Conference. With permission of the Radiological Society of North America.)

Application of Post-Mortem Cranial MRI

Post-mortem radiographs are routinely obtained in cases of suspected child abuse. Such radiographs are very sensitive for fractures. MRI, a more recent technique, may add valuable information about soft tissue injuries.

Clinical experience and several prospective evaluations of imaging techniques clearly demonstrate the utility of MRI in patients who have suffered head injury.[5-7] Blinded comparison of CT and MRI scans of the brain obtained in head injury patients have shown that CT is more sensitive for detection of fractures and that MRI is more sensitive for

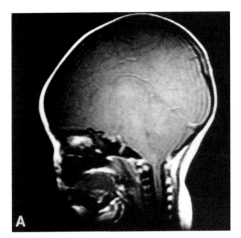 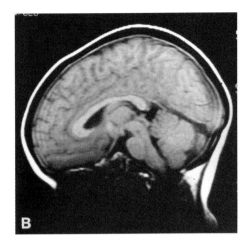

Figure 19-2   **A**: sagittal T1-weighted image shows the typical appearance of severe swelling of the brain accompanying brain death. **B**: the midline, sagittal T1-weighted image from a different post-mortem MRI study has a normal appearance in a child who died after a seizure. (From Hart, B. L., Dudley, M. H., and Zumwalt, R. E., Post-Mortem Cranial MRI and Autopsy Correlation in Suspected Child Abuse, poster presentation at 1994 RSNA Conference. With permission of the Radiological Society of North America.)

detection of extraaxial hematomas, shearing injury, and contusions.[7] Similar findings have been confirmed in the pediatric population.[8] MRI has been found useful in the investigation of child abuse in living patients.[8,9–11] The UNM/OMI investigation of post-mortem victims of trauma confirms the sensitivity of MRI for contusion, shearing injury, and subdural hematoma.[3,4]

MRI has several advantages for the study of traumatic brain injury. Many injuries resulting from trauma are accompanied by hemorrhage. Although CT is sensitive for acute hemorrhage, MRI is sensitive for both acute and later stages of intracranial hemorrhage. The single exception to this is subarachnoid hemorrhage (SAH). Despite some reports that T1-weighted MRI can detect SAH,[12] CT is generally acknowledged to be superior for this abnormality. The sensitivity of MRI for intraparenchymal hemorrhage is likely to be even higher than found in the UNM/OMI post-mortem studies, since those studies predominantly used only spin-echo sequences. Gradient-echo sequences would be expected to be even more sensitive for detecting intraparenchymal blood.

For lesions that are not hemorrhagic, such as areas of edema accompanying ischemia or nonhemorrhagic shearing injury, MRI is much more sensitive than CT. It is possible that MRI may even detect lesions not identified on autopsy, due to the sensitivity of MRI to areas of abnormal water content. One such case occurred in the UNM/OMI series, probably representing an area of ischemic damage (Figure 19-3).

The multiplanar capability of MRI offers additional opportunities to detect abnormalities with each different series obtained. In addition, some structures such as the corpus callosum are best evaluated in imaging planes other than transaxial.

The variable MRI appearance of blood with time has advantages. It is possible to indicate approximately the stage of hemorrhage and how long the blood is likely to have been present.[13,14] Forensic applications are obvious. Moreover, demonstration of intracranial hemorrhage of differing ages can be strong evidence of repeated, nonaccidental trauma.

Figure 19-3 This 15-month-old boy had been vomiting for several days prior to admission. He had a seizure, stopped breathing, and was transported to the hospital. Post-mortem cranial MRI was performed prior to autopsy. A coronal T2-weighted image demonstrates high signal intensity in the left temporal cortex (arrows). Similar signal abnormality was also present in the occipital lobes. The finding is consistent with abnormal water content, although no focal abnormalities were identified in this region on gross or microscopic examination at autopsy. Diffuse hypoxic damage was evident. (From Hart, B. L., Dudley, M. H., and Zumwalt, R. E., Post-Mortem Cranial MRI and Autopsy Correlation in Suspected Child Abuse, poster presentation at 1994 RSNA Conference. With permission of the Radiological Society of North America.)

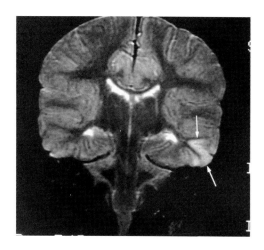

Although the sensitivity of post-mortem MRI to many intracranial processes has been confirmed, additional questions arise regarding possible limitations of a post-mortem study. In our experience, cranial MRI performed within 24 hours of death is associated with few artifacts and is very similar in appearance to routine clinical MRI studies. An obvious exception is the lack of intravascular flow on post-mortem MRI. Vascular abnormalities such as arterial dissection might be more difficult to detect, depending on the age of the dissection. There is little information available regarding how long after death MRI can be performed before tissue changes significantly alter the appearance of the brain.

The accuracy of post-mortem MRI for normal studies also appears reasonable. Although the number is small, the cases in the UNM/OMI series found not to be due to trauma can essentially serve as controls. No false positive cases were found among these or other cases in our experience.[3,4]

MRI was not found useful for the detection of optic nerve sheath hemorrhages in the UNM/OMI experience. However, those studies were not performed for that purpose, and it is possible that other pulse sequences or coils might be helpful.[3,4] Gross vitreous hemorrhage was readily demonstrated on MRI (Figure 19-4).

The severe swelling that accompanies brain death can lead to significant limitation in the ability of MRI to detect small subdural hematomas. Subdural hematomas of greater than a few cubic centimeters in volume were reliably demonstrated. However, when massive brain edema was present, very thin hematomas were identified consistently only by autopsy (Figure 19-5).[3,4]

Finally, the use of both post-mortem MRI and autopsy permits not only a comparison of findings but an evaluation of the combination of studies (Figure 19-6). Limited evaluation of CT [15] and MRI [16] of the whole body has been performed in comparison with autopsy results. However, it is clear that MRI cannot replace autopsy. The two examinations have different strengths and weaknesses. The combination of cranial MRI and subsequent autopsy, performed with knowledge of the MRI results, has distinct advantages.

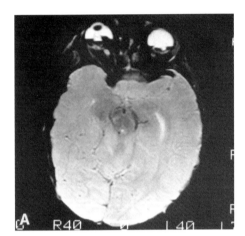
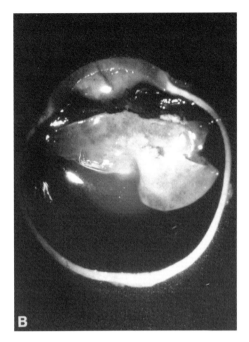

Figure 19-4   A 7-month-old girl had reportedly been dropped. Post-mortem cranial MRI showed diffuse, severe swelling of the brain. Bilateral retinal detachments and vitreous hemorrhage were visible on MRI. **A**: axial T2-weighted image, and **B**: autopsy. (From Hart, B. L., Dudley, M. H., and Zumwalt, R. E., Post-Mortem Cranial MRI and Autopsy Correlation in Suspected Child Abuse, poster presentation at 1994 RSNA Conference. With permission of the Radiological Society of North America.)

Conclusions

MRI can serve to direct the attention of the pathologist to areas of abnormality. MRI can also confirm the existence of tearing injuries that might otherwise be attributed to removal or cutting artifacts. MRI is less sensitive than autopsy for detection of extracranial injuries but has the potential to contribute greatly to the detection of intracranial and, especially, intraaxial injuries. As a practical matter, coronal imaging offers the advantage of direct comparison with brain sections. In selected cases, post-mortem cranial MRI of the brain, performed in conjunction with subsequent autopsy, can be very helpful in documenting the sequelae of child abuse.

Acknowledgments

The work discussed above includes the contributions of the author's coinvestigators at the Office of the Medical Investigator, State of New Mexico, Dr. Ross E. Zumwalt and Dr. Mary H. Dudley. Tables 1 to 3 are adapted from Reference 3, and the figures are reproduced courtesy of the Radiological Society of North America.[4]

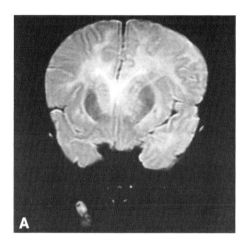 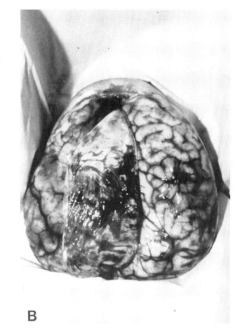

Figure 19-5   A 3-month-old child became unresponsive after being shaken. Post-mortem MRI showed diffuse cerebral edema (see Figure 19-2A) but no evidence of extraaxial hematoma. **A**: coronal T2-weighted image. **B**: at autopsy, subarachnoid hemorrhage and small subdural hematomas were present. (From Hart, B. L., Dudley, M. H., and Zumwalt, R. E., Post-Mortem Cranial MRI and Autopsy Correlation in Suspected Child Abuse, poster presentation at 1994 RSNA Conference. With permission of the Radiological Society of North America.)

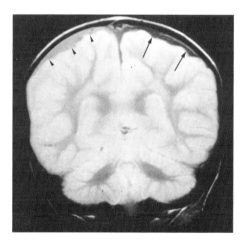

Figure 19-6   Bilateral subdural hematomas were identified on the post-mortem MRI of a 14-month-old girl who died following a "seizure." On this coronal intermediate-weighted image, the subdural hematomas (arrowheads over the right convexity and arrows over the left convexity) display different signal intensities, consistent with blood of different age. (From Hart, B. L., Dudley, M. H., and Zumwalt, R. E., Post-Mortem Cranial MRI and Autopsy Correlation in Suspected Child Abuse, poster presentation at 1994 RSNA Conference. With permission of the Radiological Society of North America.)

References

1. Caffey, J., On the theory and practice of shaking infants: its potential residual effects of permanent brain damage and mental retardation, *Am. J. Dis. Child.*, 124, 161, 1972.

2. Kempe, C. H., Silverman, F. N., Steele, B. F., Droegemueller, W., and Silver, H. K., The battered-child syndrome, *J. Am. Med. Assoc.*, 181, 105, 1962.

3. Hart, B. L., Dudley, M. H., and Zumwalt, R. E., Post-mortem cranial MRI and autopsy correlation in suspected child abuse, *Am. J. Forensic Med. Pathol.*, 17, 217, 1996.

4. Hart, B. L., Dudley, M. E., and Zumwalt, R. E., Post-mortem MR imaging in suspected child abuse: radiologic and pathologic correlation, RSNA 1994 Selected Award-Winning Scientific Exhibits, CD-ROM, 1995.

5. Sklar, E. M. L., Quencer, R. M., Bowen, B. C., Altman, N., and Villanueva, P. A., Magnetic resonance applications in cerebral injury, *Radiol. Clin. North Am.*, 30, 353, 1992.

6. Gentry, L. R., Godersky, J. C., and Thompson, B., MR imaging of head trauma: review of the distribution and radiopathologic features of traumatic lesions, *Am. J. Roentgenol.*, 150, 663, 1988.

7. Orrison, W. W., Jr., Gentry, L. R., Stimac, G. K., Tarrel, R. M., Espinosa, M. C., and Cobb, L. C., Blinded comparison of cranial CT and MR in closed head injury evaluation, *Am. J. Neuroradiol.*, 15, 351, 1994.

8. Sato, Y., Yuh, W. T. C., Smith, W. L., Alexander, R. C., Kao, S. C. S., and Ellerbroek, C. J., Head injury in child abuse: evaluation with MR imaging, *Radiology*, 173, 653, 1989.

9. Levin, A. V., Magnusson, M. R., Rafto, S. E., and Zimmerman, R. A., Shaken baby syndrome diagnosed by magnetic resonance imaging, *Pediatr. Emerg. Care*, 5, 181, 1989.

10. Alexander, R. C., Schor, D. P., and Smith, W. L., Magnetic resonance imaging of intracranial injuries from child abuse, *J. Pediatr.*, 109, 975, 1986.

11. Alexander, R., Sato, Y., Smith, W., and Bennett, T., Incidence of impact trauma with cranial injuries ascribed to shaking, *Am. J. Dis. Child.*, 144, 724, 1990.

12. Ogawa, T., Inugama, A., Shimosegawa, E., Fujita, H., Ito, H., Toyoshima, H., Sugawara, S., Kanna, I., Okudera, T., Uemura, K., and Yasui, N., Subarachnoid hemorrhage: evaluation with MR imaging, *Radiology*, 186, 345, 1993.

13. Chaney, R. K., Taber, K. H., Orrison, W. W., Jr., and Hayman, L. A., Magnetic resonance imaging of intracerebral hemorrhage at different field strengths: a review of reported intra-parenchymal signal intensities, *Neuroimag. Clin. North Am.*, 2, 25, 1992.

14. Hayman, L. A., Taber, K. H., Ford, J. J., and Bryan, R. N., Mechanisms of MR signal alteration by acute intracerebral blood: old concepts and new theories, *Am. J. Neuroradiol.*, 12, 899, 1991.

15. Donchin, Y., Rivkin, A. I., Bar-Ziv, J., Almog, J., and Drescher, M., Utility of post-mortem computed tomography in trauma victims, *J. Trauma*, 37, 552, 1994.

16. Ros, P. R., LI, K. C., Vo, P., Baer, H., and Staab, E. V., Preautopsy magnetic resonance imaging: initial experience, *Magn. Reson. Imaging*, 8, 303, 1990.

Stereolithography as a Useful Tool in Forensic Radiology

20

WOLFGANG RECHEIS, PH.D.
FERDINAND FRAUSCHER, M.D.

Contents

Introduction

Rapid Prototyping can be defined as a class of new techniques which allow conversion of a computer-aided design (CAD) file of an object into a physical model through sintering, layering, or deposition. These new techniques originated and have been primarily used in product development in industry and have a growing utilization. It is possible to create several prototypes for each progressive step in the development of a product, thus reducing the expenditure of time and money, as well as increasing the quality of the output. Since introduction of stereolithography by the Chrysler Corporation in 1987, this new technique of Rapid Prototyping has gradually come into use by the medical and anthropological communities.

In 1991, the discovery of the +5000-year-old Iceman in the Tyrolean Alps offered an excellent opportunity to adapt this technique to build an exact model of the skull. This was the first time that a stereolithographic model was used in forensic radiology.

Method — From Image Acquisition to Stereolithographic Hard Copy

Stereolithographic models of humans or animals are limited mainly to reconstruction of the bony parts. Computed Tomography (CT) is the optimal image provider, as it is possible to obtain information in all spatial dimensions, i.e., it is a volume data set consisting of up to 150 single images with a specific x-y resolution of the scanned body in the cross-sectional plane, and an z-axis resolution defined by the slice thickness. At the University

Hospital of Innsbruck the CT data set is transmitted from a Siemens Somatom Plus CT Scanner via an Ethernet connection to the external image processing workstations (SUN, SGI, Kontron). Here the most complex portion of the data processing for the stereolithographic model, the segmentation process, is performed. The individual body tissues absorb the CT radiation differently. The CT scanner displays this as a defined gray value for each pixel. In the segmentation process, each image element (pixel or voxel) has to be related to its tissue equivalent, i.e., bone, muscle, blood, etc. Numerous algorithms are used to enhance parts of the image, to connect corresponding parts, or to delete noise. The setting of specific thresholds allows the deletion of gray values that are not of interest. After segmentation, a three-dimensional reconstruction is generally made in order to visualize and inspect the results of the previously defined object.

Using a triangulation algorithm the surface of the desired object is converted into a CAD-readable format as a guide in the stereolithography process. The files are transferred via internet to Zumtobel Licht GmBH (Dornbirn, Austria) where the modeling procedure takes place. The model is produced in a vat of liquid photomonomer. A fine-meshed metal grid forms the platform for the model. After the grid is submerged just below the surface (0.1 to 0.3 mm), a computer-guided laser beam draws the outline on the thin layer of monomer, which then hardens (photopolymerization). The mesh and hardened layer are lowered into the liquid and the process repeats itself until the entire model is completed. Since portions of the model may be unconnected or free-floating during the construction, the engineer must program in temporary support structures, which are removed by hand during the finishing process.

Anthropological Examples

Stereolithographic models can be of great help in anthropology. One-to-one scale models of unique and precious objects can be produced without touching, manipulating, or destroying the original. Any number of models can be reproduced from the original data. These can be distributed to scientific groups and museums throughout the world. Building a stereolithographic model of the skull of the Iceman was one of the first major research projects of this sort.

The Iceman

A German couple hiking in the Tyrolean Alps on September 19, 1991 discovered a mummified corpse at an altitude of 10,750 ft. Multiple investigations have confirmed that the body is that of a man who lived approximately 5300 years ago. The discovery is of extraordinary importance and interest because the body had been dehydrated and frozen and thus maintained an excellent state of preservation. However, this remarkable specimen is vulnerable, and the body must be stored in a special environmentally controlled chamber with a humidity of 96 to 98% and a temperature of –6°C. All testing of the body is done as nondestructively as possible. Scientific investigation that requires removal of the body from the chamber is limited to approximately 20 min every 2 weeks. Therefore, the opportunity to precisely replicate the skull of the Iceman was enormously attractive. The rigid nature of the frozen body limited conventional radiographic examination but was not particularly detrimental for CT scanning.

The completed stereolithographic model of the Iceman's skull has displayed features of great interest to anthropologists (Figure 20-1). Further, it showed a subtle flattening of the entire left maxillofacial region, probably caused by the pressure of the glaciers. It also showed a very accurate and precise representation of a displaced tripod fracture of the left maxilla. The intersurface of the skull base was of decisive interest and could be faithfully reproduced. It is planned to produce up to 40 copies of the Iceman's skull for study by interested parties.

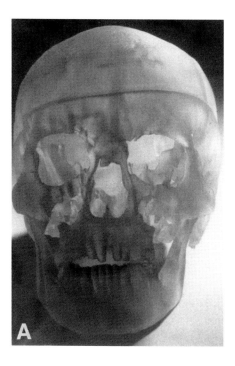

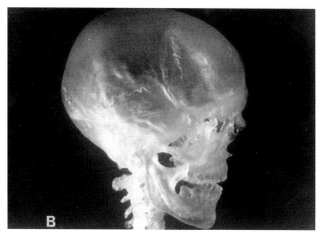

Figure 20-1   A: frontal, and B: lateral view of the stereolithographic model of the Iceman's skull.

Skulls of Petralona and Broken Hill

The use of stereolithographic models has led to totally new prespectives in the anthropological sciences. Extensive research on ancient skulls (Petralona, Broken Hill, Le Monsier, Circeo, and others), with emphasis on the endocranial morphology, has offered interesting insights into the evolution of the human brain (Figure 20-2). Until recently, anthropological examinations were restricted by the limited access to these fossils. Visualization of the internal morphology and measurements inside the skull were not possible. For example, the external morphology of the supraorbital torus appears similar in some ancient fossils (Petralona, Broken Hill, Arago 21), but reconstructions performed at the University Clinic of Innsbruck showed differences. Arago 21 has only minor pneumatization in this region, whereas Broken Hill, and to an even greater extent, Petralona, have extremely large frontal sinuses.

The use of the stereolithographic models has demonstrated further morphologic differences between these specimens. The model of Broken Hill reveals corresponding crests that appear to be less massive than those in Petralona. It was also shown that the frontal lobes of Petralona and Broken Hill are not only positioned behind the orbits, but are also

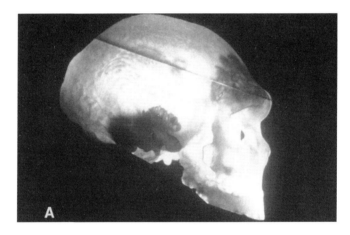

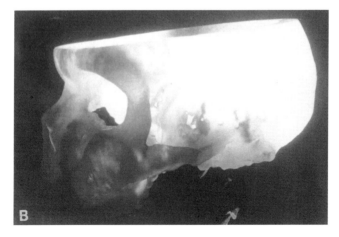

Figure 20-2   **A** and **B**: two views of the stereolithographic model of the skull of Petralona. The skull cap can be removed to allow visualization of endocranial morphology in detail.

inclined more steeply in a rostrocaudal direction than is the case for modern humans. Impressions and ridges that correspond to convolutions and sulci, respectively, on the orbital surfaces of the frontal lobes are difficult to assess due to destruction in Petralona, and are reproduced only faintly in Broken Hill. These features are pronounced in the anterior cranial fossa of Arago 21, as is also the usual case in modern humans. Such impressions have been interpreted as indicating progressive evolution of the basal neocortex. At first glance, the orbital sulcus patterns, as well as frontal lobe shape, are needed before one can assess their significance in middle Pleistocene hominids.

Applications of Stereolithography in Clinical Medicine

The exact stereolithographic models of the bony tissues of the skull are now routinely used for planning complex craniofacial and maxillofacial operations, particularly for congenital malformations. With the precision of these models, it is possible to determine osteotomy planes exactly and to form the appropriate implants. The surgeon can practice his approach, cutting the model with the same operating instruments and reconstructing the stereolithographic fragments just as he would during the operation itself. Complicated anatomy such as the orbital structures and the facial skeleton can be perfectly visualized in three dimensions (Figure 20-3). The intricacies of craniofacial malformations can be exactly understood. Regions such as the optic canal can be located and thus avoided during the operation itself. Since the model is reproducible, the surgeon has the opportunity of practicing the procedure more than once, or even testing alternative procedures. The only limitation is the cost of the model.

Since the stereolithographic model can be sterilized, it can be taken into the operating room to facilitate rapid anatomical orientation during the procedure. Surgeons have found the hands-on model to be far more helpful than the usual CT images or even three-dimensional CT images. The operating time is reduced with use of the stereolithographic model, and the accuracy and safety of the operative intervention is remarkably improved.

Accuracy of the Stereolithographic Model

To test the accuracy of the stereolithographic model, a cadaver's skull was examined in a Siemens Somatom Plus scanner using various scan protocols. The optimal image data were then utilized in the segmentation process. The stereolithographic model was measured on anthropological points and the results were compared to those determined on the skull after maceration. The model was accurate to within 0.5 mm in all spatial coordinates. The accuracy is limited only by the scan resolution (slice thickness) and postprocessing accuracy, since the stereolithographic process has an accuracy of 0.1 mm. With the introduction of new and harder acrylates, the distortion effects caused during hardening could be minimized.

Conclusions and Future Developments

For forensic purposes, it is generally accepted that facial reconstruction can be divided into four major categories: (1) replacement and repositioning of damaged or distorted soft

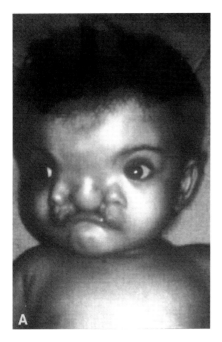

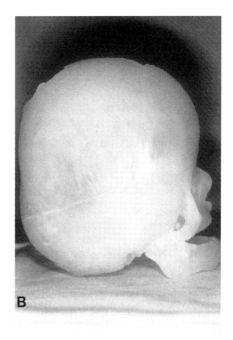

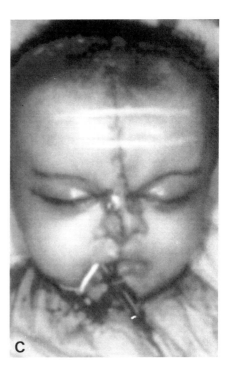

Figure 20-3 **A**: photograph of a child with severe craniofacial malformation. **B**: lateral view of the stereolithographic model used in evaluating the bony malformation and in planning reparative surgery. **C**: immediate postoperative appearance.

tissues onto a skull; (2) the use of photographic transparencies and drawings in an Identikit-type system; (3) the technique of graphic, photographic, or video superimposition; and (4) plastic or three-dimensional reconstruction of a face or a skull. Stereolithography would appear to be a promising addition to these forensic processes.

Only a few articles have been published dealing with forensic radiology and stereolithography, but the advantages of the method are unmistakable. The data acquisition is digital and can be manipulated easily with postprocessing software. The raw data can be used for three-dimensional reconstructions and even animations with specially adapted soft- and hardware, as mentioned above. Missing parts of a skull can be reconstructed on-screen and nonpertinent portions can be deleted. This can be very helpful in forensic facial reconstruction, where the lost or unknown facial features of an individual must be reconstructed, thereby aiding in the identification of unknown victims.

The value of stereolithographic modeling of anthropological objects would seem immense. True-to-life three-dimensional models of unique fossils could be generated, allowing multiple simultaneous studies. Even invasive and mechanical stress testing, as is common in industry during the product development process, would be feasible. These possibilities far outweigh the disadvantages of the high cost for computer power and software, as well as the cost of the models themselves. Currently, a skull costs between $1500 and $5000 (U.S.), depending on the size. However costs and prices will surely decrease as stereolithography becomes more popular in industry and medicine.

Bibliography

Anderl, H., zur Nedden, D., Mühlbauer, W., Twerdy, K., Zanon, E., Wicke, K., and Knapp, R., CT-guided stereolithography as a new tool in craniofacial surgery, *Br. J. Plast. Surg.*, 47, 60, 1994.

Barker, T. M., Earwaker, W. J., Frost, N., and Wakeley, G., Integration of 3-D medical imaging and rapid prototyping to create stereolithographic models, *Aust. Phys. Eng. Sci. Med.*, 16, 79, 1993.

Bill, J. S., Reuther, J. F., Dittmann, W., Kubler, N., Meier, J. L., Pistner, H., and Wittenberg, G., Stereolithography in oral and maxillofacial operation planning, *Int. J. Oral Maxillofac. Surg.*, 24, 98, 1995.

Boissonnat, J. D., Shape reconstruction from planar cross sections, *Comput. Vision, Graphics, Image Process.*, 44, 1, 1988.

Clark, K. B. and Fujimoto, T., *Product Development Performance: Strategy, Organization and Mangement in the World Automobile Industry*, Harvard University Press, Boston, 1992.

Dittmann, W., Bill, J., Wittenberg, G., Reuther, J., and Roosen, K., Stereolithography as a new method of reconstructive surgical planning in complex osseous defects of the cranial base, *Zentralbl., Neurochir.*, 55, 209, 1994.

Glenn, W. V., Image generation and display techniques for CT-scan data: thin transverse and reconstructed coronal and sagittal planes, *Invest. Radiol.*, 10, 403, 1975.

Hull, C., Apparatus for Production of Three-Dimensional Objects by Stereolithography. U.S. Patent 4,575,330, 1986.

Keppel, E., Approximating complex surfaces by triangulation of contour lines, *IMB J. Res. Dev.*, 19, 2, 1975.

Klimek, L., Keith, H. M., Schneider, W., Mosges, R., Schmeizer, B., and Voy, E. D., Stereolithographic modelling for reconstructive head surgery, *Acta Otorhinolaryngol. Belg.*, 47, 329, 1993.

Recheis, W., Knapp, R., and zur Nedden, D., Sterolithographie in Medizin und Anthroplogie, *Med. Jahrbuch*, 10, 163, 1995.

Recheis, W. and Sauerwein, E., A clinical example for Rapid Prototyping and its importance for successful optimization of production processes, Proc. Managing Integrated Manufacturing, Leicester, 1996, p. 105.

Seidler, H., Bernhard, W., Teschler-Nicola, M., Platzer, W., zur Nedden, D., and Henn, R., Some anthropological aspects of the prehistoric Tyrolean Ice Man, *Science*, 258, 455, 1992.

Seidler, H., Falk, D., Stringer, C., Wilfing, H., Müller, G., zur Nedden, N., Weber, G., Recheis, W., and Arsuaga, J. L., A comparative study of stereolithographically modelled skulls of Petralona and Broken Hill; implications for future studies of middle Pleistocene hominid evolution, *J. Hum. Evol.*, in press.

Sögner, P., Stellenwert der Stereolithographie als neue methode in radiologie und anthropologie. Dissertation der Universität Innsbruck, 1995.

Stoker, N. G., Mankovich, N. J., and Valentino, D., Stereolithographic models for surgical planning, *J. Oral Maxillofac. Surg.*, 50, 466, 1992.

Udupa, J., Goncalves, R., Iyer, K., Narendula, S., Odhner, D., Samarasekera, S., and Sharma, S., 3DVIEWNIX, An open transportable software for the visualization and analysis of multidimensional, multimodality, multiparemetric images, *SPIE Proc.*, 1897, 47, 1993.

Vannier, M. W., Marsh, J. L., and Warren, J. O., Three-dimensional CT reconstruction images for craniofacial surgical planning and evaluation, *Radiology*, 150, 179, 1984.

Wilfing, H., Seidler, H., zur Nedden, D., Weber, G., Reusshoft, H., Platzor, W., Knapp, R., Hauser, G., and Murphy, W. A., Cranial deformation of the neolithic man *Hausiabjoch, Coll. Anthropol.*, 18/2, 269, 1994.

Wolf, H. P., Lindner, A., Millesi, W., Knabl, J., and Watzke, I., Technique and applications of stereolithographic cranial models, *Fortschr. Kiefer. Gesichtschir.*, 39, 19, 1994.

zur Nedden, D., Knapp, R., Wicke, K., Judmaiser, W., Murphy, W. A., Jr., Seidler, H., and Platzer, W., Skull of a 5300-year-old mummy. Reproduction and investigation with CT-guided stereolithography, *Radiology*, 193, 269, 1994.

zur Nedden, D., Spindler, K., Seidler, H., Wilfing, H., Murphy, W. A., Hauser, G., Platzer, W., Weber, G., Wicke, K., and Knapp, R., New findings on the Tyrolean »Ice Man«. Archeological and CT-Body analysis suggest personal disaster before death, *J. Archeol. Sci.*, 21, 809, 1994.

Interesting Internet site about Rapid Prototyping: http://stress.mech.utah.edu/home/novac/rapid.html

SECTION VII

Coping with the Courts

Prefatory Remarks

So far, this treatise has dealt with history, science, medicine, and social problems in establishing a basis for forensic radiology as a field of special expertise within the forensic sciences. Now we approach the problem of interfacing this medically based forensic science with the law, and this is not always an easy fit. Perhaps we cannot expect a seamless junction between radiology, the legal profession, and the judiciary, but knowledge of the system and the rules and techniques for dealing with it can smooth out some of the rough spots as they come together. That is the purpose of this section: to relieve anxiety and to instill confidence in the forensic radiologist (especially the tyro or relatively inexperienced) as he enters our great adversarial system of justice.

The author makes no claim of legal training, a law degree, or special knowledge of the law. This section is written from the standpoint of an experienced forensic radiologist who reads a lot, listens attentively, and leans heavily on outside sources and experts. The effort here is to provide introductory background information for the colleague undertaking to act as an expert in this field. If the reader is looking for sound legal advice, he should stop right here and go call his personal attorney, or find one.

The reader who subsequently becomes involved in a case in litigation must depend heavily upon the attorney engaging his assistance and who eventually will sponsor the expert in court. If not entirely comfortable with that dependency upon the hiring attorney, the expert should decline the case and the association.

A final disclaimer: it is very difficult, and somewhat awkward to write gender-neutral text. The masculine pronoun has been used throughout this section for purposes of convenience, *not* because of chauvinism or bias. Please read every "he", "him", and "his" as "she", "her", and "hers"; the words are totally interchangeable in this text and context.

The Radiological Expert

21

B. G. BROGDON, M.D.

Contents

Introduction

The forensic scientist who deals with images or other data derived by radiological methods is, by definition, likely to become involved in court proceedings as a witness. At first this experience may be anticipated with dread and anxiety. An understanding of the process

0-8493-8105-3/98/$0.00+$.50
© 1998 by CRC Press LLC

and the rules of procedure, rules of law, and rules of evidence which establish its parameters can help to alleviate this apprehension.

A radiological scientist, like any other person, may be involved in a legal process as a "party" (i.e., as a plaintiff or as a defendant) to a lawsuit, or as a "witness" (by virtue of his five senses) to events relevant to proof of the facts at issue. In either capacity, he may be *required* to give testimony, under oath or affirmation, as an ordinary lay or fact witness — excepting Fifth Amendment protection against self-incrimination.

The fact witness can testify on the basis of personal knowledge of matters perceived through the use of his five senses. The only opinions or inferences admissible in court are those rationally based on the perception of the witness and helpful in clarifying his testimony or the determination of a fact at issue.

Testimony is the verbal statement of a witness under oath or affirmation to the trier of fact, that is, the judge or jury. Such testimony may be given orally from the witness stand, or in writing or videotaping in evidence deposition.

Evidence is any and all data presented to the judge or jury in proof of the facts at issue. It includes not only testimony from witnesses, but also records, documents, or objects.

Issues in litigation have become increasingly complex. In many cases, the matter of inquiry is of such complexity that the average trier of fact is unable to understand or come to a correct judgment upon it since it falls beyond the range of common experience or knowledge. In those cases an "expert" with special experience or knowledge may be called upon to assist the trier of fact in understanding evidence or determining a fact at issue.

This *expert witness* differs from the lay witness primarily and most importantly in that he can testify not only on the basis of personal knowledge, but also in the form of opinion. This unique privilege, and responsibility, is afforded the expert witness in support of his *raison d'etre*, his ability to translate complex scientific or technical issues into language understandable to the trier of fact who is not knowledgeable or experienced in those matters. In doing so, the expert must collect, test, and evaluate evidence, form an opinion as to the evidence, then ably communicate that opinion — and the bases from which it was derived — to the trier of fact.[1]

Admissibility of Scientific Evidence

Frye Test

For many years, the standard for admitting "scientific" testimony as evidence was the so-called "Frye Test" derived from a decision handed down by the Court of Appeals of the District of Columbia in 1923.[2] The case had to do with "the systolic blood pressure deception test", the precursor of the modern polygraph test. The lower court's refusal to admit an expert witness to testify as to the results of this test was sustained on appeal.

Counsel for the defendant argued on this admissibility:

> The rule is that the opinions of experts or skilled witnesses are admissible in evidence in those cases in which the matter of inquiry is such that inexperienced persons are unlikely to prove capable of forming a correct judgement upon it, for the reason that the subject-matter so far partakes of a science, art, or trade as to require a previous habit or experience

or study in it, in order to acquire a knowledge of it. When the question involved does not lie within the range of common experience or common knowledge, but requires special experience or special knowledge, then the opinions of witnesses skilled in that particular science, art, or trade to which the question relates are admissible in evidence.

In response to which Associate Justice Van Orsdel stated in his opinion:

Numerous cases are cited in support of this rule. Just when a scientific principal or discovery crosses the line between the experimental and demonstrable stages is difficult to define. Somewhere in this twilight zone the evidential force of the principle must be recognized, and while courts will go a long way in admitting expert testimony deduced from a well-recognized scientific principle or discovery, *the thing from which the deduction is made must be sufficiently established to have gained general acceptance in the particular field in which it belongs. (Emphasis added.)*

This rule of "general acceptance" was adopted in all of the Federal Circuits and most of the individual states.[3]

Federal Rules of Evidence

In 1975 the Federal Rules of Evidence (FRE) were adopted, and most states have adopted their own rules of evidence modeled on the Federal Rules.[3] Several of them are relevant to scientific evidence and the expert (vs. the lay) witness:

THE FEDERAL RULES OF EVIDENCE

ARTICLE VII

Opinions and Expert Testimony

Rule 701
Opinion Testimony by Lay Witnesses

If the witness is not testifying as an expert, the witness' testimony in the form of opinions or inferences is limited to those opinions or inferences which are (a) rationally based on the perception of the witness and (b) helpful to a clear understanding of the witness' testimony of the determination of a fact in issue.

Rule 702
Testimony by Experts

If scientific, technical, or other specialized knowledge will assist the trier of fact to understand the evidence or to determine a fact in issue, a witness qualified as an expert by knowledge, skill, experience, training, or education, may testify thereto in the form of an opinion or otherwise.

Rule 703
Bases of Opinion Testimony by Experts

The facts or data in the particular case upon which an expert bases an opinion or inference may be those perceived by or made known to the expert at or before the hearing. If of a type reasonably relied upon by experts in the particular field in forming opinions or inferences upon the subject, the facts or data need not be admissible in evidence.

Rule 704
Opinion on Ultimate Issue

(a) Except as provided in subdivision (b), testimony in the form of an opinion or inference otherwise admissible is not objectionable because it embraces an ultimate issue to be decided by the trier of fact.

(b) No expert witness testifying with respect to the mental state or condition of a defendant in a criminal case may state an opinion or inference as to whether the defendant did or did not have the mental state or condition constituting an element of the crime charged or of a defense thereto. Such ultimate issues are matters for the trier of fact alone. (As amended October 12, 1984.)

Rule 705
Disclosure of Facts or Data Underlying Expert Opinion

The expert may testify in terms of opinion or inference and give reasons therefor without first testifying to the underlying facts or data, unless the court requires otherwise. The expert may in any event be required to disclose the underlying facts or data on cross-examination.

Rule 706
Court Appointed Experts

(a) Appointment. The court may on its own motion or on the motion of any party enter an order to show cause why expert witnesses should not be appointed, and may request the parties to submit nominations. The court may appoint any expert witnesses agreed upon by the parties, and may appoint expert witnesses of its own selection. An expert witness shall not be appointed by the court unless the witness consents to act. A witness so appointed shall be informed of the witness' duties by the court in writing, a copy of which shall be filed with the clerk, or at a conference in which the parties shall have opportunity to participate. A witness so appointed shall advise the parties of the witness' findings, if any, the witness' deposition may be taken by any party; and the witness may be called to testify by the court or any party. The witness shall be subject to cross-examination by each party, including a party calling the witnesses.

(b) Compensation. Expert witnesses so appointed are entitled to reasonable compensation in whatever sum the court may allow. The compensation thus fixed is payable from funds which may be provided by law in criminal cases and civil actions and proceedings involving just compensation under the fifth amendment. In other civil actions and proceedings the compensation shall be paid by the parties in such proportion and at such time as the court directs, and thereafter charged in like manner as other costs.

(c) Disclosure of appointment. In the exercise of its discretion, the court may authorize disclosure to the jury of the fact that the court appointed the expert witness.

(d) Parties' experts of own selection. Nothing in this rule limits the parties in calling expert witnesses of their own selection.

These Rules from Article VII need to be read in conjunction with the Rules on relevance:

Rule 401. Definition of "Relevant Evidence" — "Relevant evidence" means evidence having any tendency to make the existence of any fact that is of consequence to the determination of the action more probable or less probable than it would be without the evidence.

Rule 402. Relevant Evidence Generally Admissible: Irrelevant Evidence Inadmissible — All relevant evidence is admissible, except as otherwise proscribed by the Supreme Court pursuant to statutory authority. Evidence which is not relevant is not admissible.

Rule 403. Exclusion of Relevant Evidence on Grounds of Prejudice, Confusion, or Waste of Time — Although relevant, evidence may be excluded if its probative value is substantially outweighed by the danger of unfair prejudice, confusion of the issues, or misleading the jury, or by considerations of undue delay, waste of time, or needless presentation of cumulative evidence.

Over the years there has been argument that FRE 702 superseded *Frye* in defining the basis for admission of scientific evidence. The U.S. Supreme Court essentially accepted this argument in what has become known as the *Daubert* rule or standard,[3] which applied to the Federal Courts in those states which follow the Federal Rules of Evidence.

Daubert

Daubert v. Merrell Dow Pharmaceuticals claimed that a drug, Bendectin, marketed by Merrell and prescribed for "morning sickness" caused birth defects in children born to women who had taken it. The case went all the way to the Supreme Court on appeal, hinging on the admissibility of a Dr. Gross and his "reanalysis" of an earlier epidemiological study. Writing for the 7 to 2 majority, Justice Blackmun considered that FRE 702 superseded the too-demanding "general acceptance" standards of *Frye*. The decision assigned a "gate-keeping" role to the trial judge in ascertaining whether scientific evidence and testimony offered the court was obtained by the "scientific method" and is relevant. Suggested factors or criteria for consideration in evaluating such "science" include, but are not limited to the following: (1) the technique or theory can be, and has been, tested; (2) peer review and publication; (3) known or potential error rate; (4) existence and maintenance of control standards for performance or operation; (5) widespread acceptance within a relevant scientific community or discipline; (6) research used as a basis of testimony must have been conducted independent of the litigation at hand.[3–5]

Daubert has engendered extensive contention and confusion in the legal profession, the judiciary, and the forensic sciences regarding standards for scientific evidence and expert testimony. A survey published in 1995[3] revealed that one year following *Daubert* there was great variation in admissibility standards in state law and state judicial rules governing most trials in the U.S. According to that author, the standards were clear or fairly clear in 39 states, fairly unclear in 5 states, and completely unclear in 6 states.

All of the above notwithstanding, there would appear to be no problem in admission of scientific evidence in the form of radiological images or data collected in the course of diagnostic radiological procedures. Further, of those "expert" witnesses proffered to explain or translate that evidence to the trier of fact, few, if any, are likely to be rejected by the court, if properly qualified as experts.

The Expert Witness

> If the law has made you a witness, remain a man of science. You have no victim to avenge, no guilty or innocent person to convict or save — you must bear testimony within the limits of science.
>
> —**Dr. P. C. H. Brouardel**
> (late 19th century
> French medico-legalist[6])

Engagement of the Expert Witness

A person with scientific, technical, or other specialized knowledge which may help the trier of fact, judge or jury, to better understand the evidence, or to better understand and determine a fact at issue in a lawsuit, can be approached by either side — plaintiff or defendant, prosecutor or defense — to serve the court as an expert witness. An expert witness can be appointed by the court (judge) with or without the consent of the contending parties. However, the expert witnesses' consent is required. He cannot be forced to serve by subpoena.

Here, for physicians and dentists and other health care providers who may have special knowledge that ordinarily would qualify them as an expert, a special exception must be noted. If that person has provided professional services to one of the parties in a lawsuit, he may be subpoenaed and required to testify as an ordinary witness. Examples would be a radiologist who performed and interpreted radiologic examinations on a patient who later becomes a party in a personal injury case, or in a corporate liability action, or a malpractice suit. In such instance, the health provider may be required to testify without compensation, but ordinarily the party calling the witness will offer compensation in order to avoid dealing with a "hostile" witness.

Parties on either side of the lawsuit can call expert witnesses of their own selection. Indeed the American Bar Association (ABA) *Model Rules of Professional Conduct* requires an attorney to seek out expert services if the client needs them. Failure to do so may be considered "ineffective assistance of counsel" or may cause counsel to be found liable for malpractice.[7]

There are further standards concerning the relations between the hiring attorney and the expert witness. Counsel must respect the expert's independence, cannot dictate the expert's opinion, and must explain to the expert his impartial role as an assistant to the trier of fact. Also, counsel is warned against paying excessive or contingency fees in order to influence expert opinion or testimony (see below). Fee splitting, or sharing of fees between counsel and expert, is explicitly forbidden.[8]

AMERICAN BAR ASSOCIATION STANDARDS
RELATING TO THE ADMINISTRATION
OF CRIMINAL JUSTICE

Standard 3-3.3 Relations With Expert Witnesses

(a) A Prosecutor who engages an expert for an opinion should respect the independence of the expert and should not seek to dictate the formation of the expert's opinion on the subject. To the extent necessary, the prosecutor should explain to the expert his or her role in the trial as an impartial expert called to aid the fact finders and the manner in which the examination of witnesses is conducted.

(b) A prosecutor should not pay an excessive fee for the purpose of influencing the expert's testimony or to fix the amount of the fee contingent upon the testimony the expert will give or the result in the case.

Standard 4-4.4 Relations With Expert Witnesses

(a) Defense counsel who engages an expert for an opinion should respect the independence of the expert and should not seek to dictate the formation of the expert's opinion on the subject. To the extent necessary, defense counsel should explain to the expert his or her role in the trial as an impartial witness called to aid the fact finders, and the manner in which the examination of witnesses is conducted.

(b) Defense counsel should not pay an excessive fee for the purpose of influencing an expert's testimony or fix the amount of the fee contingent upon the testimony an expert will give or the result in the case.

Contact and Agreements Between Counsel and Expert

The initial contact between counsel representing a party anticipating or already in litigation and an expert usually is by telephone. The expert may be approached for one or more of several reasons: the attorney may have worked with him before; the attorney may know of the expert's performance in other cases; the expert is widely known as an authority of excellent reputation in his field; the expert may have rare or unique expertise; the expert may have been recommended by other law firms; or the expert may have been selected from published lists of forensic scientists willing to serve as expert witnesses.

After the usual introductions and pleasantries, the counsel will ascertain if the expert is willing to consult on a case which may or may not be summarized briefly at that time.

In the field of forensic radiology particularly, many experts — and many attorneys — prefer that the image(s) first be seen and evaluated "cold", that is, without any introduction of bias excepting the inevitably heightened search expectations accompanying the knowledge that this image(s) ultimately may become evidence in a lawsuit.

During the initial telephone call the professional *bona fides* of both parties should be established to the extent that they can be independently verified (Dun and Bradstreet, Professional Directories, Who's Who, State and National Licensing Boards, Professional Associations, etc.). The expert can ask for an estimate of the maximum involvement that might be required of him. This is the time to bring up the subject of fee, quote fee schedules if they are set, and establish responsibility for prompt payment of those fees as service is provided. There is case law holding liable for expert witness fees a law firm hiring an expert witness on behalf of a client after the client has refused to pay.[9] There is a modern trend to hold attorneys liable for expert or other litigation provider service fees absent of an express disclaimer of responsibility.[7] If the caller seems taken aback by your fee schedule or says he has to check back with his firm or his client, watch out! He probably is underfunded.[10]

If the proposition is appealing to both the expert and the attorney, then a date can be set for the initial consultation. This should be scheduled no sooner than two working days in order to allow the expert an opportunity to check out the attorney and/or his firm. Of course, *no opinion should be expressed during the initial telephone call.*

Immediately after the initial contact, it is a good idea for the expert to summarize his understanding of the requirement for his services by mail, fax, or express letter to the attorney, including a fee schedule and a curriculum vitae (C.V.), and reconfirming the date and time for the first consultation. This letter should be sufficiently clear and detailed that it disallows room for misunderstanding and may also serve as a sort of contract should problems later arise regarding fees, etc. It has been suggested that an advanced retainer or fee be obtained for the initial consultation or opinion.[11] (The author has not found that necessary and believes a better relationship is established, with small risk, if a bill for the first service is sent immediately after that service is provided. Usually it becomes obvious early on whether or not the attorney's firm is adequately capitalized to carry the cost of long-term litigation, which may be on a contingency basis. Incremental billing by the expert as he provides services also reduces the risk of loss. Of course, if there is difficulty or delay in collecting expert fees from the hiring attorney, several remedies are available through your own attorney or the Bar Association.)

Fees

The fees charged for professional services in a forensic setting are entirely personal and not bound by any limits other than the reference to those sufficiently "excessive" to skew honesty and influence opinion (cited earlier in ABA Standards). Indeed, there is more independence and leeway in setting these fees than there is nowadays in the establishment of professional fees for patient care. Consultation with colleagues of similar stature and expertise can help in determining reasonable and customary ranges of fees for expert forensic services.

It is convenient and commonplace to charge according to time and level of activity. The time component easily is broken down into hours, quarter-hours, or even minutes. Time charges related to activity devoted to the case at hand include but are not limited to, library or bench research, consultation face to face or by "wire", correspondence and/or report preparation, travel, preparation of exhibits, review of contributing materials, etc.

The fee schedule by unit of time quite properly can vary by level and location of activity. The lowest unit charge would be for work accomplished "in house" that is, at the place selected by the expert. The next higher level of activity charged would be for deposition and might vary according to where the deposition is taken. The highest level of activity, of course, is appearance in court. Here travel and travel expenses must be considered and the time scale may change to half-day or daily increments.

It must be remembered that determination of fees by time and activity is simply a convenience, no more. The expert is not being recompensed just for his time. Rather the expert's fee is a recognition of a totality of qualification including his education, experience, research activity, scholarly productivity, rare or unique talents, communicative skills, overall reputation, the esteem of his peers as evidenced by offices and awards, personal character, professional ethics, and above all, his unimpeachable honesty and impartiality.

Finally, established or quoted fees obviously can be modified from case to case.

The First Consultation

After a mutually agreeable initial contact and the establishment of *bona fides*, comes the first consultation involving the expert and the attorney in the particulars of a specific case or question. Often, in the field of forensic radiology, this eventuates as the arrival of one or more radiographs (originals or good first copies) in the mail with or without accompanying documents or explanatory material. At other times, the attorney or his paralegal will bring the images and other material to the expert's office. In either event, the expert must not rush to an opinion. He must review and interpret the radiological images, consider any other pertinent material furnished, and formulate a preliminary opinion on the basis of all the information available to that point in time. That opinion is then conveyed to the attorney in person, through his paralegal, by telephone, or by hard-copy correspondence. Except for the latter instance, it may be best for the expert to avoid making any notes or permanent record of his deliberations up to that time, since these may be subject to discovery by the opposing party (see below). After receiving your verbal opinion, the attorney may or may not ask for a written opinion or affidavit. Also it is wise to submit a bill for services to date at this time. Most of the time this first consultation will also be the last one because the vast majority of lawsuits will be settled after some expert input is obtained.

The first consultation also affords an excellent opportunity to formulate an opinion of the attorney. Does he have a firm grasp of the case? Is he experienced in this type of litigation? Is he organized? Is he an effective communicator and time manager? Is he on a fishing trip to learn whether a case has merit? Does he try to rush or shade your opinion? Can you work together with mutual trust and respect? As the case evolves, will the attorney keep you advised of progress or stagnation, new information or changes, opposing opinion, etc.? Are there money problems?[10]

If the litigation continues there may be additional consultations face-to-face or by wire and sometimes extensive in-house preparation, review, and research by the expert. The mutually agreeable arrangement for incremental billing for these activities should be worked out in advance. As the case matures, and no settlement intervenes, the likelihood of deposition increases.

Discovery and Deposition

Discovery has been defined as the ascertainment of that which was previously unknown.[1] Thorough pretrial preparation for cross-examination requires advance knowledge of expert testimony to be presented. Discovery, in effect, is the compulsory disclosure of the expert's opinion and material associated with the formulation of that opinion. Although rules of disclosure vary somewhat among jurisdictions and between civil and criminal procedure, the expert is best advised to assume that every image, report, document, note or other material related to a case is subject to discovery by opposing counsel. Federal Rule 26 (a)(2)(B) which requires an expert to furnish the "data or other information considered by the witness in forming the opinions" could be interpreted to include almost all inter-action between the expert and his attorney, including conversation.[12]

Apart from requiring copies of all films, reports, correspondence, etc. related to the case, the principal method of discovery by opposing counsel is by deposition.

Discovery deposition is a method of taking testimony under oath but not before the court.[1] One must prepare for a deposition with the same thoroughness and seriousness as for a court appearance. Consequently, the deposition should be scheduled far enough in advance to allow for this preparation, including adequate communication between the expert and his hiring attorney. The discovery deposition will be requested by the opposing counsel. Time and location is reached by mutual agreement of the minimal number of participants required: the expert, the two opposing attorneys, and the court reporter who will administer the oath and make the legal record of the proceedings. The expert can expect exhaustive (and sometimes hostile) questions about his entry into the case, his knowledge of it, materials reviewed, and other preparation incidental to the formulation of an opinion. All questions must be answered, truthfully, unless they are unanswerable as posed, or upon the expert's attorney's advice not to answer because of his objection to the question. Since there is no judge to rule on objections, such interaction between opposing counsel is recorded and the expert is not at risk for following advice. Because the opposing side has requested the deposition and has posed the questions, there is no "cross-examination", as such, on discovery deposition. However, the attorney retaining the expert can requestion him for clarification of issues brought into the deposition by opposing counsel.

The expert may be asked if he is willing to "waive signature" upon completion of a deposition. Decline! Rather, the expert must make certain that the deposition scheduled allows adequate time for him to receive, review, correct, and approve the transcript of his deposed testimony well before the case goes to trial. Any inconsistency between testimony at deposition and in court may be used to impeach the witness or weaken his impact on the trier of fact.

Fees for discovery deposition are billed to the hiring attorney, not to the opposing counsel. When the government takes a deposition, or when the deposing party is indigent, or when the expert is court appointed, expenses and/or fees of the witness may be paid by the court.[1]

An *evidence deposition* can be requested (usually by the hiring counsel) when it is known in advance the expert cannot be physically present in court at the trial. The procedure for this deposition is much the same as for a discovery deposition except for one major difference: the expert is subject to cross-examination by opposing counsel, because the party calling the witness questions first. A minor difference is that this type of deposition is more likely to be videotaped so that the trier of fact can see as well as hear the witness if the deposed testimony is admitted at trial.

Expert Testimony in Court

As previously stated, the vast majority of lawsuits in which expert opinion in the field of radiology is solicited will be settled or plea-bargained during or after the discovery phase. Only a small proportion will come to trial, requiring expert testimony in court. Even so, every case accepted for consultation must be treated as if it will go to trial, with equally serious attention and preparation. The forensic radiologist is most likely to actually testify in court in cases of malpractice, personal injury, child abuse, and in the rare occasion of establishing identity of human remains.

Of course, the expert must be absolutely thoroughly prepared for a court appearance and take with him all notes, radiographs, or other images, and any other material needed to support the testimony — sometimes including viewboxes, since one may not be available in the courthouse. To avoid embarrassment, one's briefcase should be purged before entering the courtroom. Anything brought to the stand is subject to examination including your traffic tickets, overdue bills, bank statement, or day-old tuna fish sandwich.[11]

If visual aids such as drawings or photographic enlargements of radiologic images are to be employed, they must be reviewed for adequacy and accuracy.

Lines of anticipated questioning by counsel from both sides must have been reviewed with the sponsoring attorney. The expert may be required to disclose the underlying facts or data leading to his opinion or inference and must be prepared to do so (see Model Rule 705 above).

For the expert witness, the courtroom experience can be likened to seeing only one scene of a three-act play. Virtually never is he in attendance for jury selection, opening statements, summations, or jury instructions. In general, witnesses are not allowed in the court room during testimony by others. Consequently, the expert walks into court with no direct knowledge of previous testimony, testifies, then walks back out and is dependent upon the press for events following his appearance. [1]

To reduce waiting time outside the courtroom (and fees) the hiring counsel will try to closely estimate just when the expert will be called. But this is iffy guesswork. Trials tend to develop their own pace, and it is wise to arrive with professional or recreational reading material to while away the hours.

When finally called to testify, the expert forensic scientist should enter the court looking like one — conservatively dressed appropriate to the region and venue, neat and trimmed, with a pleasant yet dignified mien. While walking to the stand it is good to make eye contact with the judge and jury. The expert will take the stand and be sworn.

The Oath

Every witness must by oath or affirmation declare that he will testify truthfully. The form of the oath is designed to stimulate the conscience of the witness and inspire his sense of duty and responsibility to the truth.[13] However, the language of the oath requiring "the whole truth" must be interpreted within the confines of the adversary system. The witness must supply the whole truth only to the extent required by the question asked of him. The witness has no duty to go beyond the question or to answer questions unasked. Indeed, to do so may result in the answer being stricken from the record. When necessary, the witness usually can indicate subtly a wish to go further with an answer or to make additional comments. This will be picked up quickly by the perceptive attorney or by the trial judge who, of course, can question any witness.

Testifying falsely under oath can lead to perjury charges and, also, malpractice action against the expert. [4,5,13]

Qualification of the Expert Witness

After being sworn and identified the expert witness is "qualified" through a series of questions by the attorney who engaged him. This qualification will be based on the witnesses' CV and experience. If the CV is extensive, the expert should have, in advance, helped counsel winnow out the significant parts in conversation or by highlighting or abridging the CV. It has been suggested that the witness furnish sample questions to facilitate the qualification process.[14]

The expert witness does not have to be the greatest star in his field. He simply is required to have sufficient expertise to assist the trier of fact. However, the impact of testimony on the judge or jury probably is influenced by the expert's level of expertise and reputation in his field. Consequently, the attorney presenting the expert witness will lead him through a long litany of education, degrees, academic appointments, professional experiences, publications, and other scholarly productivity, professional honors, and offices, previous jurisdictions in which testimony has been admitted, and any other material reflecting favorably on the witness and by any stretch pertinent to the case. Opposing counsel may try to interrupt and truncate this exposition with an offer to "stipulate" that the witness is an expert, that is, agree to his qualifications forthwith. However, presenting counsel usually will insist on continuing the inventory of his witnesses' achievements.

When the presentation of the expert qualification is completed, the opposing lawyer has the opportunity to challenge the witness in the "*voir dire*" (from the French, meaning "to speak the truth") by bringing out matters that might prevent his qualification.[1] Following this, the judge decides admissibility of the witness.

It is improbable that anyone proposed as an expert involving testimony related to diagnostic radiology, or a product thereof, would fail to qualify. Although in 1919 an Iowa court ruled that the x-ray speaks for itself (like a photograph) and that the evidence reposed within it could be interpreted by the jury,[15] an earlier and more sensible view has prevailed:

> The evidence shows that nobody but an x-ray expert could tell anything from the plate and if they had been produced they would have done the court, the jury or the defendant's ordinary physician no good. I do not think that the doctrine that an ordinary photograph is the best evidence of what it contains should be applied to x-ray pictures. They constitute an exception to the rule concerning ordinary documents and photographs, for the x-ray pictures are not in fact the best evidence to laymen of what they contain. The opinion of the expert is the best evidence of what they contain — the only evidence.[16]

It is commonly held that almost any physician is qualified to "read" x-rays, and that any dentist can evaluate dental x-rays. Still, there is opinion that simply being a physician does not in and of itself qualify one as a competent interpreter of a diagnostic imaging study.[17] Dr. F.J. Baetjer, the first radiologist at Johns Hopkins, early emphasized:

> There is no such thing as an x-ray picture. A roentgenogram is a projection upon a photographic play of a series of shadows of varying density representing the various structures through which the rays have passed. The correctness of the diagnosis depends entirely upon the skill with which these various shadows are separated and interrupted. To interpret these shadows correctly one must know not only the appearance of the normal structure, but also the alterations that take place when there is a pathological process present … . Roentgenography is … a medical procedure based upon careful analysis and logical deductions from the shadows observed upon an x-ray plate, and translated into pathological terms. This means — and it cannot be too strongly emphasized — that the skill of a roentgenologist will vary directly with his medical knowledge: the value of the roentgenologist to the medical profession (and patient) will be based upon this fact and not upon his technical ability.[18]

The more highly qualified and specialized the expert, the more weight his opinion will carry. Most juries will appreciate that the diagnostic images must be interpreted and explained to them by a competent expert familiar with both medical and technical factors applicable to the evidence; therefore, an expert in the field of radiology will be preferred.[19] Hence, contending parties are apt to want a qualified radiologist, even a radiological subspecialist, to testify on radiological images especially if produced by one of the newer, highly technical modalities. A dentist or oral surgeon well experienced in dental radiology, or an orthopedic surgeon well versed in radiology of bones and joints, or a neurologist or neurosurgeon familiar with neuroradiological procedures, will be more easily and effectively qualified than a generalist. A physical anthropologist may qualify as an expert to testify on radiographs of the skeleton, but probably will be required to explain or document special training or experience in the use of this tool. Rarely, a technologist will be asked to testify on the production, identification, or chain of custody of images.

Direct Examination

Once qualified and admitted, the expert witness begins his testimony on direct examination by the attorney bringing him to the stand. Direct examination allows an opportunity for the expert to use his training, knowledge, experience, and special skills to present his evidence, describe it, and demonstrate how his opinion is reached on the basis of certain facts.[1] The expert is led through his testimony with a series of well-rehearsed questions designed to bring out the best in the witness and his evidence by a friendly, considerate, and understanding lawyer. This is the first opportunity for the trier of fact, judge or jury, to see and appreciate the appearance, demeanor, and communicative skills of the witness. Questions should be answered slowly and distinctly in a pleasant, confident conversational rhythm. Answers should be directed to the jury when present. One should speak loudly enough to reach the hearing-impaired juror, judge, and counsel at both tables. Although the expert witness is cast in the role of teacher to the jury, he must not be pedantic, aloof, overbearing, or smug.

> There is nothing worse than a pompous expert.
>
> —**Judge Haskell M. Pitluck**

The witness should exude an air of friendly yet dignified eagerness to be helpful. Direct eye contact with individual jurors is most desirable and effective. Levity and flippancy must be avoided at all costs.

One must expect to demonstrate images to the jury. Bring a pointer. Make sure the entire jury can see the image(s). It is acceptable, sometimes desirable, to use scientific nomenclature if it is immediately translated to lay terminology and/or thoroughly explained. The jury should be carried along in the process from interpretation of findings on the image(s) through consideration of other influencing knowledge, facts, or experience to the formulation and clear statement of the expert's opinion. Questions on direct examination tend to be open-ended, allowing the expert considerable freedom for unfettered discourse to that end, insofar as allowed by the patience of the judge and the unsustained objections of opposing counsel.

Finally, testimony on the witness stand must be in absolute consonance with previous deposition, or else an awfully good explanation for any discordance must be firmly in hand.

Admissibility of Radiological Images and Results

As already noted in Chapter 2, roentgenograms were admitted as evidence in courts in England, Canada, and the U.S. in 1896, just months after Röntgen's discovery. The admissibility of the product of a radiological examination is unlikely to be questioned in a modern courtroom. There may be a requirement to show that it was obtained by an accurate and generally recognized methodology and accurately represents the object investigated. For newer modalities such as ultrasonography, computed tomography, magnetic resonance imaging, and nuclear studies, the expert should be prepared to explain and defend the procedures in some detail.[19]

Cross-Examination

The attitudinal environment of relative comfort during direct examination with a considerate counsel coddling the witness evaporates quickly at cross-examination.

The expert has been put on the stand because his opinion is seen as favorable to the side sponsoring him, and the direct examination is designed to present that opinion in the most effective and positive manner. In our adversarial system of justice, it is the duty of the opposing counsel to tear down that testimony if possible. If direct testimony has been so good as to be virtually incontestible, or so ineffective that it poses no problem, the opposing counsel may pass the witness. That is rare.

Usually, opposing counsel will use cross-examination to weaken or impeach prior testimony or the witness himself. The witness must not react to this new setting with any change in his demeanor or attitude. The voice and rhythm of his responses should remain unaltered. The expert is empowered by the very expertise that brought him to this confrontation. No matter how hard the attorney has crammed the science and studied the specifics of the case, he will be no match for the well-prepared expert and may well be a little in awe of him.[1] On the other hand, it must be remembered that the attorney is at home in the courtroom. The expert is the visitor. And the playing field is not level, but scattered with pits and traps into which the expert must not stumble. The well-prepared expert witness will use his common sense to avoid the pitfalls of cross-examination, some of which are catalogued below, along with suggested avoidance tactics.

The Racehorse[1,11,20,21]

The cross-examiner frequently will try to rattle the witness by changing the tempo of questioning, usually by stepping up the cadence. Watch out! Don't let staccato questions tempt rapid-fire responses. Pause. Think. Answer at your established pace.

Don't let the questioner step on (cut off) your answers. Insist on being allowed to complete your reply, but pleasantly, so the jury will notice what a nice fellow you are.

Don't be lulled by a series of rapid sequential answers: "Yes, yes, yes, yes …Uh Oh!" Keep it slow.

Don't be confused by lawyer-talk or terminology at variance with scientific terms. Ask for clarification or rephrasing and qualify your answer.

Don't be bullied by "Answer Yes or No!" questions if they cannot be answered without some further qualification. Say so, pleasantly. If necessary, appeal to the judge.

If the attorney opens with, "Now you previously testified (or wrote) … ", don't buy it. Ask that the reporter read back the cited questions and answers, or that the written statement be presented for your review. Never hesitate to have a question repeated in full.

If in his hurry, or ignorance, or cleverness, the cross-examiner misstates the facts as the expert understands them, or mistakes scientific principle, don't answer the question but, rather, correct his error.

Don't let the insistence of rapid questioning distract your attention from the jury to the attorney. Try to respond to the jury on all questions.

Don't ride with a racehorse attorney. You can dismount at will and proceed at your own pace.

Don't Overreach[5,13,14,21]

Do not overblow your qualifications. Make sure your C.V. is up-to-date and error free. Exaggerations will not be well received by the trier of fact. Falsification can lead to professional disaster. You can be sure that opposing counsel has studied your C.V. with a jaundiced eye to work that end.

Don't be lured outside your scope of expertise. If you are describing cerebral edema and intracranial bleeding in a child abuse case, don't get trapped into discussing autism or head-bangers. Insist firmly and unashamedly that your special qualification is in diagnostic imaging — not pediatrics or neurology. Know your limits and do not exceed them. The jury will not think less of you.

Don't volunteer. Do not extend answers beyond the limitation of the question. Such answers may be judged irrelevant and stricken. Oration or argument may appear as partisanship to the jury. Don't overstate. The expert who tries to make more of his evidence than it is worth is unlikely to survive competent cross-examination.

Just Say "No"[11,21]

Do not hesitate to say, "No" or "I don't know" to a question if honesty demands it. A frank answer admitting a specific lack of knowledge or expertise is unlikely to do much harm and may enhance your aura of sincerity. No one is expected to know everything. A bluff successfully called by opposing counsel may cause irreparable damage.

Sensitive Issues[1,5,11]

Everyone has a few chinks in his armor — a few sensitive areas he would rather not have probed in public. One must assume that opposing counsel knows of them. They may be trivial, or ancient history, but still may be used to dull the luster of your testimony or to imply bias. How did you get involved in this case? How much are you being paid for the testimony? Do you advertise for work as an expert? Do you always, or nearly always, testify only for the plaintiff (or the defendant)? Have you been sued for malpractice? Bad debts? Did you fail licensure/specialty board examinations? Are you on retainer to this law firm? Have you practiced your testimony with your lawyer? Did you have a different opinion on a similar issue two years ago?

There are answers for all of the questions; some are easy, others require preparation. All answers should reinforce your integrity, honesty, objectivity, and the distance between the scientist and the other parties to the case.

Sometimes it is advisable to have one's own attorney bring up a sensitive issue on direct examination in order to cast the best possible light upon it. Remember that fees require no apology or explanation. They represent fair recompense for a totality of qualification. You should discuss this issue prior to trial with your retaining counsel. It should be emphasized that expert fees are not contingent on the outcome of the case.

Don't Play the Numbers[11,14]

Cross-examiners love to try to pin the expert down to numbers on issues of certainty, likelihood, ratios, chances of, incidence, etc. Usually these "numbers" questions are brought on matters with no propensity for precision. Do the best you can with them; if the question is impossible to answer, say so, and appeal to the judge if necessary. If still required to answer, try to use ranges rather than precise numbers and qualify your answer as best you can. At the same time, try not to appear wimpish or sound evasive. Watch out for "weasel words": perhaps, maybe, could be, probably, etc.

The law likes to deal with terms such as "reasonable medical certainty", "beyond reasonable doubt", or "reasonable medical probability". Unfortunately, these do not seem to have a precise numerical basis either. If you use them, be prepared to provide your own definition.

Hypothetical Questions[1,11,19]

A common courthouse tactic is to pose a question to the expert witness based on a hypothetical situation. This offers great latitude in presenting (or eroding) the opinion of the witness. In most jurisdictions, especially on direct examination, hypothetical questions must be based only on facts in evidence. Those restrictions do not apply to hypothetical questions posed on cross-examination, which can sometimes be quite fanciful and labyrinthine.

The expert must be certain he understands the question, that there are enough facts upon which to base an opinion, and that the "facts" proposed in the premise are not scientifically impossible. Do not hesitate to ask for repetition or explanation of the question. Take time in answering. Watch out for traps. On cross-examination the hypothetical question most likely will be antithetical to your previous testimony.

Learned Treatises and Textbooks[1,11,20,22]

A specific method of impeaching an expert witness is through the use of learned treatises or textbooks which are in disagreement with the expert's testimony and opinions. To be used as an instrument of impeachment, the treatise or text must be *relied* upon by the witness in reaching his opinion, or *recognized* as authoritative by the witness. Rarely, the treatise or text will be *established by other means* including the testimony of other experts or by judicial notice. The text or treatise can be read or quoted in court only when the witness is on the stand, and cannot be entered as evidence where it might be misunderstood or misused in the jury room.

The presentation of a treatise or text to the expert witness may be somewhat veiled or insidious. The witness may be asked if he knows a certain eminence in his field. Is that person reputable and authoritative? Is the witness familiar with his writings or book? Are they authoritative?

While the expert witness must be familiar with the literature and authoritative opinion in his field, he must not give a blanket endorsement to any individual or his work. The expert witness must leap between the horns of this dilemma by admitting of knowledge, and even admiration, of the person or treatise proposed, while declining total approval or agreement. The expert can label the work as out-of-date, uneven in content, controversial, or erroneous in part. The expert must ask to read for himself (not aloud) quotations, sometimes incomplete or out of context, offered by opposing counsel. The expert witness should not hesitate to disagree with quoted "authority" within the security of his own knowledge and experience. After all, the expert witness is the only expert so far qualified as such by an adversarial procedure in court. He must not give away equal billing to an absent "authority" represented only by excerpts of written work.

Taking Abuse[1,4,5,20,21]

Rarely, and usually in desperation, the cross-examiner will try to tear down an expert and his prior qualification and testimony by abusive attack. He may speak harshly, omit titles, show disdain or anger or exasperation, use aggressive body language, gesture too closely or "get in the face" of the witness. He may wisecrack, be flippant, even insulting, in order to upset or goad the witness. It is risky business, but more so for the examiner than for the witness *if* the expert stays cool.

The expert witness, already empowered by qualification and acceptance as an authority figure, must maintain the persona and power already established; he must remain wrapped in a cloak of dignified professionalism.

The judge and jury may harbor protective emotions toward the witness under assault and reproach for the aggressor. Well-placed objections by sponsoring counsel will further tip the scales against the imprudent assailant. Attorneys have been sanctioned at the bar for abuse on cross-examination.[7]

However, if the witness reacts to the abuse, takes the bait, hits back, becomes an adversary, then he will lose his standing of impartiality with the jury, becoming just another fighter in an ugly fray. In this courtroom setting, meeting force with equal force will only put the attorney in control.

Don't get into a mud-fight with a pig. You'll get mud all over you, and the pig will like it!

—Judge Haskell M. Pitluck

If cross-examination has been harmful to the expert witness and his client's case, there is one more opportunity for damage control, the *redirect examination* of the witness by the party calling him, after cross-examination. This affords an opportunity to correct possible misunderstandings by the jury, and allows reaffirmation of points that may have been blunted by opposing counsel. This will conclude the testamentary experience for the expert in this trial. He will be excused by the judge and will leave the courtroom.

Jury Charge

The expert witnesses' appearance and testimony can be effectively voided by the court. Standard jury instructions in various jurisdictions may go something like this:

Expert witnesses are like any other witnesses, with one exception — the law permits an expert witness to give his opinion. However, an expert's opinion is only reliable when given on a subject about which you believe him to be an expert. Like other witnesses, you may believe or disbelieve all or any part of an expert's testimony.[4]

An expert witnesses' testimony carries great weight and influence in the jury room.[7] At the discretion of the court relevant evidence can be excluded under Federal Rule of Evidence 403 "If its probative value is substantially outweighed by the danger of unfair prejudice, confusion of issues, or misleading the jury …".[13] Rule 403 has general application to all testimony, including expert testimony. "Expert testimony, like any other testimony, may be excluded if, compared to its probative worth, it would create a substantial danger of undue prejudice or confusion."[23]

The Verdict

In the purest sense in a perfect world, the verdict in the case just completed should be of no more interest than that of a trial scanned briefly in a newspaper or glimpsed on the evening news. After all, the expert is expected to be a scientist first and a forensic scientist second.[24] He is expected to be honest, competent, reliable, and totally objective and non-partisan.[25] However, the adversarial system works against impartiality.

The forensic scientist who gets so far into a case that he becomes a witness, surely has opinions, however objective, that support the contentions of the side bringing him rather than those of the other party. The jury probably assumes he is a partisan of the side that brings him, and opposing counsel may try to exploit this.[19]

If the expert expresses opinion contrary to the cause of the party first contacting him, then his first consultation will be his last and he is out of the case. (He must not try to sell himself to the other side at this point.[11])

Even if brought as an expert witness by the court rather than one or the other party, the forensic scientist is likely to lean more toward one side than the other as the case unfolds.

The difficulties of even-handedness and ethical behavior in an adversarial legal system are well recognized but not readily solved.[13,24–27] " 'Search for truth' in the context of the law is simply part of the process by which the goal, 'justice', is strived for. In science, on the other hand, truth is the goal."[25] The forensic radiologist is fortunate in that the evidence he works from, radiological image(s), lends itself to objectivity. The forensic radiologist then must exert every effort to remain a man of science, resolutely preserving scientific objectivity, regardless of unbidden emotion seeking to lead him astray.

> I will bear in mind always that I am a truth-seeker, not a case-maker; that it is more important to protect the innocent than to convict the guilty.[28]

—Anonymous

References

1. Kuzmack, N. T., Legal aspects of forensic science, in *Forensic Science Handbook*, Saferstein, R., Ed., Prentice-Hall, Englewood Cliffs, NJ, 1982, chap. 1.

2. *Frye v United States*, 293 F. 1073 (D.C. Cir. 1923).

3. Bohan, T. L. and Heels, E .J., The case against *Daubert*: the new scientific evidence "standard" and the standards of the several States, *J. Forensic Sci.*, 40, 1030, 1955.

4. Henderson, C., Jurisprudence: science in court, presented (with handout material) at a Multidisciplinary Symp. Uses of Forensic Sci., American Academy of Forensic Sciences, Nashville, February 20, 1996.

5. Henderson, C., Jurisprudence: science in court, presented (with handout material) at a Multidisciplinary Symp. Uses of Forensic Sci., American Academy of Forensic Sciences, Seattle, February 14, 1995.

6. Helpern, M., *Autopsy*, Signet, New York, 1979, 66.

7. Garcia, C. H., Legal and ethical considerations in using expert witnesses in litigation, *Shepard's Expert and Scientific Evidence Quarterly*, 1, 717, 1994.

8. American Bar Association, ABA Model Rules of Professional Conduct, Rule 5.4 (1) 1993.

9. *Copp v Breskin*, 782 P. 2nd 1104 (Wash. Ct. App. 1989).

10. Anon., Quoting Lewis, P. R., Experts who recognize red flags avoid cases with traps and pitfalls, *Testifying Expert*, 3, 1, 1995.

11. Stimson, P. G., Rules of evidence and document preparation for expert testimony pretrial information; Expert testimony: preparation, delivery and cautions, presented (with handout material) at Forensic Investigation of Abuse and Violence, 23rd Annu. FL Med. Examiners and 3rd Annu. Invest. Identification Combined Educational Conf., Pensacola, September 20, 1995.

12. Anon., Quoting Rothstein, P., Experts may have to disclose phone calls with case attorney, *Testifying Expert*, 3(5), 7, 1995.

13. Giannelli, P. C., Evidentiary and procedural rules governing expert testimony, *J. Forensic Sci.*, 34, 730, 1989.

14. Pitluck, H. M., A bench-eye view of expert testimony, Forensic Science Update: Crime Scene to Verdict, 4th Annu. Invest. Identification Educational Conf., Pensacola, November 15, 1996.

15. *Lang v Marshalltown*, 185 Iowa 940, 170 NW 463, 1919.

16. *Marion v Coon Construction Co.*, 216 NY 178, 110 NE 444, 1915.

17. *Raleigh v Donoho*, 238 Ky. 480, 38 S.W. 2nd 227, 1931.

18. Baetjer, F. J. and Waters, C. A., *Injuries and Diseases of the Bones and Joints*, Paul B. Hoeber, New York, 1922; quoted in: Garland, L. H., Forensic skiagraphy, *Calif. Med.*, 87, 295, 1957.

19. James, A. E. and Hall, D. J., The law of evidence and diagnostic imaging techniques, in *Legal Medicine with Special Reference to Diagnostic Imaging*, James, A. E., Ed., Urban & Schwarzenberg, Baltimore, 1980, chap. 5.

20. Anon., Quoting Whitaker, E., The O.J. Simpson trial: the cross-examination trap, dealing with the aggressive lawyer, *Testifying Expert*, 3(6), 7, 1995.

21. Donaldson, S. W., *The Roentgenologist in Court*, 2nd ed., Charles C Thomas, Springfield, IL, 1954, p. 255.

22. Donaldson, S. W., *The Roentgenologist in Court*, 2nd ed., Charles C Thomas, Springfield, IL, 1954, p. 153.

23. *United States v Schmidt*, 711 F. 2nd 595, 599 (5th Cir. 1983), *cert. denied*, 464 U.S. 1041 (1984).

24. Lucas, D. M., The ethical responsibilities of the forensic scientist: exploring the limits, *J. Forensic Sci.*, 34, 719, 1989.

25. Petersen, J. L., Symposium: ethical conflicts on the forensic sciences, *J. Forensic Sci.*, 34, 717, 1989.

26. Peterson, J. L., Forensic science ethics: developing an integrated system of support and enforcement, *J. Forensic Sci.* 34, 749, 1989.

27. Frankel, M. S., Ethics and the forensic sciences: professional autonomy in the criminal justice system, *J. Forensic Sci.* 34, 763, 1989.

28. Anon., Quotation on the wall of the Office of the Medical Examiner, State of New Mexico.

SECTION VIII

A Primer for Forensic Radiological Technology

Radiographic Equipment, Installation, and Radiation Protection

22

CHARLES W. NEWELL, ED.D., R.T.(R)
CHUCRI M. JALKH, B.S., R.T.(R)
B. G. BROGDON, M.D.

Contents

Introduction

The difficulties involved in trying to use hospital or clinical radiographic installations, equipment, and personnel for forensic investigation already have been mentioned in Chapter 3. Attempts to use mobile x-ray equipment temporarily "borrowed" from the clinical facility will meet with similar problems of accessibility and conflicting priorities. If any consistent use or benefit of forensic radiology is expected, then the medical examiner's facility (be it a one-room morgue or a separate building) needs its own in-house radiological capability. This entails dedicated space (at the very least for repetitive temporary use), radiographic equipment, x-ray films and film storage, film processing capability or availability, grids, screens and cassettes (explained later), a film identification system (see Chapter 24), and film envelopes and files for storing the archival roentgenograms.

Equipment will be discussed first because facility requirements will vary according to the type of equipment available.

X-Ray Equipment

Since most morgues do not have fixed radiographic units comparable to those found in hospital radiology departments, they often rely on mobile x-ray units to perform radiographic examinations. These are totally self-contained units on wheels that simply plug into available power supply convenience outlets (Figure 22-1). These come in a wide variety of sizes, shapes, and exposure capabilities. They are reasonably priced, and good usable secondhand units often are available from local hospitals or x-ray supply houses. Safety and dependability are important factors, but high-energy x-ray output is not so important. The main difference in equipment requirements between clinical medical radiology and forensic radiology is that the vast majority of forensic subjects don't move, breath, pulsate, or have peristalsis. Physical or physiologic motion simply is not a problem. If the exposure factors required for an acceptable single-exposure image (Chapter 24) exceed the capability of the equipment, then double exposures — or more — are possible.

Radiographic unit — Regardless of the type of unit employed, all radiographic examinations require the same components to produce radiographic images. Figure 22-2 depicts a typical arrangement of the components necessary to radiograph a patient. Not included in Figure 22-2 is the x-ray control panel which will be discussed in Chapter 24. The other components are discussed below.

X-ray tube — The function of the x-ray tube is to produce x-rays. The principal components of an x-ray tube are the filament and anode. The anode is the area of the tube where x-rays are produced. The anode is frequently referred to as the focus of the tube, and it plays an important role in producing fine detail in the radiographic image. Most x-ray

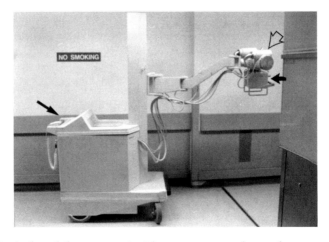

Figure 22-1   Typical mobile x-ray unit. The generator and transformer are enclosed in the tank beneath the control panel (arrow). The tube (open arrow) swings on an articulated arm and can be moved up or down on the vertical tube-stand. A collimator (short arrow) attached to the tube window limits the area exposed.

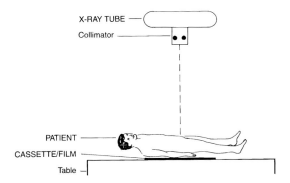

Figure 22-2 Schematic drawing of a radiographic unit.

tubes have two filaments which are designated as large and small. The small filament causes the anode (focus) to produce fine-detail images. If available, the small filament should be selected whenever fine detail is desirable. High-voltage electricity to produce x-rays is obtained from the standard power supply by means of a step-up transformer which is self-contained in mobile x-ray units. In fixed units, the generator is usually separate and sits on the floor or mounts on the wall or ceiling.

Central ray (CR) — As depicted in Figure 22-2, the central ray constitutes the center or innermost part of the x-ray beam. It is always desirable to place the central ray in the center of the film, and to the center of the body part being radiographed. Proper centering of the central ray reduces what is referred to as image shape distortion. The acronym CR will be used throughout this, and the following chapter when reference is made to the central ray.

Collimator — The function of the collimator is to restrict or limit the size and shape of the x-ray beam. In so doing, the area exposed on the x-ray film is confined to a specific area, e.g., 8 × 10 in., 11 × 14 in., 14 × 17 in., etc. The size of the collimator opening can be changed or manipulated by adjusting the horizontal and longitudinal controls located on the front of the collimator. With respect to post-mortem radiography, a rule of thumb to follow when making collimator changes is to set the collimator size to correspond with the size of the x-ray film, i.e., the collimator setting for 8 × 10 film should be 8 × 10. Following this rule of thumb will enhance image contrast, while reducing the amount of scatter radiation to the medical examiner, the assistant, and other personnel in the autopsy suite.

Other X-Ray Equipment Options

Fixed x-ray units — Ideally, there will be space and money available to have a fixed radio-graphic installation within, or contiguous with, the autopsy suite (Figure 22-3). Such units need not be very powerful or very expensive. Again, usable secondhand units may be obtained from clinical installations as they purchase newer machines or modalities, merge, or downsize. Sometimes these units can be had for the expense of disassembling, moving, and reinstallation. These fixed units will have (1) an x-ray table for holding the body; (2) a built-in tray for the film, cassette, and grid; (3) a transformer; (4) a control panel; and (5) a tube-mount by which the x-ray tube is suspended for positioning over the patient.

These are usually either floor-mounted tube hangers or ceiling hung. Either type should allow the tube to be positioned anywhere over the body (for frontal views) and anywhere alongside the body for lateral (side) views with the x-ray beam directed horizontally. Ceiling tube-mounts are desirable since they don't take up floor space and allow personnel to work from either side of the radiographic table.

Fluoroscopic units — A fluoroscopic unit in, or adjacent to, the autopsy suite is a great convenience (Figure 22-4). It allows rapid scanning of bodies for foreign objects, injuries, and unique features useful for comparison identification. The spot-filming capability allows instant radiography to permanently record findings discovered at fluoroscopy. These units also have an overhead tube-mount for conventional radiography as described above. Because of the increasing utilization of endoscopy for gastrointestinal diagnosis and the economics of managed care, the requirement for clinical fluoroscopic units has diminished substantially in recent years. Many hospital fluoroscopy units are under utilized and/or their room space is needed for the newer imaging modalities. Consequently, again, usable used equipment may be obtained at surprisingly low cost. One must realize that a fluoro-scopic installation will be more expensive, will require more maintenance, will require more skillful operators, will require more expert physicians/interpreters, and will pose greater radiation risk and protection problems for personnel.

Mobile C-arm units — There are mobile fluoroscopic units (Figure 22-5) which are commonly used in cardiorespiratory intensive care units. They can be quite valuable in mass casualty situations (see Chapter 9, Figure 9-10), but probably are not a cost-effective investment for a medical examiner's fixed facility.

Body scanners — The body scanners previously mentioned (Chapter 9, Figure 9-12) are to the best of our knowledge limited to governmental agencies and are not in use in conventional medical examiners' facilities anywhere in the U.S.

Other modalities — The newer imaging modalities, so far, have had limited use in the forensic sciences. *Ultrasonographic units* are the least expensive and are mobile to some extent, but have limited current or projected usefulness in the forensic sciences. *Computed tomography* shows promise of increasing applicability to forensic problems if the issues of cost and accessibility are overcome. CT units are becoming more plentiful and cheaper. The availability of hospital and clinical units for forensic examination may improve. Future installations of CT units within medical examiner facilities seems unlikely (in all but exceedingly rare exception) because of cost, maintenance requirements, and the necessity of highly trained high-salaried operators. *Magnetic resonance imaging* (MRI) also shows promise as a forensic tool in certain situations. However, the same considerations that jeopardize the assimilation of CT units into forensic facilities are even more weighty with respect to MRI.

Faxitron® — A unique and useful x-ray device for any radiology, pathology, or forensic science department is a small self-contained x-ray unit not much larger than a microwave oven (Figure 22-6). It has the capability of extremely fine radiographic detail. It can produce magnification radiographs. It is capable of very low exposure factors not available on conventional x-ray machines. Thus, it is extremely useful for imaging bone fragments, small parts (e.g., digits, hands, feet), biopsy specimens, non-human materials (e.g., letters, packages, clothing, etc.) (see Chapter 11, Figure 11-24). The Faxitron® is self-protected against radiation leakage and operates from standard 110 V outlets.

Film

The obvious function of film is to display the radiographic image. Thus, the x-ray film is an image receptor. Once a film is developed and the image is made visible, the film is referred to as a radiograph or a roentgenogram. Throughout this chapter and the succeeding chapter, the term "radiograph" will be used when referring to the image as depicted on an x-ray film.

Like photographic film, x-ray film is sensitive to, and affected by, a variety of factors:

1. In addition to x-rays, x-ray film is sensitive to almost any color of light. Care should be taken to protect film from light. Also, one should never leave exposed or unexposed films in an area where x-ray exposures are being made.
2. X-ray film is a sensitive medium and should be carefully handled. Folding, bending, or any form of rough handling tends to produce artifacts. Artifacts are foreign marks on the radiograph which are not the result of the patient's anatomy or pathology. In short, artifacts may interfere with the interpretation of the radiograph.
3. X-ray film is also sensitive to heat arising from heating systems, steam pipes, etc. Heat may produce excessive film blackening, which often renders the film useless. Therefore, when x-ray film is stored, it should be protected from stray radiation, light, and heat. Excessive heat and low humidity may combine to produce another artifact referred to as a static mark. Reducing the room temperature and raising the humidity level will alleviate this problem.
4. Like photographic film, the useful life of an x-ray film is determined by its expiration date. Failure to use film before the expiration date may lessen the quality of the radiograph.

Film Processing

X-ray film and photographic film share another requirement in that they both must be developed to render a visible image. Film development, or film processing as it is most commonly referred to, is perhaps the single most important step in the production of a radiograph. Film quality will be negatively affected when proper film processing is not attained. It will be preferable to handle the volume of post-mortem radiographs produced in most facilities by arranging to have them processed in the hospital radiology department — unless precluded by distance, architectural obstacles, or failed negotiation. If such an arrangement is unfeasible or unsatisfactory for whatever reasons, small automatic film processors are reasonably priced and easily installed (see Chapter 9, Figure 9-13).

However, should an automatic film processor be located in the autopsy suite, the medical examiner assistant should consult with radiology personnel regarding processor quality control procedures.

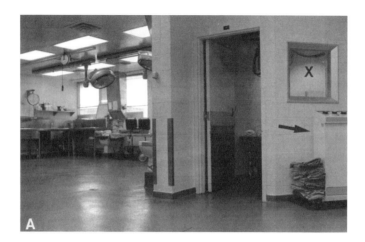

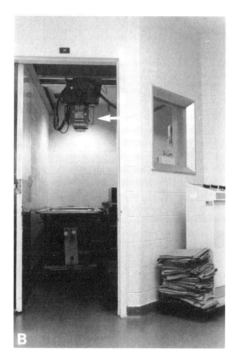

Figure 22-3   **A**: fixed radiographic installation built into a corner of the autopsy suite of the office of the Medical Examiner of the State of Alabama at the University of South Alabama Medical Center. The control panel (arrow) and viewing window (X) allow the operator to be shielded from the radiation field. **B**: bodies are positioned under a ceiling-hung tube (arrow) which can be raised or lowered. **C**: the tube is pointed downward for frontal or anteroposterior views, or **D**: to the side for cross-table lateral views.

Cassettes and Screens

A cassette is a light-tight container which holds the radiographic film (Figure 22-7). Cassettes have a labeled front and back side. The front side of the cassette must always face the x-ray tube. Cassettes typically contain a pair of intensifying screens. The function of intensifying screens is to emit light when struck by x-rays. The advantage of light emission

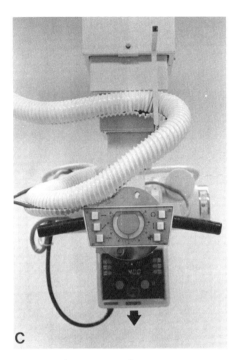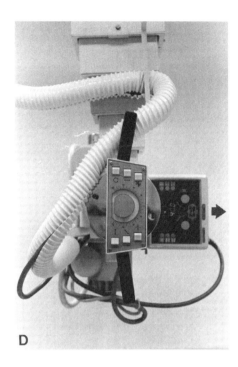

C   D

Figure 22-3 (Continued)

is that since light produces over 90% of the film blackening, less x-ray exposure is needed to produce an image. The result is less x-ray exposure to the patient and to those who perform the radiographic examination. The color of light emitted is blue or green. The manufacturer of a given screen determines the color of emission. Film manufacturers also design radiographic film to be sensitive to either blue or green light. With respect to film quality, there is essentially no difference between blue- and green-sensitive films. The same can be said for the color emission (blue or green) of intensifying screens.

In addition to differences in color emission, intensifying screens are also classified according to their speed. The speed of a screen refers to its ability to respond to x-rays and emit light (blue or green). Common screen classifications include slow, medium, and high speed. The significance of speed classifications is that higher-speed screens require less x-ray exposure than slower-speed screens to yield the same degree of film blackening. For example, a medium-speed screen requires two times (2×) more exposure than a high-speed screen. However, high-speed screens reduce the visualization of find detail in the radiographic image. The slight loss in fine detail, however, is offset by the reduction in x-ray exposure to the patient and personnel who perform radiographic examinations. Converting exposure factors to accommodate differences in screen speed will be addressed in the next chapter.

Intensifying screens can become soiled from the accumulation of dust particles or other foreign materials which enter the cassette and settle on the screen surface. Debris deposits on the screen surface prevent light from reaching the film. As a result, an artifact is produced, which always appears as a loss in film blackening corresponding to the size and shape of the dust particle or other debris. To avoid this problem, screens should be cleaned periodically with a commercial screen cleaner.

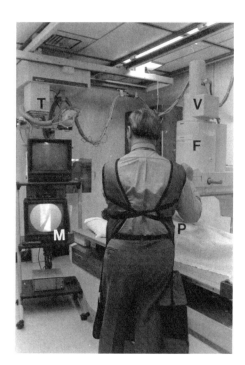

Figure 22-4   Radiographic and fluoroscopic unit. The image intensifier in the fluoroscope tower (F) can be moved in three axes to cover the patient (P). A videocamera (V) looks at the output phosphor of the intensifier and transmits the fluoroscopic image to a monitor (M). A ceiling-hung x-ray tube (T) can be moved over the patient or body for routine roentgenograms.

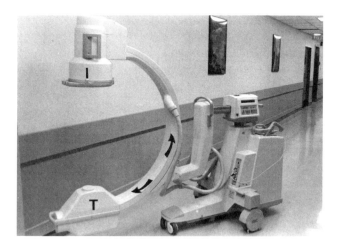

Figure 22-5   Mobile C-arm unit. The C-arm swivels clockwise or counterclockwise and the tube (T) will travel back and forth in its arc (curved arrows). The image intensifier (I) can feed into a television monitor (not shown).

Grids and Grid Cassettes

The term "scatter radiation" was previously used in the discussion regarding collimation. The production of scatter radiation occurs when x-rays enter the patient. Upon entering the patient, numerous x-rays interact with tissue molecules. Many of the x-rays are diverted (scattered) in a different direction. In fact, scatter radiation arises from the patient in virtually any direction or angle. The significance of scatter radiation with respect to

Figure 22-6   Desk-top model Faxitron X-ray unit. The controls are on top. The cabinet, below, contains the specimen and the film. (Courtesy of Faxitron X-ray Corp., 1670 Barclay Blvd., Buffalo Grove, IL, 60089.)

radiographic quality is that it produces a fogging effect on the radiograph. The fogging effect increases film blackening, which reduces image quality.

While scattered radiation cannot be totally eliminated, it can be reduced by collimating to the size of the cassette and by employing a grid. The grid absorbs scatter radiation when it is placed between the patient and the cassette. The typical grid consists of extremely thin lead strips standing on their edge. The lead strips are arranged parallel to one another and extend longitudinally from end to end (Figure 22-8). The lead strips are also separated from one another by a spacer (interspace) composed of plastic or aluminum. Since lead is radiopaque (absorbs x-rays), scatter radiation is absorbed by striking the lead grid lines at an angle. In contrast, those x-rays which approach the grid in a perpendicular manner pass through the spaces separating the lead strips. x-rays are able to pass through the interspaces because the interspace material is radiolucent (does not absorb x-rays). The close relationship existing between the lead strips and the interspaces is more fully appreciated by the fact that the number of lead strips can range from 80 to 103 strips per inch.

The grid employed in a fixed radiographic installation is permanently mounted beneath the table. In the autopsy suite, one is most likely to utilize a grid cassette. A grid cassette consists of a grid mounted to the front of a cassette. Thus, a grid cassette can be moved about to accommodate all positions and projections. However, grids are not necessary for all examinations. For example, grids need not be used in radiographic examinations of the hands, forearm, feet, or lower legs. In general, one should employ a grid whenever the body part measures 12 cm or greater.[1] The question of when to use a grid will be resolved through recommendations offered later in this and the following chapter.

Although grids improve the quality of a radiograph, they can produce problems if used incorrectly. Improper grid usage typically results in a loss of film blackening. The loss of film blackening is caused by grid cut-off. Following is a list of methods employed to avoid grid cut-off.[2]

Figure 22-7   **A**: closed cassette. **B**: opened cassette showing intensifying screens. An x-ray film lies diagonally across the screens.

1. As previously mentioned, lead strips in a grid are generally arranged parallel to one another and extend in a straight line along the longitudinal axis of the grid. For example, in a grid 14 in. × 17 in., the lead strips extend in the direction of the greatest dimension, i.e., the 17-in. direction. With this arrangement in mind, one must never angle the x-ray tube against the long axis of the lead strips. It is, however, permissible to angle the tube longitudinally with the lead strips. In fact, there will be several examples in the positioning section of this chapter which require angulation of the CR with the long axis of the grid.

2. The grid and the x-ray tube must be perpendicular to one another. If the grid is angled against the CR, significant grid cut-off will occur.

3. Some grids require a specific distance be maintained between the x-ray tube and the grid. If the distance requirement is violated, loss of film blackening will be seen

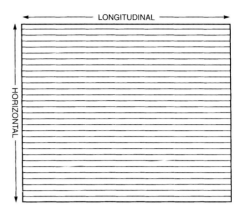

Figure 22-8 Schematic drawing of a grid (see text).

along the longitudinal edges of the radiograph. Distance requirements are indicated on the front of the grid.

4. If the CR is not centered to the longitudinal center of the grid, loss of film blackening will be seen on one side of the radiograph.

5. Grids have a labeled front and back side. If the front side does not face the x-ray tube, a distinct loss of film blackening will be seen on both sides of the radiograph.

Radiation Protection

X-rays produced within an x-ray tube represent a form of ionizing radiation. It has long been known that exposure to ionizing radiation may induce various biologic effects such as malignant disease and birth defects. Therefore, the purpose of this section is to provide those individuals who participate in post-mortem radiography with an understanding of the fundamentals of radiation protection.

Methods of Protection

A fixed radiographic installation is located in a room that typically contains a control booth barrier, which is simply a small wall extending into the room. The control booth barrier protects personnel while x-ray exposures are being made. The walls in a radiographic room are usually lined with sheets of lead. Since it is unnecessary for all of the walls to have the same thickness of lead sheeting, the level of protection varies in different areas of the room.

Walls with thicker lead sheeting allow the central ray (primary beam) to be directed toward them, and are referred to as primary barriers. Walls with thinner lead sheeting are referred to as secondary barriers. Secondary barriers are intended to protect against scatter radiation and radiation which may escape from the x-ray tube housing. The primary beam should never be directed to a secondary barrier. The control booth is usually designated as a secondary barrier.

Since most autopsy suites use mobile x-ray units, the previous discussion regarding primary and secondary barriers may not seem applicable. However, knowledge of primary and secondary barriers will assist in one's understanding of the basic tenets of radiation protection.

There are three fundamental principles (tenets) which are employed to reduce radiation exposure to both the patient and personnel. The three principles are time, distance, and shielding.[3] In the absence of a living patient, the following discussion will address reducing radiation exposure to personnel.

Time

Time usually refers to the length or duration of an x-ray exposure. The duration of x-ray exposures usually does not exceed one second. Exposure to radiation can be effectively reduced by maintaining exposure to the shortest time possible. Time also refers to the amount of time spent in an area where exposures are being made. It is therefore important to limit one's presence in the exposure area as much as possible.

Distance

In contrast to SID (source image-receptor distance), distance here refers to the amount of distance between the x-ray tube and the radiation worker. The old adage, "distance is the best protection against radiation", still holds true today. In theory, as distance increases the amount of radiation reaching the patient and personnel decreases. Since mobile x-ray units are equipped with a 6 ft. exposure cord, the operator should extend it to maximum length and stand behind the x-ray unit. This will greatly reduce exposure.

Shielding

As previously indicated, shielding serves as a protective barrier against ionizing radiation. Fixed walls surrounding a radiographic unit may provide an effective barrier depending on the materials from which the wall is built. Additional radiation barriers can be added to existing walls by lead sheathing or barium plastering. Movable barriers (Chapter 9, Figure 9-15) can be useful for personnel protection. Where structural barriers are missing or impractical, limiting the tube direction can be effective. When otherwise unprotected, personnel should wear protective apparel whenever exposures are being made. Protective apparel consists of aprons and gloves which are impregnated with lead particles (Figure 22-9). Lead aprons and gloves are intended to provide protection from scatter radiation. Since post-mortem radiography may require individuals to hold cassettes or body parts in place while exposures are being made, the use of leaded apparel will reduce exposure to personnel.

The level of protection provided by leaded apparel is greatly diminished in the presence of the primary beam. Therefore, one should never position oneself in the direct path of the primary beam. While lead aprons and gloves do provide protection against radiation, one should understand that these devices are subject to cracking and other forms of deterioration. To monitor the effectiveness of these devices, one should make periodic inspections of lead gloves and aprons. Leaded apparel may also be radiographed to visualize minute cracks in the leaded material.

In addition to time, distance, and shielding, there are other factors which can be employed to further reduce radiation exposure. These factors are discussed below.

1. Higher-speed screens require significantly less exposure than slower speed screens to produce the same film density. Any reduction in overall exposure translates into less exposure to personnel.
2. Maintaining strict collimation settings reduces the amount of scatter radiation. A reduction in scatter radiation means less exposure to personnel.

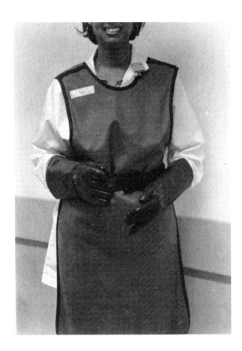

Figure 22-9   Lead apron and gloves.

3. X-ray equipment requires periodic testing and calibration to ensure the equipment is producing the desired amount of radiation. Failure to maintain appropriate equipment calibration often results in the need to repeat radiographs. The potential for increased exposure to personnel always exists when radiographs must be repeated. Consultation with commercial service technicians and radiation physicists can ensure that x-ray equipment possesses the correct components and is functioning properly.

Monitoring Radiation Exposure

Personnel should be provided with radiation monitoring devices to determine the amount of radiation received over a given period of time. Such devices do not afford protection. They are, however, useful in assessing radiation safety practices, and the possible need to divide the number of radiographic procedures performed amongst other personnel.

Personnel monitoring devices commonly employed today are film badges (Figure 22-10) and thermoluminescence dosimeters (TLD). While each of these devices has certain advantages and disadvantages, both provide a reasonably accurate measurement of the amount of exposure received by personnel. Personnel monitoring devices are routinely employed in radiology departments. Therefore, information concerning the acquisition and proper use of these devices can be obtained by contacting administrative personnel in a radiology department.

X-Ray Exposure and Pregnancy

The potential to induce congenital abnormalities following exposure to ionizing radiation has been addressed countless times in textbooks and professional journals. However, it should be noted that pregnant radiographers and radiologists routinely perform radiographic examinations and give birth to normal babies. Thus, fetal abnormalities arising

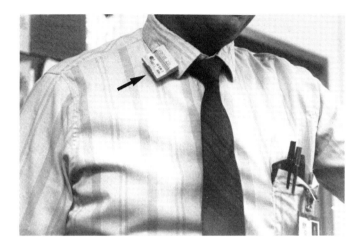

Figure 22-10   Film badge (arrow) used to monitor cumulative radiation exposure to personnel.

from radiation exposure can be avoided. With this in mind, the following considerations are offered to women who perform radiographic examinations:

1. If an employee knows or suspects she is pregnant, she should immediately inform her supervisor. Once notified, the supervisor will review the appropriate policies and procedures adopted by the institution regarding x-ray exposure and pregnancy.
2. The employee should conscientiously utilize all protective measures throughout her pregnancy, e.g., time, distance, and shielding.
3. Female employees should understand that the fetus is most sensitive to ionizing radiation during the first trimester.[4] Therefore, special attention should be given to time, distance, and shielding during this period.

Physical Layout

The physical layout of a radiographic installation in a medical examiner's facility — whether a mobile unit with movable barriers or a sophisticated radiographic/fluoroscopic unit in a separate room — should be planned with expert advice. A qualified radiation physicist should be consulted on, and approve, all renovation or new construction which will house radiation-producing equipment. This is essential for protection of personnel. Furthermore, a number of states require that all x-ray installations be periodically inspected by a qualified radiation physicist or radiation health physicist. Local requirements can be ascertained by querying the State Department of Health or the State Radiation Control Commission. The administrator or a local medical radiology department is a resource for finding a radiation physicist or radiation health physicist.

References

1. Thompson, T. T., *Cahoon's Formulating X-Ray Techniques*, 9th ed., Duke University Press, Durham, NC, 1979, p. 100.
2. Thompson, T. T., *Cahoon's Formulating X-Ray Techniques*, 9th ed., Duke University Press, Durham, NC, 1979, p. 102.
3. Bushong, S. C., *Radiologic Science for Technologists*, 4th ed., C. V. Mosby, St. Louis, 1988, p. 535.
4. Bushong, S. C., *Radiologic Science for Technologists*, 4th ed., C. V. Mosby, St. Louis, 1988, p. 543.

Radiographic Positioning

23

CHARLES W. NEWELL, ED.D., R.T. (R)
CHUCRI M. JALKH, B.S., R.T. (R)

Contents

Introduction

Consistent and accurate positioning is a key element in the overall quality of a radiographic image. This is equally true when one attempts to match ante-mortem and post-mortem radiologic images of an individual. The task of matching ante-mortem and post-mortem radiologic images becomes more complex when the remains of an individual are degraded via a myriad of environmental factors. The task, however, can be rendered less complex by producing radiographic images which closely approximate those obtained in the ante-mortem state.

Since it is common practice to perform post-mortem radiography in the absence of a trained radiographer, the focus of this chapter is to provide the medical examiner assistant with the fundamental skills necessary to produce quality radiologic images. To achieve this objective, this chapter will include terminology used in radiographic positioning, essential technical considerations, and radiographic positions to demonstrate specific anatomical

0-8493-8105-3/98/$0.00+$.50
© 1998 by CRC Press LLC

structures. Careful attention to the sections on radiographic positioning terminology and technical considerations will enhance one's understanding of radiographic positioning.

Radiographic Positioning Terminology

Positioning terminology provides a foundation for understanding and applying the fundamental concepts of radiographic positioning. Terms commonly used in radiographic positioning are assembled under various subheadings in accordance with their general usage, and are defined below.

Anatomical Aspects

Anterior — located before or in front of; generally refers to the ventral or abdominal side of the body (Figure 23-1).

Caudal or caudad — toward the tail; situated beneath the head; inferior in position (Figure 23-1).

Cephalic or cephalad — toward the head; superior in position (Figure 23-1).

Distal — situated far from the point of attachment or origin (Figure 23-1).

External — refers to a structure outside of the body.

Internal — refers to a structure within the body; opposite of external.

Lateral — pertaining to the side; structures situated away from the middle of the body or away from the median plane (Figure 23-1).

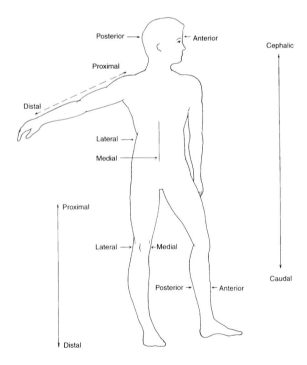

Figure 23-1   Anatomical aspects (seven references).

Medial — refers to the middle; structures located toward the middle of the body or toward the median plane (Figure 23-1).

Posterior — situated toward the back; generally refers to the back or dorsal portion of a structure; opposite of anterior (Figure 23-1).

Proximal — nearest the point of attachment or origin. Opposite of distal (Figure 23-1).

Anatomical Planes

Anatomical planes are imaginary lines which divide the body into various sections. Three of the more useful planes are defined below (Figure 23-2).

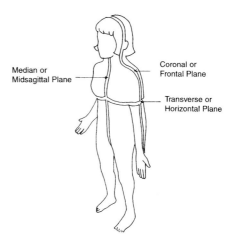

Median or Midsagittal Plane

Coronal or Frontal Plane

Transverse or Horizontal Plane

Figure 23-2   Anatomical planes.

Coronal plane — a vertical plane at right angles to the midsagittal plane which divides the body into anterior and posterior sections.

Midsagittal or median plane — a vertical plane that divides the body into right and left sections.

Transverse or horizontal plane — a horizontal plane that divides the body into upper and lower sections.

Anatomical Movement

Abduction — moving a body part away from the median plane of the body (Figure 23-3A).

Adduction — moving a body part toward the median plane of the body; opposite of abduction (Figure 23-3B).

Flexion — the act of bending a body part, such as the knee or elbow joint, which has the effect of reducing the angle of the joint (Figure 23-4A).

Extension — the act of moving a body part, such as the knee or elbow joint, which produces a straightening effect of the joint (Figure 23-4B).

Eversion — the act of turning a body part in an outward direction (Figure 23-5A).

Inversion — the act of turning a body part in an inward direction (Figure 23-5B).

Pronation — refers to placing the abdomen and chest against a flat surface, or the placement of the hand so that the palm faces in a downward direction (Figure 23-6A).

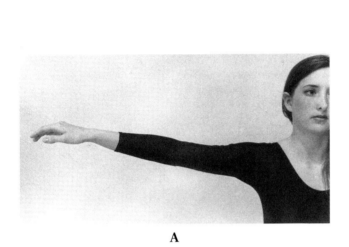

A   B

Figure 23-3   **A**: abduction. **B**: adduction.

Supination — the act of placing the back of a patient against a flat surface, or the placement of the hand so that the palm faces in an upward direction (Figure 23-6B).

Rotate — the act of turning a body part around an axis, e.g., rotating the head or the arm.

Radiographic Positions

Radiographic positioning terminology is employed to describe the actual position of the body while it is being radiographed. These terms, along with their respective acronyms, are listed and defined below.

Supine — lying on the back with the face upward (Figure 23-7).

Prone — lying on the abdomen with the face downward (Figure 23-8).

Lateral — lying on one's left or right side. It is common practice to designate lateral positions as either right or left lateral. The designation of right or left lateral is determined by which side (right or left) is placed against the film (Figure 23-9).

Oblique — a position whereby a body part is rotated to a predetermined degree between the prone and supine position. Oblique positions may be performed either upright or recumbent, i.e., lying down.

Right posterior oblique (RPO) — the model is rotated to place the right posterior side next to the film (Figure 23-10).

Left posterior oblique (LPO) — the model is rotated to place the left posterior side next to the film (Figure 23-11).

Right anterior oblique (RAO) — rotation of the body to place the right anterior side next to the film.

A

B

Figure 23-4   **A**: flexion. **B**: extension.

Left anterior oblique (LAO) — rotation of the body to place the left anterior side next to the film.

Decubitus — while decubitus means the patient is lying down, it also denotes that the x–ray beam is horizontal or parallel to the floor. Thus, the x–ray beam may enter the patient from either side (right or left), or from the anterior or posterior direction. There are also several ways to perform the decubitus position. In addition, the name of a specific decubitus position is determined by which side (right, left, anterior, or posterior) of the patient's body is placed against the x–ray film.

Dorsal decubitus — the model is supine, and the x–ray beam may enter from either the right or left side. Future reference to this and other similar positions may be referred to as a cross-table lateral projection (Figure 23-12).

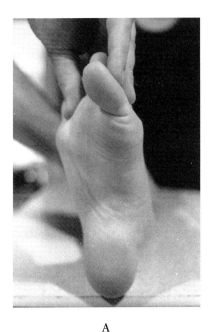

A   B

Figure 23-5   **A**: eversion. **B**: inversion.

Ventral decubitus — the model is prone, and the x–ray beam may enter from either the right or left side (Figure 23-13).

Lateral decubitus — the patient is placed on either the right or left side, and the x–ray beam enters from either the anterior or posterior direction. Once again, the name of a specific lateral decubitus is determined by which side (right or left) of the patient is resting on the x–ray film. For example, Figure 23-14 shows a model lying on her left side. Therefore, the position is referred to as a left lateral decubitus.

Radiographic Projections

The term radiographic position was previously defined as the actual position of the body while it is being radiographed. In contrast, a radiographic projection simply indicates the path of the x–ray beam as it passes through the body. In other words, the term projection describes the route of the x–ray beam as it leaves the radiographic tube, enters the patient, and exits the patient to strike the film. Projection is an important term because all radiographic examinations are identified by a particular projection. Radiographic projections may be performed either upright or recumbent. Despite the distinct difference between the terms position and projection, several illustrations previously used to depict positions are utilized again to further explain various projections in the definitions below.

Anteroposterior (AP) — in Figure 23-7 the x–ray beam enters the anterior surface and exits the posterior surface.

Posteroanterior (PA) — in Figure 23-8 the x–ray beam enters the posterior surface and exits the anterior surface.

Lateral — in Figure 23-9 the x–ray beam enters the left side of the body and exits the right side. Figure 23-9 is referred to as a right lateral projection.

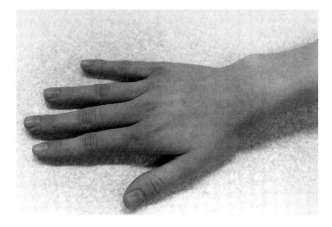

A

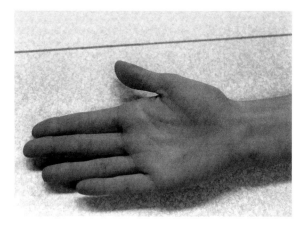

B

Figure 23-6   **A**: pronation. **B**: supination.

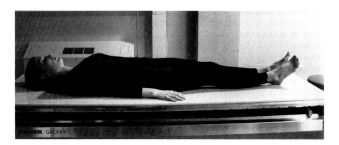

Figure 23-7   Supine (anteroposterior).

Oblique — in Figure 23-10, the model has been placed in the right posterior oblique position (RPO). Since the x–ray beam enters the anterior surface, the projection is referred to as a right AP oblique projection. In a similar manner, the position demonstrated in Figure 23-11 would be identified as a left AP oblique projection.

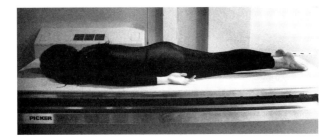

Figure 23-8   Prone (posteroanterior).

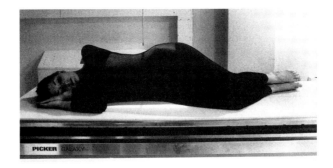

Figure 23-9   Lateral (lateral projection).

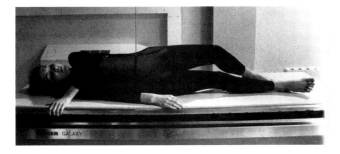

Figure 23-10   Right posterior oblique (RPO).

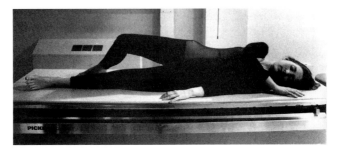

Figure 23-11   Left posterior oblique (LPO).

Axial — a longitudinal angulation of the x–ray beam along the long axis of the body (Figure 23-15).

Radiographic Positioning

Radiographic positioning entails the proper placement of an anatomical part on a cassette in a manner which yields an image that mirrors the anatomical area of interest. Much of what was addressed in the previous sections focused on positioning terminology and certain technical aspects of radiography. Reference to those sections is recommended as one reviews the radiographic positions in this section.

There are certain principles which must be observed to produce anatomically correct radiographs. Some of the more important principles are discussed below.

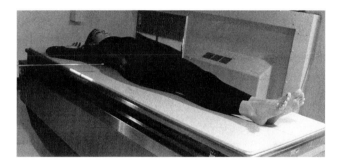

Figure 23-12   Dorsal decubitus.

Figure 23-13   Ventral decubitus.

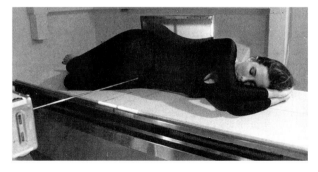

Figure 23-14   Left lateral decubitus.

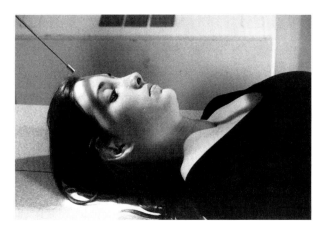

Figure 23-15   Axial projection.

1. Most radiographic examinations require two projections taken at right angles to one another. This requirement is typically fulfilled by taking an AP and lateral, or a PA and lateral projection. The AP/PA and lateral projections yield two images without superimposition of body parts (not lying on top of each other). The AP/PA and lateral projections also clarify the position and depth of a foreign body, e.g., a bullet, ingested object, etc. Thus, the AP/PA and lateral projection provides a different perspective of an anatomical part.
2. When long bones such as the lower leg or the humerus are radiographed, one should include the distal and proximal joint spaces of the long bone. The inclusion of both joint spaces of a long bone ensures the entire bone is projected on the radiograph.
3. Regardless of whether an anatomical part is placed in a supine, prone, or lateral position, care must be taken to avoid over- or underrotation of the part. In short, the part must be placed at right angles to the cassette. To ensure proper alignment is achieved, it is recommended that one use radiolucent sponges as support devices (Figure 23-16). Radiolucent sponges are available with washable surfaces, and can often be used in the place of personnel to support anatomical parts while examinations are performed. Florist's clay can be used to hold bone or bone fragments in precise position; however, florist's clay is radiopaque and care must be taken not to obscure an important area.
4. To avoid artifacts, all clothing should be removed from the area of interest. However, the medical examiner should be consulted before clothing is removed.

Survey Approach to Radiographic Positioning

Radiographs produced in the radiology department tend to focus on specific anatomical structures, such as the knee, humerus, shoulder, kidney, etc. This method would often be impractical in post-mortem radiography where, for the sake of time and other considerations, one must frequently demonstrate several anatomical structures on a single radiograph. Therefore, the initial part of this section will describe radiographic positions using a survey approach. The survey approach endeavors to include several related anatomical structures on a single radiograph. It should also be noted that the needs of post-mortem

Figure 23-16   Sandbag and Radiolucent sponges.

radiography may often be satisfied with a single AP projection. However, in keeping with the principle of providing two projections at right angles, and the importance of matching post-mortem and ante-mortem films, lateral projections are also included.

Due to the nature of post-mortem radiography, the projections described throughout this section are intended to accommodate the radiographic needs of a body in the supine recumbent position. Thus, with few exceptions, the focus of this section will be directed to AP and cross-table lateral projections. Moreover, except where indicated, the SID for all projections will be 40 in. In addition, the important aspects of each projection will be discussed under the following headings: cassette size, position of part, central ray, and structures demonstrated. A fifth heading, additional comments, will be added when deemed necessary. Finally, it should also be noted that the important aspects of each projection described below pertain to radiographic positions performed under standard conditions. Obviously, this may not always be the case in post-mortem radiography where anatomical structures may vary greatly in terms of their position, form, or composition. In such cases, one should refer to the standard positions described below, and adapt them to the given situation.

Survey Approach: Upper Extremity

AP Projection of the Shoulder to Include the Humerus

Cassette Size — 14 in. × 17 in. grid cassette.
Position of Part (Figure 23-20A)
  • The grid cassette is placed lengthwise beneath the patient, with the top of the cassette approximately 1 1/2 in. above the shoulder. Some adjustment of the grid cassette may be necessary to include the distal humerus.
  • The grid cassette must extend to the median plane of the body to include the shoulder girdle.
  • Supinate the hand to place the humerus in a true AP position.
Central Ray (CR) — Direct the CR perpendicular to the midpoint of the longitudinal and horizontal axis of the grid cassette. Collimate to the size of the cassette.
Structures Demonstrated (Figure 23-17B) — An AP projection of the shoulder girdle to include the proximal, mid, and distal portions of the humerus.

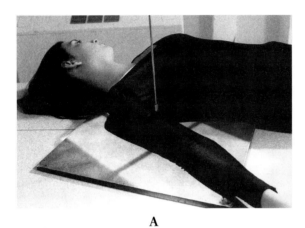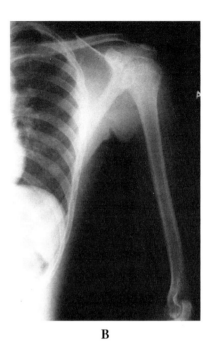

A   B

Figure 23-17   **A**: AP shoulder and humerus position. **B**: AP shoulder and humerus.

Additional Comments — In cases where the desired anatomy extends beyond the long
axis of the grid cassette, a separate AP projection will be needed to include the distal
portion of the humerus.

Lateral Projection of the Humerus

Two methods are described to demonstrate a lateral projection of the humerus.

AP Internal Rotation

Cassette Size — 14 in. × 17 in. grid cassette.
Position of Part (Figure 23-18A)
  • Adjust the cassette beneath the humerus to include the proximal and distal joints.
  • The humerus is centered to the long axis of the cassette.
  • Internally rotate the humerus to a point where the distal joint (epicondyle) is
    superimposed. Extreme pronation of the hand will usually provide sufficient
    internal rotation of the humerus. However, the hand must be held in extreme
    rotation to achieve this projection.
Central Ray — Direct the CR perpendicular to the longitudinal and horizontal axis of
  the grid cassette. Adjust the collimator to an 8 × 17-in. setting.
Structures Demonstrated (Figure 23-18B) — The entire humerus in the lateral position
  is achieved through internal rotation.
Additional Comments — The cassette may be turned diagonally if the humerus is longer
  than the cassette. In addition, an alternate projection of the entire humerus can be
  obtained by moving the arm (humerus) away from the body. This is achieved by
  placing the hand in the supine position, and abducting the humerus approximately
  90° from the midsagittal plane. A cassette is placed adjacent to the lateral aspect of

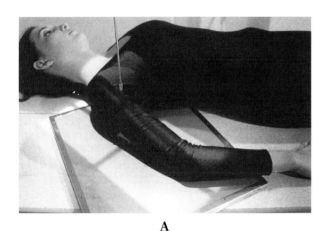
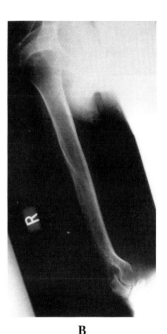

A   **B**

Figure 23-18   **A**: Lateral humerus position. **B**: Lateral humerus projection.

the humerus, and the CR is directed horizontally and perpendicular to the center of the cassette

Cross-Table Lateral of Mid and Distal Humerus

This projection excludes the proximal portion of the humerus.

Cassette Size: 14 in. × 17 in. nongrid cassette.
Position of Part (Figure 23-19A)
  • Place the cassette between the thorax and the humerus.
  • Push the long axis of the cassette as far as permitted toward the axilla.
  • The humerus should be supported by a radiolucent sponge or sandbag to ensure inclusion of the posterior aspect.
  • The hand is maintained in the supine position.
Central Ray — Direct the horizontal beam perpendicular to the midpoint of the cassette. Collimate to an 8 × 17-in. setting.
Structures Demonstrated (Figure 23-19B) — A cross-table lateral projection of the mid and distal portions of the humerus.

AP Projection of the Elbow to Include the Hand

Cassette Size — 14 in. × 17 in. nongrid cassette.
Position of Part (Figure 23-20A)
  • Adjust the cassette beneath the forearm to include the elbow joint and the hand. This may require the cassette to be turned diagonally. If so, the elbow is placed in one corner of the cassette and the hand in the other corner.

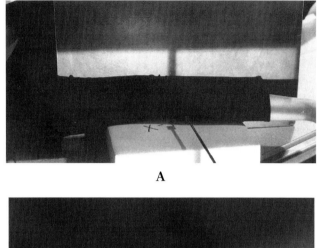

A

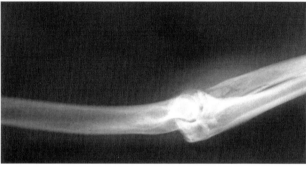

B

Figure 23-19   **A**: Cross-table lateral mid and distal humerus position. **B**: Cross-table lateral mid and distal humerus projection.

- The hand and forearm must be maintained in a supine position to achieve a true AP projection.

Central Ray — The CR is directed perpendicular to the midpoint of the cassette. Collimate to an 8 × 17-in. size.

Structures Demonstrated (Figure 23-20B) — An AP projection of the forearm including the elbow and hand.

Lateral Projection of the Elbow to Include the Hand

Cassette Size — 14 in. × 17 in. nongrid cassette.

Position of Part (Figure 23-21A)

- The elbow, forearm, and hand are elevated on radiolucent sponges or sandbags.
- The long axis of the cassette is placed between the forearm and the side of the patient's abdomen and pelvis.
- The hand and forearm must be maintained in the supine position.

Central Ray — Direct the horizontal beam perpendicular to the midpoint of the cassette. Collimate to an 8 × 17-in. size.

Structures Demonstrated (Figure 23-21B) — A cross-table lateral projection of the forearm including the elbow and hand.

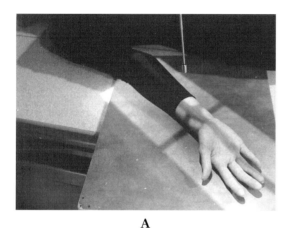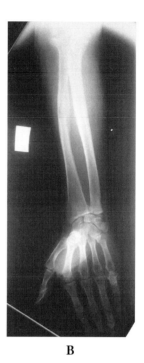

A **B**

Figure 23-20 **A**: AP forearm position to include hand. **B**: AP forearm to include hand.

Survey Approach: Pelvis and Lower Extremity

AP Projection of the Pelvis to Include Both Hips

Cassette Size: 14 in. × 17 in. grid cassette.
Position of Part (Figure 23-22A)
- A 14 × 17-in. grid cassette is placed crosswise (17 × 14) beneath the patient.
- The top edge of the grid cassette is positioned 1 ½ in. above the iliac crest.
- The median plane of the pelvis is centered to the grid cassette.
- The feet, along with the lower legs, are rotated internally. When the feet are properly rotated, they will resemble a pyramid.
- The hips are parallel to the plane of the table/floor to avoid rotation of the pelvis.

Central Ray — The CR is directed perpendicular to the center of the grid cassette. Collimate to 17 in. × 14 in. size.

Structures Demonstrated (Figure 23-22B) — An AP projection of the pelvis including both hips.

Cross-Table Lateral Projection of the Hip (Danelius-Miller Method)[1]

Cassette Size — 10 in. × 12 in. or larger grid cassette.
Position of Part (Figure 23-23A)
- The foot of the side of interest is internally rotated 15°.
- The opposite leg is raised and either placed on a support, or held by other personnel. The elevated femur should approach an angle of 90° to the plane of the table/floor.

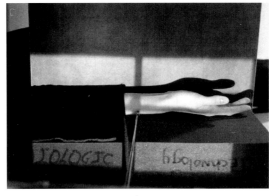

A

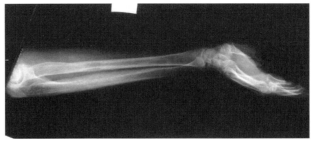

B

Figure 23-21   **A**: Cross-table lateral position of forearm and hand. **B**: Cross-table lateral projection of forearm and hand.

- The horizontal end of the grid cassette is placed just above the iliac crest and the long axis of the cassette runs parallel with the proximal end of the femur.
- The grid cassette must be held in place. A cassette holder or sand bags can be used for this purpose.
- The cassette must be maintained perpendicular to the table/floor.

Central Ray — The horizontal beam is directed cephalically to the center of the cassette. As a check, when the CR is angled in this manner it should be perpendicular to the femoral neck and the grid cassette. Collimate to 10 × 12-in. size.

Structures Demonstrated (Figure 23-23B) — A cross-table lateral of the proximal femur and hip.

Additional Comments — To avoid grid cut-off, the grid cassette must not be angled.

AP Projection of Femur

Cassette Size — 14 in. × 17 in. and 10 in. × 12 in. grid cassettes.
Position of Part (Figure 23-24A)
- Placement of a cassette for an AP femur is frequently influenced by the length of the femur. Since the length of an adult femur often exceeds the length of a cassette, two films may be required to demonstrate both joints. Two films would not be necessary if the pelvis were radiographed, as described above, and included the proximal femur. However, two AP projections are described.

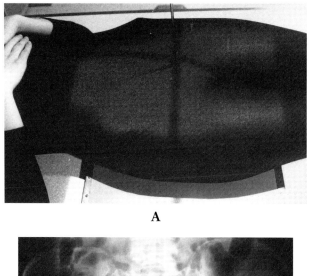

A

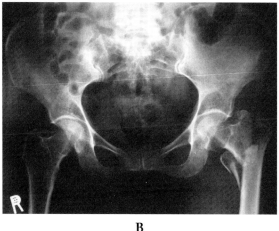

B

Figure 23-22   **A**: AP pelvis position. **B**: AP pelvis and hips.

- For the proximal femur, a 14 in. × 17 in. grid cassette is placed lengthwise beneath the patient.
- The top of the grid cassette is placed at the level of the anterior superior iliac spine (ASIS). The ASIS is a large bony prominence on either side of the pelvic bone. The ASIS lies inferior to the iliac crest.
- The long axis of the femur is centered to the cassette.
- The feet are rotated internally 15°.
- For the distal femur, a 10 in. × 12 in. grid cassette is placed lengthwise beneath the femur.
- The lower border of the grid cassette is placed ½ to 1 in. below the patella. The upper border of the cassette extends cephalad.
- Once again, the long axis of the femur is centered to the cassette.
- The foot should be directed vertically to avoid rotation.

Central Ray — For AP projections of the proximal and distal femur, the CR is directed perpendicular to the center of the grid cassette. Collimator settings for the proximal and distal portions of the femur are 10 × 17 and 10 × 12 in.

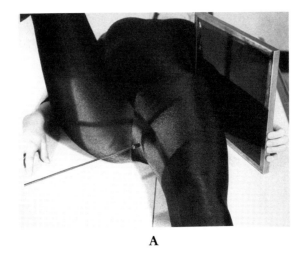

A

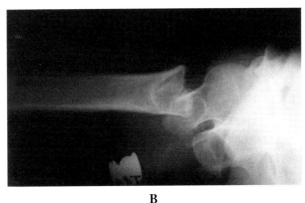

B

Figure 23-23   **A**: Cross-table lateral hip position. **B**: Cross-table lateral hip projection.

Structures Demonstrated (Figure 23-24B) — An AP projection of the femur which includes the proximal and distal joints.

Cross-Table Lateral Projection of the Femur

Cassette Size — 14 in. × 17 in. and 10 in. × 12 in. grid cassettes.
Position of Part (Figure 23-25A,B)
- Differences between the length of the femur and the cassette are addressed in a manner similar to the AP projection.
- The lateral projection of the proximal femur is performed in the same way as the cross-table lateral of the hip. The cross-table lateral hip projection was described under the heading, Cross-Table Lateral Projection of the Hip (Danelius-Miller Method).
- The cross-table lateral of the mid and distal shaft of the femur requires the long axis of the grid cassette be placed on the lateral aspect of the femur.
- The lower border of the grid cassette is placed 1/2 to 1 in. below the patella, and the upper border of the cassette extends cephalad.
- A radiolucent sponge may be placed under the femur to elevate it above the table.

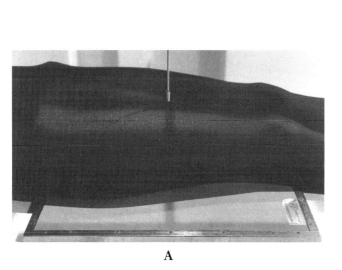
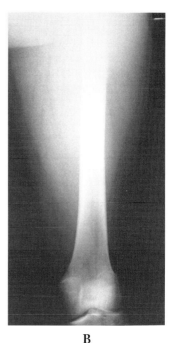

A   B

Figure 23-24 **A**: AP femur position. **B**: AP femur.

- The opposite femur is elevated high enough to avoid superimposition of both femurs (Figure 23-25A).
- When it is not feasible to elevate the leg, the grid cassette may be placed between both femurs with the front of the cassette facing the femur of interest. This method, however, will not demonstrate as much femoral shaft as when the leg is elevated (Figure 23-25B).

Central Ray — For the proximal femur, direct the CR as described in the cross-table lateral projection of the hip. For the mid and distal shaft of the femur, direct the horizontal beam perpendicular to the midpoint of the grid cassette. The collimator setting for the proximal femur is 10 × 12 in., while the setting for the mid and distal shaft is 10 × 17 in.

Structures Demonstrated (Figure 23-25C) — A cross-table lateral projection demonstrating the mid and distal shaft of the femur.

AP Projection of the Leg (Tibia-Fibula)

Cassette Size — 14 in. × 17 in. nongrid cassette.
Position of Part (Figure 23-26A)
- The foot is maintained in a vertical position to avoid part rotation.
- The cassette is placed lengthwise beneath the leg and is aligned with the long axis of the leg.
- The placement of the cassette is adjusted to include the proximal and distal joints. The cassette may be turned diagonally to accommodate longer legs. Otherwise a separate smaller cassette may be used to demonstrate one of the joint spaces.

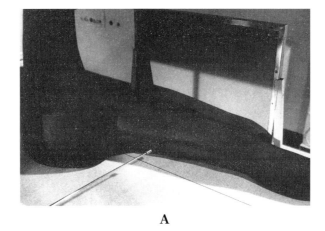

A

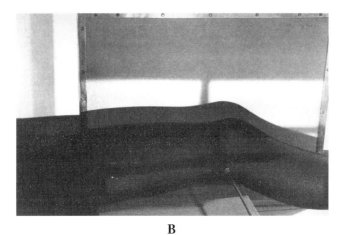

B

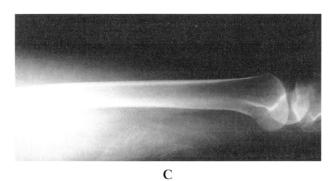

C

Figure 23-25   **A**: Cross-table lateral position of mid and distal femur. **B**: Cross-table lateral position of distal femur. **C**: Cross-table lateral projection of femur.

Central Ray — Direct the CR perpendicular to the midpoint of the cassette. Collimate to a 10 × 17 in. setting.

Structures Demonstrated (Figure 23-26B) — An AP projection of the entire tibia and fibula.

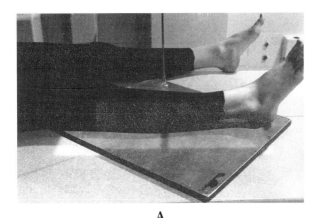
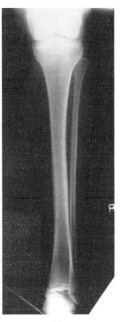

A   **B**

Figure 23-26   **A**: AP position of tibia-fibula. **B**: AP tibia-fibula.

Cross-Table Lateral Projection of the Leg

Cassette Size — 14 in. × 17 in. nongrid cassette.
Position of Part (Figure 23-27A)
- The cassette is placed lengthwise between the lower legs.
- The cassette is adjusted to include the proximal and distal joints. Since the adult tibia and fibula are often longer than the cassette, a second cassette may be needed to include both joint spaces.
- It may be necessary to elevate the leg of interest on a radiolucent sponge or sandbag to ensure the posterior aspect of the leg is projected on the film.

Central Ray — Direct the horizontal beam perpendicular to the midpoint of the cassette. Collimate to the part.
Structures Demonstrated (Figure 23-27B) — A lateral projection of the entire tibia and fibula.

Survey Approach: Chest and Thoracic Spine

Other than technical differences, the positioning requirements for the chest and thoracic spine are essentially the same. Therefore, the chest and thoracic spine will be considered together in the discussion below.

AP Projection of the Chest and Thoracic Spine

Cassette Size — 14 in. × 17 in. grid cassette.
Position of Part (Figure 23-28A)

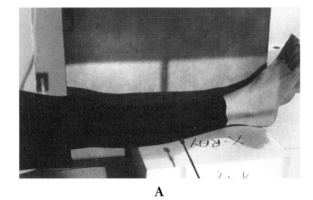

A

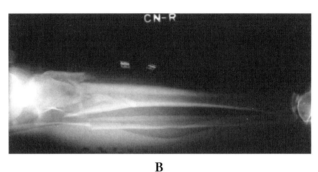

B

Figure 23-27   **A**: Cross-table lateral position of tibia-fibula. **B**: Cross-table lateral projection of tibia-fibula.

- The grid cassette is placed lengthwise beneath the thorax. The top of the cassette is about 1 ¹/₂ in. above the shoulders.
- Center the cassette to the midsagittal plane of the patient.
- The thorax should be checked to ensure that it is not rotated.
- If feasible for chest exams, both arms should be raised above the head in order to remove the scapulae from the lung field.

Central Ray — As noted previously, it is important to match ante-mortem and post-mortem radiologic images. This is particularly true when an AP post-mortem radiograph of the thoracic cavity is compared to the usual PA ante-mortem chest radiograph. To achieve comparable radiographic studies, the authors recommend the CR be angled 10 to 15° caudally to the midpoint of the longitudinal and horizontal axis of the grid cassette. The collimator should also be adjusted to the size of the cassette.

Structures Demonstrated (Figure 23-28B,C)
- An AP projection of the entire thoracic viscera should be seen without rotation.
- An AP projection of the entire thoracic spine.

Additional Comments
- In cases where the thoracic viscera is larger than the cassette, the grid cassette should be placed crosswise and the long border (17 in.) of the cassette coincides with the level of the shoulders. However, due to the occurrence of grid cut-off, this approach cannot be applied when the tube is angled. Therefore, a nongrid cassette must be employed in this instance.
- Raise the x–ray tube as much as possible for AP projection of the chest.

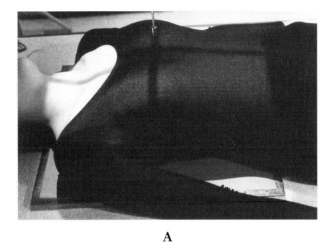

A

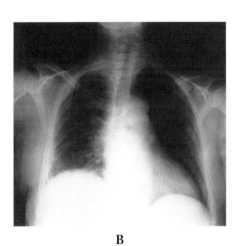

B

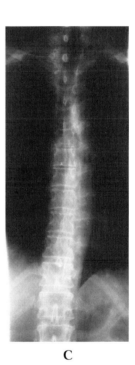

C

Figure 23-28   **A**: AP position of chest and thoracic spine. **B**: AP chest. **C**: AP thoracic spine.

Cross-Table Lateral Projection of the Chest and Thoracic Spine

Cassette size — 14 in. × 17 in. grid cassette.
Position of Part (Figure 23-29A)

- The grid cassette is held in place beside the thorax by a cassette holder or a properly shielded assistant.
- The top of the cassette is placed about 1 1/2 in. above the shoulders.
- The arms should be extended above the head.
- Center the midcoronal plane of the patient to the grid cassette.
- The patient should be elevated on radiolucent sponges to ensure proper visualization of the entire anatomy of the thoracic spine and viscera.

Central Ray
  • Direct the horizontal beam perpendicular to the midpoint of the longitudinal and horizontal axis of the grid cassette.
  • Collimate to the size of the cassette.
Structures Demonstrated (Figure 23-29B)
  • A lateral projection of the entire thoracic viscera.
  • A lateral projection of the entire thoracic spine.

Survey Approach: Abdomen and Lumbar Spine

Other than technical differences, the positioning requirements for the abdomen and lumbar spine are essentially the same. Therefore, the abdomen and lumbar spine will be considered together in the discussion below.

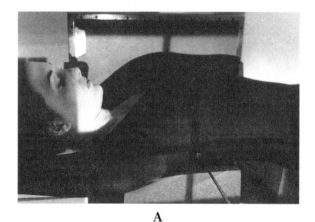

A

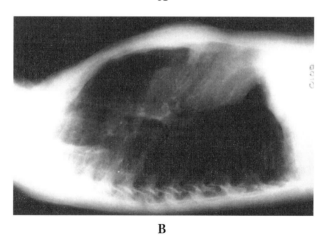

B

Figure 23-29   **A**: Cross-table lateral position of chest and thoracic spine. **B**: Cross-table lateral projection of chest and thoracic spine.

AP Projection of the Abdomen and Lumbar Spine

Cassette Size — 14 in. × 17 in. grid cassette
Position of Part (Figure 23-30A)
   • The grid cassette is placed lengthwise beneath the body.
   • The horizontal axis of the cassette is centered to the iliac crest.
   • The shoulders and pelvis must lie in the same transverse plane to avoid rotation.
   • The midsagittal plane of the body is centered to the longitudinal axis of the cassette.
Central Ray
   • Direct the CR perpendicular to the midpoint of the longitudinal and horizontal axis of the grid cassette.
   • Collimate to the size of the cassette (14 in. × 17 in.).
Structures Demonstrated (Figures 23-30B,C)
   • An AP projection demonstrating those abdominal structures situated between the diaphragm and the symphysis pubis.
   • An AP projection of the entire lumbar spine.
Additional Comments — If the patient is extremely large, it may be necessary to take two separate exposures for an AP projection of the abdomen. The grid cassette will be placed crosswise and one film will show the lower abdomen and the second film will show the upper abdomen.

Dorsal Decubitus Projection of the Abdomen and Cross-Table Lateral Projection of the Lumbar Spine

Cassette Size — 14 in. × 17 in. grid cassette.
Position of Part (Figure 23-31A)
   • The grid cassette is parallel to the midsagittal plane of the body. The grid cassette may be held beside the abdomen by a cassette holder or a properly shielded assistant.
   • The top of the iliac crest is centered to the horizontal axis of the grid cassette.
   • The midcoronal plane of the body is aligned with the long axis of the cassette.
   • The patient should be elevated on radiolucent sponges to ensure proper visualization of the posterior aspect of the abdominal viscera and lumbar spine.
Central Ray
   • Direct the horizontal beam to the midpoint of the longitudinal and horizontal axis of the grid cassette.
   • Collimate to the size of the cassette.
Structures Demonstrated (Figure 23-31B)
   • A lateral projection of the abdominal cavity and abdominal viscera.
   • A lateral projection of the entire lumbar spine.
Additional Comments — If the sacrum and coccyx are not demonstrated, the grid cassette should be adjusted caudally.

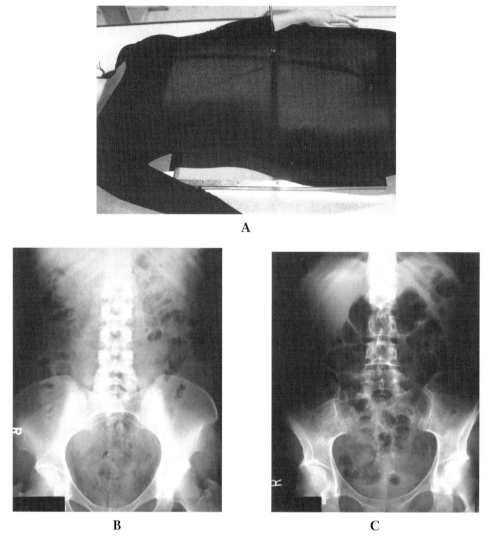

Figure 23-30 **A**: AP position of abdomen and lumbar spine. **B**: AP abdomen. **C**: AP lumbar spine.

Survey Approach: Skull (Cranium)

Proper positioning of the skull requires the application of imaginary positioning lines (Figure 23-32). The positioning lines considered most useful for post-mortem radiography of the skull, and their respective acronyms, are listed below:

1. Interpupillary line (IPL)
2. Midsagittal plane (MSP)
3. Orbitomeatal line (OML)
4. Infraorbitomeatal line (IOML)

AP Projection of the Skull (Cranium)

Cassette Size — 10 in. × 12 in. grid cassette.

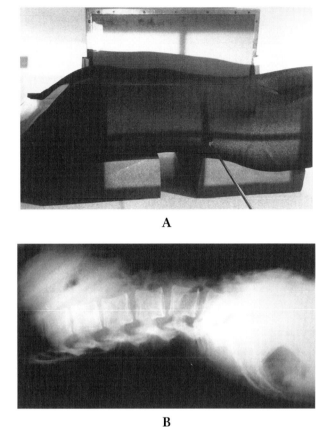

A

B

Figure 23-31   **A**: Cross-table lateral position of abdomen and lumbar spine. **B**: Cross-table lateral projection of abdomen and lumbar spine.

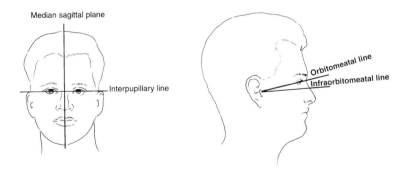

Figure 23-32   Positioning lines.

Position of Part (Figure 23-33A)
- The grid cassette is placed lengthwise beneath the skull.
- The upper border of the cassette is positioned 1 in. above the top of the skull. Note: the palm of the hand may be used to approximate 1 in.
- The MSP is centered to the long axis of the grid cassette.
- The MSP must be perpendicular to the cassette to avoid rotation.

- The OML is aligned perpendicular to the cassette. Note: it may be necessary to elevate the head on a thin radiolucent sponge to achieve the desired OML alignment.

Central Ray — The CR is directed perpendicular to the midpoint of the grid cassette. Collimate to the size of the cassette.

Structures Demonstrated (Figure 23-33B) — An AP projection of the major bony structures in the cranium.

Cross-Table Lateral Projection of the Skull (Cranium)

Cassette Size — 10 in. × 12 in. grid cassette.

Position of Part (Figure 23-34A)

- The grid cassette is placed vertically (12 in. × 10 in.) against the side of the skull.
- The upper border of the grid cassette is placed 3/4 to 1 in. above the top (vertex) of the skull.
- A thin radiolucent sponge is placed beneath the skull to ensure the posterior aspect of the skull is projected on the film.
- The MSP is aligned parallel to the grid cassette.
- The IPL is aligned perpendicular to the grid cassette.
- The IOML is aligned parallel with the long axis of the grid cassette.

Central Ray — Direct the horizontal beam perpendicular to the center of the grid cassette. Collimate to the size of the grid cassette.

Structures Demonstrated (Figure 23-34B) — A lateral projection of the major bones of the skull (cranium).

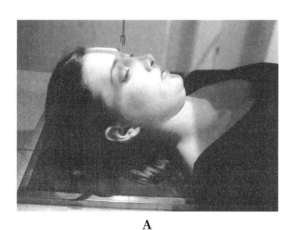

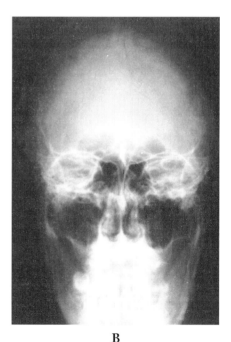

A   B

Figure 23-33   **A**: AP skull position. **B**: AP skull.

AP Axial Projection of the Skull (Towne Position)

Cassette Size — 10 in. × 12 in. grid cassette.

Position of Part (Figure 23-35A)
- Place the grid cassette lengthwise beneath the skull.
- The horizontal axis of the grid cassette is centered to the CR (see CR below). Centered in this manner usually requires the upper end of the cassette to be placed approximately 1 in. below the top of the skull.
- The MSP is centered to the long axis of the cassette.
- The MSP is perpendicular to the cassette to avoid rotation.
- The OML is aligned perpendicular to the cassette. Note: the IOML may be used. If so, see CR below.

Central Ray
- With the OML perpendicular, angle the CR caudally at an angle of 30°. Note: if the IOML is used, the CR is angled 37° caudally.[2]
- The CR enters the skull 2½ in. above the eyebrows. It exists in the area of the mastoid process.
- The grid cassette is centered to the point where the CR exits the skull. Collimate to the size of the grid cassette.

Structures Demonstrated (Figure 23-35B) — An AP projection of the occipital bone and surrounding structures.

Radiographic Positions for Specific Structures

In contrast to the survey approach, there may be occasions when projections of specific anatomical structures are desired. The positions/projections described below are intended to meet this need. However, several projections previously discussed under the survey

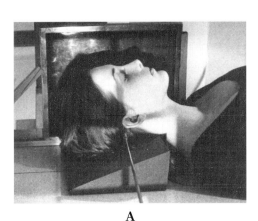
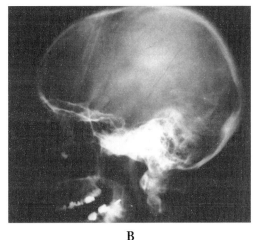

A **B**

Figure 23-34 **A**: Cross-table lateral skull position. **B**: Cross-table lateral skull projection.

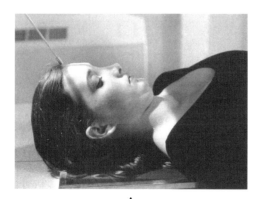
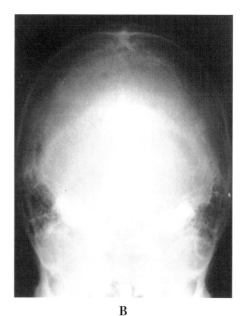

A   B

Figure 23-35   **A**: AP axial skull position (Towne). **B**: AP axial skull.

approach may also serve to demonstrate specific anatomical structures, e.g., forearm, humerus, leg, femur, pelvis, etc. Therefore, these anatomical structures will not be discussed again in this section.

Upper Extremity

AP/PA Projection of Hand and Wrist

Cassette Size — 10 in. × 12 in. nongrid cassette.
Position of Part (Figure 23-36A)
  • Place the cassette lengthwise under the wrist and hand.
  • Include distal part of forearm.
  • Fingers and hand may be pronated or supinated and placed flat on the cassette.
Central Ray
  • Direct the CR perpendicular to the midpoint of the longitudinal and horizontal axis of the cassette.
  • Collimate to the size of the cassette.
Structures Demonstrated (Figure 23-36B) — PA or AP projection of the hand, fingers, and wrist.

Lateral Projection of Hand and Wrist

Cassette Size — 10 in. × 12 in. nongrid cassette.
Position of Part (Figure 23-37A)
  • Place the cassette lengthwise under the wrist and hand to include distal part of forearm.

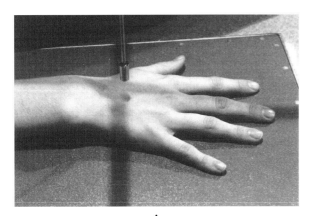
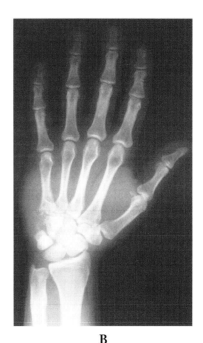

| A | B |

Figure 23-36   **A**: AP/PA hand and wrist position. **B**: PA hand and wrist.

- Rotate the hand and wrist to the lateral position. In this position, the fingers will be lying on top of one another.

Central Ray
- Direct the CR perpendicular to the midpoint of the longitudinal and horizontal axis of the cassette.
- Collimate to the size of the cassette.

Structures Demonstrated (Figure 23-37B) — Lateral projection of the wrist, hand, and fingers.

Additional Comments — The lateral projection of hand and wrist may also be performed as a cross-table lateral. If done in this manner, the hand should be elevated on a radiolucent sponge. The CR is directed horizontal and perpendicular to the cassette.

AP Projection of the Elbow Joint

Cassette Size — 10 in. × 12 in. nongrid cassette.

Position of Part (Figure 23-38A)
- Place the cassette lengthwise under the fully extended elbow joint.
- Place the elbow joint in the middle of the cassette and supinate the hand to achieve a true AP position.

Central Ray
- Direct the CR perpendicular to the midpoint of the longitudinal and horizontal axis of the cassette.
- Collimate to the size of the cassette.

Structures Demonstrated (Figure 23-38B) — AP projection of the elbow joint and distal humerus and proximal forearm.

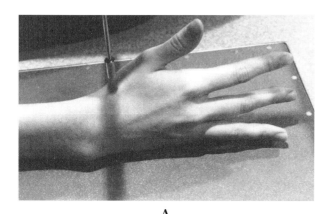 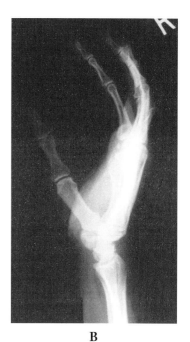

A   **B**

Figure 23-37   **A**: Lateral hand and wrist position. **B**: Lateral hand and wrist projection.

Cross-Table Lateral Projection of Elbow Joint

Cassette Size — 10 in. × 12 in. nongrid cassette.
Position of Part (Figure 23-39A)
   • Place the cassette lengthwise against the medial aspect of the elbow.
   • The elbow joint should correspond to the middle of the cassette.
   • The fully extended elbow joint should be elevated on a radiolucent sponge.
Central Ray
   • Direct the horizontal beam toward the cassette.
   • CR is perpendicular to the midpoint of the longitudinal and horizontal axis of
     the cassette.
   • Collimate to the size of the cassette.
Structures Demonstrated (Figure 23-39B) – Lateral projection of the elbow joint to
   include distal humerus and proximal forearm.
Additional Comments — A comparable projection can be obtained by extreme internal
   rotation of the forearm. In this position, the hand will be pronated and the CR is
   vertical and centered to the cassette.

AP Projection of the Shoulder Girdle

Cassette Size — 10 in. × 12 in. grid cassette.
Position of Part (Figure 23-40A)
   • The grid cassette is placed crosswise beneath the patient, with the top of the
     cassette approximately 1 1/2 in. above the shoulder.
   • The hand should be supinated.
   • The midline of the cassette is centered midway between sternum and humerus.

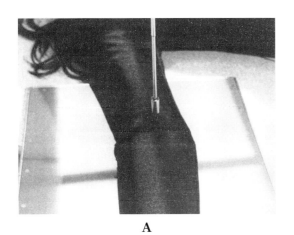
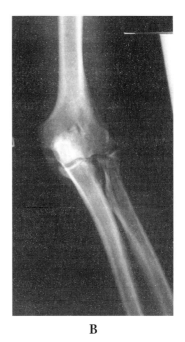

A   **B**

Figure 23-38   **A**: AP elbow position. **B**: AP elbow.

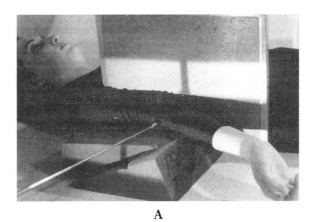

A

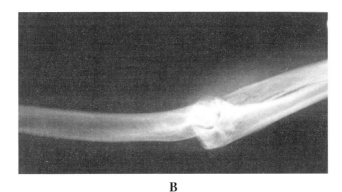

B

Figure 23-39   **A**: Cross-table lateral elbow position. **B**: Cross-table lateral elbow projection.

Central Ray
  • Direct the CR perpendicular to the midpoint of the longitudinal and horizontal axis of the grid cassette.
  • Collimate to the size of the cassette.
Structures Demonstrated (Figure 23-40B) — An AP projection of the shoulder girdle to include proximal humerus.

Lower Extremity

AP Projection of Foot

Cassette Size — 10 in. × 12 in. nongrid cassette.
Position of Part (Figure 23-41A)
  • Elevate the heel on a radiolucent sponge.
  • Place the midline of the cassette lengthwise against the sole of the foot.
  • The cassette may be supported by sandbags.
Central Ray
  • X-ray tube should be angled caudally enough to make the CR perpendicular to the cassette.

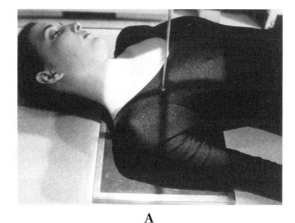

A

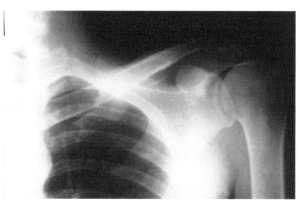

B

Figure 23-40   **A**: AP shoulder position. **B**: AP shoulder.

- Direct the CR to the midpoint of the longitudinal and horizontal axis of the cassette.
- Collimate to the size of the cassette.

Structures Demonstrated (Figure 23-41B) — AP projection of the foot and toes.

Cross-Table Lateral Projection of the Foot

Cassette Size — 10 in. × 12 in. nongrid cassette.
Position of Part (Figure 23-42A)
- Place the cassette lengthwise against the medial aspect of the foot.
- Heel should be elevated on a radiolucent sponge.
- The long axis of the foot should be centered to the middle of the cassette.

Central Ray
- Direct the horizontal beam perpendicular to the midpoint of the longitudinal and horizontal axis of the cassette.
- Collimate to the size of the cassette.

Structures Demonstrated (Figure 23-42B) — Lateral projection of the heel, foot, and toes.

AP Projection of the Knee

Cassette Size — 10 in. × 12 in. grid cassette.
Position of Part (Figure 23-43A)
- The grid cassette is placed lengthwise under the knee joint and is aligned with the long axis of the leg.

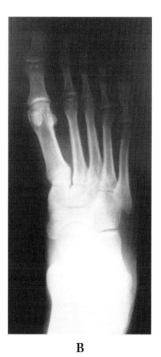

A   **B**

Figure 23-41   **A**: AP foot position. **B**: AP foot.

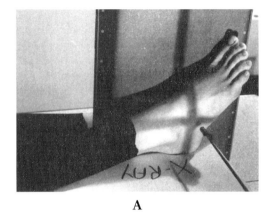

A

B

Figure 23-42   **A**: Cross-table lateral position of foot. **B**: Cross-table lateral projection of foot.

- The knee joint should be fully extended.
- The foot is maintained in a vertical position to achieve a true AP position.
- Center the horizontal axis of the grid cassette 1 in. below the patella (kneecap).

Central Ray
- Angle the CR 5° cephalad to enter at the midpoint of the longitudinal and horizontal axis of the cassette.
- Collimate to the size of the cassette.

Structures Demonstrated (Figure 23-43B) — AP projection of the knee joint to include distal femur and proximal tibia-fibula.

Cross-Table Lateral Projection of the Knee

Cassette Size — 10 in. × 12 in. grid cassette.
Position of Part (Figure 23-44A)
- The cassette is placed lengthwise between the knees.
- The fully extended knee joint should be elevated on a radiolucent sponge.
- The horizontal axis of the grid cassette is centered 1 in. below the patella.

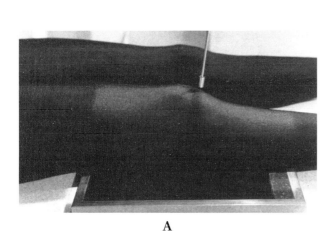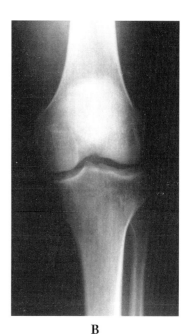

A   B

Figure 23-43   **A**: AP knee position. **B**: AP knee.

Central Ray — Direct the horizontal beam perpendicular to the midpoint of the cassette. Collimate to the size of the anatomical part.

Structures Demonstrated (Figure 23-44B) — A lateral projection of the knee joint to include proximal tibia-fibula and distal femur.

Vertebral Column

Positions demonstrating the thoracic and lumbar spine were described under the survey approach to radiographic positioning. This section will address positioning of the cervical spine.

AP Projection of the Cervical Spine

Cassette Size — 10 in. × 12 in. grid cassette.

Position of Part (Figure 23-45A)
- Place the grid cassette lengthwise beneath the neck.
- Place the upper border of the grid cassette 1 in. above the top of the ear.
- Center the MSP to the long axis of the cassette.
- To avoid rotation, adjust the MSP of the skull perpendicular to the grid cassette.
- Raise the chin as much as possible to avoid superimposition of the chin over the upper cervical vertebrae.

Central Ray — Direct the CR 15 to 20° cephalic. The CR enters the horizontal axis of the grid cassette. Note: the CR must be directed along the long axis of the grid lines.

Structures Demonstrated (Figure 23-45B) — An AP projection of the lower cervical vertebrae and the upper thoracic vertebrae.

A

B

Figure 23-44 **A**: Cross-table lateral knee position. **B**: Cross-table lateral knee projection.

Cross-Table Lateral of the Cervical Spine

Cassette Size — 10 in. × 12 in. grid cassette.
Position of Part (Figure 23-46A)
  • Place the cassette lengthwise next to the shoulder. Note: placement of the cassette next to the shoulder creates a space between the cervical spine and the shoulder (OID). Placement of the cassette in this manner is necessary to demonstrate all of the cervical vertebrae.
  • It is usually necessary to pull the arms downward to avoid superimposing the shoulders over C-6 and C-7.
  • Place the upper border of the grid cassette 1 1/2 in. above the top of the ear.
  • To avoid rotation, adjust the MSP of the skull perpendicular to the table.
  • The IPL should be perpendicular to the grid cassette. Collimate to the size of the grid cassette.
Structures Demonstrated (Figure 23-46B) — A lateral projection of the entire cervical spine.
Additional Comments — When pulling the arms down, care should be taken to exert equal pressure on both arms. Failure to do so will cause one shoulder to move upward, which will defeat the purpose of the maneuver. A SID of 72 in. is recommended for this projection.

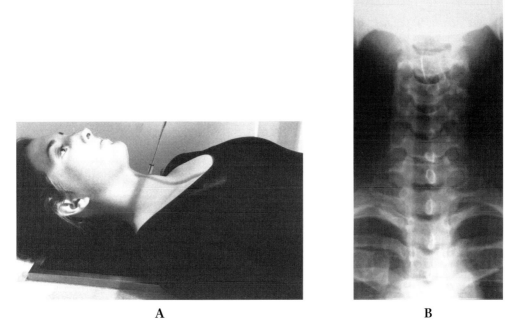

A   **B**

Figure 23-45   **A**: AP cervical spine position. **B**: AP cervical spine.

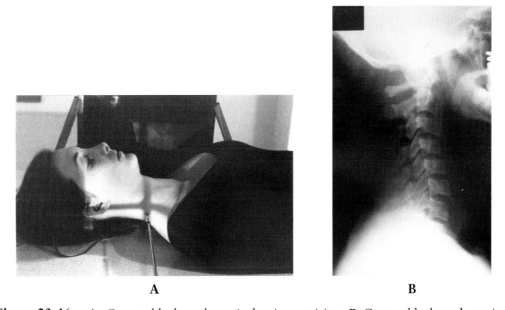

A   **B**

Figure 23-46   **A**: Cross-table lateral cervical spine position. **B**: Cross-table lateral cervical spine projection.

Facial Bones

AP Projection of Facial Bones

> *Cassette Size* — 10 in. × 12 in. grid cassette.
> *Position of Part* (Figure 23-47A)
> - Place the grid cassette lengthwise beneath the skull.
> - Place the upper border of the cassette 1 in. above the top of the skull.
> - The MSP is centered to the long axis of the grid cassette.
> - The MSP is perpendicular to the grid cassette.
> - The OML is perpendicular to the grid cassette.
>
> *Central Ray* — The CR is angled 15° cephalad to the midpoint of the cassette.[3] The CR enters the skull ½ in. above the bridge of the nose. Collimate to the size of the cassette. Note: the CR must be directed along the long axis of the grid lines.
>
> *Structures Demonstrated* (Figure 23-47B) — An AP projection of the facial bones. The petrous ridges are projected into the lower one-third of the orbit.

AP Axial Projection (Reverse Waters Position)

> *Cassette Size* — 10 in. × 12 in. grid cassette.
> *Position of Part* (Figure 23-48A)
> - Place the grid cassette lengthwise beneath the skull.
> - The MSP is centered to the long axis of the grid cassette.
> - The MSP is perpendicular to the grid cassette.
> - The IOML is perpendicular to the grid cassette.

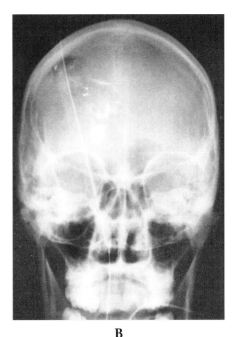

A   B

Figure 23-47   **A**: AP facial bone position. **B**: AP facial bone.

- The horizontal axis of the grid cassette is centered to the CR. Centered in this manner usually requires the upper end of the cassette to be approximately $2\frac{1}{2}$ in. above the top of the skull.

Central Ray
- Angle the CR 30° cephalic.[4] Note: the CR must be directed along the long axis of the grid lines.
- The CR enters the space between the nose and the upper teeth.
- The grid cassette is centered at the point the CR exits the skull.
- Collimate to the size of the grid cassette.

Structures Demonstrated (Figure 23-48B) — An AP survey projection of the facial bones.

Cross-Table Lateral Projection of the Facial Bones

Cassette Size — 10 in. × 12 in. grid cassette.

Position of Part (Figure 23-49A)
- The grid cassette is placed lengthwise against the side of the skull.
- The horizontal axis of the grid cassette is centered to the zygoma (cheek bone).
- The MSP is aligned parallel with the grid cassette.
- The IPL is aligned perpendicular to the grid cassette.
- The IOML is aligned parallel with the horizontal axis of the grid cassette.

Central Ray — Direct the horizontal beam perpendicular to the midpoint of the grid cassette. Collimate to the size of the grid cassette.

Structures Demonstrated (Figure 23-49B) — A lateral projection of the facial bones.

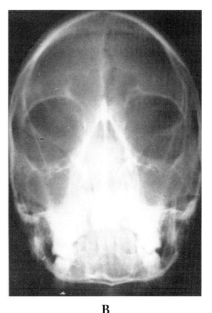

A   B

Figure 23-48   **A**: AP axial position of facial bones (reverse Waters). **B**: AP axial projection facial bones (reverse Waters).

 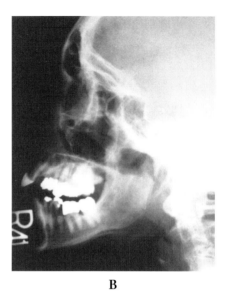

A   B

Figure 23-49   **A**: Cross-table lateral position of facial bones. **B**: Cross-table lateral projection of facial bones.

Mandible

AP Axial Projection of the Mandible

Cassette Size — 10 in. × 12 in. grid cassette.
Position of Part (Figure 23-50A)
- The grid cassette is placed lengthwise beneath the skull.
- Place the upper border of the grid cassette at the top of the ear.
- The MSP is centered to the long axis of the grid cassette.
- The MSP is perpendicular to the grid cassette.
- The OML is aligned perpendicular to the grid cassette.

Central Ray — Angle the CR 10 to 15° caudally. The CR should pass through the junction of the lips. Center the CR to the horizontal axis of the grid cassette. Collimate to the size of the grid cassette. Note: the CR must be directed along the long axis of the grid lines.

Structures Demonstrated (Figure 23-50B) — A survey projection of the mandible including the rami, angle, and body.

Cross-Table Oblique of the Mandible[5]

Cassette Size — 10 in. × 12 in. nongrid cassette.
Position of Part (Figure 23-51A)
- The cassette is placed vertically (12 in. × 10 in.) next to the side of the mandible of interest (right or left side). The head is tilted approximately 15°. Tilting the

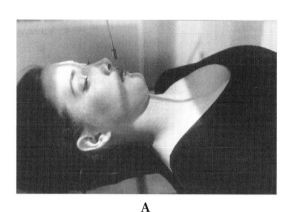
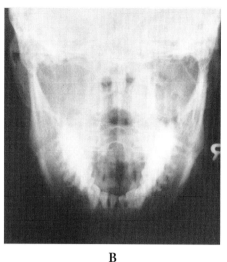

| A | B |

Figure 23-50   **A**: AP axial position of mandible. **B**: AP axial projection of mandible.

head causes the mandible to move a slight distance from the cassette. Tilting the head assists in reducing superimposition of the mandibular rami.
- Center the cassette to include the structures between the chin and the ear of the side of interest.
- Raise the chin to move the mandible away from the neck.
- The MSP is vertical.

Central Ray — The horizontal beam is directed 15 to 20° cephalically to the midpoint of the cassette. Note: both obliques are taken for comparison. Collimate to the size of the part.

Structures Demonstrated (Figure 23-51B) — An oblique projection of the mandibular body and ramus of the side next to the cassette.

Cross-Table Lateral of the Mandible

Cassette Size — 10 in. × 12 in. grid cassette.
Position of Part (Figure 23-52A)
- The grid cassette is placed vertically (12 in. × 10 in.) against the side of interest.
- The long axis of the grid cassette is centered to the junction of the lips.
- The MSP is aligned parallel with the grid cassette.
- The IPL is perpendicular to the grid cassette.
- The IOML is aligned parallel with the long axis of the grid cassette.

Central Ray — Direct the horizontal beam perpendicular to the midpoint of the cassette. Collimate to the size of the part.

Structures Demonstrated (Figure 23-52B) — A lateral projection of the entire mandible.

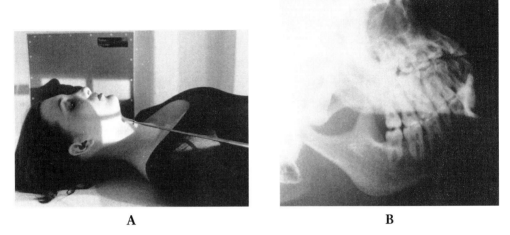

Figure 23-51   **A**: Cross-table oblique position of mandible. **B**: Cross-table oblique projection of mandible.

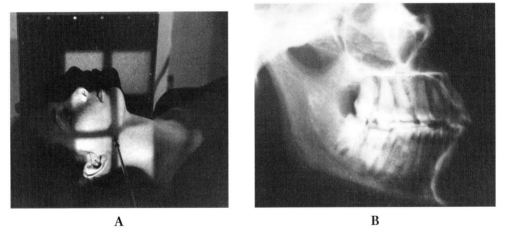

Figure 23-52   **A**: Cross-table lateral position of mandible. **B**: Cross-table lateral projection of mandible.

References

1. Ballinger, P. W., *Merrill's Atlas of Radiographic Positions and Radiologic Procedures*, Vol. I, 8th ed., Mosby-Yearbook, St. Louis, 1995, 290.

2. Ballinger, P. W., *Merrill's Atlas of Radiographic Positions and Radiologic Procedures*, Vol. II, 8th ed., Mosby-Yearbook, St. Louis, 1995, 246.

3. Ballinger, P. W., *Merrill's Atlas of Radiographic Positions and Radiologic Procedures*, Vol. II, 8th ed., Mosby-Yearbook, St. Louis, 1995, 244.

4. Ballinger, P. W., *Merrill's Atlas of Radiographic Positions and Radiologic Procedures*, Vol. II, 8th ed., Mosby-Yearbook, St. Louis, 1995, 308.

5. Swallow, R. A. and Naylor, E., Eds., *Clark's Positioning in Radiography*, 11th ed., Aspen, Rockville, MD, 1986, 243.

Bibliography

Ballinger, P. W., *Merrill's Atlas of Radiographic Positions and Radiologic Procedures,* 8th ed., Mosby-Yearbook, St. Louis, 1995.

Bontrager, K. L., *Radiographic Positioning and Related Anatomy,* 3rd ed., Mosby-Yearbook, St. Louis, 1993.

Bushong, S. C., *Radiologic Science for Technologists,* 4th ed., C. V. Mosby, St. Louis, 1988.

Carlton, R. R. and Adler, A. M., *Principles of Radiographic Imaging,* Delmar Publishers, Albany, NY, 1992.

Curry, T. S., Dowdey, J. E., and Murry, R. C., *Christensen's Introduction to the Physics of Diagnostic Radiology,* 3rd ed., Lea and Febiger, Philadelphia, 1984.

Dowd, S. and Wilson, G., *Encyclopedia of Radiographic Positioning,* W. B. Saunders, Philadelphia, 1995.

Dennis, C. A., May, C. R., and Eisenberg, R. L., *Radiographic Positioning Pocket Manual,* Little, Brown, Boston, 1993.

Meschan, I., *Radiographic Positioning and Related Anatomy,* W. B. Saunders, Philadelphia, 1978.

Swallow, R. A. and Naylor, E., Eds., *Clark's Positioning in Radiography,* 11th ed., Aspen, Rockville, MD, 1986.

Thomas, C. L., Ed., *Taber's Cyclopedic Medical Dictionary,* 16th ed., F. A. Davis, Philadelphia, 1985.

Thompson, T., *Cahoon's Formulating X-Ray Techniques,* 9th ed., Duke University Press, Durham, NC, 1979.

Wallace, J. E., *Radiographic Exposure Principles and Practice,* F. A. Davis, Philadelphia, 1995.

Production of the Radiographic Image

24

CHARLES W. NEWELL, ED.D., R.T.(R)
CHUCRI M. JALKH, B.S., R.T.(R)

Contents

Introduction

Proper execution of those positioning methods described in the preceding chapter is the first step in producing a quality radiograph. The next step, which is equally important, is to apply the correct exposure factors necessary to yield a radiograph possessing proper density and contrast. Without proper density and contrast, the usefulness of correct positioning methods is markedly diminished. This chapter will therefore address the fundamental factors affecting radiographic quality, and provide suggestions for establishing exposure factors for post-mortem radiography.

Factors Controlling Image Quality

The factors which control image quality are density, contrast, detail, shape distortion, and magnification distortion. All of these factors are essential to produce a quality radiograph. It is therefore important to understand the meaning of each factor, and its role in the formation of the radiographic image.

Density

Density refers to the overall blackness of a radiograph. If there is too much density, the image will be overexposed. If there is too little density, the image will be underexposed. In either case, the quality of the radiograph will be diminished. A radiograph must therefore exhibit a proper amount of density to demonstrate anatomical structures.

There are numerous factors which produce changes in density, and the reasons for such changes depend on the factor involved. There are several factors which affect density simply by increasing the quantity of the factor. Thus, if the quantity of a given factor is increased, density is increased. Conversely, when the quantity of one factor decreases, density will decrease. Some examples of factors affecting density in this way are as follows:

1. Exposure factors (mA, kVp, and exposure time)
2. Distance from the x-ray tube to the film
3. Size of collimator setting
4. Tissue thickness
5. Developing temperature
6. Scatter radiation
7. Pathological conditions

Contrast

Contrast is the difference between adjacent densities on a radiograph. In short, it is the difference between the black, white, and gray shades on a radiograph. The significance of contrast is that it enables one to see the difference between bone, soft tissue and other body structures. Since contrast is essentially the difference between shades of density, the same factors which affect density also affect contrast. Therefore, any change in density will usually affect contrast.

Detail

Detail is the sharpness of an image as recorded on a radiograph. Detail determines how well a small structure or minute fracture line will be visualized. Detail is often referred to as definition or radiographic sharpness. These terms are synonymous. Factors affecting detail are as follows:

1. Focal spot size
2. Distance

3. Object film distance
4. Motion
5. Screen speed

Of the factors listed above, two require further comment because they are variables which are likely to arise whenever post-mortem radiography is performed. As previously indicated, distance literally means the space or distance between the x-ray tube and the film. Since the x-ray tube is the source of x-rays and the film is the image receptor, distance is referred to as source image-receptor distance. The acronym for distance is SID, which is used throughout this and the previous chapters when referring to distance.

It is also common to find instances where a space or distance exists between the patient (object) and the film. This form of distance is referred to as object image receptor distance, and the customary acronym is OID.

The important point to be made regarding SID and OID is that both control magnification which, in turn, affects detail. Due to this relationship, one should always maintain the OID at the "least" possible distance while maintaining SID at the "greatest" possible distance. It should be noted, however, that all images possess some degree of magnification, even when they are produced under the most favorable conditions. In recognition of this fact, distance parameters have been established to standardize the degree of magnification for all radiographic examinations. Thus, absent equipment limitations or other obstacles, chest radiographs are typically radiographed at a 72-in. SID, and other body parts are radiographed at a 40-in. SID. As for OID, the practice of maintaining OID at an absolute minimum still holds true.

Shape Distortion

Shape distortion refers to instances where the shape of an anatomical structure, as projected on a radiograph, differs from its normal shape. In other words, the image is a misrepresentation of the true shape of a body part. Factors which control shape distortion are as follows:[1]

1. Angulation of the x-ray tube to the film/cassette
2. Angulation of the body part to the film/cassette
3. Angulation of the cassette/film to the body part

Shape distortion arising from angulation of the body to the film is less apt to occur because oblique projections are not routinely performed in post-mortem radiography. However, AP projections are routinely performed, and therefore careful attention should be paid to ensure the central ray is perpendicular to the film. Otherwise the image will be elongated. In addition, one should make sure the central ray is centered to both the longitudinal and transverse axis of the part being radiographed. Centering problems can be reduced by centering the body part to the cassette, and then centering the central ray to the center of the cassette. Off-centering not only produces shape distortion, but it can also cause grid cut-off when grids are employed.

Since lateral projections are employed in post-mortem radiography, attention must also be paid to proper alignment of the body part to the film. This can be easily achieved by making sure the body part and the cassette are always parallel to one another. Failure to maintain the parallel relationship between body part and cassette often yields an image that is foreshortened.

Before leaving the subject of shape distortion, it should be noted that there are numerous occasions when shape distortion is used to better visualize a body part. Angling the central ray and oblique projections are two examples.

Magnification Distortion

As the term suggests, magnification refers to the enlargement of an anatomical part as viewed on a radiograph. Factors controlling magnification are

1. SID
2. OID

Previous mention was made of the fact that all radiographic images possess some degree of magnification. To avoid greater magnification, one should adhere to the established distance parameters (72 in. for chest exams and 40 in. for all others), and maintain the OID to the least possible distance. It should be noted that the effect of OID on magnification is much greater than SID. Therefore, while there is some margin of error for SID, there is very little for OID.

Exposure Factors

Essential Exposure Factors

The fundamental components of an x-ray unit were previously described in Chapter 22. One of the components not discussed was the x-ray control panel (Figure 24-1). The control panel enables one to select or change exposure factors by manipulating various control devices. The exposure factors regulated via the control panel are milliamperage (mA), exposure time (s), and kilovoltage (kVp). These factors are discussed below.

Milliamperage
Milliamperage (mA) determines the quantity of electrical current flowing through an x-ray tube during exposure. Since mA is a quantitative factor, it controls the quantity of x-rays produced which, in turn, affects radiographic density. As the mA is increased, density is increased. When mA is decreased, density will decrease.

Fixed radiographic units have a wide range of mA settings, which are adjusted to meet the needs of a particular examination or exposure technique. Typical mA settings include 50, 100, 200, 300, 400, 500, 600, 700, 800, and 1000. In contrast, mobile x-ray units have fewer mA settings. In fact, many contemporary mobile units have a fixed or nonvariable mA. In these units, density is usually controlled or varied by a timer selector or by a milliampere-second selector.

Timer Control
As one might imagine, the timer control determines the length or duration of the exposure. Similar to mA, as exposure time is lengthened film density is increased, and vice versa. Like mA settings, the timer control has a wide range of settings. For example, timer

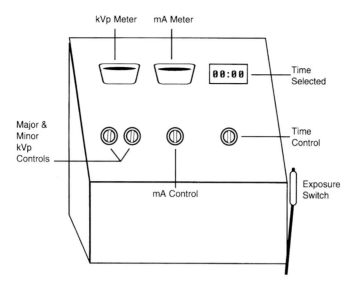

Figure 24-1 Schematic drawing of a control panel.

selections may range from a short exposure time of 0.016 s up to 1 or more seconds. For some x-ray units, including modern mobile units, the manual timer selector has been omitted. In these units, the exposure time is automatically set as one changes the milliampere-second selector. Timer selections may be expressed in one of three modes on the control panel: fractions, decimals, or milliseconds. However, if a timer selector is present on the control panel of a mobile unit, it is unlikely to be a millisecond timer.

Of the three modes listed above, millisecond settings are not useful when calculating milliampere-seconds, which is described later in this section. When confronted with this type of timer, one must convert milliseconds to a decimal or fraction equivalent. This is accomplished as follows:

1. Examples of milliseconds (ms) include 1, 2.5, 3, 4, 5, 6, 10, 20, 50, 100, etc.
2. Since a millisecond (ms) is 1/1000 of a second, placement of the ms number over 1000 converts the millisecond to a fraction. For example, 10 ms can be expressed as 10/1000 of a second. Thus, 50 ms is the same as 50/1000 of a second, and 100 ms is the same as 100/1000 of a second, and so forth.
3. As can be seen, conversion of a millisecond to a fraction often yields an unwieldy fraction. To simplify matters, milliseconds can be converted to decimal equivalents by dividing the ms number by 1000. Using the examples above, 10/1000 becomes 0.01 s, 50/1000 is 0.05 s, and 100/1000 is 0.10 s. As these examples suggest, placing a decimal point three places to the left of the last millisecond number produces the same effect as dividing the millisecond number by 1000.

Kilovoltage Control

Kilovoltage controls the penetrating ability of the x-ray beam. The penetrating ability of x-rays is often referred to as the quality of the x-ray beam. In general, higher kVp is applied to thicker and/or more dense structures, whereas lower kVp is used for thinner and/or less dense structures. Although the function of kVp is to control penetration, it also plays a secondary role in the production of radiographic density. Kilovoltage also controls the amount of scatter radiation produced in a given exposure, which can have a degrading effect on radiographic contrast.

Kilovoltage settings on the control panel typically range from 40 to 120 kVp. There are usually two kVp control selectors. One selector is designated as a major control and allows changes to be made in increments of 10 kVp. The other selector is referred to as a minor control, and it provides changes in increments of 1 to 2 kVp. Some mobile units have a single kVp control which allows changes in increments of 5 kVp, e.g., 50, 55, 60, 65, etc. Despite fewer selection alternatives, these units provide sufficient settings to achieve the proper level of kVp.

Exposure Switch

While the exposure switch is not a true factor affecting density and contrast, it is included in this discussion because it is an essential part of the control panel. The purpose of the exposure switch is to initiate the x-ray exposure. The exposure switch may be located directly on the surface of the control panel or wired directly to a detachable cord suspended from the control panel. Some x-ray units employ two switches to initiate the exposure, while others employ a single switch. Regardless of the number of switches employed, they require a two-step process to initiate the exposure. The first step requires the rotor component of the switch to be depressed. When the rotor switch is depressed, a whirring or high-pitched sound will develop in the x-ray tube. The next step requires the exposure component of the switch to be depressed, at which time x-rays are produced. Care should be taken to avoid depressing the rotor switch unnecessarily, as this will reduce the useful life of the tube.

Exposure and Distance

Although source image-receptor distance (SID) plays a significant role in affecting image magnification, it can also affect radiographic density. Briefly stated, when all of the other exposure factors (kVp, mA, s) remain constant, density can be **increased** when the SID is **reduced**, and **decreased** when the SID is **increased**. While the preceding statement is accurate, small changes in distance will not significantly affect density, e.g., 6 to 8 in.. However, since distance parameters have been established over the years for routine radiographic examinations, one should adhere to established distances to avoid magnification-related problems. Moreover, exposure factor recommendations in this chapter are based on specific distances.

Calculating Milliampere-Seconds

A milliampere-second (mAs) is the product of mA and exposure time. Collectively, mA and exposure time control the quantity of x-rays produced. As a result, mA and exposure time directly control radiographic density. The acronym mAs will be used throughout this chapter when reference is made to milliampere-seconds.

Since mAs is the product of mA and exposure time, mAs is determined by the formula $mA \times s = mAs$. This formula is applied in the following examples.

Time in Fractions
200 mA × 3/20 s = 30 mAs
300 mA × 1/60 s = 5 mAs
100 mA × 1/10 s = 10 mAs
200 mA × 1 s = 200 mAs

Time in Decimals
300 mA × 0.3 s = 90 mAs
100 mA × 0.1 s = 10 mAs
200 mA × 0.5 s = 100 mAs
400 mA × 0.3 s = 120 mAs

Time in Milliseconds
200 mA × 100 ms (0.1 s) = 20 mAs
100 mA × 50 ms (0.05 s) = 5 mAs
400 mA × 20 ms (0.02 s) = 8 mAs
600 mA × 4 ms (0.004 s) = 2.4 mAs

Note: milliseconds must be converted to fractional or decimal equivalents to calculate mAs.

As previously indicated, some x-ray units employ a mAs selector in the place of separate mA and time controls. In these units, the mAs selector is simply adjusted to the proper level of mAs. For other units, one must select the mA and exposure time to produce the correct mAs. Regardless of the system employed, the correct mAs must be selected to achieve the proper radiographic density.

Adapting Exposure Factors

While KvP, mA, time, and SID are the primary factors affecting density and contrast, there are secondary factors which affect density and contrast as well. Two secondary factors which often vary in terms of their effect upon radiographic density are grids and screens. Since screens differ in accordance with their speed, one must adapt the mAs from one screen speed to another screen speed to produce the same density. In the same way, there are different types of grids, and therefore the mAs must be changed when different grids are employed to maintain equivalent density. Understanding the process of changing exposure factors to accommodate differences in screens and grids will enable one to adapt exposure factors whenever changes such as these occur.

In addition to adapting exposure factors to accommodate differences in screens and grids, one must also understand how and when to adjust mAs and kVp. Differences in part thickness and density of an anatomical structure are two of the more common reasons why kVp and/or mAs must be adjusted. Changing the kVp or mAs is also the way to correct over- or underexposed films when radiographs must be repeated. Methods used to adapt exposure factors to various circumstances are described below.

Screen Conversions

The speed of intensifying screens was typically designated as slow, medium, and high speed. This designation no longer holds true since there are more than three speeds available. As a result, the speed of an intensifying screen is designated by a specific number. For example, the medium-speed screen is now identified by the number 100. The number 100 is now the standard against which all intensifying screens are compared. Thus, a 200-speed screen is twice as fast as the 100-speed screen, and a 50-speed screen is one-half the speed of a 100-speed screen. Some of the screen speeds available today are shown in Table 24-1.

Table 24-1 Speed Values and Conversion Factors

Speed Values	Conversion Factors
50	0.5
100	1
200	2
400	4
600	6
800	8

Modified with permission from *Kodak Health Sciences Publication*, Eastman Kodak Company, Rochester, NY.

The speed values listed in Table 24-1 can be used to match radiographic density when changing from one screen speed to another. This is accomplished by employing the conversion factors listed in Table 24-1. The conversion factors were obtained by converting the 50 speed value to 0.5, and deleting the zeros in the remaining speed values. The conversion factors are placed in a formula to calculate screen speed changes as shown below.

$$\text{Original mAs} \times \frac{\text{Original Screen Value}}{\text{New Screen Value}}$$

Examples of screen conversions are shown below:

1. Original factors: 20 mAs employing a 100-speed screen
   New factor: 50-speed screen

$$20 \text{ mAs} \times \frac{1}{0.5} = 40 \text{ mAs}$$

   The mAs is **doubled** to maintain the same density.
2. Original factors: 10 mAs employing a 200-speed screen
   New factor: 400 speed screen

$$10 \text{ mAs} \times \frac{2}{4} = 5 \text{ mAs}$$

The mAs is **reduced** by one-half to maintain the same density.
3. Original factors: 30 mAs employing a 50 speed screen
   New factor: 200-speed screen

$$30 \text{ mAs} \times \frac{0.5}{2} = 7.5 \text{ mAs}$$

The mAs is **reduced** by a factor of 4 to maintain the same density.

As one can see, as the screen speed value increases the mAs must be reduced to maintain the same density, and vice versa. If the speed of the screen being used is not known, one should contact a representative from a commercial film/screen company.

Grid Conversions

Grids differ from one another in accordance with their grid ratio. Grid ratio is essentially a ratio of the height of the lead strips to the distance between the lead strips. The distance between the lead strips is actually the interspace, which is filled with radiolucent material. The relationship between lead lines and interspaces is expressed as a ratio, such as 6:1, 12:1, etc. The ratio of a grid is printed on the front of the grid. An important point to remember is higher-ratio grids absorb more scatter radiation than lower-ratio grids. Common grid ratios are shown in Table 24-2.

Table 24-2   Grid Ratios and Conversion Factors

Grid Ratios	Conversion Factors
No grid	1
5:1	2.5
6:1	3
8:1	4
10:1	4.5
12:1	5
16:1	6

Modified with permission from *Characteristics and Applications of X-Ray Grids,* Liebel-Flarsheim Company, Cincinnati, OH.

Although higher-ratio grids absorb more scatter radiation, they also require more x-ray exposure (mAs) to yield the same density when compared to lower-ratio grids. In fact, grids of different ratios require different amounts of mAs to produce the same density. In addition, whenever the exposure factors applied to a grid must, for whatever reason, be applied directly to a screen (no grid), the mAs must always be reduced. When variables such as these are encountered, one must change the mAs to maintain the same density. This can be achieved by applying the conversion factors in Table 24-2. The formula for grid conversions is quite similar to the one applied to screen conversions. The formula is expressed as follows:

$$\text{Original mAs} \times \frac{\text{New Grid}}{\text{Original Grid}}$$

Examples of grid conversions are shown below:

1. Original factors: 30 mAs employing a 6:1 grid
    New factor: 12:1 grid

$$30 \text{ mAs} \times \frac{5}{3} = 50 \text{ mAs}$$

    The mAs is **increased** by 20 to maintain the same density.
2. Original factors: 10 mAs employing a 5:1 grid
    New factor: no grid

$$10 \text{ mAs} \times \frac{1}{2.5} = 4 \text{ mAs}$$

    The mAs is **reduced** by 6 to maintain the same density.
3. Original factors: 50 mAs employing an 8:1 grid
    New factor: 16:1 grid

$$50 \text{ mAs} \times \frac{6}{4} = 75 \text{ mAs}$$

    The mAs is **increased** by 25 to maintain the same density.

The examples above illustrate that grids with different ratios cannot be interchanged without making appropriate changes in mAs. However, one can confidently utilize a variety of both screens and grids by applying the mAs conversion factors for screens and grids.

Milliampere-Second and Kilovoltage Adjustments

Both mAs and kVp can be adjusted to accommodate a variety of exposure factor needs. Examples include correcting for over- or underexposed radiographs and for the numerous variations which exist amongst patients. Since there is a direct relationship between mAs and density, there are a few fundamental considerations to keep in mind:

1. If the mAs is doubled, the density will be doubled. If the mAs is tripled, the density will be tripled, etc. For example, if 50 mAs is changed to 100 mAs, the density will be doubled. In the same way, if 50 mAs is changed to 150 mAs, the density will be three times greater.
2. If the mAs is cut in half, the density will be reduced by one-half. If the mAs is reduced by a factor of 3, the density will be reduced to one-third of the original, etc. For example, if 50 mAs is changed to 25 mAs, the density will be reduced by one-half. Similarly, if 50 mAs is reduced to 16 mAs, the density will be decreased by two-thirds.

The question of how much to increase or decrease the density in a given situation can only be answered once one has acquired sufficient experience in making mAs adjustments. However, it is important to note that it requires a **minimum** change of **30%** in mAs to see a visible change in density. This is referred to as the 30% rule.[2] Examples of the 30% rule are shown below. (**Note: Only the mAs is changed.**)

1. If an exposure of 50 mAs produces a radiograph that is slightly underexposed, what is the **minimum** amount of mAs necessary to correct the image?

$$30\% \times 50 \quad = 15$$
$$50 + 15 \quad\quad = 65 \text{ mAs (the new mAs)}$$

2. If an exposure of 100 mAs produces a radiograph that is slightly overexposed, what is the **minimum** amount of mAs necessary to correct the image?

$$30\% \times 100 \quad = 30$$
$$100 - 30 \quad\quad = 70 \text{ mAs (the new mAs)}$$

In actual practice, the majority of mAs changes will be greater than 30% (50%, 100%, etc.). Thus, 30% is simply the **minimum** starting point for making exposure changes using mAs.

The kVp can also be used to make changes in density. While there are other ways to effect changes in density using kVp, the authors have found the 20% kVp rule to be an effective method. The 20% rule is based on the premise that a 20% (0.20) increase in kVp will produce a doubling effect on density. Likewise, if the kVp is reduced by 20%, the density will be reduced by one half. Other variations in the 20% rule include increasing or decreasing the kVp by 10% (0.10) to yield a 50% increase/decrease in density. While a 5% (0.05) change in kVp will produce a 25% change in density, such a change has little significance in the clinical setting. Examples of the 20% rule are shown below. (**Note: only the kVp is changed.**)

1. A radiograph employing 10 mAs at 70 kVp is judged to be 100% overexposed. Solution:

$$70 \text{ kVp} \times 0.20 = 14$$
$$70 - 14 \quad\quad\quad = 56$$

The new exposure factors are 10 mAs and 56 kVp.
2. A radiograph employing 20 mAs at 80 kVp is judged to be 50% underexposed. Solution:

$$80 \text{ kVp} \times 0.10 = 8$$
$$80 + 8 \quad\quad\quad\quad = 88$$

The new exposure factors are 20 mAs and 88 kVp.

While the 20% rule can be used to effect changes in density, one should understand that changing the kVp affects image contrast. Significant changes in image contrast may be considered objectionable under certain circumstances. In addition, anatomical structures require a minimum or effective kVp. Effective kVp refers to the minimum kVp required to penetrate a given structure.[3] Thus, the 20% rule must be applied with effective kVp in mind. As with mAs changes, the amount of kVp change applied to a given situation can only be determined following sufficient practical experience.

Structure Thickness and Density as Factors in Radiographic Density

As the term suggests, structure thickness refers to the thickness of a body structure. Variations in body thickness are particularly evident in the chest and abdomen. In general, thicker structures require greater exposure factors. For exposure factor determinations, thickness is measured in centimeters by employing a measuring device referred to as a caliper (Figure 24-2). The technique chart presented later in this chapter provides exposure factors which are based, in part, on the measurements of anatomical structures. Some areas will list specific measurements while others will list measurements in ranges of centimeters. To utilize the chart effectively, one must correctly measure the structure. The correct procedure to follow is to measure the area of the part through which the central ray will pass. This area is typically placed in the center of the cassette.

With experience, it will not be necessary to measure parts such as the hands, wrist, feet, etc. unless there is an obvious decrease or increase in a body part. One should always measure the chest and abdomen, including thoracic and lumbar spine examinations. The density of a structure refers to how close the atoms or molecules of a structure are bound together, i.e., the compactness of a structure. Hence, bone has a higher/greater density

Figure 24-2   Radiographic caliper.

than fat. Depending on the quantity of each, muscle, blood, and water often exhibit similar densities. Air has the lowest density. Higher-density structures absorb more x-rays and require more exposure (kVp and mAs) to yield satisfactory radiographic densities. The opposite is true of less dense structures. The thickness and density of a structure are major considerations in the selection of exposure factors. This is particularly true in post-mortem radiography where the lungs are not inflated with air, or instances where the tissues are gas-filled due to decomposition or dehydrated from incineration. Variables such as these require special consideration. A few suggestions are offered below.

1. Despite the other suggestions which follow, one should understand that it is virtually impossible to determine or quantify many of the variables which may arise based on a visual inspection of a cadaver. With this in mind, it is strongly recommended that one take a single projection, and then review the radiograph to evaluate what changes, if any, should be applied to the succeeding radiographs. One can then apply the previously described mAs or kVp rules to make the appropriate corrections. A film taken for this purpose is referred to as a scout film. Providing one employs the corrections properly, the scout film is the best method for ensuring the remaining radiographs are correctly exposed. The time spent in reviewing the results of the scout film will, in the long run, reduce the time for the overall procedure by decreasing the number of repeat films.

2. With less certainty than the scout film method, there are some rules of thumb which can be helpful in establishing exposure factors for a number of physical variables as described below.

   a. For a lung containing water or other fluid, one can increase the original mAs by 35 to 40%, or increase the original kVp by 6 to 8.

   b. Freezing greatly increases tissue density and causes "ice artifacts".[4] If possible, bodies should be thawed before radiography. Trial exposure on frozen tissue should begin with a 40 to 50% increase in mAs or an increase of 8 to 10 kVp.

   c. For gas-filled tissues, one can decrease the original mAs by 30%, or decrease the kVp by 5 to 6.

   d. Incinerated and/or dehydrated body parts require a decrease in the original mAs of 30 to 40%, or a decrease in the original kVp of 6 to 8.

   e. Denuded bones or skeletal remains require a substantial reduction in mAs. Two suggestions are offered below:

   • All extremities require the mAs to be reduced by one-half of the usual mAs applied to extremities. A nongrid cassette is employed for all exposures.

   • The remaining skeletal parts can be radiographed employing a mAs ranging from 2 to 4. A nongrid cassette is employed for all exposures.

   • The suggested kVp range for all exposures is 60 to 70.

Single-Phase and Three-Phase Generators

In the event a three-phase generator is used for post-mortem radiography, a simple conversion method can be employed: to convert single-phase exposure factors to a three-phase x-ray generator, simply reduce the original mAs by one half. Thus, the mAs for a three-phase generator will be one-half that of a single-phase generator.

Technique Chart

The exposure factors listed on the technique chart below match the positions/projections described in the preceding chapter. The exposure factors were developed to meet the needs of a particular radiographic unit. It is doubtful this chart, or any other technique chart, will completely satisfy the exposure requirements for all conditions or all x-ray units. This is particularly true in light of the previous discussion regarding structure thickness and density. Thus, the technique chart should be considered only as a guide. In short, it is the beginning point from which the medical examiner assistant can formulate his/her own exposure factors. Hence, the suggestion of taking a scout film is equally applicable to the technique chart.

Prior to using the technique chart, one should make note of the type of generator used, screen speed, and grid ratio. Any differences between these factors and those employed at another site can be equalized by applying those conversion factors discussed in this chapter, e.g., screen values, grid conversions, etc. Differences in equipment performance can also be equalized by applying mAs and kVp adjustments. However, the suggested SID should not be changed. Once all of the conversions are made, any further changes should be made by changing either the mAs or kVp, but not both.

Finally, it should be noted that the chart is divided into anatomical regions. Adjacent to each region is a listing of projections appropriate for a specific region. The mAs and kVp listings are based on measurements of the thickness of an anatomical structure. The measurements are listed as a range of centimeters, which correspond to a specific projection. The measurements listed for each anatomical region usually vary when the projection changes. Should the thickness of a part to be radiographed measure above or below the centimeter ranges listed, one can increase or decrease the kVp by 2 for each centimeter of variation. For example, if a structure measures 12 cm and the listed centimeter range is 8 to 10, the kVp can be increased by 4 to accommodate the difference in thickness. One would subtract 4 kVp if the structure measured 6 cm. Hence, kVp should be varied by 2 kVp/cm to accommodate changes in thickness.

The technique chart below was prepared using the following equipment:

- Single-phase x-ray unit
- 400 Screen/film system
- 8:1 Grid with 103 lines per in.

Film Identification

Film identification refers to the placement of information on a radiograph which serves to distinguish one patient from another. Film identification is also used to determine which extremity (right or left) was radiographed, or to indicate a patient's right or left side. Proper film identification plays an important role when older studies must be compared to more recent examinations. In this regard, film identification is an inherent part of the record-keeping system. Examples of data ideally included in film identification are listed below.

1. Date of examination
2. File, case, or accession number
3. Name (if known)

TECHNIQUE CHART

Region	Projection	Cm. Range	mAs	kVp	Grid	SID
Hand and Wrist	AP/PA	3-5	3	55-58	No	40"
	Lateral	3-6	3	60-62	No	40"
Forearm	AP	6-8	3	62-64	No	40"
	Lateral	7-9	3	64-68	No	40"
Humerus	AP	6-10	20	62-66	Yes	40"
	Lateral	6-10	20	66-70	Yes	40"
Shoulder	AP	10-14	20	64-66	Yes	40"
Foot	AP	5-8	3	60-62	No	40"
	CTL	6-9	3	64-66	No	40"
Tibia-Fibula	AP	9-13	3	75-78	No	48"
	CTL	8-12	3	72-76	No	48"
Knee	AP	10-13	20	66-70	Yes	40"
	CTL	9-12	20	62-66	Yes	40"
Femur	AP	15-18	25	72	Yes	40"
	CTL	14-17	25	70	Yes	40"
Hip	AP	15-20	40	76	Yes	40"
		21-25	60	76		
		26-31	100	80		
	CTL	23-28	125	85	Yes	40"
Pelvis	AP	15-20	40	76	Yes	40"
		21-25	70	76		
		26-31	125	80		
Lumbar Spine	AP	15-20	50	72	Yes	40"
		21-25	100	76		
		26-31	200	80		
	CTL	20-25	100	80	Yes	40"
		26-30	200	85		
		31-36	300	85		
Thoracic Spine	AP	15-20	50	75	Yes	40"
		21-25	100	78		
		26-31	150	80		
	CTL	19-24	75	80	Yes	40"
		25-31	150	80		
		32-37	225	85		
Cervical Spine	AP	10-13	20	68	Yes	40"
	CTL	10-13	20	90	Yes	72"
			10	90		48"
Chest	AP	15-20	4	100	Yes	48"
		21-25	8	100		
		26-31	12	100		
	CTL	19-24	12	100	Yes	48"
		25-31	24	100		
		32-37	36	100		
Abdomen	AP	15-20	40	72	Yes	40"
		21-25	80	76		
		26-31	150	80		
	CTL	20-25	80	80	Yes	40"
		26-30	160	85		

TECHNIQUE CHART (continued)

Region	Projection	Cm. Range	mAs	kVp	Grid	SID
		31-36	240	85		
Skull	AP	18-21	30	80	Yes	40"
	CTL	14-16	30	68	Yes	40"
	AP Axial CR 30° Caudal	18-21	30	85	Yes	40"
Facial Bones	AP CR 15° Cephalad	18-21	30	78	Yes	40"
	AP Axial CR 30° Cephalic	18-21	30	80	Yes	40"
	CTL	14-16	25	70	Yes	40"
Mandible	AP CR 15° Caudal	17-20	25	76	Yes	40"
	CTL Oblique	8-12	8	66	No	40"
	CTL	14-16	25	70	Yes	40"

Note: Should a grid be deleted from the above suggested exposure factors, one must apply the grid conversion factors discussed previously in this chapter.

4. Date of birth (if known)
5. Gender (if known)
6. Race (if known)
7. Name of institution
8. Initials or numbers indicating person making the radiograph

The radiograph may eventually be admitted as evidence and the entered information is part of the chain of evidence.

Since lead is radiopaque, lead letters are placed on the front of a cassette to indicate a variety of information, e.g., right or left side, right or left leg, etc. Lead numbers are used whenever it is necessary to record information in numerical form. Lead may also be fashioned into arrows. Lead arrows are used to indicate when a patient is upright or, in conjunction with an R or L, to indicate which side of the patient's body is directed upward.

There are several ways to get information onto the radiograph. Informational data can be printed or written (legibly) directly on the film with a permanent-ink ball-point or felt-tip pen or felt marker immediately after film processing. This will not prevent errors in side-to-side location of the body or part. That must be done before the film is exposed using lead markers (see above).

Lead letters and numbers can be used to enter informational data as the film is exposed. If "R" or "L" markers are included, then the problem of lateralization also is solved (Figure 24-3).

Data such as those listed above may be placed on a film by a device referred to as an identification printer or camera. The printer requires the use of cassettes with small metal windows located in the corner of the cassette. The window is referred to as an ID blocker. The ID blocker has two functions: to block or prevent x-rays from reaching the area of the film directly beneath the blocker, and to automatically open when placed in the printer. When the ID blocker is placed in the printer and opened, light passes through an index card, and information previously typed on the card is printed or flashed on the film. Figure 24-4 illustrates the ID printer system described above.

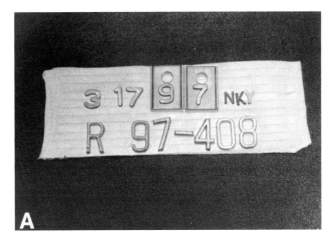

Figure 24-3   A: lead numbers placed on adhesive tape providing data (left to right, top to bottom): month, day, year, initials of person making the exposure, right side of body, accession number. The tape is placed face-down (sticky-side down) on top of the cassette before exposure. Exposed and processed films are viewed as if facing the patient or body. Therefore, if the lead data images are readable, **B**: the x-ray beam direction was posteroanterior; if the numbers and letters are backward, **C**: the beam was directed anteroposterior.

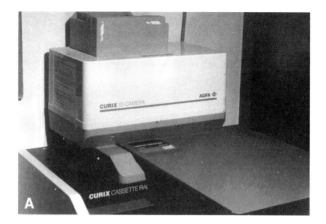

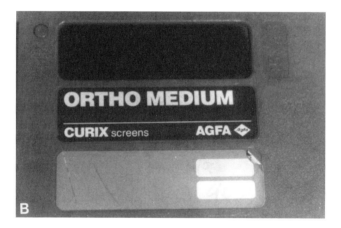

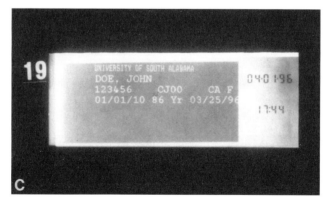

Figure 24-4 **A**: ID printer with cassette in place. **B**: ID blocker. **C**: exposed and processed film showing imprinted data.

While ID printers and lead letters serve an important function, they must be properly utilized to achieve their intended purpose. A few suggestions are offered below regarding the proper use of film identification devices.

1. Care must be exercised to prevent the placement of anatomical structures over identification markers or the placement of ID devices beneath anatomical areas of interest. Should either of these occur, anatomical structures may be hidden.

2. It is important to identify the correct side of a patient's body. In the supine or prone recumbent position, one can identify either the right or left side of the body. For instance, if one decides to mark the right side, then a right lead marker must be placed on the right side of the patient's body. Examinations which allow discretionary placement of film markers to indicate a patient's right or left side when the patient is in the prone or supine position are listed below. In addition, the examinations listed below limit the discretionary placement of right and left markers to AP and PA projections.
   - Cervical spine
   - Chest
   - Thoracic spine
   - Abdomen
   - Lumbar spine
   - Pelvis

3. It is important to remember that right and left markers are also used to differentiate between body parts which are often identical in their radiographic appearance. Examples include the right or left foot, leg, thigh (femur), hand, forearm, etc. Other body parts possessing a right and left side or segment include the skull and mandible. As one can see, proper use of right and left markers is essential to correctly identify body parts.

4. Previous mention was made to the use of lead arrows to indicate direction. The use of lead arrows is typically restricted to upright and lateral decubitus positions. For upright positions, the arrow is placed on the same side as the R or L marker and it is directed cephalad. When used for the lateral decubitus position, the arrow is placed on the side opposite to the side the patient is resting on, and is directed upward. For example, in a left lateral decubitus, the patient rests on the left side. The lead arrow is placed next to a right marker located on the patient's right side, and is directed away from the patient's left side. The arrow simply indicates which side of the patient is up.

5. For lateral and cross-table lateral projections, the correct procedure is to identify the side of the patient placed against the cassette. For example, if the cassette is next to the patient's right side or if the patient is lying on the right side, then a right marker should be placed on the cassette.

6. The placement of lead markers in oblique projections is the same for those examinations previously listed under supine or prone positions, e.g., chest, lumbar spine, abdomen, etc. However, when a body part, such as a hand, wrist, or leg is placed in the oblique position, one must identify the part with the appropriate right or left lead marker.

Lead markers of all kinds should be taped to the cassette *before* exposure factors are selected and the exposure is made. The ID printer is used to flash information onto the film immediately after the film is exposed *and* before processing.

References

1. Thompson, T., *Cahoon's Formulating X-Ray Techniques,* 9th ed., Duke University Press, Durham, NC, 1979, p. 130.
2. Thompson, T., *Cahoon's Formulating X-Ray Techniques,* 9th ed., Duke University Press, Durham, NC, 1979, 170.
3. Thompson, T., *Cahoon's Formulating X-Ray Techniques,* 9th ed., Duke University Press, Durham, NC, 1979, 229.
4. Notman, D. N. H., Anderson, L., Beattie, O. B., and Amy, R., Arctic paleoradiology: portable radiographic examination of two frozen sailors from the Franklin expedition (1845-1848), *Am. J. Roentgenol.,* 149, 347, 1987.

Bibliography

Bushong, S. C., *Radiologic Science for Technologists,* 4th ed., C. V. Mosby, St. Louis, 1988.

Carlton, R. R. and Adler, A. M., *Principles of Radiographic Imaging,* Delmar Publishers, Albany, NY, 1992.

Characteristics and Applications of X-Ray Grids, 1989, Liebel-Flarsheim Co., Cincinnati, OH.

Curry, T. S., Dowdey, J. E., and Murry, R. C., *Christensen's Introduction to the Physics of Diagnostic Radiology,* 3rd ed., Lea & Febiger, Philadelphia, 1984.

Devos, D., *Basic Principles of Radiographic Exposure,* Williams & Wilkins, Philadelphia, 1995.

Kodak Health Sciences Publication, No. M3-138, 1984 and No. M5-15, 1993, Eastman Kodak Co., Rochester, NY.

Thompson, T., *Cahoon's Formulating X-Ray Techniques,* 9th ed., Duke University Press, Durham, NC, 1979.

Wallace, J. E., *Radiographic Exposure Principles and Practice,* F. A. Davis, Philadelphia, 1995.

Index